College & University
Business Administration

College & University Business Administration

Third Edition

National Association of College and University Business Officers • Washington, D.C.

Copyright © 1974 by the National Association
   of College and University Business Officers
One Dupont Circle
Washington, D. C. 20036

Printed in the United States of America

Library of Congress Cataloging in Publication Data

National Association of College and University Business
   Officers.
   College & university business administration.

   First ed. (1952-55) by the National Committee on the
Preparation of a Manual on College and University Business
Administration.
   Bibliography: p.
   1. Universities and colleges—Business management.
I. National Committee on the Preparation of a Manual on
College and University Business Administration. College
and university business administration. II. Title.
LB2341.N38 1974   658'.91'378   73-92074
ISBN 0-915164-00-0

Contents

Foreword

Publication of this revision of *College and University Business Administration* carries forward into a new time, and in an entirely new way, an effort that has been of singular significance to higher education and one that the American Council on Education views with understandable satisfaction.

This revision is addressed to a new era in higher education management and to a future that certainly will bring more changes than we now can see. Yet the authority of *College and University Business Administration* springs from a most interesting past in which certain dedicated college and university business officers, for whose vision and initiative we still are grateful, developed studies of management principle that were published by the American Council. Two of my predecessors were writing notes such as these when the Council produced earlier editions of this work. President Arthur Adams prepared the forewords to the original volumes of 1952 and 1955 and President Logan Wilson the foreword to the single-volume revision of 1968. Now I, looking back at this history and ahead to the new needs and obligations of college and university management, can try only to contribute an additional perspective.

The new *College and University Business Administration* is published, as it will be hereafter, not by the American Council but by the National Association of College and University Business Officers. I think this altogether appropriate, for it is in the professional field represented by the National Association that so large a part of management experience is to be found and it is there that the professional focus properly belongs.

With this volume the American Council on Education now transfers to the National Association a responsibility in which the Council will continue to have a large interest. This revision is published at a time that higher education is striving as never before to achieve greater effectiveness in the management of its resources. The times call for a professional reference devoted to management principles; the member institutions of the Council will look to the new *College and University Business Administration* for guidance in this important field.

ROGER W. HEYNS
President
American Council on Education

Preface

THIS NEW EDITION of *College and University Business Administration* is in direct line of descent from publications that occupy a special place in the literature of higher education administration. The earlier volumes that established the title not only have been used for years by colleges and universities as their own basic references in the field of management, but are cited in the codes and regulations of many states as proper authority for the design of financial accounting and reporting systems of academic institutions. The present edition is of that pedigree.

The texts herein are far more, however, than mere revisions of earlier works. There is the same dedication to identification and statement of management principle, but in other respects this *College and University Business Administration* is something almost entirely new—new in sponsorship, in scope of coverage, and in breadth of professional contribution. Its publisher is the national association that represents the professional interest in management; it touches many topics that were until recently unknown or only lightly considered in the higher education context; and finally, this edition has had in its development the assistance of more persons than ever was possible before. The authority of the text thus is not merely inherited, it is enhanced.

A GLANCE AT THE BEGINNINGS

The effort for improved business administration of colleges and universities in the United States is an outgrowth of several developments: (1) the movement toward efficiency, which affected all aspects of organizational activity, beginning about 1890, (2) the increased interest and activities of businessmen in higher education, (3) the growth of the accounting profession, and (4) the survey movement, which evolved into the "self-survey" and the modern, introspective "management by objectives." Since the 1890s, certified public accountants have been active in higher education, and many have been active in seeking "generally accepted standards" in colleges and universities.

Two very successful businessmen were outstanding in their continuing interest and philanthropy: John D. Rockefeller, Sr. and Andrew Carnegie. Mr. Rockefeller was especially interested in the second University of Chicago, beginning in the 1890s. As a result, that university was one of the first to have a "business manager"; it also had one of the first "auditors." This was Trevor Arnett, who published the first unit costs in higher education. He also wrote what is considered the first generally accepted book in the field, *College and University Finance,* published by the General Education Board in 1922. Copies were sent to every college and university in the country.

Mr. Rockefeller developed a practice of inviting the officers of the University of Chicago to discuss the university's plans for the following year: what funds were expected, their sources, and their purposes. This was one of several forerunners of budgeting as it is practiced today in colleges and universities. The General Education Board, created by Mr. Rockefeller, provided the funds to write and publish the interim and final reports of the Morey Committee (1930-1935). Later, the Rockefeller Foundation provided funds to support the work of the committee that compiled and published the first *College and University Business Administration* ("Volumes I and II"). The various Rockefeller foundations have steadily supported the efforts of colleges and universities to achieve better business administration.

Andrew Carnegie, in the early 1900s, developed the Carnegie Foundation for the Advancement of

Teaching, and selected Dr. Henry S. Pritchett, President of the Massachusetts Institute of Technology, as the president of this foundation. One of Dr. Pritchett's first steps was to seek a definition of a "college or university," and soon after this he initiated one of the first efficiency studies of such an institution. Morris Llewellyn Cooke, one of the outstanding "efficiency experts" of that time, administered the program, which included a cost study. About the same time, Dr. Pritchett provided his auditor, Harvey S. Chase, C.P.A., of Boston, with a number of financial reports of colleges and universities in an effort to develop a standard form for reporting the financial facts of these institutions; pamphlets resulting from this study were published in 1910 by the Carnegie Foundation as "Standard Forms for Financial Reports of Colleges, Universities, and Technical Schools." This foundation thus sponsored the first endeavor toward standard reports, as well as the first survey.

The Carnegie Foundation supported the Educational Finance Inquiry Commission of the American Council on Education in 1921, resulting in a thirteen-volume publication in 1925. It supported the Morey Committee, beginning in 1930, the work of the Council's Financial Advisory Service in the late 1930s, and together with the Rockefeller Foundation, it furnished funds to the National Committee on the Preparation of a Manual on College and University Business Administration (known as the Manual Committee).

Since the 1890s there have been many studies, published and unpublished, on college and university administration and costs. Beginning in 1913, the U.S. Office of Education was a leader in the survey movement, from which numerous cost studies were developed. One of these, in 1929, was the monumental survey of land-grant colleges and universities. This led Dr. Arthur J. Klein, who was chief of the Division of Higher Education of the U.S. Office of Education, to press for something resembling standard practices in accounting for colleges and universities.

As a result, and in response to growing demands from colleges and universities for authoritative guidance in the accounting and reporting field, the American Council on Education organized in 1930 a National Committee on Standard Reports for Institutions of Higher Education (the Morey Committee, mentioned above). Chairman of the committee was a man widely acknowledged as a leader in the profession, Lloyd Morey, Comptroller (and later President) of the University of Illinois, who in that same year published his own pioneering textbook, *University and College Accounting.*

Dr. Morey appointed Thad L. Hungate, Comptroller of Teachers College, Columbia University, who had worked with Trevor Arnett, to examine approximately 100 financial reports from institutions of higher education. This work was published by the committee, and also served as Mr. Hungate's master's thesis at Teachers College. The committee then issued a series of pamphlets on various aspects of college and university accounting. One listed as author W. B. Franke, C.P.A., who had a large practice among colleges and universities. This pamphlet, "Suggested Forms for Internal Financial Reports of Colleges and Universities," was Bulletin No. 5, published by the National Committee in 1932. Three other C.P.A.'s joined Mr. Franke in this study: Lloyd Morey; Gail A. Mills, who had helped Dr. Morey write his book, and who later was to be the long-time Comptroller at Princeton University; and F. L. Jackson, who for many years was Vice President and Treasurer at Davidson College.

As the committee worked, it was increasingly in consultation with representatives of the Association of American Colleges, the American Association of Collegiate Registrars, and other organizations. The committee's final report, *Financial Reports for Colleges and Universities,* was published by the University of Chicago Press in 1935. The editorial committee of this publication was composed of Lloyd Morey; E. S. Erwin, of Stanford University; and George E. Van Dyke, then a graduate student at the University of Chicago and a former student-employee of Dr. Morey's. The committee not only produced the first set of "standard" guidelines, but pointed to other ways in which professional guidance might be provided.

Following publication of *Financial Reports,* the American Council on Education established a Financial Advisory Service, a consultative and reference project (mentioned above in reference to the Carnegie Foundation). First administrator of the Service was George Van Dyke, who was followed by J. Harvey Cain, long-time Comptroller of the Catholic University of America, and others. Twenty-one pamphlets were published under the auspices of the Service, which operated until the advent of World War II.

Much of the impetus for improvement of management practices during this period came from the two regional associations of college and university business officers then existing: the Central Association (then the Association of Business Officers of the State Universities and Colleges of the Middle West), organized in 1912, and the Eastern Association (then the Asssociation of University and College Business Officers of the Eastern States), organized in 1920. The members of these associations were drawn together by a common need to discover generally acceptable ground rules for conducting business and financial affairs. Such interests, thus germinating, would grow in the ensuing years into the far more elaborate and sophisticated professional programs that would be required to cope with problems of management in an entirely new age. In this movement the American Council was a centralizing force. Long before there was a national organization of business officers, the Council was the rallying point for those leaders of the profession who, sharing their knowledge and experience, contributed voluntarily to developing the studies of management principle of which the Council was sponsor and publisher.

THE SEARCH FOR MANAGEMENT PRINCIPLE

It was in this period that *College and University Business Administration* was conceived. The authority of *Financial Reports* was unquestioned. But the success of that guide suggested that there might be developed a publication of similar authority, but broader in scope, touching all major areas of business and financial administration. The question was discussed at the 1937 meeting of the Central Association of College and University Business Officers. In 1938 representatives of four regional associations—the Central and the Eastern, the Southern, which had been organized in 1928, and the Western, organized in 1936—met in Pittsburgh to form a body called the National Committee on the Preparation of a Manual on College and University Business Administration. The chairman was J. C. Christensen, of the University of Michigan. The movement thus begun continued during World War II with the support of grants to the American Council, in 1942 and 1943, by the Carnegie Foundation. The four regional associa-

tions also contributed to the fund, as did the Association of Business Officers in Schools for Negroes (later the American Association of College and University Business Officers) that had been organized in 1939. Through such an essentially informal mobilization the groundwork was laid for activities that would follow World War II.

In 1946 Thad L. Hungate's doctoral dissertation, *Financing the Future of Higher Education,* was published by Columbia University. Included in this work was a new unit: cost of professional instruction. In 1950 Harvey Sherer's master's thesis, under the direction of Lloyd Morey, was published at Urbana. This was a comparative study of the Morey Committee's recommendations and the financial reporting practices in 1948. Also in 1950, Mr. Sherer was appointed by the Manual Committee to revise the 1935 volume *Financial Reports* in the light of his findings; his work for the committee ended with Volume I.

THE ORIGINAL "VOLUMES I AND II"

The work of the National Committee on the Preparation of a Manual proceeded from the date of the first grant, 1942, until publication of *College and University Business Administration* had been completed by the American Council in 1955. The manual was in two volumes, the first, published in 1952, covering the principles of financial accounting and reporting and the second those other aspects of college and university management clearly within the realm of the business officer's interest and responsibility. Not surprisingly, the publication was universally referred to in the profession as "the manual" or "Volumes I and II."

Associated with the development of Volumes I and II were persons who had achieved or would attain positions of professional leadership. Thomas E. Blackwell, then Vice Chancellor and Treasurer of Washington University, was appointed editor in 1946. Arthur W. Peterson, Vice President for Business and Finance at the University of Wisconsin, represented the American Council as chairman of the Executive Committee, the original membership including Lloyd Morey and E. S. Irwin; L. H. Foster, Jr., Tuskegee Institute; A. M. Graham, Winthrop College; and A. S. Johnson, Rutgers University. Later, during the preparation of Volume II, the membership included E. S. Irwin and L. H. Foster, Jr.; John F. Meck, Dartmouth College; W. T. Middlebrook, the University of Minnesota; and Clarence Scheps, Tulane University. Ralph S. Johns headed a special committee of five from the American Institute of Accountants (now the American Institute of Certified Public Accountants) that provided consultation on accounting and auditing. Mr. Blackwell's Editorial Committee for Volume II included Mr. Middlebrook, Mr. Peterson, and George Van Dyke, then Assistant Comptroller of the Rockefeller Foundation, who would himself serve as Editor when the time came to revise the volumes. (Far more comprehensive acknowledgments of all who contributed to these efforts will be found in the prefaces to the volumes.) Expenses of executive committee operations were defrayed by the Commission on Financing Higher Education, an organization sponsored by the Association of American Universities and financed by grants from the Rockefeller Foundation and the Carnegie Corporation.

THE FIRST REVISION: *"CUBA* (1968)"

The time for revision arrived shortly. There had come into existence in 1956 the National Federation of College and University Business Officers Associations, predecessor to the National Association, and by 1959 the Board of the Federation formally recognized the need to create a mechanism for revision. In 1960 a national committee was established under the chairmanship of Dr. Scheps, but it was not until 1964, when financing finally was obtained by the American Council, that the new group could proceed. Financing during the course of the project came from the American Council itself, from the American and regional associations of business officers, the U.S. Office of Education, the Teachers Insurance and Annuity Association, the International Business Machines Corporation, and the General Electric, Shell, and United States Steel Foundations.

The Scheps group was called the National Committee to Revise Volumes I and II, *College and University Business Administration.* Mr. Van Dyke was appointed full-time editor, serving thus until his retirement in 1966, when he was succeeded briefly by John M. Evans, of the University of Connecticut, who was throughout the chairman of the Editorial Subcommittee. Members of the subcommittee were Kenneth R. Erfft, Duquesne Uni-

versity; Robert B. Gilmore, California Institute of Technology; R. W. Kettler, State University of New York; Bruce J. Partridge, Johns Hopkins University; Fred S. Vorsanger, American Council on Education; and Dr. Scheps. The national committee itself was composed of some thirty business officers, consultants, and representatives of other organizations including the American Institute of Certified Public Accountants and the U.S. Office of Education.

An early decision of the national committee was to combine into a single volume the new revision of Volumes I and II. Many business officers provided drafts of chapters and scores of others contributed readings and comments. This work went forward for three years. The Editorial Subcommittee, handling drafts and manuscripts, met monthly on weekends from May 1964 to March 1967, and while the costs of operations were covered by outside support, the time and effort were volunteered by committee members. The single-volume revision was published by the American Council in 1968. It became known almost at once as *"CUBA* (1968)." About 17,000 copies were sold before the book went out of print in 1973.

THE SECOND REVISION: *"CUBA* (1974)"

The National Association's office was established in Washington in 1967, some months before the 1968 revision was published. Already it was clearly recognized that further revision should be anticipated, perhaps in five years, and that the national office now provided an operating base of a kind that had not existed before. Even then there was the hope that the National Association could become the publisher of future revisions, but the professional machinery first had to be organized. Accordingly, National President James J. Ritterskamp, Jr. appointed a new Committee on the Revision of the Manual under the chairmanship of Robert B. Gilmore, Vice President for Business and Finance at Caltech.

By 1971 the Manual Revision Committee had developed certain general procedures for the preparation of materials. The drafting of preliminary texts was given to those professional associations or National Association committees having primary interest, experience, or authority in the various management fields. These associations or committees were invited to assign authors to produce draft texts. When the drafts were submitted, they were given a preliminary evaluation by voluntary groups appointed to serve as short-term subcommittees of the Manual Revision Committee, each to deal only with its particular subject, and many including in their membership a consultant from outside the college and university field also participating voluntarily. When the manuscripts were further revised, the texts then were exposed to sixty to eighty business officers. Manuscripts completing such exposure were adjusted as necessary and forwarded, finally, to the National Association's Board of Directors for approval for publication.

Because of the central importance of the financial accounting and reporting functions, there had been, since the time of Volumes I and II, close liaison between the college and university business professionals and members of organizations representing certified public accountants. By 1970 the National Association had established its Accounting Principles Committee, designed to become in the college and university field the equivalent of the AICPA's former Accounting Principles Board. This committee, headed first by Gilbert L. Lee, Jr., of the University of Chicago, and later by W. Harold Read, of the University of Tennessee, performed a most important early service by establishing a close working relationship with the AICPA's Committee on College and University Accounting and Auditing which, under the chairmanship of Daniel D. Robinson, of Peat, Marwick, Mitchell & Co., was developing a new AICPA guide, *Audits of Colleges and Universities.* Through the Accounting Principles Committee and through its liaison representatives to AICPA, Dr. Scheps and Mr. Gilmore, the National Association participated in the early drafting of the guide, and in 1972 assisted directly in the exposure of the draft text. When the AICPA guide was published in 1973, the text so closely reflected a general professional consensus that copies of the publication were distributed by the National Association to its members.

In preparing to assume responsibility for publication of *College and University Business Administration* the National Association faced first the challenge of mobilizing professional resources, then the less familiar tasks of organizing staff, proce-

dures, and support for publication itself. In each of these fields it had a truly magnificent assistance and cooperation.

Professional participation was very broad. All of the Association's "program" committees—those dealing with specific areas of management concern or levels of institutional interest—were deeply involved in the processes of developing or evaluating manuscripts. The four regional associations were similarly engaged, not only in the exposure of manuscripts but in organizing discussions at annual meetings and workshops of substantive issues related to accounting and auditing. Further, fourteen associations having interests in the field of college and university business were directly engaged in the preparation of manuscripts or in evaluating or exposing the manuscripts finally produced.

From 1969 until 1973 the responsibility for developing and recommending publication plans rested primarily upon the Manual Revision Committee under the chairmanship of Mr. Gilmore with the counsel of the Publications Committee under the chairmanship of Vincent Shea, of the University of Virginia. In 1973 these two committees were combined into an enlarged Publications Committee headed by Kurt M. Hertzfeld, of Amherst College. It was this committee that pushed to conclusion the review of manuscripts and the final act of publication.

The long process of preparation was one necessitating special support, financial and otherwise, that the Association was ill-equipped to provide. The financial support came in the form of special awards by the Ford Foundation, the United States Steel Foundation, Inc., and the General Motors Corporation, and for this assistance the Association and its member institutions continue to be grateful. This gratitude will be shared, certainly, by all who find in *College and University Business Administration* the management assistance it is designed to offer.

Elsewhere in this text there appear the names of persons, committees, and associations contributing to this effort. In acknowledging their work the Association is aware that there are other persons who also have in some way lent support, advice, and encouragement. Thanks go to them, too, with the assurance that their interest always will be welcome. There still will be much to do in the future.

Part 1

Business Administration in Higher Education

Business Administration in Higher Education

THE ADMINISTRATION of colleges and universities and the management of their resources are functions which, although they call for all the skills and qualities of judgment common to management in other fields, nevertheless are fundamentally and necessarily different in essential forms and motivations.

The difference stems from the nature of the college or university as an institution of importance to society and to which there is an inherent public commitment. The difference is subtle and therefore frequently overlooked. Any college or university, whether it is "public" or "private" or whether its support comes from any imaginable combination of appropriations, capitation grants, gifts, tuition, investments, or endowments, is a unique management entity. It is unique in that the "user" of its product, the student, is not expected to pay all of its costs and that resources are expected to be expended as fully as is possible, judiciously, to achieve educational goals. The difference is something more than that the college or university is "nonprofit" and thus is not asked to earn profits for owners or shareholders. Society's commitment to higher education is a mandate to the institution to use its resources for purposes of great social importance. The task of college and university management is to insure the wise and most effective use of resources for such purposes.

In a Changing Environment

The environment in which colleges and universities function must be considered in a discussion of their administration. The changes of recent years in higher education were caused by many factors, among them inflation and a reduction in the rate of enrollment growth.

Prior to World War II, the United States never experienced a sustained general rise in prices without later experiencing a commensurate fall in prices. Existing price data suggest that the average annual compound increase in prices from about 1820 to 1913 averaged around two-tenths of one percent. The price rise in World War I was followed by price decreases that reached their nadir in the 1930s. No such decrease followed the price increases of World War II. Rather, except for moderate inflation during most of the 1950s and early 1960s, inflation generally has grown progressively more acute.

Higher education fares poorly in times of inflation; increases in revenues invariably lag behind increases in cost. Educational institutions thus are hard pressed merely to "keep up" in terms of claims on real revenue. At issue is whether higher education can achieve significant increases in productivity. Some argue that effectiveness and economic efficiency are antithetical to an educational environment. One point, however, is acceptable to most: given the prospect of continued inflation and growing competition for scarce resources, productivity gains may be important to the survival of many colleges and universities.

The decline in the rate of enrollment growth in the early 1970s was greater than predicted by most of the experts. This decline may indicate a significant, long-term change in the proportion of young people in higher education. It may indicate a fundamental change in the nature of education beyond the secondary level or it may be only a temporary deviation in traditional educational patterns.

The enrollment growth pattern is an important phenomenon with which educational administrators must reckon. Powerful pressures for institutional growth occurred in the late 1940s and continued through the 1960s. The response of the nation's colleges and universities was dramatic: the capacity crisis was met and students were accommodated. The price of this expansion, however, was that many institutions became burdened with fixed charges in the form of heavy bonded indebtedness and other recurring obligations. Geared for additional growth that did not materialize, they were caught short by the decline. Unless the decline in growth is temporary, it could threaten many institutions that have excess capacity.

At the least, analyses of demographic and enrollment data suggest that institutions of higher education should plan for the future on a comprehensive and continuous basis. The outlook for enrollment (coupled with that for inflation) makes control of resources in higher education an urgent matter. Priorities must be established in light of these realities, and good administration can increase the options open to institutional policy makers.

INSTITUTIONAL ORGANIZATION

A college or university is a diverse community, composed of members such as students, teachers, researchers, administrators, secretaries, technicians, salespeople, groundskeepers, and custodians. Each person in this community is related, directly or indirectly, to one or more of the primary functions of the institution—instruction, research, or public service—and every policy decision made by the managers in the community should be weighed in terms of how it affects these three functions as well as other pertinent aspects of the institution. An institution's form of organization should be determined in a manner that will most efficiently and effectively enable it to achieve its mission.

The Governing Board

The apex of the organization is the governing board. The powers of the governing board are contained in the charter or in the legislative acts establishing the institution. In public institutions board members usually are appointed by the governor of the state or the parent governmental body and in some cases they are elected by popular ballot. In many private institutions the board is self-perpetuating, although some members may be elected by the alumni or by affiliated professional societies. In church-related institutions, the members often are elected by the legislative body of the religious denomination or are appointed by its

executive officers. The titles most commonly used for the governing board are "board of trustees," "board of governors," and "board of regents."

The governing board has full and final responsibility for the conduct of operations of the institution. This responsibility usually includes:

1. Selection and appointment of the president of the institution.
2. Appointment of faculty and administrative officers, on the recommendation of the president.
3. Approval of long-range plans.
4. Determination of all major policies.
5. Approval of the operating and capital budgets.
6. Seeking the funds necessary to permit the institution to operate and to fulfill its mission.
7. Approval of legal documents.
8. Representing the institution to the public.
9. Acting as a final authority on institutional matters.

The President

The president or chancellor, as chief executive officer, is responsible to the governing board for the administration of all affairs of the institution. It is the president who implements board actions and provides leadership and stimulation for innovation and high morale in the institutional community. He also supplies initiative and direction for the strategic institutional planning of programs and resource requirements. It is his further responsibility to see that the objectives of the institution are coordinated, evaluated, and controlled.

Although the president delegates authority to other officers, he may have one or more staff assistants for work that relates directly to his office. Assistants to the president may be responsible for such functions as institutional research, consortium arrangements, legal counsel, legislative liaison, or communications with the board.

The Administrative Officers

Although no single form of organization applies to all institutions, there are at least four major functional areas to be administered in a college or university. These are: (1) instruction, research, and public service, (2) business and financial management, (3) student services, and (4) institutional development, including fund raising, public relations, and alumni relations. All of these are interrelated, and the goals of the institution will be achieved only if there is an awareness of interdependence and a spirit of cooperation among the administrators responsible for these functional areas.

Not all institutions have an officer for each of these areas. In many institutions, however, these officers are: (1) a chief academic officer, usually referred to as dean of the college, provost, or vice president for academic affairs; (2) a chief business officer, typically designated as the business manager, controller, or vice president for business and finance (or business affairs); (3) a student services officer, who may be identified as dean of students or vice president for student services; and (4) a development officer, often referred to as director of development or vice president for development (or community relations). Smaller institutions may effectively combine responsibility for two or more functions in one person. Larger institutions may have additional officers for other functional areas, such as research or continuing education. The authority delegated to each officer is determined by the president and approved by the governing board, if not prescribed in the charter of the institution.

The primary responsibility of the chief academic officer is to formulate and implement the educational goals of the institution. He confers with department chairmen or deans in the employment of faculty, in determining entrance and degree requirements, and in the continuing study of curricula. In the university there may be various divisions, colleges, and schools, each headed by a dean or other academic officer. The director of the library usually reports to the chief academic officer.

The primary responsibility of the chief business officer is to manage the business and financial affairs of the institution. He sets the style and tone of the office and determines the broad policies of all institutional functions relating to business and finance. Above all, he is responsible for creating the systems and selecting and training the personnel to make the systems work effectively. The chief business officer is the financial adviser to the president and the governing board, and is often treasurer of the corporation.

The primary responsibilities of the student services officer include such activities as admissions, student records, counseling, health services, student aid, social and athletic programs, student government, student publications, placement, and various aspects of auxiliary enterprises.

The primary responsibility of the development officer is fund raising, but in some institutions, he is also responsible for public relations, communication with federal agencies, and alumni relations. These functions include radio, television, and newspaper coverage; institutional publications; homecomings; dedications; and mailings to alumni, foundations, and corporations, with associated record keeping.

The number of persons reporting directly to the president may be more or less than the four officers responsible for the major functional areas. The major functions should be coordinated through an administrative group, typically comprised of the officers who report to the president, often called the president's cabinet, which should meet at regular intervals.

The officers generally are considered to be appointed on a continuing basis, even though they serve at the pleasure of the president and the governing board. Some boards reelect officers periodically. They are not granted tenure in their administrative positions, but may have achieved tenure by virtue of their academic position, which they retain.

Forms of Organization

Any institution of higher education requires some type of governing body and a chief executive, although organizational structure varies according to individual tradition, mission, size, and whether the institution is a college or university, public or private, two-year or four-year. Some states have commissions of higher education that coordinate the administration of all state colleges and universities and, in some cases, of private institutions as well. This ordinarily does not affect the organizational structure of the institution itself, which may employ either a unitary or multiple form of organization.

In the unitary form of organization, which is the more common of the two types, authority and responsibility are centralized in the president. Authority is delegated by the governing board to the president, who in turn delegates authority to officers responsible for major functional areas. These officers report to the president, who alone reports to the board. The chief business officer works closely with such committees of the governing board as the budget committee, investment committee, finance committee, buildings and grounds committee, and those committees involved in long-range planning and construction. An officer who works directly with the board in the unitary form of organization does so as a representative of the president, and at the president's discretion.

In the multiple form of organization, officers in addition to the president receive a delegation of authority from the board, and report to it as well as to the president. Under this form, the chief business officer is responsible directly to the board for the business and financial affairs of the institution.

A third form of organization is the modified unitary form, in which the chief business officer is responsible directly to the governing board only in a fiscal reporting capacity. For all other functions, he reports to the president.

In addition to appointing the president, the governing boards of institutions organized on the unitary plan usually appoint the chief academic officer and chief business officer. In such cases, these officers should be appointed and terminated by the board only on the recommendation of the president. Whether or not they are appointed by the board, the chief academic officer and chief business officer should participate in meetings of the board, and the president should be permitted to invite other officers as well.

By working harmoniously, the chief academic officer and chief business officer can be of immeasurable value to the president and the institution. They should work closely together on many tasks, such as preparation of the budget, determination of faculty and staff levels, and new facilities. Cooperation between the two officers can significantly aid the president in long-range planning and allocation of resources.

THE RANGE OF MANAGEMENT RESPONSIBILITIES

The lines of responsibility and the management specialties within the institution's division of business affairs are found in various forms and balances as institutions vary by type and by levels and forms of support and as organizational patterns reflect institutional needs with regard to the size of the academic community, the size and character of the physical plant, the geographical or community environment, and even the institution's history, tradition, and perception of its role and mission. The management function is responsive to, and in a sense must tie together, all the interlocking elements of institutional life. The function is a "business" function only in the sense that it is concerned with management of and accounting for financial and physical resources—with the handling of funds and of endowments and investments and of expenditures for salaries and wages, for operation of the physical plant, for supplies and equipment, for housing and food services, and so on. Yet these are the "business" elements essential to the institution's existence, and thus the overriding responsibilities of the division of business affairs are (1) to keep the accounts and make reports through which the total activity becomes intelligible and (2) to bring to the administration of the college or university an intelligent and sympathetic awareness of how or whether resources are being used to advance educational goals.

No organization chart of the division will, in itself, set out clearly the measures of responsibility essential to successful and effective management. The lines of responsibility and authority will show primary relationships, but the effectiveness of the whole will depend, as in other fields, upon the leadership and upon the degree to which professional skills are brought together in the service of the institution. There may be one chief business officer, a "Vice President for Business and Finance," for example, or two, a "Vice President for Business" and a "Vice President for Finance." But there must be an essential unity in the way affairs are conducted and there must be participation by the officer or officers in planning and policy determinations. The "business" organization must be so constructed that it links the various management sectors of the institution and, with trained staff and with proper accounting and financial data-gathering systems, prepares itself to give to the administration both information and informed counsel.

The distinctions between "business" management and "financial" or "fiscal" management are not altogether clear and are, in fact, largely subject to institutional definition. The characteristic organization is one that combines in a single entity, under a single officer, all or most of the business and financial functions. It is in the large or complex educational organizations that separations of responsibility have become necessary and apparent, so that some institutions or systems have separate offices for business management, for financial management, for budget, for personnel administration, or for planning, each having responsibilities that touch the traditional "business" field. Without reference to specific organizational patterns, however, the range of responsibilities in management may be outlined as follows:

Administrative Management: Institutional planning, design and operation of management information systems, fiscal administration of sponsored programs, management of risk-reduction and insurance programs, legal services, management of student aid funds, and administration of personnel programs, including faculty and staff benefits and labor relations and collective bargaining.

Business Management: Purchase of supplies and equipment, administration of auxiliary enterprises and service activities, development of the physical plant (operation, maintenance, planning, design, and construction), and management of security and safety programs.

Fiscal Management: Administration of endowment and similar funds, management of investments, budget preparation and budgetary accounting, internal control and audit, and institutional research and resource management.

Financial Accounting and Reporting: Development and maintenance of the basic financial accounting and records systems and preparation of financial reports and analyses.

If it is possible to sift from the foregoing the direct and primary responsibilities expected to be assumed by the chief business officer, the functions include these:

1. Management of all financial operations of the institution, including design of the systems, preparation of reports, conduct of financial analyses, and provision of appropriate controls and audits.

2. Participation with the president and the chief academic officer in preparation of the institutional budgets.

3. Management of the physical plant, routinely in its operation and maintenance and, with other officers, in planning, design, and construction decisions.

4. Management of personnel programs.

5. Management of purchasing, stores, and property control systems.

6. Management, or financial control within institutional policy, of auxiliary enterprises and service departments.

Although student aid programs may be administered by another officer, the business officer is responsible for the custody of student aid and scholarship funds. Legal counsel often is assigned to his office. He may be, under policies established by the trustees, the manager of investments or the administrator of endowments, all such operations being reportable in the institution's financial statements. He authenticates institutional contracts, administers the funds of federal or other sponsored programs, and assumes responsibility for utility systems, safety and security programs, and traffic, parking, and communications.

Effectiveness in the business function depends, finally, on clear statements of policy and procedure. The articles or statutes establishing the institution may set certain basic guidelines or requirements. Whether they do or not, institutional bylaws should incorporate such a section. For continuing operations there should be manuals that set out policy, fix responsibilities, and describe the procedures—and the ranges and limits—of business and financial management.

QUALIFICATIONS OF THE CHIEF BUSINESS OFFICER

The chief business officer, as one responsible for managing the resources of the institution, must bring to the task high technical competence, a considerable administrative ability, and a grasp of, and a liking for, the elements of the educational environment that make his role as a manager unlike any other. He must be equipped by training and experience to assume large responsibilities and must be professional in viewpoint.

The chief business officer's academic preparation must be of appropriate depth. Typically, this includes a degree in business administration, although the degree may be in another field. In addition, the officer often is a certified public accountant and/or has a master's degree in business administration, and in more cases than ever before, he has earned, or is earning, the doctorate. Whatever the avenue or level of preparation, training in accounting is essential, for development in the business office context requires familiarity with the accounting and reporting functions. The chief business officer must be, above all, the kind of person who, dedicated to learning, uses every opportunity for the improvement of professional knowledge and skills.

As an administrator, the chief business officer should have both the strengths of the executive and the capacity to work comfortably and effectively as a counselor to the trustees and to the president of the institution. The officer should be not merely a compiler but an interpreter of data and financial information. Because a principal contribution to the institution will be in helping to determine how resources are used to achieve primary goals, the officer should be a person who not only comprehends academic objectives but appreciates them as personal goals. The chief business officer should be an effective communicator in the administrative councils of the institution, in relationships with the faculty and other members of the academic community, and with those who comprise the staffs of the business organization. The officer should be sensitive to questions of human and public relations and should be able to represent the institution before any audience interested in its mission, goals, achievements, or courses of action.

Business officers of such breadth are not rare. They are to be found, in fact, in many institutions —many in the smaller institutions in which they personally are dealing with all of the major management responsibilities, others in the large or multicampus institutions where their roles may be more specialized. The ideal of the chief business officer is that person who, working within the framework of his institution's own policies and objectives, seeks constantly to help the institution make the most of its resources while in his campus and community relationships he makes himself an example of dedicated service. Business officers of that caliber have influences beyond the limits of their institutional roles and, in their professional relationships, have influences on the development of higher education itself.

NEW DIMENSIONS

The climate of the present decade is one of shift and change in higher education, the challenges to management enlarged by new perceptions of what constitutes education beyond the secondary level. It is, in fact, no longer either sufficient or accurate to limit discussions of management to the management of institutions of traditional form. Because of new perceptions of the scope of the educational process, the commitment now is seen as including all of "postsecondary education," a concept that the public and the institutions have only begun to define. There is a vast curiosity about what is spent on education and how institutions are financed and what they do with their funds. The single certainty is that, whatever the outcome, the need for sound, responsive, and responsible management will continue to grow.

In contemplating the organization and administration of institutions of higher education, it is natural to speculate on the forces in motion and the prospects for change. No such speculation can reflect all such forces, much less the shapes they may take, but new dimensions such as these may affect the functions of college and university administration in the future:

1. Institutional governance and policy making may take new forms. Colleges and universities may become more politicized, more subject to external controls, as not only students but alumni and other constituencies become more interested in sharing institutional controls.

2. In the face of increased competition for scarce resources in an increasingly crowded world, the public may become more critical of higher education's share of the resources.

3. Society increasingly may favor pragmatism

and vocational orientation in education, resulting in new and different institutional programs.

4. Internal operation of colleges and universities may be characterized by increasing tension among interest groups within the institutions.

5. Renewed commitment may be necessary with regard to equality of opportunity.

6. Unconventional educational institutions may emerge, some of which may be profit-oriented, to serve a public whose needs may not be met by traditional institutions.

This list typifies the challenges and indicates the direction of higher education in the United States and other countries. Administration of colleges and universities promises to become more important and more difficult than ever before. Such a development makes good administration essential.

Part 2

Administrative Management

Institutional Planning

PLANNING IS AMONG the most important responsibilities of a college or university administrator. It is the act of identifying, specifying, and selecting alternative goals, objectives, and courses of action for accomplishing the mission of the institution. To avoid confusion between ends and means, there is a sequence of levels at which planning decisions should be made: from philosophy to objectives to programs to organization to staffing to facilities to financing.

A statement of mission, purpose, or philosophy should precede all planning efforts. Although typical mission statements are written in general terms, an effective statement should be sufficiently specific that it can condition each planning decision; that is, each planning decision should derive from this statement. The statement provides direction and integrity in planning, and makes possible the definition of goals and objectives to realize the mission.

"Mission" refers to the broad, overall, long-term purpose of the institution; "goal" implies something less remote than mission, more definitive and capable of achievement in a certain period of time (perhaps five to ten years); "objective" implies something tangible, which can be reached in a shorter period of time than a goal.

The statement of mission should provide guidance on such questions as:

1. What is the philosophy of governance?

2. What are the priorities of the institution?

3. What are the roles of instruction, research, and public service in the institution, and how should they interact and reinforce one another?

4. Are degree programs oriented toward liberal education, professional ends, vocational ends, or next degree level?

Regardless of the tradition, mission, or size of an institution, planning occurs whether or not it is specifically provided for. It may be formal or informal, and goals may or may not be documented. To be most effective, however, planning must be organized and goals must be realistic and well-defined.

PRINCIPLES OF PLANNING

Four principles are vital to the planning process:

1. The organization for planning must reflect total institutional commitment.

2. The planning process must anticipate and facilitate the action that is to follow; that is, it must generate action.

3. The planning process itself must be planned and it must be continuous. The master (program) plan for a college or university should be a living document that is updated at least annually in the regular course of evaluation and reporting, program projection, budget projection, and operation. For maximum effectiveness, it should be available to everyone associated with the institution.

4. A key to effective planning is involvement, which enhances commitment to achievement. Plans must be developed with the understanding and cooperation of those responsible for execution of the plans, in collaboration with their supervisors, their peers, and those whom they supervise who also will be involved in implementation.

A number of factors have combined to make the planning process in colleges and universities more elaborate and complex than formerly. Among these are the increasing size and complexity of institutions, the increase in numbers and kinds of persons and organizations to whom institutions are accountable, the growth and proliferation of federal and state programs of assistance to institutions of higher education (plus increased dependence upon support from those programs), and the availability of methods and techniques, such as PERT (Program Evaluation and Review Technique), management by objectives, program budgeting, and computer simulation, which make it feasible to plan more elaborately and to base planning decisions on greater amounts of information.

The four principles that underlie the planning process can be augmented by several others. These may be summarized as follows:

5. Planning should be integrated with the management function, especially the processes of budget development, reporting, evaluation, and other aspects of management.

6. The planning-management system must have built-in checks and balances leading to realism in planning and to responsible execution.

7. The planning process must be reinforced and undergirded by an adequate data base that is organized and programmed to make available for planning decisions the consideration of many alternatives and the consequences of alternative choices. Such techniques as program budgeting and the use of projection models and specialized computer programs should be evaluated and utilized when necessary and feasible.

8. Resources for planning must be provided. Although many of the employees of a college or university are involved at one point or another in the planning process, there should be one person who, on behalf of the president, is responsible for the planning function, and who will have the time and be furnished the resources to proceed with the planning process. In some cases the institution may find it desirable to secure the assistance of outside consultants, particularly in the initial stages of developing a planning project. Even the large university is likely to be unable to employ, on a full-time basis, all the specialists it would like to use. Planning therefore must utilize the most efficient balance of resources — people, time, and money.

9. Planning by individual units must be coordinated by the person responsible for the planning function.

The planning function can be implemented without a special office to support, supervise, or monitor it; but to operate this way requires an overt, institutional commitment of its senior administrators to recognize, reward, and sponsor planning as part of all administrative activity. If there is a planning office, its staff should be cognizant of academic administration planning.

For the planning process to be successful, it must be integrated, or interlocked, with all the other activities that bear directly on the implementation of plans, such as reporting, evaluation of performance, and development and adjustment of budgets.

The interlocked planning-budgeting-evaluation-reporting pattern should include a system of checks and balances leading to realistic planning and responsible performance. In order to achieve accountability, plans must be expressed in terms of achievement, not only by the person responsible, but by supervisors, and even by persons outside the institution. If the persons who project plans for a given unit, expressing these in terms of objectives, know that their performance subsequently will be evaluated in terms of their accomplishment of these objectives, they will be influenced to be realistic or even modest in the objectives they write. On the other hand, if they know that their budget requests must be justified in terms of the plans they write, they know that it will be self-limiting and self-defeating to make the plans too modest. Handled appropriately, the planning-budgeting-reporting-evaluation pattern can maintain effective checks and balances leading to ambitious, optimistic planning.

Planning helps to provide long-term visibility of the impact of present decisions, better exposes the financial reality of possible alternatives, allows the detection of trends, focuses on a broad spectrum of programs rather than on incremental funding, and, most importantly, links achievement and cost.

THE PLAN FOR THE PLANNING PROCESS

As previously stated, the planning process itself must be planned. If an institution does not have an annual program planning-budgeting-evaluation-reporting cycle in operation, its approach to initiating such a cycle should involve the development of a program master plan expressed in terms of specific objectives and incorporating provisions for annual revision of the plan, for budget development, and for evaluation and reporting. This cycle, not necessarily annual, is the normal and almost unavoidable sequence of planning, budgeting, evaluation, and reporting that takes place in most colleges and universities, whether or not they use management by objectives or other management tools. This sequence exists to some degree in every institution, although it may be highly unsystematic and subjective; that is, someone makes plans for programs to be offered (program planning), someone determines the allocations of funds for programs (budgeting), someone exercises some judgment concerning results of the programs (evaluation), and in most institutions, there is some reporting of results achieved.

In most cases it will be advantageous to develop a method for the master plan development program and to review this in detail with everyone involved in the planning process, beginning with the senior administrators of the institution, revising and improving the method in response to suggestions received. The results of this process should identify each task to be performed in the development of the master plan, the person or persons responsible for the completion of each step, the date on which it can be initiated (by virtue of the completion of all tasks that must be completed before it), the date on which it is to be completed, and the way it relates to subsequent tasks.

It is essential that the presentation to the various administrative officers, department heads, and other involved persons begin with a rationale for the development of the master plan and for the procedure to be used in producing it. This presentation also should indicate the constraints that apply and the relationship to existing policies or statements of mission of the institution. Above all, it is essential that commitment result from the presentation of the plan and its refinement in consultation with the persons involved in the planning process.

Once the overall plan is completed, subplans for each of the major units of the institution should be developed and combined into a single document. A summary of the completed document, including timetables for implementation of specific projects, then should be published and distributed widely, to identify the commitments of the persons involved and to establish the time schedule for which they are responsible, individually and collectively.

ROLE OF THE SENIOR ADMINISTRATORS IN INSTITUTIONAL PLANNING

When the objective of planning and the primary activities of the planning function affect the institution as a whole, the president of necessity becomes the chief planning officer. He is the key person in the planning process, whether a staff member or a line officer is responsible for its organization and implementation. The value the president places on the planning process determines how effective and workable the plan will be. He should provide adequate time throughout the year to meet and to discuss planning with the other senior administrators. This is one means that leads to commitment and involvement. Because the planning process is involved with academic planning, budgeting, and management, and frequently with state, regional, and national planning, it must have the specific direction of the president. The president is the person most aware of the effect of interactions between internal and external conditions. These interactions may affect programs, tuition rates, liaison with other institutions, salaries, enrollment policy, and investment strategy. It is the president who must make the critical decisions among alternative needs. Because budgets normally are incremental, at some point incremental changes may become less than productive for an institution. The president is the only administrator with broad enough authority and responsibility to break this chain, if such action is necessary.

A planning office—as distinct from a planning function—relates to the senior administrators in the following manner:

1. When planning crosses several jurisdictions, it falls under the purview of the president. In this case the planning office operates as

staff, with responsibility for seeing that a plan is realized; or it operates as line, with authority to develop a plan for implementation. Even though the planning office administers and expedites the planning process, the president must take the lead in establishing the rationale for the planning process.

2. When planning is within a given jurisdiction, the planning office should provide staffing as needed and provide a communications mechanism to the administrator involved. However, the president must help to resolve impasses that arise because of the many interdependent steps, handled by different groups or units, that are involved in the planning process—especially in the development of a master plan.

Each of the line officers who report to the president, and are therefore responsible for individual major units of the institution, has a dual role in the institutional planning process. As a member of the administrative council (or other similar entity) of the institution, he must participate in the development of the overall planning process, contributing to its refinement so that it is effective for the entire institution. In particular, he must work with the officer responsible for planning, the other senior administrators, and the president on those aspects of planning that involve more than one of the major units, and which therefore require responsible participation.

In addition, it is axiomatic that he plan for missions, tasks, and processes in his own unit. Senior administrators should possess the ability to write plans in terms of objectives, as mentioned above, and also should provide such training to those members of their staffs involved in planning for the unit.

Each senior administrator must support and interpret the rationale for the planning process, make sure that those responsible to him recognize that within his unit all persons will be expected to participate in the planning process, that budget requests will be weighed in relation to the extent to which the plans support them, and that performance will be evaluated in terms of achievement of objectives that appear in the plans. He also must establish guidelines and priorities within

his own unit for those in the subunits to follow in the development of their plans. To do this effectively, he must delineate the role of his area of responsibility and that of his staff in the context of the mission of the institution. Staff members must understand how they fit in the total plan.

RELATIONSHIP OF OPERATING BUDGET TO INSTITUTIONAL PLANNING

A crucial step in the planning process is the projection of available resources and the application of this projection to objectives, programs, organization, staffing, and facilities plans. "Adjusted" plans should result in specific final goals and the pattern for financing, including projected budgets and capital requirements.

In practice, the planning process usually is limited to the consideration of changes or additions to programs already in operation and the modifications of organization, staffing, and facilities required for those changes. An exception occurs when an institution sets out to develop a new master plan, reviewing its educational philosophy and restudying its objectives anew. To a lesser or greater degree, it may approach the development of program plans as if no programs were already in existence, deferring any study of the practicability of eliminating unnecessary programs or adding new ones that will be required.

What should happen in the planning process is that all proposed program changes should be reviewed annually in terms of the specific, established objectives of the institution, as reflected in the master plan. These objectives should be reviewed annually for relevance to the philosophy and purposes of the institution. This can happen only if the master plan of the institution is a current document, reviewed continuously and updated at least once a year.

An important role of the chief business officer in the planning process is to provide an appropriate perspective on the relationship of resources to plans. Prior to the initiation of the budget cycle, the chief business officer must brief the president on the projected financial picture so that the guidelines provided by the president in initiating both the planning and budget cycle may afford a maximum of opportunity for innovative planning while remaining within realistic limitations. The counsel and guidance of the chief business officer also will be needed by the president when budget requests must be adjusted.

Several management techniques are useful in providing effective interlocking of the planning and budgeting processes. The use of projection models, either computerized or manual, can facilitate the development of budget projections that reflect with reasonable accuracy various program elements and their interrelation and interdependence. They also can broaden the perspective in which planning decisions are made, by making it possible to organize and use vast amounts of relevant data in considering alternatives and answering questions about the future.

The relationship between planning and the operating budget can be handled most effectively if budget development and budget projections can be delineated in both program budget and object class patterns. The use of crossover techniques (for converting from a program budget to an object class budget and vice versa) with a computerized simulation model can be a distinct advantage.

RELATIONSHIP OF INSTITUTIONAL RESEARCH TO INSTITUTIONAL PLANNING

The needs of the planning function should be supported by institutional research, whether or not there is an office for either of these functions. The minimum requirements of an acceptable institutional research program for a college or university should include the following:

1. A data bank containing adequate information about students, faculty, and staff; financial resources; physical plant; and the programs and research conducted by the institution.

2. An information system that organizes the data bank for effective use, accessibility, and flexibility.

3. A program of regular studies providing consistent support to the planning process.

4. Provision for specific attention to the evaluation of new programs and research projects, so organized as to go into action whenever programs or projects are added.

5. Provision for support services to faculty members and others interested in conducting institutional studies, especially evaluations of the instructional process.

6. Adequate manpower and resources for implementing ad hoc studies needed in connection with specific planning decisions.

Educators need better ways to define, describe, and measure educational output. Quantitative measures are easy to identify, such as semester hours of credit awarded and number of students graduated. Qualitative indexes are much more elusive.

Institutions of higher education in the United States tend to use one of two conceptions of quality or, in most cases, a blend of the two. One of these, the idea that the quality of an institution is measured by the academic level of its graduates, was derived from the European tradition of higher education. When this tradition is followed, the quality of an institution is affected as much by its admission policies as by the quality of its instructional program. The other conception of quality in an educational institution is more in keeping with American traditions generally, that is, the quality of an educational institution is measured primarily by the difference in the student between the time he enters and the time he leaves. Within this perspective the open-door junior college, the highly selective liberal arts college, and the comprehensive university all may be of high (or low) quality, according to their performance.

The chief academic officer, in addition to making sure that planning in his own unit is centered on instruction and its results, must stimulate and support faculty participation in institutional research. His budget, or that of a research committee, should include funds for faculty (or faculty-supervised) research aimed specifically at the instructional process.

RELATIONSHIP OF STATE, REGIONAL, AND NATIONAL PLANNING TO INSTITUTIONAL PLANNING

When an institution is part of a state system of higher education, its own planning must relate specifically to the planning done for the state system, and must fit within the context of that planning. It can strive for individuality and distinctiveness, but only within the limits imposed by the state system. Although private institutions theoretically are free to make their own plans, such plans are likely to have greater success if they fit into national, state, and regional planning in higher education. By coordinating their plans with those of other entities, private institutions may best serve their own interests and promote the common good.

The pattern of federal support to higher education makes it impossible for any institution to proceed independently in institutional planning, as opposed to and fitting into state and regional planning. Regional planning, through the regional accrediting associations, the regional compact agencies, and other organizations, is having increasing impact on institutional planning.

Nearly all the states have established agencies with statutory responsibility for statewide planning and coordination of higher education.[1] Their influence and responsibilities can be expected to increase significantly as a result of enabling federal legislation.

The growth of voluntary-membership organizations referred to as consortia is also impressive. In addition, there are many examples of specific interinstitutional cooperation. Few institutions can afford to ignore opportunities to share resources, facilities, and expertise with other institutions as they plan for the future. National planning through the American Council on Education and other voluntary organizations provides needed perspective for institutional planning.

SYSTEMS MODELS AND PROGRAMS

The use of management information systems and, in particular, simulation models is a rapidly growing development. Unit cost analysis, space utilization studies, simple projection models, and other tools useful in management have been used in institutions of higher education for several decades. The computer makes possible the combination of an extensive array of such tools in coordinated systems providing consistent, timely information support for planning and management decisions. However, these systems must not

be allowed to become ends in themselves. Their primary purpose is to make it possible for management decisions to be made more wisely, more accurately, and on a more reliable schedule.

At its simplest a management information system consists of a data base, a set of procedures for maintaining and updating that data base, and a set of programs (manual or computerized) for extracting useful information from the data base. At a more sophisticated level the management information system may include an extensive computerized set of models capable of simulating many aspects of college operation. Such a system makes possible the informed consideration of a wide variety of alternative choices in administrative decision making. By informed consideration is meant consideration in which the implications of the various choices, and their probable effects, are clearly apparent.

At the most sophisticated level of computer simulation, many of the models for the programs of an institution are combined into one model— or very few models—in which the effects of quantifiable changes in one part of the program are reflected appropriately in most of the others. Thus, a question about the effect of a specific change in faculty size—for example, to reduce the student-teacher ratio—conceivably might reflect itself (in such a model) in changes in space and equipment requirements, custodial and maintenance services, instructional salaries, support service salaries, classroom utilization, anticipated budget for the faculty dining room, and even such elusive factors as student attrition rates and some indexes of student achievement. This is not to say that in any existing model it will accomplish all the above, but that models can be devised that relate all quantifiable factors whose relationships one can estimate to a reasonable degree. The effectiveness of a given model depends on the accuracy with which such relationships can be estimated and the extent to which the factors included (and the outputs chosen) are relevant to the management decisions that need to be made.

Six major purposes can be served by systems models and programs:[2]

---

[1] "Cooperation: Voluntary vs. Statutory," *Planning for Higher Education,* Vol. 2, No. 1 (1/4), February 1973, p. 1.

[2] William A. Shoemaker, *Systems Models and Programs for Higher Education,* (Washington, D.C.: Academy for Educational Development, April 1973).

Management information systems for current operations collect and utilize data needed to provide information and means of control for daily or periodic transactions such as cash balances, payroll records and disbursements, alumni contributions, and student grades.

Management information systems for planning organize and analyze data needed for long-range planning and for projecting goals, needs, and procedures, such as the cost of various instructional programs, the cost of various enrollment levels, the cost of instructional procedures, and the resource allocation required to support such projections.

Simulation emphasizes the interrelationship in the quantifiable factors of higher education which will result from various assumptions about the learning environment, such as enrollment growth or decline, changes in instructional procedures, changes in faculty composition and compensation, and overhead costs.

Procedural or process models attempt to use PERT techniques to organize and structure the flow or process of decision making and planning to encompass all essential steps in a time-flow sequence, including consultation with interested groups, decision making, and resulting action.

Comprehensive tailored models define the specific needs of a particular college or university and then apply one of several different models to the development of projections or simulation appropriate to that institution.

Exchange services serve as clearinghouses for the exchange of information about computer programs developed in particular colleges and universities and encourage systems applications by promoting an exchange of actual computer programs.

Institutions planning to initiate management information systems or simulation models for the first time should begin at an elementary level, gaining experience with single-purpose parts of such systems or models and proceeding from the simple to the complex. Many persons experienced in this field believe that attempts to model an entire institution are impractical. They feel that no model should be made so large or complex that it does not represent a relatively closed system, one that

is understandable and definable. Certainly, an extensive set of mini-models, each designed for a specific purpose and understood in all its limitations, is better than a complex model whose credibility, relevance, and flexibility will be limited.

Once it is decided that a comprehensive, "off-the-shelf" model or system is to be used, the utmost care is required to make sure that the model selected is well-suited to the institution. The model must be sophisticated enough to accommodate all the facets of the institution's programs to be represented, yet it must not be too complicated to apply to the particular institution. Unless the institution has on its staff, or plans to employ, those who are experienced in the use of simulation models, it may be advisable to employ a professional firm to install the system, instruct staff members in its use, and guide the institution during the initial period of its use.

CONCLUSION

Success in planning and its implementation depend equally on the president of the institution and on the capabilities of those who are responsible for this activity. It is common, particularly in small institutions, for the leadership and inspiration of the institution to be so centered in the person of the chief administrative officer that the planning process is accomplished without the involvement of many members of the staff, and without any student involvement. This method cannot possibly do justice to the requirements of effective planning in larger institutions.

Accountability of institutions of higher education is to those within as well as without. Each member should have a full, free opportunity to understand what the institution is trying to do, what he has a right to expect in connection with what he is trying to do, and what his responsibility is in contributing to the operation and success of the institution. Accountability in this sense cannot be brought about, or even approached, without broad knowledge of the planning process. There should be participation in the development of plans by those responsible for implementation of those plans. The planning process should bring about commitment, and plans should be developed and expressed in such a way as to make possible the evaluation of their accomplishment.

Management Information Systems and Data Processing

COLLEGE AND UNIVERSITY administrators require relevant, accurate, and current information on many different activities in order to make decisions, provide for efficient operation, and plan the future of their institutions. Different situations demand different systems: a large university probably will automate more of its transactions than a small college, and more complex institutions have organizations and enterprises that may require systems having unique capabilities.

A *management information system* is an organized method of providing past, present, and projection information related to internal operations and external intelligence. It supports the planning, control, and operational functions of an organization by furnishing uniform, [timely] information to assist the decision process.[1] The design of such a system should begin with documentation of the requirements of management for information that is needed and that will be used. *Data processing* is the collection and handling of data, maintenance of files, and production of reports.

Although modern management information systems usually presume the use of electronic data processing equipment, such a presumption is unwarranted in situations where manually oriented systems are justified under cost-benefit analysis. Use of a computer can be one of the most expensive ways to obtain information, and is one of the easiest ways to get an information overload. The feasibility of electronic data processing should be based not on net cost reduction, but on the economic advantages of making more complete information available to managers, resulting in better decision making.

The essential ingredients of manual and computer-based systems are the same: personnel, data input and organization, data storage and processing, and information output. A manual system has clerks, operations manuals, sets of procedures, and ledgers and files. A computer-based system also uses clerks, operations manuals, and sets of procedures, but in addition has a processing unit, programs, and data files. In maintaining and manipulating the data of the organization, computer-based systems as well as clerks can perform the following operations:

1. Identify a specific file and classify its contents.
2. Selectively extract information from, insert it into, or alter it in, specific individual records within a file.
3. Transfer records from one file to another or rearrange them within a single file.
4. Do routine updating and computations on the data in a file.
5. Search for particular characteristics in records within the files and keep a check list of all records possessing this characteristic. (An example would be all overdue accounts.)
6. Make low-level decisions on the basis of data, usually by automatic comparison of the data with some prearranged, alterable standard. (An example would be to compare inventories to specified stock levels and issue an order for supplies when inventories fall below these levels.)

For routine report production, a computer-based system has potential advantages over a manual system in terms of speed, size (the ability

[1]Kennevan, Walter J. "MIS Universe," *Data Management,* September 1970.

to manipulate large data files), and accuracy, particularly when large amounts of data must be summarized and presented. For special reports, or for a report whose need was not anticipated, a manual system is sometimes more efficient and flexible than a computer-based system if the quantity of data is small and/or response time is a criterion.

Persons responsible for management information systems must be able to influence data processing from the transaction level to the user level. Both management information and data processing systems require planning, organization, and a high level of technical and administrative skills. Administrators must be aware of trends in personnel sophistication, hardware (equipment), and software (operating systems and applications programs) to insure the effectiveness of a computer-based system. A management information system must have the understanding, involvement, and support of the chief administrative officers to be successful. Additionally, this will help to insure that administrative data processing requirements are compatible with other computational needs of the institution. Only then is it possible to develop systems that satisfy the information needs of the entire institution in a way that prevents wasteful and confusing duplication.

INFORMATION REQUIREMENTS

The management functions of planning, control, and operation are widely dispersed in colleges and universities. Claiming a role in the management process are faculty and students, deans, academic department chairmen, administrative unit managers, and central administrators; each has his own perception of the needs for information. However, management information system activities in higher education generally have focused on the needs of central academic and administrative offices and on the colleges and departments.

Planning information should be provided to the president, vice presidents, deans, department chairmen, and managers of each administrative unit. Enrollment forecasts and their implications concerning resources are one of the major planning concerns. Other information required relates to (1) students, sponsors, and other institutional users, (2) personnel, facilities, equipment, supplies, travel, student aid, and other resources used,

and (3) instruction, research, and public service projects that consume resources supplied by sponsors or other users in meeting institutional objectives.

Control information should be provided (usually by the department responsible for the function) when exceptions occur. For example, the admissions officer would receive from the management information system major variances in admissions patterns, or the officer responsible for budget control would receive from the system major variances between budgeted and actual expenditures. This aspect of control should be a part of the more detailed control provisions of the operational data systems for the specific area.

Operational information typically is provided to:

1. Financial and accounting officers—receipts and expenditure accounting, budgetary accounting, purchasing, student aid and loan accounting, inventory records, cost data, and portfolio management data.

2. Academic administrative officers—faculty workload information.

3. Registrar and admissions officers—admissions, registration and enrollments, courses, course scheduling, grades, transcripts, and degrees.

4. Personnel officers—personnel data, payroll, employee benefits, tax data, personnel budget, and applicant-position data.

5. Alumni and development officers—alumni records, gift acknowledgment, and related accounting.

6. Facilities planning officers—building inventory records, utilization reporting, and space planning models.

7. Research administration officers—proposal records, grant and contract reporting, and related accounting.

8. Managers of major public service operations —records associated with cooperative extension services, community service programs, and ticket operations.

9. Librarians—cataloguing, purchasing, and circulation.

10. Directors of physical plant and auxiliary enterprises—scheduling and acquisition, usage and costing records required for janitorial services, maintenance, housing, food

services, college stores, and similar operations.

11. Planning, budgeting, and institutional research officers—information in support of major external reporting requirements, integrated cost studies, and resource use and prediction models.

In order to meet the diverse operational needs of these groups, many institutions have developed a large number of separate systems. Frequently each system is designed to meet the needs of a particular manager, resulting in a total system in which the relationships among separate systems are not well-defined. For example, the period for reporting fee payments and the definition of a full-time student used by a cashier or bursar for fee-paying purposes may differ considerably from the period and the definition of a full-time student used by the registrar for academic degree purposes.

ORGANIZING THE MANAGEMENT INFORMATION AND DATA PROCESSING FUNCTIONS

There are many ways in which the management information and data processing functions can be organized within a college or university. Some institutions have user committees for management information and/or data processing systems design. Operations and applications programming may be performed by personnel of an internal or external service bureau, of an administrative data processing center, or of a combined research and instructional center. Institutions also may find it useful to share personnel and facilities for the programming and production control functions of all or certain sections of a management information system.

As previously noted, manual data processing of part or all of the data for a complete management information system is sometimes more cost-effective than electronic data processing. However, because most management information systems are automated, the remainder of this chapter assumes such systems; the principles apply to both methods.

Functional responsibilities and the assignment of those responsibilities to qualified persons with sufficient authority to perform are more important than the organizational structure that logically follows. In general, one office should be responsible for management information systems design and coordination. It should report at a level at least equal to that of the primary users, but should not report to any one of these users. The director of the office should be able to communicate effectively with all levels of management.

The best data processing organizational structure is one that encourages the users of information to work together for their mutual benefit and at the same time fosters the appropriate and judicious use of hardware and software technology in meeting both user and institutional management needs for consistent, reliable, and timely information in a cost-effective manner. There are myriad possible combinations. Evidence that a structure is working includes:

1. A recognized and agreed-upon plan for management information and data processing systems development.

2. Reasonably well-balanced development of systems among various user groups.

3. Clearly defined priorities, assignments, and deadlines.

4. Timely and accurate production of scheduled reports.

5. Awareness on the part of users of the relationship of their data and needs to the data and needs of others.

6. Lack of dependence on specific individuals with respect to data or systems by having programs adequately documented.

7. Capability of readily responding to a majority of integrated information needs such as those of the Higher Education General Information Survey (HEGIS), the National Science Foundation Research Survey, or the Information Exchange Procedures of the National Center for Higher Education Management Systems (NCHEMS).

8. Ability of users and management analysts to retrieve and arrange data in meaningful ways for their purposes within a reasonable time.

9. A general awareness of costs and alternatives, and evidence that these play a part in deciding to continue or terminate an activity.

FUNCTIONS REQUIRED FOR DEVELOPMENT OF DATA PROCESSING SYSTEMS

The functions required to develop and operate data processing systems that support a management information system include:

1. Management Systems Design—developing the overall requirements for organizing pertinent past, present, and projection information for use in planning and control, and coordinating to see that the needs of management are met in operational systems.
2. Management Data Coordination—
   a. Insuring that definitional consistency is maintained among the various sources of data, including the definition of data elements. *Example*: What is a full-time-equivalent student?
   b. Insuring the structural translation of data. *Example*: Does the student system report data to HEGIS in the same way that the personnel system does?
   c. Insuring the appropriateness of a given time. *Example*: Were first-semester fees divided by first-semester enrollments, not summer-session enrollments?
3. Management Data Control, Analysis, and Security—providing the coordination between the management question and the appropriate sources of data for answers to those persons authorized to receive them.
4. Data Processing Systems Design—developing the systems requirements for collecting and handling of data, maintenance of files, and production of reports that meet institutional management needs and the operational needs of users.
5. Applications Programming—preparing, testing, documenting, and maintaining the programs used in a data processing system and specifying the operating instructions and production control procedures appropriate to the programs.
6. Operations and Systems Programming—providing the hardware and general system software such as schedules, utility routines, and compilers necessary to serve the development needs of applications programmers and the production needs of operating systems.
7. Production Control—scheduling and progress monitoring of data processing jobs from the time a request is received until the user receives the requested information.
8. Facilities Management—meeting the specialized requirements of computing facilities for climate control, constant power sources, alternate facilities to provide processing back-up, adequate equipment maintenance, efficient arrangement of equipment, and effective methods for accomplishing equipment conversions.
9. Security—providing both data and facilities protection from intentional and unintentional actions that would result in damage to the institution.

In addition, the general management and support functions of directing, staffing, scheduling, training, budgeting, and reporting are required for these functions.

USE OF DATA PROCESSING IN DEVELOPING MANAGEMENT INFORMATION SYSTEMS

When used most effectively, data processing can support three kinds of activities:

1. Basic transaction processing and control—to meet the needs of unit managers in performing specific tasks.
2. Comprehensive profile and exception reporting—to meet the needs of program managers in seeing the interrelationships, history, and status of data from a variety of related units, and to meet the needs for external reporting.
3. Projection information processing—to meet the needs of planners in evaluating policy alternatives by applying forecasting, simulation, and other analytical tools to stored data.

Data processing can provide the desired management information systems reports, but independent, internal control by other departments is an essential part of the system.

An effective management information system must have the capability to transcend organizational boundaries. One way to accomplish this is to develop a generic grouping of related tasks into a series of systems and subsystems that support operational needs and, through the use of common elements, provide for comprehensive data. Such a management information system might be designed around three major systems, with related subsystems as follows:

1. Resource Management Information—to collect and store data and provide reports about sources, inventories, needs, acquisitions, allocations, and activities or usage of resources and evaluations as reflected by the organizational structures by which resources are acquired and assigned. Typical examples of subsystems are:
   a. Personnel.
   b. Facilities.
   c. Equipment, supplies, and materials.
   d. Finance.
2. Student-Sponsor-Patron Information — to collect and store data and provide reports about the prospects, selection, preferences, contributions, activities, and evaluations of students, sponsors, and other users of the programs of the institution. Typical examples of subsystems are:
   a. Students.
   b. Government, industry, and foundations.
   c. Alumni, parents, and patrons.
   d. Participants, clients, and patients.
3. Program Management Information—to collect and store data and provide reports about the programs of the institution. Program information includes goals, contents, capacity, demand, requirements, schedules, and evaluations of a program, and is augmented by relating to the resource management and user-sponsor-patron systems. Typical examples of subsystems are:
   a. Instruction.
   b. Research.
   c. Public service.
   d. Academic support.
   e. Student services.
   f. Institutional support.
   g. Operation and maintenance of plant.
   h. Scholarships and fellowships.

Whatever the design of the management information system, a plan is required that will address both organizational and programmatic needs for information.

Data Base Management Systems

One of the most promising technical developments for the use of data processing to support management information systems has been the introduction of data base management software programs. A variety of these is available commercially, and each has its own advantages and disadvantages. These programs generally:

1. Provide for the creation and maintenance of complex files (data bases) in a very flexible way. New elements or partial files can be added readily.
2. Require that a dictionary of common terms be developed for each data base and that the dictionary term be used in any application program that accesses the data base.
3. Provide for cross-relating different files in a way that is obvious to the programmer.
4. Provide for security protection of whole files, segments of files, or key data elements so that they can be accessed only by authorized users.
5. Support batch or on-line processing. Batch processing permits the uninterrupted processing of different jobs by organizing them before processing; on-line processing permits the user to enter or access data quickly, by means of peripheral equipment, without the need for writing a program or requesting a report.
6. Support reporting languages that can be used to meet unplanned requests.
7. Support the use of translation tables to convert data from an institutional format into externally required formats.

The implications of this technology are particularly important in the systems development and program maintenance areas. The use of a data base language requires a comprehensive approach to defining data needs. However, it facilitates use of the system both by those supplying data and by those drawing authorized data from the system. It also simplifies the design problem of adding new data elements to a file, since all that generally is required is to supply a name to the dictionary, to relate the new element to other elements, and to provide sufficient storage space for the data to be supplied.

In theory, application programs such as a payroll report program or a grade report program become independent of the file because they access only those parts of the file that contain the elements needed to operate the program, and need no longer be concerned with all the elements in a file. Prior to data base languages, for example, an expansion of the personnel file to add a new data element, such as the equal employment opportunity code, required a change to every program that used that file to reflect, at the least, the new format. With a data base language the only programs affected by a new data element are the ones that require that element for reporting.

Program maintenance also is simplified when data elements are to be redefined or eliminated. Because a common dictionary of terms is required to access the data base, it is relatively simple to discover which programs are using the data element in question.

Data base management is not the only alternative. Many benefits of a data base approach—adopting common definitions, requiring programmers to use these terms, and using comprehensive definition of data bases—can be gained without incurring the increased software costs and hardware sizes that may be necessary to support a data base management language. However, the concept of data base management has considerable importance, and institutional managers should consider carefully whether it may be appropriate or useful for their needs.

Creating Systems from Applications

The most common method for achieving a management information system is to successively integrate existing applications. For example, a typical pattern of development of a student information system has been to:

1. Relate programs supporting student fee accounting to programs supporting registration and grade reporting.
2. Relate programs supporting admissions to those supporting registration so that common data can be passed through.
3. Relate fees collected for housing and other enterprises to fees collected for instruction so that more comprehensive bills can be prepared.

4. Automate transcripts of grades by providing history files.
5. Add automated student scheduling between the admissions and registration-grade reporting system with appropriate links to the fee assessment and payment process.
6. Develop a link to the alumni system so that student data can be passed through.

This approach has its merits, in that each step supports clear-cut objectives of specific users at a given time and corresponds to the increased ability of data processing equipment to deal efficiently with larger programs and larger files.

The integration of existing applications, while pragmatic in concept, has created maintenance problems at the data processing level, where large numbers of programs have been linked together and where inflexible procedures have been written into the basic logic of programs to account for differences that existed among applications at a given time.

Both data processing personnel and users have been frustrated by the apparently constant and insurmountable problems of adapting these systems to changes in requirements or to new technology. This has led to significant interest in developing new, major systems. Student systems and personnel systems have received the greatest attention because they represent the amalgamation of the greatest number of different suppliers and users of data.

Summary

Every college or university has a management information system, whether or not by design. The use of electronic data processing and the degree of its sophistication may depend on such factors as specific applications, resources available, and the size or complexity of the institution. Regardless of the system being planned or in use, the management information function should be administered by one office, and to be successful, must have the full and continuing involvement of the chief administrative officers. It is only in this way that the system will have maximum efficiency and will meet the information requirements of the entire institution.

Risk Management and Insurance

RISK is uncertainty concerning the probability of an occurrence—in the context of higher education, the occurrence of financial loss not offset by opportunity for gain. Risk management consists of identifying risk and analyzing ways of treating, controlling, and funding risk. Specifically, administrators of higher education are charged with preserving an institution's assets—human, physical, and financial—at the lowest cost to the institution. A program employing techniques of risk management can be more cost-effective than a program limited to insurance purchase. The ultimate evaluation of a program of risk management is success in preventing personal injury and property loss, while reducing the cost of risk to a minimum.

Although a relatively new business concept, risk management has been used effectively to enhance profitability. Lack of the profit motive may account for the slower growth of this managerial technique in higher education. However, colleges and universities have become aware of the long-range benefits of a sound risk management program as a result of a period of crisis in the late 1960s involving availability and cost of insurance.

STATEMENT OF POLICY

An essential first step in treating risk is the development of a written statement of objectives and limitations. Such a policy statement must emanate from the governing board, but as a practical matter must have its origins in the administration of the institution. This responsibility generally rests with the chief business officer. It is his function, together with his staff, to develop a policy statement for presentation to the board, where it should be discussed in order that board members understand fully the policy's implications.

Ideally, this statement expresses philosophically the objectives of the institution in managing risk. This includes the limitations of risk and possible loss that can safely be retained as well as the extent to which resources can be devoted to various techniques for treating risk. It is desirable that the statement be flexible, general, and permit practical administration without regular recourse to the governing board. Also, there should be periodic review of the policy statement to adjust to changing conditions.

The policy statement must clearly delegate authority for its implementation to the institution's administration, including identification of the risk manager. Alternative approaches are available for risk identification and management.

THE RISK MANAGER AND HIS FUNCTION

Because of the scope of his job, the chief business officer is the risk manager for most institutions. So many individuals in the institution are affected by risk management that the task of coordination cannot satisfactorily be assigned, referred, or transferred to others except in the case of a large institution, where the function may warrant a specialist or even an entire department devoted to managing risk. It is not necessary that direct line authority be established from the risk manager to all those executing policy. The risk manager must be someone with direct access to senior management, and the position must be defined so as to effect policy implementation.

Whether the risk manager is the chief business officer or a specialist on his staff, identification of risk is the first task. A review of financial statements and property and other records will indicate physical assets to be preserved, although an up-to-date evaluation for risk management purposes is often necessary. The manager must be informed of new building plans and changes in space utilization. Accounting officers, legal counsel, physical plant directors, and academic administrators are among those to be consulted. Outside the staff are external auditors, insurance and risk consultants, insurance brokers, and insurance company specialists in various fields. The identification process is never-ending; the lines of communication must be kept open, but the risk manager should exercise initiative to keep abreast of changes that might affect risk handling.

RISK CONTROL

Once risk is identified, it should be analyzed and evaluated. There are several options open to the manager. He should never overlook the possibility of eliminating or abating the risk. Illustrative of this is the correction of dangerous physical conditions by the safety specialist. Identification is possible before an accident occurs. Designation of a safety officer and property preservation specialist is essential. Regardless of the size of the institution and the depth of the risk manager's experience, consultants may be required. Many firms offer such a service, and some insurance companies and major insurance brokers also provide this expertise. As with most insurance policies, the premium base provides a level of loss prevention service. It is the institution's responsibility to secure this help and see that it is used effectively.

The Occupational Safety and Health Act of 1970 has resulted in increased risk reduction efforts. The alert risk manager should see in the Act an opportunity to reduce risk on a scale not possible before. In many cases, laws act as a stimulus for making major capital expenditures that might have been deferred otherwise. The Act gives the force of law to practices and conditions of employment widely recognized as desirable, but too expensive. The Occupational Safety and Health Administration (OSHA) has added fines and penalties to accompany the Act. Institutional recognition of OSHA requirements and how to fund and implement them should challenge the risk manager; the Act should be a code for risk reduction.

All private institutions are subject to the Act. Many state-supported or related schools are exempt until their state has enacted a law acceptable to the federal government as a substitute for the

Act. These state regulations will affect public institutions and will be enforced by state inspectors much as federal law requires. For a detailed treatment of this subject, refer to the chapter "Safety."

An aid in avoiding risk is careful review of contracts for obligations to indemnify, insure, or save harmless. Often such provisions are "boiler-plate" and may be subject to negotiation. Inability to manage a risk may require a chief business officer to modify some activities in order to conform to the institution's statement of risk management.

Transfer of risk is a technique too often associated only with the purchase of insurance. Another vehicle for transfer is the type of contract mentioned above. The risk manager must be alert to ways to impose on others the risk of a given operation where it is justifiable. On construction operations in which the builder is not directly supervised, risk generally is transferred to the contractor by "hold harmless" clauses. Leases for real estate should be scrutinized for proper transfer of liability and property risks when appropriate. Relative bargaining position of the parties may dictate whether transfer of risk is possible, but even if possible, such transfer is not always advisable.

RISK FUNDING

Those risks that have been identified, cannot be eliminated, and have not been transferred by contract must be deliberately not insured, self-insured, or insured commercially. The risk management concept dictates that all three—no insurance, total self-insurance of risk, and retention through use of deductibles (described in the section "Deductibles")—be weighed carefully in light of the budget, peculiar financial needs, investment policy, and experience of administrators. Before deciding among the three alternatives, a careful analysis of risk, including a history of losses, is necessary. Self-insurance without an adequate program of loss prevention or control can be a costly error.

In a normal situation glass breakage is a non-insured risk. Physical damage to vehicles and theft of movable equipment are other risks that might not lend themselves to insurance, depending on the financial situation of the institution and the loss history. The probability factor cannot be overlooked.

Self-insurance offers one advantage over not insuring. It produces a record of risk cost that is otherwise lost. One must recognize the administrative cost as part of the overall risk cost. Self-insurance may be funded from the annual operating budget or a funded reserve established and carried year to year, depending on the ability and needs of the institution. Business interruption, direct property damage up to a given level, and limited crime loss lend themselves to self-insurance. Liability risks that are insured economically and serviced for claims on a first-dollar (no deductible) basis seldom lend themselves to self-insurance.

Some states and institutions have examined the feasibility of pooling certain risks. A state may self-insure most risks and provide a self-insurance program to its entire college and university system. If any generalization can be made, it is that the combination of self-insurance and retention through deductibles offers opportunity for savings after careful study by risk managers.

INSURANCE

Insurance consists of sharing the risks of possible catastrophic losses from specified hazards by a group of "individuals." Each member, or policyholder, within the group agrees to pay a portion of the losses suffered by other members of the group. In this way, the annual cost to each policyholder of such contingencies is reasonably predictable, while removing uncertainty about facing larger costs of assuming individually the results of a catastrophe to property. The larger and more widespread the risk-sharing group, the more mathematically predictable are the anticipated losses in any given period.

In exchange for the benefits gained by spreading the risk among many individuals, the policyholder must pay not only his share of the estimated cost of catastrophes predicted to occur to members of the group during a future period of time, but also his share of the operating costs of the organization.

Several factors enter into the amount of insurance premiums. The total amount collected in premiums must cover (1) anticipated claims for losses of policyholders during the following year, determined on mathematical and statistical bases, (2) operating expenses of the company, (3) agents' commissions, and (4) any amounts retained by the company or paid to stockholders. The total cost is reduced by earnings on investment of reserves and other funds of the insurance company.

No insurance company escapes the economics of this formula. Lower costs to educational institutions can be realized only by purchasing insurance from companies that operate economically. Companies that have selected risks wisely, that have held down operating expenses and commissions, and that have reduced or eliminated dividends to stockholders may offer satisfactory protection to colleges and universities at minimum cost. Insurance should be purchased on the basis of these factors—not because of friendship, patronage, or reciprocity.

Agents and Brokers

Although agents work on behalf of insurers and brokers work on behalf of insureds, the terms are used synonymously in this text. The largest insurance volume on a national scale is placed through agents and brokers. There are advantages in dealing with an agent or broker having available within his organization marketing skills as well as claim and loss prevention engineering services that can be used directly or coordinated with an insurance company. Although there may be advantages to retaining a local agent or broker, an existing relationship does not preclude securing competitive prices.

Agents and brokers traditionally have been compensated by a commission paid by the insurance company, which varies with the line of insurance. This is changing, however, and more brokers have been willing to perform services for a specified fee on large accounts, rather than to rely on commission. In smaller institutions the percentage commission is undoubtedly a fair means of compensating the broker for his knowledge and skill. The risk manager-insurance buyer must determine for himself in each instance what the commission amounts to and whether he is receiving fair services for the money spent.

The Underwriter

The insurance company's decision on accepting the risk and on the price to charge is the function of the underwriter. Although many types of insurance are priced from a manual, it is generally true that there are numerous variables or credits possible. The underwriter's analysis of the risk is an essential point. In many instances he receives his information from the agent or broker or, in the case of a direct writing company, from a salesman. It is desirable to invite the underwriter to the institution, as a full understanding of the local situation is valuable.

Considerations in Selection

The relationship between an institution and an insurance company should be long-term. Assuming the quality of service is satisfactory, an accepted minimum guideline is three to five years of continuous coverage before testing the market. Different timing might be appropriate, however, depending on market conditions.

For the large insurance purchaser, competitive positions between stock insurance companies and direct writers, including many mutual companies, probably are indistinguishable. A thorough survey of prospective companies by the insurance purchaser or his broker should include direct writing and mutual companies. Brokers have access to these types of firms as well as all others, even though mutual companies do not pay a commission. It is anticipated that the purchaser will pay a fee to the broker for his services if a company other than one offering a commission is selected.

From time to time, any insurance program should be reviewed by one of several methods. Some institutions operate on the assumption that they have a lasting broker relationship, which dictates that the broker participate in designing specifications and solicit all proposals from insurance companies.

Another school of thought suggests competition among agents and brokers as well as insurers. This generally requires that the specifications be designed by the institution. Often this complex job is best done by a consultant; many such experts sell no insurance but work for a fee. Design of specifications should produce a clear, insurance-term description of coverages desired. These specifications should enable production of proposals that may be compared fairly, and yet should be flexible enough to permit an innovative insurer to do the best job possible. Insurers should be

required to present a comprehensive illustration of services to be provided, by whom they will be performed, and what personnel are present at each servicing location. It is not out of order to ask any insurer not previously known to the institution to name other institutions of higher education he services in order to facilitate a "service after the sale" inquiry, and to evaluate familiarity with the field. Price and breadth of protection are critical factors.

Selection of the brokers to compete is an exacting process. They should demonstrate an interest in the account, with scope of service offered and experience of personnel proper points of judgment. Proximity of a service office is desirable. If possible, the broker should know something about a similar institution's risk management and insurance problems. Finally, the broker should demonstrate familiarity with the concepts of risk management.

Adequate time should be allowed from issuance of specifications until proposals are due. This should be at least thirty days, and longer if the risk is large or complex. It is best to allow a month to evaluate proposals.

In general, insurance coverages should be thought of and discussed in terms of the types of risks. The two major divisions are property insurance and casualty or liability insurance.

Property Insurance

Building and Content Valuations. Institutions with standard fire and extended coverage are insured at actual cash value (ACV). Generally, actual cash value is defined as replacement cost new less depreciation. Risk managers should be aware that most financial reports show historical cost of buildings and depreciated cost of capital contents. To prevent over- or under-insuring property, the risk manager may want to have an appraisal by one of the many firms offering this service. Once completed, an annual index can be used to update original appraisals.

Deductibles. The deductible amount of an insured loss is that portion borne by the insured before he is entitled to any recovery from the insurer. The deductible may be for each loss, an annual amount of losses, or a combination of both. The purpose of the deductible is to eliminate the relatively small and frequent losses from insurance coverage. The business officer should carefully appraise the ability of the institution to fund loss through increasing deductibles. He should retain as large a risk as feasible, based on history of loss, present efforts at loss prevention, and market requirements. However, considerable premium savings may be possible for a relatively small increase in the deductible.

Perils. It is desirable to insure the broadest spectrum of perils by purchase of "all risk" or "difference in conditions" insurance which, instead of naming perils, insures against all risks except those specifically excluded. Such exclusions include war, nuclear reaction, and wear and tear. The alternative is to insure against specific risks such as fire, sprinkler leakage, and radioactive contamination.

Property insurance includes protection against direct financial loss due to insurable perils as well as protection against indirect loss occasioned by direct loss. Examples of business interruption insurance include loss of dining services receipts and housing revenue through fire or disablement of a central steam boiler.

Other components of the property insurance package may be transit insurance, covering merchandise and purchases while in commercial movement and other types of floater (or movable property) coverage on institutional assets, either in movement or on premises. Special property insurance is available on data processing systems and can apply to both hardware coverage and media coverage, which refers to processing loss as a result of direct damage.

Not to be overlooked is boiler and machinery insurance, the greatest feature of which is intensive loss-prevention inspection service for steam boilers, hot-water generators, moving mechanical equipment, and electrical systems. It protects against direct loss to equipment, to the enclosing building, and to bodily injury if such coverage is desired, as well as indirectly to use and occupancy.

Casualty Insurance

Casualty or liability insurance usually concerns losses caused by personal injury as well as the liability of the insured for such injury or for property damage. Casualty insurance is as important as property insurance in protecting the assets of an institution. In a sense, it is a much more complex

insurance problem, since this coverage is designed to protect the institution against liability imposed by law. Common law doctrines vary from state to state as does statutory law. Immunity from tort liability is granted in some states to eleemosynary institutions. Public colleges and universities in certain states enjoy protection from tort liability under the theory of sovereign immunity. Long-standing legal concepts change, so no institution should consider its condition static.

For those institutions with statutory or common law immunity from suits, additional caution is necessary. Although the corporate institution indeed may enjoy some immunity, individual faculty and staff members may not. There is an increasing tendency for litigation directed against an individual as well as an institution. This creates tension and uneasiness among employees unless they are assured of protection or defense at the institution's expense. All such liability policies should contain an endorsement prohibiting the insurance company from invoking the defense of immunity without specific written consent.

The heart of a liability program is a comprehensive, general liability policy. It is usually desirable to insure all employees and agents, including board members, acting on behalf of the institution, in order that such persons if named individually without the institution will be granted a defense. This is, of course, a policy decision. The standard policy grants protection to the university for claims arising from its position as a landlord, including all of its operations both on and off premises.

Certain extensions of the customary scope of the policy are essential. One such extension is contractual liability on a broad-form basis. This protects against liability not imposed directly by law but is assumed voluntarily under a contract other than a property lease. Other essential coverage is the so-called personal injury endorsement. This extends protection for claims from physical or bodily injury to the areas of libel, slander, and false arrest and can be extended to include dissemination of information that may cause damages.

Workmen's Compensation. Each state requires an employer to indemnify an employee against certain types of losses resulting from a work-connected injury. Such laws grew out of reform in the first decade of the twentieth century, depriving the employee of the right to sue in tort and guaranteeing stipulated benefits without proof of negligence. Some consider this a staff benefit, but most authorities agree it more closely resembles casualty insurance in terms of its financial impact on the institution.

This impact varies with the benefit level of each state. The important point is that in some jurisdictions such as California, New York, and New Jersey, the financial impact of compensation liability can be substantial. Such liability is generally insured. Even in those cases where self-insurance programs are maintained, it is wise to reinsure upper-level liability for catastrophic losses.

In those cases in which an institution chooses to insure its entire liability, several forms are available. For the smallest institutions, the manual rates are applied to payroll. The premium is set by experience of similar employers in the state. Larger institutions may secure experience-rated policies. These contrast the individual institution's experience over a three-year period with similar employers and provide a credit or debit factor to manual rates. The largest institutions generally find it advantageous to insure under a restrospective rating plan in which roughly twenty percent of the experience-rated premium is retained by the insurance company. The balance of the premium is determined by the actual claim payout, modified by certain additional charges for claim cost and taxes; thus an individual pays his own way. All such plans have a maximum annual premium. The twenty percent retention includes the cost of pure insurance for exposures that the insurance company cannot pass back to the policyholder in the retrospective premium plan. For an institution large enough to qualify for a retrospective plan, this is usually an excellent vehicle for securing the proper credit for a good safety program and other efforts aimed at curtailing employee injury.

In some jurisdictions, a state monopoly is the only source of insurance. This form of insurance is regulated carefully everywhere. Still, it is essential that experts be employed to evaluate the most advantageous plan for a given institution and the insurance company best able to furnish the invaluable loss-prevention engineering and claims services that must be a part of the workmen's compensation program. This protects both the institution's finances and the right of employees to prompt and fair treatment after injury. Many compensation insurers operate in only one state and due to efficient, specialized operations, offer substantial dividends to selected policyholders. This coverage deserves complete investigation, since workmen's compensation often represents a significant budgetary cost.

It is important that possible endorsements to the compensation policy be evaluated. Examples are voluntary compensation endorsements, all-state coverage for employees subject to a jurisdiction outside the state of primary work, foreign coverage for faculty members who may be abroad, coverage under the Jones Act, longshoremen and harborworkers' compensation program, or federal maritime jurisdiction.

Crime Insurance

Careful attention should be given to blanket coverage of all employees to prevent financial loss due to their activities. Most crime policies can include additional protection for loss of money due to burglary, robbery, holdup, forgery, and counterfeit money. The policies, including their limits of liability, must be tailored to the needs of the institution. This requires careful scrutiny by financial officers, auditors, and agent or broker.

Unemployment Compensation

This liability is new to most institutions of higher education and resulted from federal government pressure on the states to make nonprofit employers subject to the law. It is intended to discourage unnecessary expansion and contraction of staff and can be costly if not well-managed. Students usually are not covered; faculty contracts should be so written that faculty members with contracts for teaching in the subsequent fall are not eligible to claim unemployment compensation benefits during the summer months.

Management of this risk dictates prudent personnel practices, especially in larger institutions, which may be laying off employees in one department while hiring in another. Close coordination and rethinking of the economics of some summer layoff practices are necessary. Careful documentation of discharge for cause is elementary in controlling this risk. Funding generally permitted includes either reimbursement to the state for actual benefits paid to former employees or payment of a payroll tax, which is normally experience-modified. Thoughtful but prompt attention must be paid to each claim for unemployment compensation when notice is received from state employment offices.

Student Accident and Health Insurance

Almost every institution has a program to provide such group insurance to its students. It may be mandatory or optional. In a few instances student groups administer and purchase such coverage. In others the institution itself directly purchases the coverage on behalf of students. Many innovations are being made in the type of insurance coverage available in this complex, competitive market. The choice often varies with the amount spent and the size of the institution.

Statistics is the key to effective student health insurance. The agent or broker handling this coverage should provide detailed claim statistics for joint analysis of the price structure. This insurance usually is written on a very low company overhead compared to casualty or property insurance and has all the advantages of mass merchandising econ-omies. It behooves the institution, on behalf of its students, to make sure the price is equitable.

SUMMARY

Each institution must adopt a policy statement for treating risk. This statement should be used in analyzing risks. Authority for managing the treatment accorded the risks identified should be centralized.

Only after the risk manager has completed a program of reducing and eliminating risks, assumed or funded risk, and transferred certain risks to others should the residual risks be transferred to an insurer.

Careful attention must be paid to selection of the insurance company intermediary and the competitive marketing of the institution's insurance. Coverage is best bought on the broadest possible basis after the assumption of maximum risk. Insurance may be grouped into property coverages, casualty (including workmen's compensation) coverage, crime coverage, and insured benefits. (Except for student accident and health insurance and unemployment compensation, more detailed information on insured benefits can be found in the chapter "Faculty and Staff Benefits.")

Administration of Sponsored Programs: Instruction, Research, and Public Service

INSTRUCTION, research, and public service are the primary functions of American higher education. The degree to which each college or university fulfills any or all these functions depends in large measure on the goals of the institution, its size, and availability of resources. Funds for attainment of these functions come from various sources such as student fees, state government appropriations, gifts, income from endowments, and extramural support (grants and contracts, principally from agencies of the federal government, corporations, foundations, and voluntary health agencies).

POLICY AND PROGRAM IMPLICATIONS

Grants and contracts provide a significant portion of the total revenues of many institutions and are the primary source of support for research projects. Society and institutions have benefited greatly from the availability of such funds, as they advance knowledge, aid training of new scholars, and provide support for expanded facilities. However, administrators must consider the real and potential impact these funds can have on their institution. If these resources are permitted to become an integral part of the financial fabric of an institution, any significant withdrawal could create substantial academic, administrative, and fiscal problems. Acceptance of these funds is accompanied by a requirement for strict accountability, and involvement in sponsored programs imposes demands on facilities and staff, which must be weighed carefully.

The foregoing should be considered in policy decisions as to the level and type of sponsored program activity the college or university will pursue. The business officer should be cognizant of the resource implications associated with extramural support in order either to advise appropriate officials adequately when policy decisions are under consideration or to provide leadership in their formulation and management. Regardless of the extent to which the institution engages in sponsored programs, the effect of such funding in the context of overall institutional objectives and the administrative requirements imposed by sponsoring agencies are a matter of direct concern to the business officer.

Grants and contracts, the devices for authorizing sponsored programs, are awarded to institutions, not to the individuals responsible for the conduct of programs. Although grants and contracts normally are awarded to institutions because of special competence of staff members, the institution assumes full legal responsibility for the programs and for fulfilling sponsoring agency requirements. It is therefore essential that every effort be made to insure that sound management practices and prudent fiscal policies are followed in administering these resources.

ORGANIZATION

Formal policies and procedures for handling sponsored programs are essential whenever there is any significant volume. Such policies and procedures, which should involve the business officer and those in the academic community at an early stage, should be developed with the cooperation of all segments of the institution to insure compliance with sponsor requirements as well as maintenance of institutional integrity.

One of the initial steps in negotiation and administration of grants and contracts is the development of an appropriate functional structure.

Institutional support activities required for the administration of sponsored programs include proposal preparation, review, and submission; grant and contract negotiations; purchasing; development and negotiation of indirect cost rates; maintenance of accounts and records; management of inventions and copyrights; affirmative action programs; protection of rights of human subjects and welfare of animals; preparation and submission of reports; administration of cash flow information; and compliance with other grant and contract conditions. A major task of organizing is coordination of all persons involved.

The academic staff is responsible for preparation and review of at least the technical part of proposals, performance of the work, preparation of technical reports, and many other activities. The business or administrative structure should be designed as a service and coordinating operation.

The coordination required for a successful system of sponsored programs should begin with the president or principal officer of the institution, where the various lines of responsibility and authority converge. Below the president there can be a variety of organizational frameworks. There is perhaps only one key element common to all: a proposal for a project constitutes an offer and, legally speaking, may become a binding contract (whether called a grant or a contract) if the sponsor accepts. The final approval of the proposal thus cannot be taken lightly and should be made by a duly authorized officer of the institution. Often there are differences between the initial proposal and the grant or contract received, or there are terms and conditions not previously specified. In that case, acceptance of the resulting grant or contract also should be made by a duly authorized officer. Other actions such as vouchers, financial reports, and final settlements also may require an authorized officer's signature.

DIVISION OF RESPONSIBILITY

The office can fit into any of the following frameworks, or a combination of them, since absolute generalizations are impossible.

No Separate Office

When the volume of sponsored programs within an institution is small, there may not be sufficient justification for establishing a special office to handle the administrative responsibilities. In certain circumstances, even when the volume is large, assignment of the various responsibilities to regular departments, divisions, and officials may be preferable in order to avoid multiplying the lines of responsibility within the organization. In either case, it is essential that each responsibility be clearly defined and assigned, with sufficient time and personnel for each. It is important that those who handle the business and legal problems involved have adequate training, inasmuch as these problems are not only substantially different from those encountered in other aspects of educational institution administration, but also are often more complicated, particularly in government contracts.

When there is no special office for handling sponsored programs, the business office normally will administer the business and financial details, and the academic divisions or departments will be responsible for the scientific and technical aspects. The institution's legal counsel may assume legal and contractual responsibilities.

There are many situations, however, that involve business and scientific as well as legal aspects, such as inventions and patents. Making and reporting an invention is primarily a responsibility of researchers, although there should be procedures and reminder services to facilitate reporting. Negotiation of contractual provisions for inventions and patents is a business and legal matter, and agreements regarding disposition of inventions must be prepared to be legally enforceable and must be executed by the research staff. The question of patenting must be decided, and the contract conditions must be complied with before the institution receives its full payment for performance of the research.

Therefore, close liaison is necessary among the business office, the office responsible for legal matters, and the dean, department head, or project leader to insure that the institution undertakes only obligations it can fulfill and to insure that these obligations are met.

Separate Office

In larger institutions there is often a separate office for handling many administrative aspects of sponsored programs. These programs generally include all three functions (instruction, research, and public service), but sometimes only research. Fellowships also may be a responsibility of the same office. In some institutions the person responsible for the separate office reports to the chief business officer; in others, to a senior academic officer. In rare instances he may be responsible to a vice president in charge of fund raising. Any of these arrangements work, but the detailed responsibilities may be somewhat different. In any event, and most importantly, there should be well-defined duties known both within the institution and to all sponsors.

The internal organization of an office for sponsored programs is complicated. There are broad functional responsibilities that cut across projects, such as patents and copyrights, human subjects, animal care, security, property management, and occupational safety and health. There are individual project management responsibilities, including preparation and submission of proposals, negotiation and acceptance, monitoring, and closeout. A competent person can specialize in one or more broad functional areas and still handle a group of individual projects.

Fiscal and accounting responsibilities for sponsored programs may be assigned to an office for sponsored programs if the person responsible for the office reports to the chief business or fiscal officer. More often they are not. In either case it is an important responsibility of the office to assist in obtaining prompt, meaningful project cost statements for principal investigators and for the office itself to insure effective project management. The office for sponsored programs should monitor costs carefully and anticipate and act upon potential overruns.

Committee or Board

Sometimes a committee or board is established for the general overview of sponsored programs, particularly for sponsored research. Approval by the faculty for establishment of such a committee or board has a salutary effect in terms of acceptance. Both academic and business interests should be represented, but more than seven or eight members will tend to make it unwieldy. The executive officer for such a committee frequently is the director of the office for sponsored programs.

Major functions of this committee include periodic development and review of statements of policy or procedure covering various aspects of sponsored programs such as criteria for acceptance, proposal procedures, security, and patent policy. The committee also may find it desirable to review specific proposals above a certain dollar level or with unusual implications. Subcommittees can be established in areas such as patents and copyrights, human subjects, professional non-faculty personnel, and even for allocation of internal research funds and institutional grants.

Separate Corporation or Foundation

In some instances, primarily in state-supported institutions, it is desirable or even necessary to establish separate corporations or foundations to accept and carry out sponsored programs. The reasons include limitations in charter or authorizing legislation that prevent or hamper conduct of such work, state fiscal regulations and purchasing procedures, or the desirability of having a separate corporate entity handle patents and other types of transactions in addition to sponsored programs.

The separate foundation may operate on a basis comparable to a sponsored program office within the institution, or it may take on additional or fewer responsibilities. The legal, contractual, and operating relationships between the foundation and the institution must be established on a more formal basis and require somewhat more detail than when an office within the institution has the administrative responsibility. Foundations that service multicampus institutions must be specially organized and staffed to mitigate the distance problem; generally, an authorized representative of the foundation should be placed at each campus to facilitate liaison.

PROPOSAL, NEGOTIATION, ACCEPTANCE, AND IMPLEMENTATION

Because all sponsored programs are based on agreement to perform, the process necessarily requires a formalized application and acceptance procedure. This includes presentation of ideas, negotiation of terms of award, acceptance, and structure for administering the projects. Only a properly designated official or his designated representative should be able to obligate the institution or amend the terms or conditions of a grant or contract.

Proposals

The Principal Investigator. The sponsored project must have a principal investigator or director, who should be free to select his subject matter within the limits of institutional policy and to formulate independent findings and conclusions.

The investigator's or director's role is predominant in performance of the project. He should devote a significant portion of his time and effort to the undertaking. The institution is responsible for fostering an environment conducive to the project.

Proposal Preparation. Proposal preparation is basically the responsibility of the investigator. However, depending on an institution's size, the volume of sponsored activity, and the individual investigator's commitments, support services may be necessary to the efficient production of proposals.

Basic services include typing and reprographics. Administrative staff familiar with budgeting and cost projections should be available to assist investigators in preparation of fiscal elements of the proposal. Ideally, these same persons would be responsible for administration after a grant or contract is awarded. In addition to their accounting and budgeting knowledge, administrative managers should be familiar with the proposal guidelines and administrative regulations of the institution and the sponsor, and serve as the points of contact with institutional officers responsible for approving, endorsing, and forwarding the proposal to the sponsor.

Reviews. Proposals should be reviewed and formally approved by department chairmen, deans, or laboratory or institute directors. The business aspects of any proposal also should be reviewed by the business officer or his delegated representatives. Factors considered in proposal review may include:

1. Eligibility of the Investigator—Is the individual initiating the proposal eligible under the rules of the institution to be a principal investigator?

2. Educational Component—Does the proposal include an educational component that contributes to the academic program of the institution and provides training and support of students?

3. Freedom to Publish—Is the investigator free to publish his findings without restriction?

4. Presence at the Institution—Will the proposed activity require the investigator to be absent from the institution for extended periods of time? Is such absence warranted?

5. Percentage of Effort—Is the amount of effort committed by the investigator consistent with his other duties?

6. Human Subjects—If the proposed research involves the use of human subjects, does the research protocol comply with governmental requirements and with assurances filed by the institution?

7. Care of Laboratory Animals—If warm-blooded animals are to be used in the conduct of the research, have provisions been made to insure adequate and humane care in accordance with prescribed institutional and legal standards?

8. Budgets—Is the budget sufficiently detailed and consistent with the subsequent accounting to be rendered for actual costs? Have all potential cost items been covered in the estimated budget?

9. Staff Benefit and Indirect Cost Rates—Have the institution's staff benefit and indirect cost rates been properly applied and included in the proposed budget?

10. Radiation Hazards—In the event that the proposed activity contemplates use of materials or devices that may pose a radiation hazard, such as isotopes or radiation-producing machines, is there evidence of appropriate planning for safety and control?

11. Safety and Health—Does the proposed project comply with the federal Occupational Safety and Health Act and state industrial safety regulations?

12. Patent Agreements—Have the sponsor's patent terms been considered? Are patent agreements on file for all persons who may be in a position to make, conceive, or first use inventions, improvements, or discoveries under the project?

13. Copyrights and Rights in Data—Have the sponsor's copyright and rights in data

terms been considered? Are they acceptable?

14. Insurance—Does the proposed activity pose any special property or liability insurance questions?

15. New Staff—Will the proposed activity require new staff? Would such expansion be consistent with the institution's plans?

16. Space and Equipment—Can the project be housed within existing space? Is it adequately equipped? If not, are requirements for additional space and equipment consistent with the institution's plans?

17. Cost Sharing—Is any cost-sharing commitment made in the proposal accurate and consistent with the institution's plans and budgets?

18. Long-Term Commitments—Does the proposal commit the institution to continue the proposed activity beyond the period of sponsor funding? If so, do budgeting and planning appropriately support such commitments?

19. Security Restriction—If there is a security restriction, does this conflict with institutional policy?

Final Approval and Submission. A proposal should not be initiated unless the institution is prepared to undertake the work, nor should the same proposal be submitted to different sponsoring agencies concurrently unless this procedure is known to each prospective sponsor. The sponsor should be notified immediately if the institution, after submitting a proposal, finds itself unable to conduct the program under the conditions originally proposed.

Although many proposals are submitted in expectation of receiving a grant rather than a contract, increasing complexity in grant instruments makes prudent a thorough final review, approval, and institutional endorsement. Depending on the organizational structure of the institution, final approval should be made by the official who is delegated signatory authority by the governing body of the institution.

Solicited Proposals. Proposals solicited by government agencies or private organizations require close scrutiny. The solicitation, usually a Request for Proposal (RFP) or Request for Quotation (RFQ), results in a contract more often than in a grant. Acceptance of the proposal by the soliciting agency precludes further negotiation of terms included or incorporated in the request.

Solicitations generally are made for very specific lines of inquiry or for an end product that does not necessarily contribute to the objectives of the institution. Because terms of solicitations often contain provisions appropriate for industry, they should be screened carefully to insure that necessary negotiations take place prior to submission and that all changes and exceptions to the terms of the solicitation are documented in the submission.

Negotiation

In the process of applying for support from extramural sponsors, negotiations take place at various stages to establish the scope of the activity to be pursued and the terms and conditions under which work will be performed. In many cases negotiations occur prior to formal submission of a proposal for agency support. These negotiations frequently take place between the principal investigator and an agency program official, and generally involve matters such as scope of work or objectives of the contemplated activity. However, it is incumbent on the business officer or sponsored programs administrator to caution principal investigators against negotiating on such matters as administration of funds received, since conflicts with institutional policy may develop that make subsequent negotiations extremely difficult. These are usually concerns of the business officer or sponsored programs administrator, and concessions on agency requirements that conflict with institutional policy should be made only by such officer or administrator after appropriate consultation with the principal investigator.

Once the proposal is submitted, the terms and conditions governing work under sponsored program agreements normally are established in negotiations between the sponsoring agency and the institution. The responsible administrative officer must take the initiative in requesting the sponsor to modify provisions to accommodate policy needs of his institution, again coordinating, when appropriate, with the person responsible for conduct of the project and with other officials of the institution. Requests for such modifications should be a condition for acceptance of the award or agreement. Since it is legally responsible and liable for the program, the institution must insist that the sponsoring agency contact directly the appropriate responsible institutional representative, not the individual faculty member, to negotiate terms and conditions of the agreement. Faculty members also should be informed that they cannot commit the institution.

It is essential in arriving at equitable and satisfactory agreements that institutional officers or representatives responsible for negotiation become thoroughly familiar with the sponsoring agency's manuals, circulars, letters of instructions, and other publications. Institutional officers should maintain close liaison with neighboring institutions participating in similarly sponsored activities in order to benefit from their experience.

Acceptance

Many grants do not require acceptance by an authorized official of an institution; based on the proposal submitted, the grant becomes a binding contract when awarded. Some grants and all contracts require acceptance by an authorized official. Regardless of the sponsor's policy regarding acceptance of grants, it is good institutional policy for all grants to be accepted.

Implementation

Following the award the institution should establish an institutional project number consistent with its chart of accounts. From the agreement a central administrative office should prepare an abstract containing the following information:

    Project title
    Institutional project number
    Sponsor
    Sponsor's project number
    Department
    Principal investigator
    Location
    Dates
    Total budget
    Patent conditions
    Budget for line items such as salaries, wages, equipment, travel, etc.
    Indirect cost rate
    Type of agreement
    Cost-sharing requirements

    Prior approval requirements
    Billing requirements
    Reporting requirements
    Property provisions
    Other special information

A copy of the abstract should be provided to every party having any responsibility for the project. On receipt of the abstract the accounting department takes steps to issue operating reports for the project.

The principal investigator and any offices concerned should be furnished a copy of the complete agreement to insure their understanding of its provisions. The institution, through its established procedures, should authorize certain individuals to commit funds against the project. Commonly the principal investigator and one other person, such as the department head, are designated to sign documents that commit funds.

The budget contained in the proposal normally constitutes the project's initial operating budget. By administrative determination the institution may make the budget more detailed than was set forth in the proposal. An administrative office should monitor expenditures for allowability of costs under terms of the agreement, as well as for adherence to the budget. Responsibility for compliance with terms of the agreement rests first with the principal investigator. Especially for a faculty member assuming responsibility as a first-time principal investigator, it is important to provide written instructions. Preferably these instructions should be part of a broader manual, defining the investigator's responsibilities, with emphasis on budget adherence and making only authorized expenditures.

TYPES OF SPONSORS

There are a great number and variety of organizations sponsoring research and other programs at colleges and universities, from large federal agencies to small private foundations. It is practical, however, to group all sponsors into four general categories:

1. Federal government.
2. State and local governments.
3. Private industry.
4. Private foundations and voluntary agencies.

The largest single sponsor is the federal govern-

40

ment, with programs supported by such agencies as the Department of Defense, Department of Health, Education, and Welfare (which includes the National Institutes of Health, the Office of Education, and the National Institute of Education), National Science Foundation, National Aeronautics and Space Administration, and the Atomic Energy Commission. The category of state and local governments includes the fifty states as well as all lower government units such as cities, counties, townships, boroughs, and school districts.

Private industry includes all profit-making organizations, large or small, national or local.

The last category includes all sponsors that operate on a nonprofit basis and are not government agencies. Private foundations are required by law to dispense their assets philanthropically. Voluntary agencies such as the American Cancer Society and American Heart Association generally are supported by public contributions.

Usually, sponsored programs are identified with the sponsor who makes the award rather than with the original source of the funds. Thus it is possible for a local government agency to make a grant to an institution with funds obtained from the federal government, with the institution considering the local government as the source of the funds.

TYPES OF INSTRUMENTS

There are two basic types of instruments—grants and contracts—used by sponsors to fund extramurally sponsored programs.

Grants

The head of each agency of the federal government empowered to enter into contracts for scientific research is authorized by Public Law 85-934, September 6, 1958, (42 USC 1891) to make grants to institutions of higher education and other nonprofit organizations whose primary purpose is the conduct of scientific research. The intent of this legislation is to provide a mechanism for supporting research programs without imposing administrative restrictions generally included in most contract instruments.

There are some advantages in using the grant as an instrument for supporting research or other programs. The work description is generally written in broad, flexible terms; it is less likely to im-

pose publication restrictions, and title to equipment purchased with grant funds usually rests with the grantee, although it may be conditional.

There are also disadvantages in using the grant for sponsored programs. The grant instrument functions as a "fixed ceiling" agreement, and since any unexpended funds usually revert to the sponsor, it is subject to downward revision only. Unexpended balances on one project may not be used to offset an overrun on another.

Practically every federal agency awarding grants has a grant manual incorporated into the grant by reference, the terms and conditions of which are binding. Over the years these manuals have expanded until they now cover grantee activities in great detail. Because of this detail, grants are not necessarily more flexible or easier to administer than contracts.

There is a tendency for some investigators (and on occasion the grantor) to consider a grant as a gift or contribution. The Comptroller General of the United States stated in his opinion B-149441, December 6, 1962, that "the acceptance of a grant creates a contract between the government and the grantee under which the moneys paid over to the grantee, while assets in the hands of the grantee, are charged with the obligation to be used for the purposes and subject to the conditions of the grant. Clearly, the United States has a reversionary interest in the unencumbered balances of such grants, including any funds improperly applied."

Private foundations and voluntary agencies use grants almost exclusively. Many foundation grants are less restrictive than those from the federal government; however, voluntary agencies are somewhat more restrictive, particularly regarding inventions and patents. Industrial organizations occasionally make grants but are more inclined to use contractual agreements.

Contracts

The government contract was developed primarily to purchase tangible items. As a procurement instrument it includes many clauses based on statutory requirements or agency regulations that are not applicable to procurement of basic research. Although some clauses may be considered inapplicable, it is incumbent upon the business officer or sponsored programs administrator to be aware of their content, since they may contain restrictions unacceptable to the institution, thus requiring negotiation.

With notable exceptions such as contracts with the Office of Naval Research, contracts sometimes are considered to be slightly less desirable than grants as a research instrument for several reasons: (1) the description of work is generally more restrictive, (2) the performance period and report requirements may be less flexible, (3) there is a greater tendency to evaluate performance by results (positive results cannot be guaranteed in basic research), (4) there is a stronger likelihood of encountering such unacceptable terms and conditions as "technical direction" and "publications restrictions," and (5) there is a greater possibility that the government will retain title to equipment.

The federal government has developed several types of contracts, which range from cost reimbursement to firm-fixed price. The various types are based on the degree of responsibility assumed by the contractor for the cost of performance, which ranges from minimal for cost reimbursement to full cost responsibility for a firm-fixed price contract. There are several incentive-type contracts between the two types identified above, the use of which depends on such criteria as the profit factor or the uncertainties of contract performance.

The Armed Services Procurement Regulation, which generally favors fixed priced contracts (ASPR-3-402), concludes that cost-type contracts may be better suited for procurement of research from educational institutions (ASPR-3-403). ASPR-3-403 states that "in cases where the level of contractor effort desired can be identified and agreed upon in advance of performance, negotiations of a firm-fixed price level of effort contract may be appropriate."

Basic Agreement

The basic agreement is an instrument that contains all the standard contract clauses applying to future negotiations between the parties. The Office of Naval Research, National Aeronautics and Space Administration, National Institutes of Health, and the Air Force are among those that use the basic agreement. Each contract or task order negotiated describes the scope of work, performance period, price, and any special conditions applicable to the particular project. The basic agreement is incorporated by reference. Each task order is considered a separate contract and upon completion is closed out by submission of the final technical report, invention report, and completion voucher. The audit and retention of records requirements apply to each task order and are not related to the date of the basic agreement.

Cost Sharing

Educational institutions have been required for many years to share in the costs of government sponsored grants. Initially the cost sharing was accomplished by limiting the indirect costs the institution was permitted to recover, first by agency regulation and later by statute. In 1966, the limitations on indirect cost reimbursement were omitted from appropriation legislation; instead, a requirement that grantees share in the costs of each project on more than a token basis was imposed on grants for research projects. In 1970, a somewhat different statute on cost sharing was incorporated in the Independent Offices (which include the National Science Foundation and the National Aeronautics and Space Administration) and Housing and Urban Development appropriations, which added the requirement to certain contracts as well as grants.

The Office of Management and Budget in December 1970 issued Circular No. A-100, "Cost Sharing on Research Supported by Federal Agencies," which provides basic guidelines for cost sharing and specifies that cost participation by educational institutions, when required, normally should be at least one percent of the total project cost. Implementing regulations are issued by each funding agency. Cost sharing may be accomplished by making a contribution from nonfederal sources to any element of the project, direct or indirect, provided that the costs would otherwise be allowable. Cost participation may be determined for each individual project, or there may be an institutional agreement for aggregating cost sharing for all projects sponsored by a particular agency.

Private foundations and voluntary agencies normally require cost sharing, frequently in the form of limitations on indirect cost reimbursement. Full cost reimbursement is generally available from industry.

CONDITIONS OF PERFORMANCE
FOR GRANTS AND CONTRACTS

All grants and contracts have certain conditions, some quite simple and others greatly detailed. Since they are binding on the institution, all affected institutional officers and staff should be aware of their requirements and take necessary measures to comply. Some provisions are general as they apply institution-wide; others apply only to individual projects. In the absence of such conditions, the policies of the institution must be observed.

Costs

In sponsored programs there are both direct and indirect costs. Direct costs include the salaries and wages of those working on the project, expenditures for equipment and materials, and other expenses specifically identified with the project. Indirect costs are those that cannot be specifically identified with the project, but which are just as real as direct costs. They include an allotted share of such items as operation and maintenance of the plant; departmental, college, and institutional administration; library operations; charges for use of equipment and facilities; and certain more general expenses that are to some degree attributable to sponsored programs. Many costs may be classified as either direct or indirect (but not both), and practices vary among institutions. The primary reasons for the variations in practice are the differences in accounting procedures and in forms of organization.

The Executive Office of the President, Office of Management and Budget, under OMB Circular No. A-21, in the past has issued principles for determining costs applicable to research and development and educational services performed by educational institutions under grants and contracts with the federal government.[1] These principles are incorporated in various regulations such as the Federal Procurement Regulations (FPR) and the Armed Services Procurement Regulation (ASPR).

Indirect costs are difficult to establish with precision. Unless they are reimbursed by sponsoring agencies for such costs, institutions must use their own resources, which diverts support from other educational objectives. It is obviously impracticable to determine indirect costs separately for each research project. An indirect cost rate or rates usually expressed as a percentage of salaries and wages or modified total direct costs should be computed annually for the various sponsored programs of an institution in accordance with appropriate government regulations. To apply these rates to federal grants and contracts, it is necessary to have them audited by and negotiated with the cognizant federal agency, appointed under the provisions of OMB Circular No. A-88 to represent all federal agencies in this and other audit matters.

Indirect cost rates may be established either on a provisional basis, subject to later negotiation, or on a predetermined or fixed basis. When rates change as a result of negotiation, agreements that specify provisional rates should be reviewed to incorporate the new rates. The rates established may or may not be utilized in connection with non-federal sponsored programs, depending on the policy of the sponsoring organization.

Cost Accounting Standards Board

An amendment to the Defense Production Act of 1950, signed by President Nixon on August 15, 1970, created the Cost Accounting Standards Board, chaired by the Comptroller General of the United States, as an agent of Congress. The amendment directed the Board to "promulgate cost accounting principles followed by defense contractors and subcontractors . . . in all negotiated prime contract and subcontract national defense procurements with the United States in excess of $100,000." The Board was authorized to make rules and regulations to implement cost standards and was directed to require all contractors, as a condition for contracting, to disclose in writing their cost accounting practices and to agree to a price adjustment for failure to follow disclosed practices or any standards issued by the Board. Jurisdiction of the Board extends only to contracts

---

[1] Effective April 15, 1973, the division of the Office of Management and Budget responsible for promulgating and issuing various circulars on costing and administrative practices was transferred to the General Services Administration. Henceforth, circulars such as A-21, A-88, and A-100 will be designated as GSA Circulars when they are revised or amended.

negotiated for "national defense," defined in Title VII of the Defense Procurement Act.[2]

Cost Accounting Standards Board regulations have been issued, implementing disclosure requirements prescribed in the 1970 legislation, including the Disclosure Statement forms to be used by contractors and subcontractors in setting forth their accounting practices. A disclosure statement was initially required only of contractors with very high volume but will eventually be applied to all contractors of negotiated defense contracts over $100,000. The statement includes data on methods of charging direct costs, criteria used to charge indirect costs, practices relating to capitalization and depreciation, and "other costs and credits" such as employee fringe benefits, deferred compensation, and insurance. Regulations also prescribe a contract clause to be included in negotiated prime and subcontracts covered by the disclosure requirement. This clause requires that disclosed cost accounting practices and applicable standards promulgated by the Board be followed.

Colleges and universities are considered defense contractors in their contractual relationships with the Department of Defense, Atomic Energy Commission, and National Aeronautics and Space Administration and are therefore subject to the rules and regulations, including cost accounting standards, issued by the Board.[3] The Board has assured contractors that standards promulgated recognize the unique characteristics of institutions of higher education. When appropriate, the Board can grant exemptions from individual standards. Chief business officers should be familiar with the detailed regulations and requirements of the Board as published in the *Federal Register* and by other reporting agencies.

Human Subjects

The Department of Health, Education, and Welfare has established a single set of requirements with respect to any funded activity that places an individual at risk, and requires an institution to abide by certain protective rules. Most universities extend these rules to guide all research involving human subjects regardless of the source of funding.

To provide the necessary mechanism for evaluation of planned and current research, the institution should organize a committee on human subjects. Generally, this committee evaluates proposed research projects to insure that the methods and techniques used are adequate to protect the rights of subjects, that the risks to the subjects are outweighed by potential benefits, and that informed consent of the subjects is obtained when necessary. The legal and ethical liabilities involved are substantial and make mandatory a well-organized committee with clear lines of responsibility and authority.

Animal Care

Educational institutions have a legal responsibility under Public Law 91-579 to provide adequate care and humane treatment for warm-blooded animals used in experimental research.[4] For an educational institution to meet its minimal legal and ethical obligations it should have a committee for laboratory animal care to review animal care procedures and assure compliance with high standards. A doctor of veterinary medicine (DVM) must be included on this committee.

Personnel

It is generally a result of accepting federal funds, mainly through grant and contract awards, that requirements relating to personnel (both employees and students) are imposed on the institution. These requirements are defined in the specific terms and conditions of a grant or contract, in federal legislation, and in executive orders. They

---

[2]Application of these cost accounting standards to contracts other than for defense, though not required by law, has been mandated by regulation of the General Services Administration. However, colleges and universities were exempted from this regulation, at least temporarily.

[3] Since Board standards in 1973 were applicable to negotiated defense contracts in excess of $100,000, there was a potential for conflict with the cost principles prescribed in OMB Circular No. A-21 as applied to other grants and contracts. However, agreement was reached with the Office of Management and Budget to make appropriate modifications of Circular No. A-21 as standards are published to provide a single reference to uniform costing principles and practices for colleges and universities.

[4]The Department of Health, Education, and Welfare published a *Guide for the Care and Use of Laboratory Animals (NIH73-23)*, which defines humane care in professional terms and describes facilities that provide humane care. The recommendations in the *Guide* are used by the American Association for Accreditation of Laboratory Animal Care in its accreditation program.

cover such matters as equal employment opportunity; equal pay for equal work; wages, hours, and working conditions; job listings; nondiscrimination in student admissions and financial aid; and student unrest. Some of the requirements apply regardless of the size of the institution and the scope of federal funding; others have applicability according to size and scope. Many requirements also may extend to private companies engaging in campus construction or to those providing major campus services. Failure to comply with requirements may result in cancellation of grants or contracts, disqualification for future awards, or financial penalties.

State laws governing educational institutions also must be observed. These differ from state to state and sometimes differ from federal laws. Therefore, careful examination and continued surveillance of legislative action is essential.

Quality of Management

Sponsoring agencies are concerned with the effectiveness of systems by which colleges and universities manage the resources entrusted to them. Evidence of this concern is the Department of Health, Education, and Welfare's management evaluation program, which is discussed in its two volume publication *A Program for Improving the Quality of Grantee Management,* issued in June 1970. The plan incorporates certain measures of performance for eight management systems against which the institution's management practices can be reviewed and evaluated.

Uniformity and Consistency in Administrative Requirements

Since the publication of the Bureau of the Budget's Westrate Report in 1966,[5] concerted efforts have been made to bring about greater consistency and uniformity among federal agencies in administration of grants and contracts. An outgrowth of this effort was the issuance of OMB Circular No. A-101, which established policies and procedures in certain areas of administration for

research agreements with educational institutions.[6]

Deviations from these requirements are kept at a minimum by establishment of formal procedures within each agency, which provide for approval of deviations for individual agreements by the head of the agency or an officer designated by him. The Office of Management and Budget is consulted or informed by each agency regarding class deviations applied to all similar agency research agreements. The circular contains detailed policy statements regarding review and direction of the research effort, approval procedures for expenditures under research agreements, vesting of title to equipment, and advance payments. These policies and procedures became effective after March 31, 1971, for new awards or extension of existing awards with additional funds. Amendments and additions to the circular may be made as new requirements arise.

Statement of Work

Each grant or contract document sets forth what is to be performed as a condition of the award. This provision in contracts, generally labeled "Statement of Work," contains:

1. A detailed statement of all elements of the work to be performed, which may be prefaced by a general statement of the project objectives.

2. A schedule setting forth the reports, technical data, and all other deliverable end items required under the contract.

3. Generally, a level-of-effort or a best-efforts commitment when work is to be performed on other than a completion basis.

Such statements in grants are generally less formal and specific than in contracts.

Changes in the scope of work described in a grant or contract rarely can be made without prior approval by the sponsor. On occasion some contracts will contain a changes clause giving the sponsor the right to change unilaterally the scope of work or the specifications. This in effect gives the sponsor a degree of technical direction of

---

[5] This report, officially titled "The Administration of Government Supported Research at Universities," was based on a study by Lee Westrate, which disclosed among other things a need for greater uniformity of agency administrative policies.

[6] Subsequent efforts by an interagency task force under OMB auspices may bring about even greater consistency. This could apply to all nonprofit institutions and would not be confined, as is Circular No. A-101, to research programs.

the work, which many institutions consider unacceptable.

Purchasing and Subcontracting

Government contracts may contain requirements pertaining to purchasing and subcontracting usually absent from government grants and from agreements with private organizations. In addition to the prior approval requirements mentioned elsewhere in this chapter, an institution may have to agree to accept conditions pertaining to utilization of labor surplus area enterprises, small business enterprises, and minority business enterprises. If purchasing is accomplished through the regular purchasing office of the institution, which is the normal practice, the staff of that office will require instruction in these matters.

In addition to the above, purchase orders under government contracts require a number of special terms and conditions. These are best handled with an attachment to purchase orders issued under government contracts, including the following:

Examination of records
Renegotiation
Federal, state, and local taxes
Equal opportunity
Compliance with laws and regulations (which should be named, such as Buy American Act)
Contract Work Hours Standards Act
Listing of employment openings

It is desirable to have an attorney familiar with government contracts prepare the forms recommended for the purchase order attachment.

Government contracts define subcontracts as including purchase orders, but for the purpose of this discussion subcontracts are defined as those procurement instruments which are not on a fixed price basis or are for research or development, or both. Virtually all these require sponsor approval and inclusion of many of the same terms and conditions as in the prime contract. Subcontracts under grants also should include applicable requirements from the grant document or applicable grant manual. Auditing of subcontracts on a cost-type basis can be a problem unless the sponsor accepts responsibility.

Subcontracts as defined here require substantially more negotiation than fixed price purchase orders. Each subcontract must be separately tailored, and most require careful administration dur-

ing the period of performance. For these reasons it is often more practical for the sponsored programs office, rather than the purchasing office, to handle negotiation, preparation, and administration of subcontracts.

Prior Approvals

All government grants and contracts, and some from nongovernment sources, contain requirements for prior approvals in a variety of instances. Some of the most important of these relate to:

Change in the approved scope of work
Change in the principal investigator
Changes in budget
Purchases above a specified amount
Purchase of equipment
Building construction or alteration
Subcontracts for research and development
Foreign travel
Consultant agreements

Institutional procedures applying to these matters should be developed with care. It is particularly important to determine the degree of centralization of responsibility for compliance with and maintenance of records relating to these requirements. The records of approvals granted usually must be available for audit.

Accounting

Generally accepted accounting and reporting procedures for colleges and universities should be followed in the management and administration of sponsored programs and projects. In addition, the accounting system should provide for application of cost principles and standards on a consistent basis as prescribed in OMB Circular No. A-21. Familiarity with the provisions of A-21 and policies and regulations of sponsoring agencies on allowability of costs is essential. The system should be responsive to billing and reporting requirements, which vary among agencies.

Adjustments among budget categories should be controlled, since restrictions on such action vary considerably among agencies. Budget control is also important to avoid overruns, which may affect institutional resources, or underruns, which may indicate performance levels below commitments to agencies.

Separate accounts for each project should be

established and monthly expenditure statements provided on a timely basis to aid the sponsored programs administrator and his staff in effective management of resources and in preparation of reports. These records should be retained as required and made available for government or other special audits. It should be noted that the fiscal period for grants and contracts is not necessarily related to the fiscal year of the institution.

Audits

Expenditures incurred under grants and contracts as well as the management systems employed to administer the institution are subject to audit by sponsoring agencies. In addition, the proposal for indirect cost rates to be applied to federally sponsored programs is subject to audit prior to negotiation of acceptable rates.

The cognizant federal agency appointed under the provisions of OMB Circular No. A-88 is assigned to each institution to represent all federal agencies in the performance of audits. An institutional representative should be designated to provide liaison with the auditors. He should establish a working relationship with the auditors so that he is notified of their activities at the institution. Arrangements also should be made for exit interviews upon completion of audits for advice on findings.

It should be noted that audit findings are advisory to the appropriate agency, and that resolution of problems of management or disallowances is generally negotiated with the appropriate agency official, not the auditors. Certain major agencies, such as the Department of Defense, Atomic Energy Commission, and Department of Health, Education, and Welfare include appeals procedures in their regulations to accommodate situations in which audit findings cannot be resolved with agency representation.

An audit by the cognizant federal agency does not necessarily constitute a final audit of the records. The U.S. General Accounting Office reserves the right to audit, within the legal retention period, any records pertaining to disbursement by any federal agency.

Payments

Several methods are employed by federal agencies to pay educational institutions under spon-

sored programs. Depending on the practices of the individual agency and the dollar volume of the programs, payments may be made in advance, in installments, or upon submission of invoices after costs have been paid. OMB Circular No. A-101 encourages federal agencies to make advance payments in reasonable amounts to educational institutions whenever practical in all cases where the agency is authorized by law to do so.

The Treasury Department's letter of credit procedure is an advance payment method commonly used. Treasury Circular 1075 establishes the policy regarding advance financing of federal programs. The procedures are detailed in Treasury Fiscal Requirement Manual, Part VI, section 1020, under which payment to the institution with respect to allowable costs is made. Submission of form TUS 5401 results in deposit of funds to the institution's commercial bank account to meet actual cash requirements.

Advance payments also may be made through a three-party advance payment agreement among the government sponsoring agency, a commercial bank, and the institution. Under this arrangement the agency deposits funds in a commercial bank account to be drawn on by the institution to pay costs of the sponsored programs. The amount advanced normally is based on expenditure level, time required to prepare the institution's billings, and period required for payment by the appropriate agency disbursements officer.

Without involving a commercial bank, arrangements for advance payments occasionally can be made directly with a sponsor. The sponsor also may elect to make installment payments. The schedule of payments usually is established in advance by the agency at the time the agreement is awarded. In the event the sponsor does not approve the use of any of the above payment methods, the institution will find it necessary to submit periodic invoices in such detail as required to obtain reimbursement for project costs.

Records

Acceptance and use of funds from government sponsoring agencies generally are accompanied by an obligation to keep intact and accessible the records relating to receipt and expenditure of such funds. Also frequently required are records such as those relating to property acquisitions and maintenance of the property. These records and any other pertinent books, documents, and papers are usually subject to audit by sponsoring agencies or their authorized representatives, and, in the case of federal funds, by the U.S. General Accounting Office. Retention periods for these records generally can be found in applicable statutes, regulations, or terms and conditions of agreements.

Equipment

In the acquisition of equipment financed from grant or contract funds, one must look to the terms and conditions of the agreement, appropriate regulations, and agency policy, since prior approval almost invariably is required for acquisitions exceeding a specified dollar value. A further condition to acquisition may be a determination that no existing government or institutional property is available to fill the particular need.

Vesting of title to equipment in the institution and accountability for the equipment are variable factors set forth in agency policy statements and regulations. These should be reviewed for constraints on use of equipment as well as maintenance, reporting, identification marking, and disposition requirements.

Inventions and Patents

Nearly every contract and many grants for sponsored research contain provisions governing reporting and disposition of inventions and patents. Such provisions are used less frequently in nonresearch projects. Government agencies generally have firm policies concerning inventions and patents, leaving little or no opportunity for negotiations. However, some agencies such as the Department of Defense, the Department of Health, Education, and Welfare, and the National Science Foundation leave title to inventions with the grantee or contractor (with a nonexclusive license to the government) if the latter has an approved patent policy.

In many cases the government will assert its right to title. In some instances, however, it may be easier to persuade the agency to waive title. (The National Aeronautics and Space Administration is an example.) Voluntary agencies also have fixed policies regarding disposition of inventions and patents, but most private, nonprofit organiza-

tions such as private foundations have no restrictions. In grants and contracts from industrial organizations, there is usually latitude for negotiation.

An established institutional patent policy for the administration of inventions and patents affects the extent to which grant and contract patent conditions are acceptable to or negotiable by academic institutions.

All professional persons participating in a sponsored program should sign an agreement to comply with grant or contract (or grant manual) provisions specifying sponsor acquisition rights in inventions and patents. It is the participation that matters, not the source of the faculty member's salary or the graduate student's stipend. The legal consideration cited in the agreement thus should not be salary or stipend but furnishing of funds, facilities, and services. A standard agreement covering all types of grant and contract conditions is simpler to administer than separately tailored agreements.

Periodic review of all grants and contracts containing invention disclosure requirements is desirable and often required. A summary invention statement may be sent to every principal investigator on the anniversary date of his grant or contract, or all summary invention statements may be sent out at the same time. (The latter is simpler to administer.)

Some institutions, particularly those with a substantial volume of research, employ patent counsel to review reports and sometimes even notebooks to keep current with inventions made and to handle patent applications promptly. Strictly speaking, whether or not there is patent counsel, individual invention disclosures should be made promptly without waiting for an annual summary invention statement. Principal investigators frequently need to be reminded of this.

If the institution does not employ patent counsel, an individual on the staff should be reasonably knowledgeable in the patent field so that he can advise research staff members. Agreements with nonprofit management firms such as Battelle Development Corporation and Research Corporation are helpful in evaluation of inventions and, if patentable, in their management.

Any subcontract or consultant agreement involving research or development activity must contain a clause covering inventions and patents

48

similar to that in the prime contract, grant, or grant manual unless the sponsor approves a different arrangement. However, it is generally possible and most desirable in government grants and contracts to pass the enforcement task to the government.

Publication, Copyrights, and Data

Publication of results of sponsored programs is far more important to colleges and universities than inventions and patents. Most institutions refuse to accept grant or contract terms giving a sponsor the right to veto or censor publication, although a delay of up to four months may be acceptable in the event foreign patenting is important. Some institutions accept classified contracts for reasons of national security in the interests of faculty members whose scientific specialties are in classified areas. Special contract clauses are available that recognize the differences between academic institutions and industrial concerns in security matters. In nonclassified areas, it is considered contrary to the Freedom of Information Act for federal agencies to prevent publication.[7]

Problems with restriction on publication almost never arise with private nonprofit agencies and foundations. Industrial sponsors are another matter. Institutions rarely give industrial sponsors the right to veto publication because of faculty and graduate student interest in and dependence on publication and because of the basic educational obligation to disseminate knowledge. However, it is in the interests of both parties to agree to make no reference to the other in any publication, publicity, or advertising without prior approval.

Data usually refers to recorded information regardless of form or characteristic and is normally subject to copyright. "The following types of material now or in the near future may be subject to copyright:

1. Books, journal articles, texts, glossaries, bibliographies, study guides, laboratory manuals, syllabi, tests, and proposals.
2. Lectures, musical or dramatic compositions, and unpublished scripts.

3. Films, filmstrips, charts, transparencies, and other visual aids.
4. Video and audio tapes and cassettes.
5. Live video or audio broadcasts.
6. Programmed instruction materials.
7. Computer programs.
8. Other materials.

"Although copyright law does not specifically mention computer programs, the U.S. Copyright Office has recognized since 1964 that computer programs are copyrightable, and numerous programs have been copyrighted."[8]

Most federal agencies normally ask only for a royalty-free, nonexclusive license for reproduction and use of copyrightable material. Additional controls may be sought when the specific object of a grant or contract is the production of copyrightable material. As with inventions and patents, an agreement pertaining to copyrightable material should be obtained from all professional personnel participating in sponsored programs having requirements for disposition and licensing. Again, the legal consideration should be provision of funds, facilities, and services. If possible, having a single agreement covering both inventions and copyrightable material is an administrative advantage.

There should be a footnote for any publication in a copyrighted journal or book, giving the sponsor the required license for reproduction and use.

Reports

Upon completion of a sponsored project there are reporting requirements that must be satisfied. These requirements vary among sponsoring agencies, but most government projects require the following reports:

1. A Final Technical Report on the work accomplished during the period of performance.
2. A Final Report of Inventions disclosing inventions made under the project, since in many cases determination of patent rights may rest with the sponsor. It is often necessary to certify whether or not an invention

[7] House Committee Report "U.S. Government Information Policies and Practices—Administration and Operation of the Freedom of Information Act" (Part 5), Hearings before a Subcommittee of the Committee on Government Operations, House of Representatives, 92nd Congress, 2nd Session, March 20, 23, 24, 27, and 28, 1972.

[8] "Copyrights at Colleges and Universities," Washington, D.C., National Association of College and University Business Officers, 1972.

has been made during the course of a project.

3. A Final Equipment Report of equipment purchased, fabricated, or furnished by the sponsor during the project.

4. A Final Financial Report that sets forth all expenditures and other financial data (such as cost sharing contributions) for the project.

Some of these reports, particularly 1 and 4 above, also are required by nongovernment sponsors. In addition to final reports, various periodic reports such as those on inventions, equipment acquisitions, project progress, and expenditures frequently are required, particularly by federal agencies. Terms and conditions of grants and contracts as well as agency policy should be reviewed carefully for such requirements. In some cases continued funding of projects is dependent upon timely submission of required reports.

Security

If compliance with government security regulations is a requirement of certain sponsored programs, an administrative officer or reliable staff member should be designated as security officer to supervise such compliance. He should be responsible for keeping the institution informed of all security regulations of sponsoring agencies. He should insure that safeguards are available for mail and storage facilities, and arrange for internal security procedures. He also should aid in acquiring facility clearance so that classified information may be obtained from the federal government by faculty members who have a need to know, arrange the necessary visit clearances for staff members attending meetings, and perform all other duties necessary to insure the institution's compliance with security regulations.

Miscellaneous Requirements

In addition to the specific requirements identified above, there are other administrative requirements frequently imposed as conditions of accep-

tance and use of funds. The business officer or sponsored programs administrator should be cognizant of these requirements to assure that adequate policies and procedures exist within the institution to satisfy them.

Closeouts and Terminations

The closeout, or completion, of a sponsored project is a regular occurrence. Termination of a project before its scheduled completion date, however, is quite different; it happens much less frequently, but it is important that policies and procedures exist to minimize the impact on finances and morale should termination occur.

An institution cannot expect to be reimbursed for costs incurred (with rare exceptions) beyond the closeout or completion date of a grant or contract notwithstanding verbal promises made for additional funding and time extension, or commitments made to personnel or suppliers by the institution. Close monitoring is therefore necessary as a project completion date approaches, and when a renewal proposal has been submitted, to verify whether the renewal will actually occur.

Terminations as stated are different from closeouts or completions. For government grants and contracts OMB Circular No. A-21, paragraph J. 45, "Termination Costs Applicable to Research Agreements," outlines the costs that will be paid after the termination date. In addition, paragraph J. 36, "Severance Pay," must be taken into consideration. When persons are terminated because of a sponsored project termination, severance pay is dependent on written and reasonable personnel policy statements that are institution-wide, not merely limited to government sponsored projects.

Suspensions, sometimes known as Stop Work Orders, are occasionally included in the provisions of federal agreements. They amount to temporary termination, with obligation to resume work if the suspension is lifted. Most institutions refuse to accept such clauses, since persons in colleges and universities, particularly faculty and students, cannot readily be shifted back and forth among different projects or different fund sources.

Legal Services

INSTITUTIONS OF HIGHER EDUCATION have become increasingly involved in litigation and other legal matters, with a consequent need for more legal services. Among the reasons for this involvement are greater sophistication in legal analysis, such as in the changing treatment of the privilege versus rights concept; the enactment of social legislation applicable to colleges and universities, such as the Fair Labor Standards Act (including the Equal Pay Act), Titles IV, VI, VII, and IX of the Civil Rights Act of 1964 (as applied by the Higher Education Amendments of 1972), and the Occupational Safety and Health Act; the advent of labor relations and collective bargaining; and the dependence of many colleges and universities on federal financial aid and contracts. These factors and others have resulted in a significant increase in the aggregate body of law that influences colleges and universities. This body of law is updated constantly by court decisions and changes in law.

A law in its broadest sense may be defined as a rule, adherence to which is enforced by governmental action. Sources of law are the U.S. Constitution and acts of Congress, as well as their state, commonwealth, and territorial counterparts. The term "law" also may include municipal ordinances, as well as administrative regulations and orders validly adopted by a public agency (in the case of public institutions of higher education, the general orders of the governing board and of its chief executive officers). There are often administrative procedure acts that govern administrative rule-making, usually through specific notice and hearing provisions. Typically, these statutes allow an exception for "internal organization." Counsel should be consulted to determine the applicability of these laws to particular proposed actions and to insure that any action taken is in compliance.

Through the administrative chain of delegation, actions of deans and academic councils also may have a limited effect as "laws," depending on the authority given these officers and bodies. Not infrequently, such actions have acquired a sort of "common law" development, through which their force and effect often are grounded on practice and acceptance, with resulting expectations that decisions made within traditional authority will be honored unless clearly overruled by higher authority. Thus, a faculty member cannot lightly disregard academic and ethical decisions of these bodies, and the university often is "estopped" from doing so because of reliance by others.

Least understood as "law" are private engagements entered into in such a way as to entitle the parties, and those claiming under them, to invoke the aid of governmental processes to enforce adherence or to remedy a breach when it occurs. Contracts are the most obvious examples, but there are many others, such as conveyances, deeds of restrictions, trusts, and simple gifts. Technically, only the rules that authorize resort to governmental process to enforce these transactions are "laws," but the substantive effect is that the provisions of the transactions themselves become "laws" with respect to parties who are bound by them.

The internal rules of business, especially those of large corporations, take on many aspects of legislation, although usually without a due process analogue. Governments also contract, and when they do, they usually are bound to honor their engagements as any private entity is bound to do. A notable exception is the case of a contract entered into in excess of governmental power, usually because of failure to meet some procedural requirement. The traditional view is that this failure voids the contract. But this is an area in which the law is undergoing change; it is becoming increasingly common for courts to "estop" the government from excusing compliance with contracts on such grounds, when there has been reasonable reliance on the other side and no major public policy violation would result from the government's performing under the contract.

If contracts and corporate rules of internal management and practice are recognized as a kind of law, the rules of governing boards, presidents, deans, and others in private institutions of higher education also must be included. Such engagements will not be enforced if doing so would result in government aid of policies that violate fundamental law. This is illustrated by *Shelley v. Kraemer,* in which the U.S. Supreme Court held that state court enforcement of racially restrictive covenants would violate the Fourteenth Amendment.[1]

Because an institution's contracts with its staff are often "contracts of adhesion" made under circumstances in which the employee has little or no bargaining power with respect to contract terms, the traditional disinclination of courts to interfere on the campus has been tempered in such cases with a reluctance to allow the university to excuse its own adherence to a rule on the basis of an "escape hatch" provision permitting change of anything at any time. An interesting example of this principle is *Greene v. Howard University,* in which a federal court held a university to its published undertakings to faculty, notwithstanding general handbook language to the effect that all rules were subject to change.[2]

LEGAL COUNSEL

A unique function of the lawyer is to counsel with respect to the possible legal consequences of a given course of action. Further, the lawyer should advise the client of the degree and quality of risk of a proposed action, and help develop a range of alternatives designed to accomplish a policy objective with a minimum of risk.

An institution may employ legal counsel on its staff or it may retain counsel outside the institution. There are advantages to each. Staff counsel will be more aware of the institution's particular prob-

lems, and may be expected to devote full attention to the institution because there will be no competition from other clients. On the other hand, outside counsel often may perceive aspects of a problem not known to the staff. Sometimes both staff and outside counsel are employed. Staff counsel can be available on a daily basis for most of the institution's legal problems, while outside counsel may be retained for trial litigation and occasional, specialized matters such as patents.

Legal counsel may report to the president or chancellor or to another administrative office. The office of counsel should be situated organizationally so as to insure its integrity and ability to meet all the institution's legal requirements.

In some states the state attorney general's office acts as legal counsel for public institutions.

SELECTED LEGAL PROBLEMS

Few enterprises are so varied in the kinds of transactions in which they are involved as are institutions of higher education. In addition to their primary functions of instruction, research, and public service, such institutions buy and sell real property and securities, manage radio and television stations, employ thousands of persons in an extremely wide range of occupations, operate complex businesses and residence facilities, and employ substantial security forces. The discussion that follows reflects the rules in most states in significant, substantive areas of concern to institutional administrators. There may be local exceptions and there almost always are local applications, for which counsel should be consulted.

Governance and Delegation of Authority

Each institution has some kind of fundamental, legal instrument that establishes the basis of its legal existence, its mission, and the composition and powers of its government. Many of the older, private institutions have charters in the literal sense. In the case of some private institutions the fundamental instrument is a trust. Some public institutions and a few private colleges and universities are recognized by specific constitutional provision. The usual case is that of statutory provision

---

[1]334 U.S. 1, 68 S.Ct. 836 (1948).

[2]412 F.2d 1128 (D.C. Cir. 1969).

for public institutions and articles of incorporation and sometimes a kind of license for private institutions. These fundamental instruments almost invariably provide for a governing board, typically composed entirely or principally of laymen. Public board members usually are appointed by a high executive authority, such as the governor, although in some cases they are elected. Boards of private institutions normally are self-perpetuating.

Within the ambit of the governing "charter," a board has full authority to govern the institution. Courts historically have been reluctant to overturn decisions of governing authorities and those acting under them, particularly on questions of academic program and policy. Despite the erosion of the deference principle in the courts, there is still considerable judicial restraint to intrusion in such areas, at least where constitutionally prohibited classifications and constitutionally protected rights are not involved.

With authority, members of governing boards assume commensurate responsibility and, possibly, liability exposure. There has been a considerable expansion in the liability exposure of board members of publicly held corporations, and this development may be expected to have its effect in higher education. That impact may be felt principally in private institutions, where its form may parallel the liability of charitable trustees for prudent management of the trusts within their charge. In the case of public boards, the general doctrine of immunity for discretionary acts performed within the scope of authority may continue to shield trustees and regents from personal liability.

No governing board can manage without extensive delegation. However, the board is responsible in a legal sense (even if its members are not answerable by way of personal liability) for whatever its officers, agents, and employees do under its authority. In view of the board's ultimate responsibility for the affairs of the institution, the extent and limits of its delegations should be clearly stated. For board committees, this usually is done through bylaws or rules of procedure. Beyond that, it normally is accomplished by a broad grant of authority to a chief administrative officer, with certain specific limitations.

The board's actions in delegating authority need not be renewed as the composition of the board changes. In the absence of a specific provision to the contrary, the governing board is a continuing body whose contracts can and do bind it for future years, and whose policies continue until changed by the board itself.

Finally, delegations may be terminated, and the act of a board in authorizing an agent—administrative officer, faculty council, or committee—to act for it does not necessarily deprive the board of authority to act itself concerning the matter delegated.

Personnel

Termination and Layoff of Faculty. Higher education is almost unique in its tradition of shared authority in major aspects of its work. The faculty typically is charged with major responsibilities in such areas as curriculum, standards for student performance, and its own selection and retention. In an age tending to increased formality and challenge, there is increased reason to codify the scope and procedure for the exercise of this authority, and the reserved power of the executive or board to disagree.

The concept of collegiality in academic decision making has been challenged particularly by collective bargaining and in the application of constitutional principles of due process. The effect of collective bargaining is still in doubt. The use of this "industrial" form of employer-employee relations in higher education has produced unique and sometimes difficult problems, such as the definition of who constitutes "management." For a detailed treatment of this subject, refer to the chapter "Labor Relations and Collective Bargaining."

Principal constitutional issues were framed at public institutions in the context of procedural and substantive rights of probationary faculty members who are not retained on probation or awarded tenure. Questions to be considered are whether such members are entitled to a specification of charges and a hearing at which evidence in support of and rebuttal to the charges can be presented, and, if so, whether the other attributes of a trial, such as confrontation and cross-examination, representation by counsel, and a formal record, also are required; and what the difference is between probation and tenure, since these things also are necessary to separate a tenured faculty member "for cause."

The problem is complicated by the established

constitutional principle that the government cannot exercise its discretion in an unconstitutional manner. Thus, it could not refuse to retain a faculty member because of race or religion, nor could it do so because of the exercise of constitutionally protected rights—such as exercise of freedom of association by joining a labor union—on the part of the faculty member. From this, it has been argued that unless a statement of reasons for nonretention is given, the faculty member cannot know whether the reasons for nonretention are constitutionally proscribed. Further, without a hearing, the member cannot know whether the reasons stated are the real reasons.

These issues were addressed by the United States Supreme Court in the landmark cases, *Board of Regents v. Roth* and *Sindermann v. Perry*, both decided in 1972.[3] In *Roth*, the court held that where a year-to-year probationary faculty member has been given no legal right to a fresh or continuous appointment (the usual case), he or she has no vested *property* interest in continued employment. As a result, denial of a new appointment does not constitute a taking of property in derogation of the Fourteenth Amendment. Nor does the faculty member suffer an impairment of *liberty*, unless the denial of reappointment is accompanied by what are, in effect, charges of immoral, dishonest, or other heinous conduct. A conclusion that the faculty member lacks academic suitability is not enough to constitute such a charge. Where charges of heinous conduct are made, the faculty member is entitled to a hearing, but because of the absence of a property interest, the hearing is only "to clear his name," not to gain reinstatement (unless, of course, local rules or laws call for reinstatement in such a case; the U.S. Constitution does not).

Sindermann arose in a different context. In that case, there were substantial allegations that the reason for nonretention was the exercise of constitutionally protected rights. In addition, the local faculty manual was so ambiguous on the question of tenure that there was a real question as to whether it existed. A decision favorable to the faculty member on either issue could result in his reinstatement, and the court found the allegations sufficient to warrant trial on both.

There are substantial indications that most institutions of higher education in the United States have concluded a period of rapid growth. While this is not applicable to all colleges and universities, many institutions face problems of staff reduction if only because of changes in the academic disciplines that students are entering.

Administrative regulations should clearly state the rules on layoff. Typically, layoff is triggered by a decline in students, which requires a consequent reduction in the number of faculty members needed for their instruction and academic supervision. Institutional administrators must determine whether to wait for a decline in number of students before reducing the number of faculty members, or to begin layoff in reasonable anticipation that a decline will occur. Also to be considered are standards that will guide the layoff, such as questions of seniority, breaks in service, and the possibility of split assignments or transfers from one discipline to another.

Termination and Layoff of Support Staff. The principles regarding terminations and layoff of faculty are pertinent to support staff as well, although details of their application are different. Governance of support staff is usually far closer to general government, civil service, or corporate models than it is to academic governance. Local laws as well as an institution's internal policies and labor contracts must be consulted for questions concerning personnel issues of support staff.

Regardless of whether it is faculty or support staff, if financial reasons are given for reductions in force, it is essential that very careful documentation be available to support proposed actions.

Affirmative Action and Nondiscrimination

In pursuit of national policy to end discrimination on the basis of race, sex, national origin, color, and religion—and the effects of such discrimination—the federal government has moved in a number of ways having particular impact on higher education. There are three principal sources of federal authority in this area: the U.S. Constitution and the original Civil Rights Act enacted shortly after the Civil War; recent legislation, particularly the Civil Rights Act of 1964; and the power of the federal government to condition

---

[3]408 U.S. 564, 92 S.Ct. 2071 (1972) and 408 U.S. 593, 92 S.Ct. 2694 (1972), respectively.

grants and contracts on compliance with affirmative action programs.

The first of these, the U.S. Constitution, is the basis of the breakthrough efforts to bar government actions in aid of discrimination.[4] Both the Constitution's "Civil War Amendments" (13-15) and contemporary legislation are used as the basis for court action in this area. The statute most often utilized is the Civil Rights Act of 1964, as amended in 1972. That law enacted nine titles, of which four are of particular interest to higher education.

Titles IV and VI are applicable principally to students and to candidates for admission, and will be discussed further. Titles VI and IX are administered by the Office of Civil Rights of the Department of Health, Education, and Welfare. Title VI bars discrimination on the basis of race, color, or national origin (not religion or sex) in federally assisted programs of employment, and Title IX comprehensively bars sex discrimination of students in applications for admission and in employment by institutions of higher education.

Title VII declares it an unlawful employment practice for any employer with fifteen or more employees to discriminate with respect to any "benefit of employment" on account of the applicant's or employee's race, color, religion, sex, or national origin. The enforcing agency for Title VII is the Equal Employment Opportunity Commission (EEOC), which is established by that Title. It has broad powers to investigate complaints, to attempt to bring about compliance through conciliation and, failing that (and subject to deferral to qualified state or local agencies for sixty days), to institute litigation. If the employer is a public agency, the EEOC must act through the attorney general in instituting court action. If no action is taken by the EEOC, the attorney general, or a local agency, the person aggrieved may institute an action within ninety days after the Commission has so notified him.

The institution also must be concerned with the Equal Pay Act of 1963, made applicable to higher education by the Education Amendments of 1972. This law requires that equal wages be paid for equal work. Neither men nor women may be paid less than the opposite sex for an equal job. "Wages" are defined comprehensively to include all forms of compensation. "Equality" is determined by examination of effort (a measurement of physical or mental exertion), responsibility (the degree of accountability required for performance), and working conditions (whether any difference is of a kind customarily taken into consideration in setting wage rates). Enforcement is by the Wages and Hours Division of the Department of Labor. There are many other statutes bearing on the subject, including Titles VII and VIII of the Public Health Act, as amended by the Comprehensive Health Manpower Act and the Nurse Training Act of 1971.

First applied (in recent years) to federally assisted construction through the Philadelphia Plan, an approach using the government's contract power bars race, sex, color, religion, and national origin discrimination, and requires programs of affirmative action to remedy the effects of past discrimination. The principles are formulated in the President's Executive Orders 11246 and 11375, and detailed in the *Higher Education Guidelines* (issued in 1972), and in a series of regulations concerning affirmative action plans set forth in Chapter 60 of Title 41 of the Code of Federal Regulations (notably, Revised Orders 4 and 14).

In broad terms, affirmative action plans call for institutions to determine, through statistical data, whether they are "underutilizing" women or minorities (that is, whether fewer are employed than might reasonably be expected, based on those available in the relevant labor market) and, if such underutilization exists, to establish goals and timetables (not quotas) for the elimination of this underutilization. There are other important aspects of affirmative action, including anti-anti-nepotism policies, sick leave provisions, selection criteria, and many more. Enforcement resides with the Office of Federal Contract Compliance of the Department of Labor and, by delegation, with the Office of Civil Rights of the Department of Health, Education, and Welfare for institutions of higher education.

Affirmative action and nondiscrimination are rapidly developing areas of law in which there are unsolved major issues, including due process rights of institutions when threatened with a loss of federal contracts or with other sanctions, questions of

---

[4]See: *Brown v. Board of Education,* 347 U.S. 483, 74 S.Ct. 686 (1954) and 349 U.S. 294, 75 S.Ct. 753 (1955).

privacy and confidentiality, preferences ("reverse discrimination"), and job qualifications and testing.[5] Certain regulations on these issues have been extant for some time, and others have been issued more recently. Still evolving is the extent of the institution's discretion with respect to test validation and to employment practices that have a "disparate effect," that is, which reject greater numbers of women or minorities than might be expected by chance. This is an area in which legal counsel is very useful. The institution may be involved with many agencies, both federal and local, and may risk various sanctions (including back pay, termination of federal contracts, and injunctive action) in its efforts to act with justice and to comply with applicable laws and regulations.

Influence of Federal Programs

One of the most significant developments affecting higher education has been the advent of substantial federal programs. Included may be student aid, grants and contracts from many agencies, and support for both academic and academic-related facilities.

There are federal standards governing overtime and premium pay (Fair Labor Standards Act), safe working conditions (Occupational Safety and Health Act), hiring the handicapped (Vocational Rehabilitation Act), age discrimination (Age Discrimination Employment Act), unemployment insurance, and others. The National Labor Relations Board has asserted jurisdiction over private institutions of higher education, if engaged in interstate commerce under the Board's "yardstick." There are also Environmental Protection Agency orders, as well as conflict of interest rules issued by the Department of Health, Education, and Welfare, which affect institutions that may hire former employees of that Department. Most of these have their analogues in state and local legislation, with which institutions also must be concerned.

Such regulations present many legal problems. An example is the liability exposure to the federal government for breaches in grant agreements or failure to exercise due diligence in recovering loans made under federal programs. Many public and private agencies have grant and contract clauses that need to be examined by institutions before acceptance of a grant or contract. For a detailed treatment of grants and contracts, refer to the chapter "Administration of Sponsored Programs: Instruction, Research, and Public Service."

Student Affairs

Discipline. The relationship of the student to the institution once was explained in terms of the now-outmoded privilege-right dichotomy, wherein the student had a *privilege* to attend college, which the college had a *right* to terminate at any time, or by the related doctrines of *in loco parentis* or *parens patriae,* both long since out of favor with the courts.

Dixon v. Alabama State Board of Education[6] established the right of students to a hearing bearing at least "the rudiments of due process" before a conduct expulsion or other serious disciplinary action could be taken. The precise content of the "rudiments" still may be disputed, but it is clear that, at a minimum, the student is entitled to:

1. A clear statement of charges of the alleged misconduct.
2. A hearing at which the evidence against the student is presented.
3. An opportunity to challenge such evidence, and to present evidence in rebuttal.
4. At least a summary record, and a fair decision based on the record.

More also may be required. If the institution has counsel (or someone legally trained) to present its position, the student is entitled to the same (but at his or her own expense).[7] The student may be entitled to a list of witnesses to be presented in support of the charges and to a summary of their evidence. Technical rules of evidence and other judicial rules—such as those restricting the scope of cross-examination—are not required, and most courts have concluded that the code of conduct need not be so precisely drawn as to qualify as a criminal statute.[8] However, "conduct unbecoming" rules may yet present problems.

---

[5]See: *Griggs v. Duke Power Co., 401 U.S. 424, 91 S.Ct. 849 (1971).*

[6]294 F.2d 150 (5th Cir. 1961), *cert. denied,* 368 U.S. 930 (1961).

[7]See: *French v. Bashful,* 303 F.Supp. 1333 (E.D.La. 1969).

[8]See: *Esteban v. Central Missouri State College,* 415 F.2d 1077 (8th Cir. 1969), *cert. den.* 398 U.S. 965, 90 S.Ct. 2169.

While courts continue to be chary about challenging institutional discretion in matters of discipline, they have not hesitated when substantive constitutional rights are perceived to be involved. Thus, courts have held that an institution could not punish a student for constitutionally protected expression (although it could punish the student for expression that violates carefully prepared and valid rules of time, place, and manner, or that presents an immediate danger of physical disruption).[9] Similarly, institutions are severely limited in their authority to discriminate in recognizing student clubs and in providing institutional resources and facilities for such clubs.[10]

Discrimination. Several of the provisions of the Civil Rights Act of 1964, as amended in 1972, are particularly applicable to students and to candidates for admission.

Title IV bars denial of admission or continuation of students at a "public college" on grounds of race, color, religion, or national origin; it is enforced by the Department of Justice. Title VI bars race, color, or national origin discrimination in any program receiving federal assistance; the sanction is termination of assistance, at least for the particular program.

Title IX prohibits sex discrimination in any program or activity benefiting from federal financial assistance. It is specifically applicable to discrimination with respect to students, applicants for admission, and employees.[11] It seems clear that an institution receiving federal grants could not discriminate on the basis of sex in any program directly aided by such grants. Thus, students could not be denied admission to programs on the basis of sex, much less denied entry into a "sex-stereotype" professional program. Conduct rules—for example, lockout—also would appear to have to apply equally to men and women.

Property

An institution is usually one of the major property owners in its area, and often has substantial holdings in other locations as well, such as outdoor science laboratories, farms, and properties for investment. Unlike most owners of real property,

colleges and universities usually are exempt from property assessment with respect to academic and academic support facilities. This typically is not true in the case of investment property, or with respect to special assessments for direct support of services such as street lighting; local law must be consulted in both instances.

Public institutions may resort to eminent domain to acquire additional property either under their own authority or through an appropriate governmental unit in the same jurisdiction. Many states accord the same privilege to private, nonprofit schools. The usual rule is that state-operated institutions are not subject to local ordinances governing the use of property. Thus, in many states a state university need not secure a building permit to erect a facility on a campus within the boundaries of a city or county. However, advice of counsel should be sought to examine the particulars of the local rule.

Law enforcement is an area in which even the state institution is subject to local jurisdiction. Typically, city police officers have full powers to enforce state laws anywhere in the city (federal enclaves excepted in certain cases), including a college or university, whether it is public or private, state or local. County sheriffs have similar powers over institutions outside city limits. In short, even though a college or university may have its own security personnel who are empowered to exercise the authority of police officers within institutional boundaries, the campus is not a sanctuary from local law enforcement personnel. Local police do not need permission to enter the campus in the course of their duties, although when circumstances permit, considerations of comity may prompt them to notify institutional authorities of their intention. Both institutional and local police are subject to Fourth Amendment limitations against unreasonable searches and seizures.

The institution is well advised to have a working agreement with local authorities covering how each will act in given situations in cases of concurrent jurisdiction. This should not be left until an emergency occurs.

Campus authorities may enter a dormitory room

---

[9]See: *Tinker v. Des Moines Independent Community School District,* 393 U.S. 503, 89 S.Ct. 733 (1969).

[10]See: *Healy v. James,* 408 U.S. 169, 92 S.Ct. 2338 (1972).

[11]Draft regulations were issued for notice and comment on 20 June 1974.

under appropriate circumstances for purposes of health or safety and enforcement of dormitory rules. Counsel should be consulted with respect to the circumstances justifying such entry as well as the drafting of pertinent dormitory license or lease provisions.

Patents and Copyrights

Patents. Legal questions concerning patents sometimes call for the help of an outside expert, since few institutions find it practical to have staff patent counsel. Patents can be awarded only by the federal government and foreign sovereigns. Generally, only the inventor may apply for a patent, and this usually is done with the cooperation of the employer. Institutions experienced in the administration of patents often have attorney-prepared agreements with faculty and staff in which the employee, associate, or consultant agrees to assign his or her patent rights to the trustees under stated terms and conditions, usually including a formula for division of royalties. These agreements typically give ownership to the trustees and sometimes provide for the possibility of release of proprietary rights to the inventor under appropriate circumstances. The invention must be submitted in a proper, delineated form to the institution through an administrator, committee, outside consultant, or some combination of these, which then may elect whether or not to file a patent application.

If a college or university pursues a patent, it may bear all or most of the development costs. If the inventor pursues the matter, he or she bears the full costs of securing the patent and of any further development.

Ownership of patent rights developed in the course of employment belongs to the employer by virtue of the implied agreement of employment to invent. However, implied agreements are subject to difficult problems of proof, and therefore such employment arrangements and the ownership of patent rights virtually always are expressed in writing. "Shop rights" to an invention arise when an inventor uses an employer's facilities to create or to perfect an invention. They amount to a non-exclusive license appurtenant to the business,

which is royalty-free. They are the lowest form of license and give an employer slight protection against others who may use an invention. An express agreement is always preferable to reliance by the employer on these common law rights.

Patent applications must be filed within one year from first publication of the invention, and it usually takes two years or more after filing a patent application to secure a patent. Application for a patent may give the inventor (and his or her assignees) a "patent pending" status in the interim. This gives notice to would-be users of their potential liability should the patent be issued, and the inventor can contract for what is, in effect, a waiver of rights during this period (a kind of license).

There are a number of important questions in patent law still in the process of development, chiefly revolving around what is an "invention" for patent purposes. Generally speaking, processes are patentable but laws of nature, including mathematical expressions of scientific facts, are not.[12]

Copyrights. A copyright is an exclusive right to prohibit others from copying a delineated literary work. Willful infringement of a copyright is a crime, and plagiarism is a serious academic offense. Infringement may be remedied by private suits for damages (but only if two copies of the copyrighted material are filed with the Register of Copyrights) or by other civil relief. A professor has a common law copyright in his or her own lectures. The professor, through appropriate court action, may prevent students or others from marketing notes of his or her lectures. The institution has probable standing to join the faculty member in these efforts.

Recent principal legal questions for colleges and universities have concerned the right of an educational or research institution to copy a copyrighted scientific work for use of its own personnel. The Court of Claims has upheld a limited right to do so as an aspect of "fair use."[13] Counsel should be consulted for the limitations of this exception.

Gifts, Taxes, and Consortia

Both public and private institutions are dependent upon, and actively encourage, gifts. For the

[12]*Gottschalk v. Benson,* 409 U.S. 63, 93 S.Ct. 253 (1972).

[13]*Williams and Wilkins Company v. United States,* ___F.2d___(Ct.Cl., 1974); 42 LW 2282, *cert. granted,* U.S. Sup. Ct.

public institution, the giving program is often the "margin of excellence" which, when added to the base of taxpayer support and student fees, permits it to enhance its programs. For the private college or university, the program often is essential to survival.

The unrestricted gift presents few legal problems. Most substantial gifts, however, are burdened with some kind of trust. Depending on trust conditions, the institution as trustee may have broad discretion with respect to programs to be benefited, may or may not pool the gift with others, may or may not be permitted to use principal, and may or may not be able to charge overhead costs to the trust.

All private colleges and universities should be certain that their Internal Revenue Code tax-exempt status is current and is in the most favorable classification. In general, gifts of capital gain appreciated property and tangible personal property (the property itself, not merely the right to its use) may be given to institutions that qualify under Internal Revenue Code Section 501(c)(3) with the donor entitled to a deduction (up to percentage limitations specified in the Code) of the appreciated value (not merely the donee's basis) if, in the case of personal property, the property is related to the exempt function of the donor. Certain gifts of charitable remainder and income interests in trust also may be made, with the donor entitled to a current deduction, if Treasury rules are scrupulously followed.[14]

Tax counsel will be able to advise the institution how to tailor its giving program so as to make it as attractive as possible to potential donors. But the institution's lawyer should not at the same time act as counsel to donors, who should have their own counsel.

Closely allied to these tax problems are tax issues presented by consortia—combinations of two or more entities engaged in a particular and limited enterprise. The necessity to achieve maximum use of scarce resources increasingly has compelled institutions to find ways of sharing certain kinds of facilities and programs. The tax problem stems from refusal of the Internal Revenue Service

to accord favorable tax treatment to income from certain of these joint efforts, despite authority contrary to its position.[15] Thus, if Institution A and Institution B each operates its own laundry, serving its own needs exclusively, no income is realized on account of funds transferred on the books of account to the laundry function. But if the institutions combine their laundry resources into a single operation, to be owned jointly by them in order to realize the benefits of an economy of scale, money paid to the laundry is taxable income to that enterprise, even though it serves no other customers. Attempts are under way to change that result by legislation.

Information Systems

Institutions steadily are becoming more involved in the collection and retrieval of data through automated systems. Three legal problems involved are noted here:

1. Privacy. Considerable quantities of confidential information relating to individuals often are stored in computers. Depending on particular circumstances, the deliberate revelation of such data may constitute actionable invasions of privacy. A negligent revelation, such as failure to maintain adequate security systems, may become actionable as the law develops in this area.

2. Contracts for acquisition of hardware and softwear. Multimillion-dollar agreements have been negotiated with little or no involvement of counsel by the institution; this approach may benefit vendors that do use attorneys, to the disadvantage of the institution. Institutional administrators should thoroughly understand the conditions proffered by vendors, develop their own provisions, and take advantage of all the legitimate negotiating leverage they may have. Legal counsel is only one of many factors indispensable to that result.

3. Regulation. The federal government and many states are considering legislation that in some instances would heavily regulate the

---

[14]Internal Revenue Code Section 170 *et seq.*

[15]*Hospital Bureau of Standards and Suppliers, Inc. Association v. United States.* 158 F.Supp. 560 (Ct. Cl., 1958) *cert. den.* (1958).

automated information handling process. This regulation usually has as its goal the protection of privacy, and in many instances establishes criminal sanctions for noncompliance. The form of regulation (whether by commission or by direct application to the operator) inevitably will generate legal problems, not only as to compliance, but also as to the basic form of the regulation itself. Overbroad regulatory language can have a significant impact on extensive university capital investment for research and administration by computer process.

Separately Incorporated Auxiliary Enterprises

Institutions often find it useful to have certain educationally related functions operated by entities legally distinct from the college or university. Common examples are college stores, college unions, and food services, and in some instances the entire student organization.

These operations present special problems of unemployment and disability insurance exemption, of tax-exempt status for both income and property tax purposes, and of assuring their legitimacy as separate entities. The separate entity becomes a problem when the institution and the auxiliary organization are different in name only. Institutions whose management is coterminous with the management of the auxiliary enterprise may find both categories of activity subject to similar rules and regulations of the institution.

Torts and Liability

Nearly all public institutions formerly enjoyed an immunity from liability for most of their torts. Thus, persons injured on account of negligent operations of the institution could not recover for their injuries—at least, not from the institution. Many private schools enjoyed analogous exemptions developed under one or more of three common law theories.

Most of these immunities no longer exist. Courts and legislatures largely have eliminated the public institution's sovereign immunity in cases of nondiscretionary torts such as negligence, although there usually are claims and notice provisions that

plaintiffs must follow. Also, charitable immunities formerly available to private institutions have all but disappeared. The institution therefore must be concerned for its tort liability exposure. The Occupational Safety and Health Act (and state laws enacted in conformity with it) also expands the ambit of liability exposure to the institution.

Classically, courts designated persons who entered the property of another as "business invitees," "bare licensees," "trespassers," or as falling into some intermediate classification. The duty of care the property holder was bound to exercise was reduced as one moved down the scale: thus, a trespasser often was protected only against deliberate injury. In time, this categorization proved unsatisfactory, as was shown by the engrafting of multiple exceptions and qualifications ("attractive nuisance" is a familiar example). The modern view is to inquire as to what safeguards are reasonable in light of *all* the relevant circumstances, including the severity of risk, the foreseeability of harm, the likelihood that persons will be on the property, and the cost and practicality of avoiding or abating the danger, such as by posting notice of the danger or by fencing off.

Determination of Which Institutions Are "Public"

Institutions of higher education are categorized as "public" or "private," with different legal consequences attached to each. Public institutions are subject to all the constitutional limitations implicit in the concept of "state action": they cannot discipline students in violation of due process principles, and cannot decline to retain employees on grounds prohibited by the U.S. Constitution, such as the exercise of constitutionally protected expression. But these institutions enjoy a partial immunity from suit in federal court under the Eleventh Amendment; their officers usually are personally immune under state law for "discretionary" acts and have the protection of tort claims acts procedures. The public institution also may be in a favorable tax position as a potential donee, and is often beyond the authority of local ordinance. On the other hand, the private institution is not subject to the plethora of laws limiting the extent and procedure of exercise of powers by government.

It is arguable that an otherwise "private" institution that receives substantial public financial support—as most do, directly or indirectly—is sufficiently infused with "state action" as to make it public. As is true in other areas, courts are unlikely to take a rigid attitude on this issue. Thus far, they have been liberal in finding "state action" where discrimination is involved[16], but slow to do so on questions of procedural due process.[17] Moreover, "state action" is a constitutional concept, and has not been applied to questions of the public or private nature of the institution for purposes not involving the Fourteenth Amendment, which makes most of the provisions of the Bill of Rights applicable to the states.

ADHERENCE TO LAW

Institutions of higher education, as inheritors of a very special and precious tradition of integrity, and as preceptors, have special reason to scrupulously honor the letter and spirit of the law. This is demanded not only by principles of fairness, but also by the necessity of maintaining the wide support that is requisite to their well-being. To paraphrase an apt law review variation on a comment by Justice Holmes, if it is said that persons must turn square corners when they deal with institutions of higher education, it is hard to see why these institutions should not be held to a like standard of rectangular rectitude in their own affairs.[18]

---

[16]See: *In re Girard College Trusteeship*, 386 Pa. 548, 127 A.2d 287 (1956), overruled *Pennsylvania v. Board of Directors of City Trusts*, 353 U.S. 230 (1957); 391 Pa. 434, 138 A.2d 844 (1958); *cert. den.* 537 U.S. 570 (1958); *Commonwealth of Pennsylvania v. Brown*, 392 F.2d 120 (3d Cir. 1968), *cert. denied*, 391 U.S. 921, 88 S.Ct. 1811 (1968).

[17]See: *Grossner v. Trustees of Columbia University*, 287 F.Supp. 535, 547 (S.D.N.Y., 1968); *Wahba v. New York University*, 492 F.2d 96 (2d Cir., 1974); but see: *Belk v. Chancellor of Washington University*, 336 F.Supp. 45, 46 (E.D.Mo., 1970).

[18]48 Harv. L. Rev. 1299, quoted in *Farrell v. County of Placer*, 23 C.2d 624, 628 (1944).

Student Aid

THE USUAL FORMS of financial aid to college and university students, administered through the institution, are scholarships, fellowships, assistantships, grants, loans, part-time employment, and special arrangements for the payment of tuition and other charges. This segment of the financial affairs of the institution, affecting the welfare of individual students as well as the institution, requires judicious and effective administration.

ADMINISTRATION

Administration of the student aid program is a responsibility of both academic and financial officers. Broad policies and procedures for award and administration of student aid should be adopted by the institution. These may be based on recommendations of a committee of representatives from academic departments, admissions and student aid offices, student personnel office, business office, and student body. Such a student aid committee should determine, in areas of its concern, standards and requirements relating to academic and other qualifications of applicants and methods used to appraise their financial needs.

An officer should be appointed to implement student aid policies and coordinate the work of the program, although graduate fellowships and assistantships usually are administered by a separate office, such as the graduate school or the student's academic department. In small institutions the student aid function may be a principal part-time assignment of the officer. In large institutions or those with significant student aid budgets, a full-time administrator and supporting staff are required.

Within the framework of approved policies, the student aid officer should be responsible for administering the program, including such procedures as receipt of applications for all forms of financial assistance, evaluation of financial need and qualifications of applicants, and decisions concerning the amounts and kinds of student aid to be granted. Although the business officer should be responsible for receipt, custody, and disbursement of all funds for student aid and for all aspects of their accounting and fiscal reporting, many federal student aid programs require accounting and fiscal reporting by the student aid officer.

To comply with laws pertaining to aid funds, student aid officers and appropriate staff in the business office must review periodically, and become acquainted with, provisions of federal, state, and local laws and regulations as they relate to all forms of payments to students. Under federal regulations, a student who receives federal aid funds may not be paid amounts that exceed his computed need, including income from any source. An institution that fails to comply with this restriction may be liable to repay the amount of "overmet need" to the government. Whenever possible, there should be a data bank of information for each student, indicating the amount and type of aid from institutional as well as outside sources.

Information describing the total student aid program should be published in convenient, comprehensible form. The publication should include kinds of aid available, general rules and regulations in granting aid, qualifications and eligibility requirements applicable to special funds and types of aid, methods of applying for aid, and procedures to be followed in arranging for deferred payments of fees and charges. Information on loan funds should include interest rates, repayment schedules, and obligations of borrowers.

While financial need in most cases is the basic criterion for granting student aid, many institutions consider other factors such as academic achievement, vocational objectives, and leadership potential. All students seeking aid should be required to complete the appropriate application form, which solicits such information.

Professional financial analysis services, such as the College Scholarship Service and the American College Testing Program, are available to evaluate family financial circumstances to determine the support to be expected from the family. At the student's request, results of these evaluations are sent in confidence to institutions for use in determining the amounts of financial assistance needed by the applicant.

FORMS OF STUDENT AID

In order to make the most effective use of their student aid funds, institutions typically grant assistance to a student through a "package" of aid, which may include a combination of scholarship or grant and self-help such as loan or work. Adjustments in the amount and composition of the package are made from year to year as the financial and academic circumstances of the applicants or the resources of the institution change. Some institutions award aid for the entire period of study unless circumstances change; others require annual application.

Scholarships and Fellowships

Scholarships, which generally are awarded to undergraduates, are based on scholastic achievement and/or financial need, and rarely cover total educational expenses. Some scholarships are awarded for academic excellence or special talents in specific areas, regardless of financial need.

Fellowships, which are awarded to graduate students, usually are of larger amount; traditionally, applicants have not been required to demonstrate financial need. Scholastic excellence has been the important criterion, but some institutions are introducing the need factor as costs rise and funds become scarce.

Recipients of scholarships and fellowships are not expected to render service to the institution as a consideration for their awards, nor are they expected to repay them.

Foundations, fraternal orders, religious groups, and similar agencies often grant scholarships and fellowships directly to students they select, based in many cases on information supplied by the institution. Student aid officers should cooperate with such organizations but should suggest that, whenever possible, the standards, qualifications of students, and other regulations of their institutions be followed.

Institutions are sometimes asked to accept gifts to which the term "scholarship" is applied, but with the donor reserving the right to designate the recipient. Such receipts cannot be treated as scholarship funds, and donors should be informed that their funds are being accepted as agency funds for use of the designated students. Donors should be notified that such funds are not gifts to the institution and therefore are not tax-deductible.

Assistantships

Assistantships, like fellowships, usually include tuition remission for graduate students, but the award, or stipend, is generally less than that of a fellowship. Unlike fellowships, however, assistantships require performance of services, which should be charged as expenses of the department in which the work is performed, regardless of the basis on which recipients are selected.

Grants

Grants typically are awarded to students with special talents—music and art students, athletes, and others—usually without regard to scholastic achievement or financial need. Grants also may be mandated by law, such as the federal opportunity grant programs and many state "scholarship" programs.

Loans

There has been an emphasis on self-help, particularly student loans. This has been caused partly by the expanded availability of loan funds from federal sources, which provide loans at subsidized interest to students meeting certain need criteria. In addition to federal programs, there are state and private programs of loans with subsidized interest. Loans also are made directly to students by agencies outside the institution. As with scholarships from outside sources, colleges and universities should cooperate with the organizations and encourage them to observe the institution's standards, policies, and regulations in administering loan funds.

The revolving fund is the usual type of institutional loan fund. When a loan is repaid by the recipient, it is again made available for lending. Interest on loans, if any, is added to the fund to help cover occasional losses and to insure perpetuity of the loan fund.

Long-term loans are granted to students whose needs for assistance are sufficiently great that the amount of gift-aid funds and employment available is not sufficient to meet the students' entire needs. Long-term loans generally do not require payment of interest while the student is attending school (or the interest is paid for the student), but do carry an interest charge during the repayment period. Short-term loans are maintained by some institutions to provide immediate funds for emergency purposes. The amount that can be borrowed usually is small, and the repayment period may vary.

A student should be granted a loan only after review of his application form, a personal interview by the appropriate college officer, and the execution of a loan note, which must contain pertinent information regarding truth-in-lending laws, according to applicable statutes. In addition to other information about the student, the application form should disclose all sources and amounts of income of the applicant for the following year, estimates of expenses during the year, and amount of loan requested. Names, addresses, and telephone numbers of references and a cosigner, if there is one, must be furnished. This information is valuable in locating borrowers who fail to keep the institution informed of changes of address. On a loan made to a minor, a cosigner may be necessary to enforce the legal right to collect the note according to laws of the state in which the institution is located. Ordinarily, responsibility for approving a loan rests with the student aid officer.

The administration of loans approved is a responsibility of the business officer. He should verify authorizations and terms of loans, ascertain that recipients have no outstanding delinquent accounts, prepare the notes, and issue checks payable to students for the amount of the loans. Checks should be endorsed by students, even though proceeds from loans are to be paid immediately to students' accounts. The issuance of checks to students who borrow funds, which also requires their subsequent endorsement, emphasizes the business nature of the loan.

Since it is the duty of the business officer to collect loans, he should insure that both an initial and an exit interview are held with recipients of student loans. At the exit interview, stress should be on the student's obligation to pay any interest stipulated, to repay the loan, and to keep the institution advised of his correct address and name changes. A written agreement should confirm interest payments and the schedule for repayment. A monthly schedule is often best.

The business officer is responsible for developing an efficient system for collecting student loans. Advance notices of interest and principal payments due should be sent regularly by the business office or billing agent to all borrowers. Notices of payments made, which also show the balance of unpaid principal, and reminder letters should originate in the business office. Telephone calls to delinquent borrowers produce satisfactory results. Data processing equipment is effective in preparing bills and statements, notices and requests for payment, analyses and reports on student loan fund activities, aging of loan notes, and other phases of accounting and reporting for student loan funds. A number of institutions use banks and billing agencies for the administration of collection of student loans.

An institution that accepts funds to be lent to students, regardless of the source, accepts the responsibility for administering the funds effectively. When a student is granted an aid package that includes a loan, it must be made clear to the student that the loan portion is an obligation that eventually must be repaid.

Part-Time Employment

Part-time student employment often is incorporated in the student aid program. Students seeking aid may be expected (although not required) to accept part-time employment, loans, or both as part of their self-help obligation. Ideally, the part-time employment function is vested in the student aid office.

The student aid office should refer students to prospective employers. Final selection of students to be employed should be the responsibility of those in areas where the students will work. Part-time or temporary work for students, with wages paid entirely from institutional or agency funds, is common to most institutions. Financial need is not always a prerequisite for institutional employment, and placement may depend on the student's interest and job skills. Supervisors of student employees, regardless of source of funds, should insist on prompt, efficient, and conscientious performance. Failure to require satisfactory performance is a disservice to students as well as to the institution.

The College Work-Study Program was established by the federal government to increase the availability of jobs, thus helping needy students finance their college education. Employment opportunities are available for students with demonstrated financial need to earn a portion of their college expenses in part-time, on- or off-campus work while they attend college. College Work-Study Program funds may be used to subsidize up to eighty percent of a student's wages, with the balance to be paid by the institution or employer, whether on- or off-campus.

Deferred Payment Plans

At colleges and universities, arrangements can be made for students and parents to pay tuition, fees, room and board charges, and other expenses on a deferred payment plan. Deferments usually are for short time periods—not beyond the end of the current semester or term or, at most, beyond the end of the academic year.

A charge should be assessed against those using a deferred payment plan, such as interest on the unpaid balance of the bill or a flat fee for each deferred payment. If financial assistance is necessary for longer periods of time, the student or parents should be advised to apply for a long-term loan.

Although deferred payment plans are a part of the total student aid program, they should be handled through the business office because academic factors and financial need determination generally are not involved. Institutions wishing to restrict deferred payments to students with a genuine need for deferment may channel such applications through the student aid office for need determination and cash flow analysis. If the program of deferred payments is understood by students and is well-administered by the institution, collection problems are minimized.

Arrangements for deferred payments should be in writing, and the payment agreement form signed by the student and/or his parents. The agreement should indicate amounts to be paid, dates on which payments are due, interest rate, and penalties to be incurred in case of failure to meet payments on the dates specified.

Described as deferred payment plans, loans are offered by many agencies and banks. By such plans, parents may pay the cost of tuition, room and board, and other charges in monthly installments over a period of years. These plans may include insurance on the life of the employed parent for the full amount of the contract.

Personnel Administration

PERSONNEL ADMINISTRATION is a systematic approach to manpower recruitment, utilization, compensation, and development. When fully and properly implemented, it creates an environment that is conducive to, and facilitates the accomplishment of, the goals of the educational institution in the most effective manner. A well-developed program of personnel administration can:

1. Assist administrators in clarifying the organization of the staff and workload in their departments.
2. Enable administrators to develop and maintain fair and equitable compensation policies and practices.
3. Facilitate staffing of the organization with competent employees.
4. Insure that the institution complies with federal and state laws relating to employment and maintains data for federal, state, and local personnel audits and reports.
5. Assist employees in understanding the organization and in identifying with it.
6. Encourage and assist department heads and supervisors in initiating and maintaining orientation, training, and development programs that will make it possible for employees to understand what is expected of them, to perform their work efficiently, to develop their skills and abilities, and to achieve their full potential.
7. Help employees motivate themselves to work together productively.
8. Facilitate communication among administrators, supervisors, and employees about personnel matters.
9. Provide procedures for resolving grievances.
10. Assist administrators in interpreting and reacting to concerns of employee organizations, unions, and special-interest groups.

Personnel administration is usually a *staff* function, but may include certain *line* functions. Those involved in personnel administration participate in the development and implementation of institutional personnel policies and practices by working with other institutional administrators and supervisors. The personnel administrator should, of course, play a very active part in helping initiate these policies and practices. A personnel officer may have direct administrative authority over certain institutional employees in order to insure compliance with federal and state laws.

The need for consistent application of personnel policies, laws, and government regulations throughout the college or university is of such importance that it dictates centralization of the entire institutional personnel function. This is especially true with respect to the impact of federal and state legislation regarding equitable employment practices, which must apply equally to all employees. Since the influence of the personnel operation affects all segments of the college or university, responsibility for establishing and implementing the institutional personnel program must be assigned to a major administrative officer. In a small institution this assignment may be given to someone who has other administrative responsibilities. It is important, however, that there be a clearly identifiable personnel operation or function.

Historically, the chief business officer normally has been responsible for promotion and development of what was identified as personnel administration in the institution, usually as it related to nonteaching employees. Academic administrators have been responsible for largely unstructured personnel activities related to the academic staff. Regardless of this separation of functions, it is advisable for the chief academic officer to avail himself of the specialized assistance of the personnel officer when it is required. Much overlapping of duties, confusion, and unwarranted expense can be avoided, however, by centralizing all personnel administration under one officer. Centralization can best be accomplished by making the personnel operation responsible directly to the highest practical level of authority.

An institutional decision as to whom the chief personnel administrative officer should be responsible must therefore be made in the context of individual workloads, capabilities, and personalities. The decision should be based on how the personnel program can best serve the institution. As conditions change, reorganization may be required.

Regardless of organization structure there should be specific action by the governing board of the institution, which defines the broad objectives of the personnel program and the major features of its relationships and structures. The personnel program is much more likely to be better received and greatly strengthened in its utilization if there has been employee participation in its development and if provision is made for employee committees or councils for communication and advisory purposes.

Key functions of a comprehensive personnel department include position classification; compensation and benefits; employee relations; recruitment, selection, and promotion; affirmative action programs; orientation and training; performance evaluation; organization and manpower planning and development; labor relations; records; and sometimes, safety. Each of these functions should be considered and evaluated separately; however, in practice they should be organized to blend into a totally effective program.

POSITION CLASSIFICATION

A classification plan provides a method for grouping individual positions together under common class titles and descriptions and is basic to all programs and processes in personnel administration. It also is essential for insuring and documenting equal employment opportunity. The selection of a plan presupposes sufficient analysis of the organization and positions to determine the factors for job evaluation. Techniques involved in establishing and maintaining a classification plan as a

basic tool include:
1. Writing and verifying, by on-the-job audits, individual position descriptions.
2. Sorting positions into a classification structure.
3. Outlining class specifications and relative values.
4. Delineating use of class specifications—for example, as a basis for budget preparation and personnel programs and procedures.

COMPENSATION AND BENEFITS

Compensation and benefit plans provide a systematic approach to establishing salary levels for positions, establishing practices relative to vacations, holidays, leaves, insurance, and retirement, maintaining equitable relationships among positions based on levels of responsibility, recognizing competitive salaries paid in the labor market, maintaining salary and benefit levels that permit recruitment and retention of personnel, and affording a means of rewarding improved or meritorious performance. Because compensation and benefits represent total employment cost, each program must be developed and evaluated in the context of total compensation.

Careful consideration must be given to the most effective use of the institutional dollar—in the form of take-home pay, pay for nonproductive time, insured income in case of loss of pay because of disability or layoff, delayed compensation to be paid after retirement, or indirect income through "job niceties" such as inexpensive parking. Basic to the development of all compensation and benefit plans is a determination of the institution's financial resources and its ability to support the various benefit plans, many of which become far more costly than was anticipated at the time of original adoption.

Compensation and benefit plans are implemented by acceptable techniques applied to such established basic principles as:
1. Internal equity among all classes of work in the classification plan.
2. External equity with rates paid by other organizations in competition for the supply of qualified applicants.
3. Cost-of-living changes.
4. Performance.
5. Length of service.

EMPLOYEE RELATIONS

Maintaining consistent application of policies and practices, thus tending to prevent personnel problems and grievances and helping to solve those that occur, requires an effective liaison and communications program among staff, faculty, and administrators. Employee relations includes administration of factors affecting morale and such matters as discipline, seniority, layoff, and rehiring. Involved in this activity are:

1. Development of the personnel function as one of advice and counsel on personnel matters.
2. Education and training of department heads and supervisors.
3. Communication of personnel practices and policies through explanations by supervisors and through the use of handbooks, training programs, meetings with employees, and other appropriate media.
4. Establishment of a formal procedure for handling employee grievances.

RECRUITMENT, SELECTION, AND PROMOTION

The recruitment and selection of nonteaching employees was one of the earliest functions of personnel administration in colleges and universities. Recruitment and selection procedures should include a systematic program for securing qualified applicants and for recommending applicants who are best qualified for a vacant position. It is no longer considered adequate for an institution to rely on recruitment procedures in which an applicant must take the initiative in seeking employment with the institution; the institution must take the initiative in securing applications from individuals who might not be reached through the traditional procedures of referrals and general advertising. A recruitment program must acquaint employees with existing vacancies and assist in the transfer or promotion of current staff members. Qualifications to be considered include not only technical skills and abilities, but also traits or qualities that are needed to bring strength and balance to both the operating unit in which the vacancy exists and the overall institution.

Screening and selection procedures must be carefully developed and implemented, with equal concern for the rejected applicants as well as those selected. Proper validation of all screening and selection procedures is extremely important in meeting compliance standards established for equal employment opportunity and affirmative action programs.

AFFIRMATIVE ACTION PROGRAMS

Federal regulations make it imperative that imaginative programs for affirmative action be developed at each employment level to provide equal employment opportunity and advancement to all individuals regardless of race, color, religion, sex, age, or national origin. These efforts may include:

1. Analysis of legal requirements.
2. Promulgation of a formal statement, to be adopted by the governing board, of policies and practices of the institution, without bias as to race, color, religion, sex, age, or national origin.
3. Programs for implementation of these policies and practices.
4. Sensitivity training for administrators, supervisors, and present employees.
5. Special recruitment of women and the culturally disadvantaged.
6. Orientation and training programs especially designed, for example, to assist culturally disadvantaged employees in becoming part of the working community.
7. Training, conducted both on and off the job, and upgrading.
8. Follow-up and evaluation procedures.
9. Effective liaison with appropriate compliance review agencies.

ORIENTATION AND TRAINING

Orientation and training programs provide services to the new employee in adjusting to the employer and the work unit, to the employee in developing skills, abilities, and knowledge relating to promotional opportunities, and to the administrator and supervisor in implementing such activities. The programs should be developed after searching out stated needs for training and development activities. Needs may range from reading and writing for illiterate employees to skill training, such as typing, or sensitivity training and professional development. These services, which can be provided within or without the institution, by the employer or by other agencies, may include:

1. Centralized orientation sessions to assist new employees in identifying with the college or university.
2. Centralized training programs on business and academic policies and procedures, office practice techniques, supervision, and other skills usable by employees throughout the organization.
3. Technical assistance to departmental administrators and supervisors in development of departmental orientation and training programs that assist employees in becoming acquainted with the department and its work methods.
4. Training supervisors in how to supervise and train employees.
5. Administration of educational assistance programs for enrollment of employees in developmental courses in vocational schools, colleges, and universities.
6. Encouragement of attendance in appropriate professional meetings and workshops.

PERFORMANCE EVALUATION

Performance evaluation is often thought to be a mechanical process for determining who will be given a pay raise. Performance evaluation can be used in making such decisions, but a good performance evaluation program will serve many other, equally important purposes. It can:

1. Help employees see how their work appears to supervisors.
2. Assist employees in improving their performance.
3. Assist supervisors and management in analyzing the effectiveness of the organization and its operations.
4. Help supervisors and management in identification of employees who should be considered for development, promotion, transfer, or dismissal.
5. Increase employee morale by providing a means of communication with management.
6. Assist in attainment of departmental and institutional goals.

Performance evaluation is a continuing process, but there should be provision for periodic formal review. There are several approaches that can be used in the design of a performance evaluation system:

1. Employee characteristics analysis.
2. Task performance analysis.
3. Management by objective.

ORGANIZATION AND MANPOWER PLANNING AND DEVELOPMENT

Systematic reviews of staffing requirements are necessary in order to implement recruitment, promotional, and transfer patterns for existing staff. The program should be designed to promote internal movement of promotable staff members, to encourage individual employee development by planned movement within the organization or by training, and to analyze such factors as:

1. Skills and abilities required for all positions in the institution.
2. Skills and abilities of present employees.
3. Turnover of employees in each class of work.
4. Growth trends of each department of the organization and implications of patterns upon future personnel needs.
5. Projections for recruitment, development, and promotional programs.

LABOR RELATIONS

Labor relations is an increasingly important activity in personnel administration. At one time only maintenance, service, and craft and trade employees were thought to be interested in unionization. Perhaps there is no group of employees, including administrators, that has not given some thought to the advantages and disadvantages of unionization. In the event that bargaining units exist or are a possibility, consideration of the relationship between the union and the college or university should include:

1. Determining the labor relations philosophy of the governing board and the senior administrators of the institution.
2. Obtaining legal counsel and labor relations consultation as circumstances dictate.
3. Defining the bargaining unit or units.
4. Determining the issues that will be negotiable.

5. Negotiating with union representatives.
6. Presenting the institutional points of view to the employees involved, to other institutional staff members, and if the situation warrants, to the general public.
7. Implementing the provisions of a negotiated contract.
8. Keeping the administration informed of pertinent events and trends.

For a detailed treatment of this subject, refer to the chapter "Labor Relations and Collective Bargaining."

RECORDS

Development of a centralized system of employee records is an integral part of a personnel program. Such a system serves the operating and legal needs of all personnel programs and the statistical needs of personnel managers, personnel research, and administration, with particular emphasis on budget planning and administration. Record systems should be established and continually evaluated concerning:

1. Nature of records required.
2. Record systems available for utilization.
3. Record retention policies.
4. Legal requirements regarding record keeping.

Because personnel records are an essential part of the institution's management information system, they should be integrated with it to the extent practicable.

SAFETY

A well-developed safety program is required of all educational institutions by federal as well as by many state laws. The personnel department may be responsible for administering the institutional accident prevention program, including record keeping, and for providing training in safety measures. Adherence to safety principles will reduce accidents, improve quality of service, and often reduce the cost of operations. Elements of a safety program include strong administrative support; active supervision; constant search for, and correction of, physical defects and unsafe practices; and training of employees in safety measures.

Claims under workmen's compensation and disability laws should be processed through the personnel department, which also should be assigned responsibility for maintaining records and preparing reports required by law.

For a detailed treatment of this subject, refer to the chapter "Safety."

Faculty and Staff Benefits

BENEFITS have become a significant part of total compensation, and they often are key elements in union negotiations. The personnel department normally is responsible for administration of the benefits program, and also should conduct periodic reviews of the program and recommend changes as appropriate.

Because benefit programs are costly and complex, careful planning is essential. The entire compensation program must be surveyed when new plans or programs are considered or existing ones are revised. For example, it would be inappropriate to establish retirement or disability benefit levels without considering the substantial benefits available from social security and other statutory programs, such as workmen's compensation or, in some states, temporary disability plans.

One method of regarding the total benefit package systematically is through functional benefit planning. Such planning may utilize a simple matrix with the various benefit plans listed along one axis and the various contingencies along the other, thus revealing needs, duplications, and unnecessary coverage.

A continuous communication program is an integral part of the administration of the benefits program. Communications would include information about benefits available, proposed changes, new features of existing plans, and cost to the employer (or value to the employee in dollars). Generally, a message is most effective if it can be presented to the employee's spouse as well as to the employee. Annual reports concerning the benefits program as it pertains to the individual employee are an effective means of communication; these usually are mailed to the employee's home.

Although benefit programs historically have been considered a means to attract and retain employees, they are now important aspects of compensation and are recognized as employee entitlements through which certain social and individual needs are met. Such programs in educational institutions usually include medical, disability, life insurance, and retirement benefits. Other programs offered by some institutions include remission of tuition, housing, periodic health examinations, travel and personal accident insurance, recreational and cultural events, leaves of absence, and credit unions.

INSURED PLANS OR DIRECT COST PROGRAMS

Medical Care

The medical care plans of colleges and universities usually fall into two categories—basic hospital-surgical-medical plans and major medical coverage. The hospitalization plans normally provide benefits for inpatient, semiprivate accommodations, such as room and board, special diets, general nursing service, use of operating room, and drugs and medicines. The surgical-medical plans cover physician fees, laboratory tests, X rays, electrocardiograms, etc. Payments usually are based on fee schedules, which are fixed or "reasonable and customary." These plans either provide for payment of claims directly to the hospital or doctor, such as Blue Cross-Blue Shield, or reimburse the insured for payments made to the hospital or doctor.

Major medical plans are designed to meet the costs of catastrophic or extraordinary medical expenses. Such plans normally carry large benefit amounts ($25,000 to $50,000) per family member, and reimburse usually eighty percent of covered expenses not reimbursed by a base plan or exceeding a deductible amount. Typically, the cost of these plans varies more with the deductible selected than with the maximum benefit specified. Basic hospital plans also can be written to include provisions for major medical coverage.

A coordination of benefit (C.O.B.) clause should be included in health care plans because such clauses tend to eliminate double reimbursement of benefits.

All full-time employees should be eligible for participation in the medical care program at the time of employment. In order to avoid selection against the insurance company, eligibility for enrollment is limited specifically to the first month or two of employment, with an open enrollment period held annually. Although most institutions pay for employee coverage only, the trend is to pay a part of the full cost of dependent coverage also.

Introduction of medicare has increased health protection resources for persons age sixty-five and over. Consideration should be given to continuing the institution-sponsored health care program into retirement. Such coverage should be available to the retiree or spouse on an employee-pay-all basis as a minimum commitment, with the institution paying for all or a portion of the coverage if financially feasible. Institutional payment of the medicare part B premiums also can be considered important financial assistance for the retiree. Of course, such assistance must coincide with the philosophy of the institution.

Efficient claims handling is essential to health care programs, as prolonged processing can be a source of annoyance to the claimant and the institution. Procedures must be established to expedite claims handling and to control costs.

Short-Term Disability Income

Most colleges and universities provide salary continuation programs with schedules of limited duration. These programs frequently provide full salary for a certain period, the duration of which usually depends on length of service. For example, an employee may accumulate one day of sick leave per month of service.

One drawback to this type of plan is that the employee may feel he has "earned" the sick pay and therefore is entitled to it upon termination or retirement; however, most institutions do not recognize "earned" sick pay for this purpose, and the conditions of the benefit should be stated in a handbook.

Short-term disability plans sometimes are insured (accident and sickness insurance), but more frequently are self-insured, that is, paid out of current funds.

Long-Term Disability Income

Although most periods of disability are of short duration, disabilities of longer duration may present a virtually hopeless financial situation. Protection against long-term disabilities should, after a suitable waiting period, provide adequate benefits to at least age sixty-five. In addition, contributions to the retirement plan should be continued during the period of disability in order that income will be adequate upon retirement. The plan should include a method of adjusting disability income to meet rising living costs and standards. An institution also may consider contributing toward the disabled employee's health and life insurance coverage.

In establishing disability plans or revising existing ones, consideration must be given to benefits from other institution-sponsored programs and from government programs, such as social security and veterans' benefits.

Disability programs are often part of retirement plans. Other disability programs are insured, and some are self-insured and administered. The specific terms of a disability plan should be stated formally so that employees may learn exactly what is available in case of disability.

Life Insurance

Life insurance programs available at colleges and universities usually consist of term insurance rather than types of coverage that accumulate cash reserves. Such insurance is written on a group basis and is issued without medical examination, provided a minimum percentage of the group participates in the plan. In establishing a new life insurance plan, or in reviewing an existing plan, consideration should be given to such factors as classes of personnel to be included, age groupings, waiting periods, amounts of insurance, sharing premium costs, and continuing insurance after retirement. Life insurance plans should include all permanent, full-time employees, either as a single group or in selected classifications. Participation should be available at the time of employment or after a reasonable waiting period.

Amounts of insurance may be determined in

various ways. One method is to provide the employee, regardless of age, with insurance of a fixed amount or of a stated multiple of the basic salary or wage. Premiums usually increase with age in this case. Another method is to hold the premium constant but to decrease the insurance as the age of the individual increases. Participants frequently are permitted to elect, at their own expense, additional insurance above that provided in the basic schedules.

Other benefit variances provide survivor life insurance benefits that more nearly fit individual needs. This program typically provides a dependent spouse and/or children with a monthly income in lieu of lump-sum distribution. This benefit is a percentage of monthly earnings, payable to the spouse until death, remarriage, or a given age, such as sixty-five, with children's benefits usually continued until the youngest child reaches a given age, such as twenty-three.

As the employee approaches retirement age, the need for high financial protection usually is reduced and the emphasis of protection normally shifts from the group life insurance plan to the retirement and death benefits available from a retirement plan. Group life insurance can provide the protection needed by employees during high-expense years at a reasonable cost. It seems to make little sense to provide a substantial amount at the death of an individual who has no dependents.

The cost of life insurance plans may be shared by the institution and the participants, or it may be assumed in full by the institution. If group life insurance is term insurance, coverage ceases a short time after the insured member leaves the institution. The employee usually has the right to convert this insurance to a permanent, individual policy without medical examination during a designated period and at the premium rate established, based on age at the time of conversion. Some institutions provide continued life insurance protection after retirement, frequently at a substantially reduced level. The cost of this extended coverage is relatively high in terms of benefit dollars.

The amount of group life insurance typically does not represent an individual's entire insurance portfolio, but rather an important base that may be supplemented by personal programs.

Accidental Death Insurance

Many colleges and universities offer accidental death and dismemberment insurance (AD&D), which pays specified indemnity amounts if the individual dies as the result of an accident or if he sustains the accidental loss of sight or of parts of the body. Although many institutions have AD&D provisions in their life insurance plans, there is danger of misleading the employee to assume that his insurance protection is greater than it is. An employer is responsible for making sure that the full amount of group life insurance is paid for death from sickness as well as accident.

Retirement Plan

The retirement plan is basic to the benefits program and, of all benefit plans, usually represents the largest single financial commitment. In determining the adequacy of a retirement plan, consideration must be given to such factors as:

1. Classes of personnel to be included.
2. Amount of retirement income to be provided.
3. Waiting periods.
4. Retirement age and/or length of service.
5. Average age of employees and employment turnover.
6. Vesting, or ownership of retirement benefits.
7. Sharing of costs.

Retirement plans generally were designed to provide employees with income in addition to social security after retirement from the institution under whose program the payments were made. Retirement plans funded under TIAA-CREF are the most common exceptions to this practice, as they provide for transfer (or portability) of benefits from institution to institution. Retirement plans frequently provide different benefits and means of funding for various personnel groups, such as faculty and technical, clerical, and service staff. Such differences should be based as much as possible on the different needs of these groups.

Requirements for Participation. Many retirement plans require a waiting period before technical, clerical, and service staff are eligible (or are required to participate), while plans for members of the faculty and administrative officers frequently require relatively short waiting periods. The waiting period may be based on age, length of service, or a combination thereof. There is, however, a trend toward shortening or eliminating the waiting period for nonfaculty employees.

Participation in the retirement plan should be mandatory during the major portion of an employee's working years. This means that compulsory participation should occur near the age of thirty or thirty-five. Consideration can be given to immediate participation for a new employee who already has a retirement contract such as TIAA-CREF, assuming that the employing institution is willing to contribute to such a contract.

Although participation may be made optional for those in service at the time a new plan is implemented, it is better for the employee as well as the institution if participation is required immediately. Prior service credit for participants can be provided when a new plan is installed, based on age, length of service, or a combination thereof.

Arrangements for meeting the cost of retirement plans vary widely among institutions. The cost may be divided between the institution and participants or it may be assumed by the institution.

Age at Retirement. Retirement plans should specify an age for retirement. Early retirement is often to the mutual advantage of both the institution and the individual. Arrangements for early retirement should be considered carefully according to individual circumstances. Provisions may be made for extension of service in individual cases at the option of the institution. Unless controlled, however, extensions may become the rule rather than the exception. Therefore, extensions should be made for renewable periods of one year, subject to approval, often by the governing board, which should indicate clearly that extensions are not automatic and that retirement is not postponed indefinitely, but will occur on a certain date.

Integration with Social Security. The substantial increases in social security benefits and coverage, as well as commitment to adjust benefits to changes in the cost of living, make it essential that social security benefits be considered an integral part of retirement planning and funding. An appropriate plan must meet whatever criteria of benefits and cost have been established, considering institutional sources and social security. Frequently, higher contributions are made on salary above the social security base than on the salary subject to social security taxes. This arrangement tends to provide higher-paid participants with retirement benefits similar to those available to lower-paid participants when related to salary.

Level of Retirement Benefits. The level of retirement income to be provided should be decided by institutional policy and should be reviewed periodically. The retirement plan should reflect changes in the compensation of participants. It also should provide suitable arrangements for participants to contribute when leaves of absence without salary are granted, so that the steady accumulation of benefits will not be interrupted.

If the objectives of the plan are to be realized for both the early and the later years of retirement, the retirement income should be protected as much as possible against the effects of inflation. One method of achieving this is through use of the variable annuity contract. Premium payments under such contracts are invested in common stocks on the assumption that the cost of living and the yield from common stock investments follow similar trends. Such retirement contracts provide periodic payments to retirees in amounts that historically have reflected the changing value of the dollar's purchasing power.

Ownership of Benefits. Participants usually acquire vesting rights at some time during their term of employment, depending on various conditions such as age and/or number of years of participation. "Full vesting" means that if a participant leaves the employer before retirement, he retains the right to all the benefits purchased by the employer's contributions as well as his own. A participant is less than fully vested if he has not met the age and/or length-of-service requirement for full vesting. The retirement plan should not allow a retiring or terminating participant to receive a cash settlement in lieu of a retirement annuity. The accumulated funds should be kept intact to be used solely for their intended purpose, that is, to provide retirement or death benefits. However, it might be desirable to pay out a small portion of the accumulated funds upon retirement; TIAA-CREF permits payment of up to ten percent at the option of the retiree.

When a retirement plan is initiated, it is desirable to provide for those who have served the institution for many years, but who will not meet the years-of-service requirement before reaching retirement age to achieve an adequate retirement income, either under the regular provisions of the new plan or through a special program. The purchase or commitment for prior service is often very costly. Therefore, it sometimes is not possible to achieve full coverage for prior service and thus insure that benefits are made available uniformly to all.

Some institutions administer the retirement plan completely, from investing the funds to sending monthly payments to retirees. Normally the services of an actuarial consultant are obtained to advise on appropriate funding of the plan.

Exclusion Allowances. Internal Revenue Service regulations make it possible, under a formula, for an employee to have his salary reduced or to forgo an increase in salary in return for the purchase by the institution of a fully vested, nonassignable annuity contract for him.[1] This option may prove helpful to older employees who are thus able to give up a portion of current income to build a greater retirement benefit and reduce their current tax liability. Other benefits such as group life insurance normally are determined by the base salary and not the "reduced" salary.

Options. Retirement plans should provide a number of options for paying retirement benefits, so that the retiring participant can select a suitable annuity and provide for spouse or other beneficiary. The plan should not require final selection of the option prior to the retirement date.

Pre-Retirement Counseling. The transition from active to retired status can be traumatic. Pre-retirement counseling ideally should begin ten years prior to retirement. At that time, one should consider the implications of retirement—financial, legal, health, geographic, and housing.

Approximately one year prior to retirement, individual conferences should be held to explain various benefit options available under the retirement plan as well as disposition of health and life insurance benefits. The fact that there are income tax implications also should be mentioned, so that the employee may seek professional counsel if necessary. The employer does not use these conferences to advise the employee about which option to select, but rather to present him with the facts necessary to make a knowledgeable decision. The personnel department is usually responsible for pre-retirement counseling.

TIAA-CREF

Many educational institutions provide employees with retirement, life insurance, medical insurance, or a combination thereof through TIAA-CREF. There are many other companies that provide these services competently and efficiently, but TIAA-CREF is mentioned because of its predominance in providing these services for higher education.

CREF provides retirement benefits based on common stock investments. TIAA provides fixed-dollar retirement annuities. Subject to the provisions of an employing institution's TIAA-CREF retirement plan, participants may allocate their premium payments (including the institution's contributions) between TIAA and CREF in any proportion, including full allocation to either company. The purpose of the TIAA-CREF system is to provide a retirement income more responsive to economic change than a fixed-dollar annuity alone and less volatile than a variable annuity alone.

Social Security

Employees of most colleges and universities have been covered by social security since 1954, although the public institutions of a few states have elected not to participate. Social security provides significant benefits for retirement, disability, death, and medical expense.

Workmen's Compensation

Workmen's compensation plans usually are highly regulated by individual states. However, it benefits employers to take internal measures that reduce the cost of workmen's compensation. One of the most effective steps is establishment of a safety committee whose recommendations are accepted and implemented. (For a detailed treatment of this subject, refer to the chapter "Safety.") Requirements of the Occupational Safety and Health Act make this almost mandatory for covered employees. To avoid misunderstanding, employees

---

[1] In 1973 the maximum amount permitted under IRS rules to be paid into a retirement plan was twenty percent of salary.

and supervisors must know the procedure to follow in case of accident.

The cost of workmen's compensation plans is borne by the employer and is related to the claims incurred. Workmen's compensation insurance may be purchased from an insurance carrier or a plan may be self-administered by the college or university. When insurance is purchased, the premium is based on claims experience plus the cost of administration. With a self-administered plan, the university makes claim payments directly to the claimant.

Unemployment Compensation

The "Employment Security Amendments of 1970," followed by separate amendments to each of the fifty state employment security acts, extended unemployment compensation coverage to institutions of higher education as of January 1, 1972. Although this program varies from state to state, the cost of unemployment compensation is related to claims incurred. This cost can be minimized by establishing and following sound personnel procedures, particularly documenting reasons for termination and establishing a procedure for interviewing all terminating employees. Two areas requiring special consideration are an information system that allows claim forms to be completed and returned on a timely basis and an employment procedure that can offer reemployment to persons terminated within the college or university. A system of requisitioning to fill all open positions is implied in the latter procedure.

INDIRECT COST PROGRAMS

Because such benefits as vacations and holidays usually are included in the budget as part of salaries, they do not appear as a separate cost. However, there is a cost in terms of lost work time, which is a significant factor in planning workloads. Institutional policies regarding pay for time not worked influence recruitment and employee relations. The most common indirect cost benefits are vacations, holidays, leaves of absence, and sick leave.

Vacations

This benefit usually is influenced by practices of other institutions and commercial firms in the regional labor market. Vacation benefits for staff members normally are related to length of service. Often there are increases in the length of the benefit at the fifth, tenth, and twentieth years, but the practice varies widely. It is important, however, to apply the benefit consistently for all staff members at an institution.

Holidays

There are both national and state legal holidays. Holiday practices vary widely from state to state, and laws of the applicable state should be reviewed before stating the practice. Many institutions recognize certain legal holidays and add so-called "floating holidays" to their schedules in accordance with the particular need of the organization and the desire of the employees.

Leaves of Absence

Most colleges and universities have a practice regarding leaves of absence. Reasons for such absences may be personal need, education, pregnancy, or military or sabbatical leaves. In most instances, the salary is suspended but benefits and seniority continue during the period of the leave if the employee returns to work within a specified time. Often there are conditions such that if the employee works elsewhere during a leave, he is terminated. (Veteran's rehire privileges apply in cases of military leave.) Pregnancy leaves should be considered in light of the federal "Sex Discrimination Guidelines." The benefit normally is granted with permission of the department head and the personnel officer.

Sick Leave

Insurance companies sponsor plans that provide pay for absences due to illness, and several states have statutory plans. These plans often are part of a comprehensive health insurance program. However, many institutions have self-insured sick leave, based on length of service—for example, one day for each month worked to a maximum of ninety days. A thorough analysis of an organization should be made before instituting self-insured arrangements, and conditions such as "bona fide illness or accident only" and "no pay in lieu of unused sick time" should be described clearly.

REVIEW OF THE BENEFITS PROGRAM

Every institution should review its benefits program periodically to determine its effectiveness and to adjust the program to changing conditions. For nonfaculty employees, the trend is toward industry-type benefits that usually are considered compensation, such as shift premium pay, holiday pay, jury duty supplementary pay, National Guard supplementary pay, and meal allowances.

One method of maintaining an awareness of the latest developments is to subscribe to one of several reports. There are also several organizations that handle only college and university insurance problems.

Labor Relations and Collective Bargaining

LABOR RELATIONS refers to the relationship between the administration of an institution (management) and organized faculty and staff (employees) together with organizations to which faculty and staff belong. Collective bargaining, an important facet of labor relations, refers to negotiations between representatives of organized employees and the institution to determine such matters as salaries and wages, hours, work rules, and working conditions. The relationship between the administration and any organized faculty or staff is critical not only to negotiations of a labor-management contract but also to the efficiency of the institution, demands made on the time and energy of key administrators, and prospects of work disruption.

This discussion of labor relations and collective bargaining includes the following:

1. Labor Legislation
2. The Bargaining Unit and the Institution
3. Negotiating the Contract
4. Administering the Contract

LABOR LEGISLATION

Of utmost importance to the administration's relationship with faculty and staff is the nature and extent of labor relations legislation, which establishes the right of employees to organize and be represented exclusively by labor organizations for the purpose of collective bargaining. Private and public institutions are not covered by the same laws, but in states having enabling legislation, the expansion of unionization among personnel of public institutions has been greater than in states without such legislation.

Private institutions, except those with operating revenues of less than $1 million, are subject to the National Labor Relations Act (1935) as amended by the Taft-Hartley Act (1947) and the

Landrum-Griffin Act (1959); thus their labor relations will involve the National Labor Relations Board or one of its regional offices. Public institutions in many states are subject to somewhat similar state statutes. State laws, however, vary from each other and from federal laws both substantively and procedurally. For example, foremen, supervisors, and managerial personnel in private institutions are not protected by the National Labor Relations Act as amended, but some states have granted them the right to bargain collectively on the same basis as the rank and file, but in separate units. (The Board has criteria to determine who is a supervisor.) Private institutions should familiarize themselves with the Act and public institutions should know their state labor laws—prior to evidence of organization.

In states with no applicable laws, some institutions have granted union recognition, resulting in formalized collective bargaining or less formal "meet and confer" discussions of such matters as working conditions, salaries, and benefits. Decisions to enter into such forms of labor-management relations should have the approval of the governing board.

Illegal Practices

The National Labor Relations Act and most state labor relations laws set restrictions on employers and unions so that employees' rights are protected. Violations of these restrictions comprise "unfair labor practices." For example, any person acting as an agent of an employer, directly or indirectly (not only administrative personnel, but any person acting in a supervisory capacity, to the lowest supervisor level) may not legally:

1. Threaten employees with loss of jobs or benefits if they join a union, or promise benefits if they do not join a union.

2. Threaten to discontinue an operation or department if a union is organized by these employees.

3. Question employees about their union activities or membership under conditions that tend to restrain or coerce employees in their free choice.

4. Spy on union gatherings or give the impression of surveillance of such activities.

5. Grant wage increases or other benefits deliberately timed to defeat self-organization among employees.

6. Take an active part in organizing a union or committee to represent employees or bring pressure on employees to join a "company union."

7. Show favoritism to one of two or more unions competing to represent employees.

8. Take an active part in or foster an action initiated by institutional employees to decertify a union.

Many management activities concerning unions are permitted by the Act, however. Prior to selection of a union, management may:

1. Continue all operations and policies in a normal manner and insist that no organizing activities be carried on during working hours. (However, employees may discuss unionization during off-duty periods.)

2. Withhold or express its views concerning unions and collective bargaining as long as the message does not contain a threat of reprisal or promise of benefits.

3. Explain advantages or disadvantages of belonging to a union.

4. Discuss employee benefits and compensation plans and compare them with those enjoyed at other institutions.

5. Explain economic facts on which the institutional budget is developed and resources allocated.

6. Explain representation election procedures for determining the union's right to represent employees.

7. Urge employees to vote in the election because the majority of those voting determine the outcome, which is binding on every employee in the proposed unit.

8. Point out that employees may vote for or against the union even though they may have signed a membership card (or did not sign one).

9. Correct false or confusing statements made by union organizers or others concerning institutional or related matters.

Labor organizations also are forbidden under the National Labor Relations Act and the labor relations laws of some states to engage in practices designed to restrain or coerce employees in the exercise of their rights "to join or assist a labor organization or to refrain from so doing." For example, unions may not:

1. Tell employees they will lose their jobs unless they support the union's activities.

2. Cause or attempt to cause an employer to engage in discrimination against an employee in any way that tends to encourage or discourage union membership.

3. Make an agreement that requires an employer to hire only members of the union or persons "satisfactory" to the union—a closed shop. (However, a requirement that employees become members within a specified time after they are hired is legal in most states—a union shop.)

4. Picket in numbers such that nonstriking employees are physically barred from entering grounds or buildings.

5. Threaten bodily injury to nonstriking employees or commit acts of force or violence on the picket line.

6. Engage in secondary boycotts or jurisdictional strikes.

THE BARGAINING UNIT AND THE INSTITUTION

The bargaining unit is the specific group of employees the union seeks to represent for the purposes of collective bargaining and the resolution of grievances. Usually the union files a petition describing the unit with the appropriate labor relations agency at the state level. In most instances, labor relations laws provide for such agencies to determine appropriate units on a case-by-case basis according to legislative intent or administrative guidelines. Occasionally parties will agree mutually on the unit definition which, if legal, may be approved by the appropriate state or federal administrative agency — for example, the National Labor Relations Board. The agency also resolves disputes over inclusion or exclusion of particular groups of employees.

Examples of bargaining units identified by types of staff or faculty entering into conventional collective bargaining are:

Maintenance, custodial, grounds, and food service employees

Clerical and secretarial personnel

Security personnel

Foremen and supervisors

Middle management personnel

Teaching and research assistants

Interns and residents (in medical schools and hospitals)

Faculties (separate bargaining units for law schools)

Doctors, dentists, nurses, and pharmacists

Librarians (professionals and paraprofessionals)

Radio and television technicians

If the union and the employer are unable to agree on the unit, or the unit agreed on is not acceptable to the agency having jurisdiction, the agency conducts a hearing to examine the facts and arguments before making a decision binding on all parties. The criteria under state laws for examining these facts sometimes vary significantly from those of the National Labor Relations Act. The following are examples of the more frequently accepted criteria:

1. The extent of community of interest among employees — similarity of skills, working conditions, supervision, and/or uniform personnel policies such as wage and salary administration and employee benefits.

2. The history of collective bargaining at the institution, if any.

3. The desires of the employees.

4. The geographical separation of employees and the organizational structure of the institution.

5. The effect of the proposed unit on efficiency of the institution.

6. The nature of the work performed. (Security personnel such as police and guards are

required to be excluded from any other group. Under the National Labor Relations Act, professional and nonprofessional employees are not included in the same group unless the professionals vote in favor of such grouping.)

Supervisory and nonsupervisory employees are not combined in a single unit, although differences of opinion may develop as to whether certain persons have sufficient supervisory responsibilities to justify their exclusion—for example, department chairmen elected by the faculty and who serve on a rotating basis. Under the National Labor Relations Act, supervisors are excluded from provisions of the law and therefore may not be in any unit certified by the National Labor Relations Board at a private institution. However, many state laws permit foremen or supervisors to have separate units. Some institutions have given informal recognition to supervisory units, although they are not legally required to do so.

College and university administrators should not underestimate the importance of determinations regarding bargaining units. The size and composition of such units will influence the outcome of representation elections, the nature of proposals requested by the union at the bargaining table, the efficiency of operations, and the added demands on time and energy. It is often easier for unions to recruit a majority in a small unit than in a large one. When there are several units of employees represented by different unions at an institution, strong competition among the unions seeking to negotiate the most favorable contract often results in a multiplicity of proposals and problems not otherwise expected. Some institutions have many units, although the majority of institutions with collective bargaining agreements have no more than two or three units, and often only one.

Institutional Policy Decisions

Good management requires that institutions adopt, change, and implement personnel policies on a continuous basis and solicit ideas from and communicate with staff and faculty. Once union membership cards are circulated or union meetings are organized, the administration often is restricted in its actions, depending on statutory provisions.

From the organizing step to administration of the agreement, options are available to the administration in each phase of the development of labor relations. Decisions on these options should achieve specific purposes, based on an awareness of the probable consequences of alternative propositions. Among the more fundamental decisions are these:

1. What is the institution's attitude toward collective bargaining with its employees? Favorable? Neutral? Opposed?

2. If the institution does not consider unionization desirable, at what stage will steps be taken to minimize the prospects?

3. Is the attitude toward union activities the same for faculty members as for custodial and maintenance personnel?

4. Does it matter whether the various employee groups choose to be represented by several different unions in separate bargaining units rather than in one overall unit?

5. Are there matters that the administration believes should be exclusively management's right to decide? Or is it willing to negotiate on any issue?

The trustees and senior administrators of some institutions have chosen to maintain a neutral position and have publicly acknowledged that the decision for or against unionization was a choice to be made solely by the affected employees. In other instances institutions have seemed to favor selection of one union over another, which may be illegal or improper. In other cases, aggressive efforts have been successful in discouraging unionization. Institutional policies may vary with the type of employees being organized, such as faculty, security personnel, maintenance workers, and custodians, but the policies should be weighed carefully since they have implications for the future.

Once the decision is made, implementation must be consistent with relevant laws, if any, concerning the employer's conduct and that of the union during the period of recruitment of members. First-line supervisors may be questioned by their employees about the institution's position on collective bargaining, the union's campaign commitments, the peer pressures being exerted, the laws governing the representation election, and the benefits and disadvantages of union membership. To avoid misunderstanding and possible charges of unfair labor practices, such questions should be anticipated and written replies developed for use by all supervisory personnel. In some cases it may be advisable to refer questions to a designated person who is knowledgeable in labor law.

Determination of Employee Interest in Collective Bargaining

When there is a question of employee desire for union representation, the National Labor Relations Board, or its counterpart established by state statute, normally conducts a secret ballot election. Prior to the election, voter eligibility must be determined. For example, should part-time employees be included? Other decisions concern the date and hours the polls will be open, number and location of voting places, designation of institution and union observers, and other procedural matters.

Federal representation elections normally are not held in response to a union petition for certification as the exclusive representative unless the union first has evidence of support by at least thirty percent of the employees involved. Proof of support for a union is furnished to the administrative agency, not to the institution, and may be in the form of membership cards, dues deduction authorizations (check-off form), or signed petitions designating the organization as the employees' bargaining representative.

The employer, however, may and sometimes does voluntarily recognize the union as the bargaining agent without an election, but except under unusual circumstances, it is wiser to require the potential membership to vote. Also, the administrative agency may order an employer to recognize a union based only on evidence of majority interest if the agency finds that the employer's unfair labor practices have made a free-choice expression by employees in an election impossible. The advantage of having an administrative agency conduct an election is particularly important if problems arise as a result of the election, such as unfair presentation of issues, possibility of tampering with ballots, or intimidation of voters.

Employee Communication

Institutions that have an established pattern of communication with employees and their families, regardless of union activity, have a distinct advantage over those that do not. Institutions should not wait to communicate with employees until an organizing drive begins or when negotiations break down. Further, the historical pattern of employee communications is important to prove the legitimacy of the institution's motives and to avoid being charged with unfair labor practices.

NEGOTIATING THE CONTRACT

Pre-Negotiations

In preparing for negotiations, the administration should establish a policy committee, decide who will serve on its negotiating team, who will be the spokesman, and what authority the policy committee will have. Labor counsel should be retained. Each side has full responsibility for determining who will represent its interest in negotiations. There are no restrictions on the composition of the committee or qualifications of its members, and selection of union or management representatives is not a bargainable issue. Someone on the bargaining team must be assigned the responsibility for taking notes, and each side must be responsible for its own note-taking.

The negotiating teams need not be numerically equal, although generally there are three to five persons on each side of the table. Larger committees may exist when the union or institution is inexperienced in collective bargaining, but larger teams are generally less productive in negotiating sessions. Resource staff should be used during negotiations as needs arise.

The spokesman for the institution usually coordinates the planning and preparation for the bargaining sessions, development of management's proposals and counterproposals (together with supporting arguments), and determination of the strategy of the bargaining process. He also is the communicating link with senior administrators and trustees.

Essential to effective collective bargaining is the accumulation of extensive economic and competitive personnel practices data. The data should include current and proposed wage and salary rates, costs of each type of employee benefit, and any proposed changes. Evaluation of contract proposals should include a test of their effect on management's rights. It is axiomatic that management should seek to maintain maximum flexibility, since almost every issue negotiated in collective bargaining is designed directly or indirectly to limit such flexibility. The institution's policy committee should determine in advance the negotiator's latitude on issues, which must be broad enough to negotiate the best contract possible.

Good Faith Bargaining

The National Labor Relations Act requires "the performance of the mutual obligation of the employer and the representative of the employees to meet at reasonable times and to confer in good faith with respect to wages, hours, and other terms and conditions of employment." It also provides for "the execution of a written contract incorporating any agreement reached if requested by either party, but such obligation [to meet and confer in good faith] does not compel either party to agree to a proposal or require the making of a concession." Historically, the latter provision has been subordinated to the former.

The National Labor Relations Board has found employers unlawfully refusing to bargain in good faith when they have practiced dilatory tactics; refused to meet with "outsiders" serving on the union committee; effected changes in wages, employee benefits, or working conditions without prior discussion with the union or without the parties having reached an impasse in negotiations; or bargained with individuals in disregard of the union representatives. The Board and most state agencies require the employer to furnish to the unions upon request relevant financial, wage, or personnel data considered necessary for effective bargaining and the processing of grievances. However, an employer has considerable latitude in gathering its information, which does not have to be in the exact form requested by the union.

A union bargaining or striking to gain illegal demands, such as a closed shop agreement against an institution covered by the National Labor Relations Act, is not bargaining in good faith. Other examples of union improprieties are inequitable representation of nonunion members employed in the bargaining unit for which the union is the exclusive representative, requiring the employer to favor union members over nonunion members (as in promotions), and coercion of the employer in selecting its bargaining or grievance representatives.

The Unique Characteristics of Faculty Collective Bargaining

A unique characteristic of faculty collective bargaining in higher education results from the concept of academic governance and the nature of policy decisions in which faculty senates, councils, or departmental or divisional committees have participated. Many such subjects would be outside the scope of industrial collective bargaining. The dichotomous representation of faculty interests by both unions and senates may thus need to be determined by the National Labor Relations Board or state agencies.

Although the overlapping is mutually acceptable, the National Labor Relations Board and the courts ultimately may delineate the mandatory issues subject to faculty collective bargaining at private institutions. Nevertheless, administrators and many faculties are confronted with other difficult decisions concerning the residual roles of senates, councils, and committees. The "separation of powers" dilemma is confused further by the accepted labor relations theory that although certain matters are exclusively management's to decide, the effects of such decisions on the terms or other conditions of employment are bargainable issues.

For the service and support staff, the more conventional categorization of mandatory, permissible, and illegal bargainable issues should pose few problems, except to the extent that the broader faculty bargaining concepts may become applicable to that group also.

Impasse Procedures: Mediation, Fact-Finding, and Arbitration

Labor-management disputes, after questions of representation have been resolved, are of two basic types:

1. Disputes over "rights" granted by an agreement usually concern the interpretation or application of provisions of a contract, subject to redress under the grievance procedure. (These disputes are discussed in the section "Grievance and Arbitration Procedures.")

2. "Interests" disputes involve matters being negotiated or renegotiated, and are an integral part of the collective bargaining process.

A negotiations impasse occurs after many issues have been agreed upon or dropped as "demands" and the parties have reached a point past which further progress seems unlikely.

Mediation. At this point, the union and the institution may seek a mediator to join the parties and help effect the basis for an agreement. Under the National Labor Relations Act, the parties are required to advise the Federal Mediation and Conciliation Service (FMCS) and any state or local dispute settlement agency that a dispute exists if no agreement has been reached within thirty days after giving notice of the end of a contract. The FMCS staff then usually communicates with the union and institution representatives but does not become involved unless it seems evident a strike may develop or the parties jointly invite participation. In the public sector federal law does not apply, although some states have a comparable mediation service. Even though the Act is not applicable to public institutions, the FMCS will try to assist if both the labor organization and the institution request its services.

As the word "mediation" suggests, the mediator seeks a voluntary compromise or reconciliation of the differences. He has no authority to direct a settlement, only to persuade and cajole. His broad experience often can be helpful in suggesting alternative propositions, one or more of which may be mutually acceptable. Also, the mediator sometimes can assume blame when face-saving is a barrier to a settlement.

As in other phases of labor relations and collective bargaining, there are effective as well as harmful methods of utilizing the mediation process. The union's international representative, who is frequently at the bargaining table assisting the local union committee, may be highly experienced in utilizing a mediator. He may know how to proceed, especially if the institution spokesman is also knowledgeable and understands the subtleties of the action.

Fact-Finding. In the public sector, where strikes

often are prohibited by law or court decisions, there is a trend toward a statutory requirement that the parties enter into a fact-finding hearing—an infrequent procedure in the private sector except in certain emergency labor disputes covered by federal law.

A fact-finder or a panel of fact-finders usually is expected to recommend the basis of a fair settlement after hearing and weighing the evidence. Although fact-finding may be productive, the process is time-consuming and demanding, as objective data and information must be gathered and prepared for introduction through witnesses, and arguments and rebuttal testimony must be considered. Extreme care must be exercised in the selection of a fact-finder.

Recommendations of fact-finders serve as a form of mediation in that usually there is no binding advance commitment by either party to adopt the recommendations. Thus, the process lacks finality, and may create further tensions if one party accepts and the other rejects all or part of the proposed settlement. However, rejection of recommendations normally requires a position statement.

Arbitration of "Interest" Issues. Essentially the same quasi-judicial process is involved in *advisory* arbitration of "interest" disputes. The decision is not binding, but may be found acceptable for political, psychological, or economic reasons. *Binding* arbitration differs from fact-finding primarily in that a settlement is imposed on the parties, which they accept as final and binding. This process, in the absence of enabling legislation, often raises questions of the legality of such delegation of responsibilities when used by public authorities.

In the public sector, if fact-finding or arbitration is expected, negotiations should be adapted to the union's probable course of action. Some negotiators seldom reach an agreement before having exhausted all available mediation, fact-finding, or arbitration forums. Other negotiators may hope to gain more from impasse procedures than they can achieve through collective bargaining; or the leadership of the labor organization may think the recommendations of fact-finders or the decision of the arbitrator will aid them if there is dissension within the union, or if union officers face strong opposition in a forthcoming election.

Strikes, Secondary Boycotts, and Jurisdictional Disputes

Good management requires that all institutions expand their emergency action plans (which operate during such disruptions as severe weather, power failures, and riots) to anticipate labor disputes that could result in strikes, slowdowns, mass call-ins for sickness, or picketing by unions involved in secondary boycotts or jurisdictional controversies. Private institutions may obtain relief through the regional office of the National Labor Relations Board against secondary boycotts, jurisdictional strikes, and certain forms of picketing.

Such planning should include expected reduction in staff, difficulties in obtaining supplies and services, pickets seeking to keep nonstrikers from entering and leaving the institution, possible violence or threats of violence, and attention from the news media. Public institutions also should expect involvement, directly or indirectly, by the legislators, governor, and other government officials.

During strikes at public institutions, there are legal actions to be considered. In the case of secondary boycotts or jurisdictional disputes, legal recourse often is indicated. Some of the more conventional solutions are compulsory arbitration, prescribed fact-finding procedures, and injunctions. Injunctive procedures may be the remedy for wildcat strikes in violation of no-strike agreements signed by private institutions.

Terms of Agreements

The length of time the signed agreement will be in effect without further bargaining is an important consideration for the institution, union, and employees. In the early years of collective bargaining in industry, contracts often were written for one year, after which issues were subject to renegotiation. Progressively the terms lengthened to two years, then three years or even longer. In a majority of multiyear agreements, all provisions remain constant for the full term, except perhaps wages. Agreements usually make provision for additional wage or salary adjustments of negotiated amounts to become effective at the beginning of the second and third years, or there may be a provision permitting renegotiation of wages only (under a wage-reopener clause) on the anniversary date each year. However, there are techniques for administering the contract during multiyear agreements, such as letters of understanding, in which both sides agree to certain terms. During periods of wage and price controls, unions frequently seek shorter agreements so that they may negotiate more generous contracts if or when controls are lifted.

There are advantages to multiyear agreements. Under National Labor Relations Board rules, exclusive rights of representation by an incumbent union cannot be challenged by another union during the first three years of an agreement. This restriction minimizes prospects of unrest and disruption, which are sometimes by-products of jurisdictional campaigns by rival unions, and provides some stability and continuity to the labor-management relationship. (If it is an unsatisfactory relationship, it also prolongs the dissatisfaction, as there can be no decertification election during the same period.) The institution generally is free from further demands for two or three years even though wages may be increased as indicated above. If the agreement provides for a predetermined wage adjustment in the second and third years, there should be no further negotiations for the entire period. There are substantial advantages to the administration in not being confronted with annual, time-consuming arguments and threats of strikes.

There are exceptions to the argument favoring long-term contracts. For example, when negotiating a contract for the first time, mistakes in judgment and language (omissions, commissions, and ambiguities) may occur, and some provisions of the contract may prove unsatisfactory. Such errors are extremely difficult to correct or negotiate out of the agreement. Few mistakes, except those in building design, have a greater life expectancy, and because of this some institutions elect to sign only a one-year agreement in the beginning.

A second exception exists in the case of public institutions that do not have taxing authority but that are dependent on year-to-year legislative appropriations. Such institutions may not enjoy the same latitude on long-term agreements as do private institutions. However, some public institutions have negotiated multiyear agreements.

Bargaining with Multiple Entities

Occasionally either or both parties may find it desirable to combine with others. Association-type bargaining exists when there are two or more institutions; council-type bargaining exists when there are two or more unions and a single employer; there also can be multicampus bargaining in a university system. There are many complexities, implications, advantages, and risks involved in these combinations, but all find some acceptance. There is less competition among unions when they are jointly participating in negotiations, but there is difficulty in reaching mutually satisfactory agreements for several institutions or even several campuses of one system. One modified format that long has had currency in industry is the "master agreement" covering uniformly the major topics for all groups, supplemented by appropriate "local agreements" that speak to needs of a particular campus or group of employees.

ADMINISTERING THE CONTRACT

After the agreement is typed (usually by the institution) and then reviewed by both parties, it is customary for it to be printed and a copy furnished to employees and supervisors at all levels. The reproduction cost of employees' copies may be borne by the union, the institution, or both; this is a negotiable issue. It is important that the management staff be familiar with provisions of the agreement. Orientation sessions to discuss new or changed policies may be indicated. A single administrative officer should serve as contract administrator or coordinator. The terms of the signed agreement, which are enforceable either through the grievance-arbitration process or through the courts, should not be taken casually. The union and the employer may, of course, negotiate written deviations from the contract or enter into letters of understanding to clarify specific issues.

Placement of Collective
Bargaining Responsibility

Collective bargaining may be the responsibility of various offices. The extent of centralization or fragmentation of the function will vary, depending on such factors as experience and competence of the staff, awareness and appreciation of the long-term consequences of decisions reached, the size of the institution, its history of collective bargaining, and applicable federal and state laws.

Under labor relations statutes, the spokesman for either party in collective bargaining must have authority to negotiate. Employers may be in violation of laws and guilty of unfair labor practices if their representatives do not have authority to negotiate, but only to issue policy statements from the employer. This does not mean the representative should have plenary authority, but the authority granted to the negotiator is a factor in deciding whether the employer is acting in good faith.

Disregarding legal obligations, successful negotiations probably require a senior administrator to serve as spokesman for the institution. Employees wish to have their needs considered by senior management and they desire evidence of concern from this level. The institution's spokesman should have stature and be able to explain effectively and convincingly the institution's problems. In effect, he serves as spokesman for the president. He must be well-informed and willing to discuss a wide range of subjects in considerable detail with employees and their representatives during negotiations, grievance meetings, and casual conversations.

There is no single, best, or perfect organization for the collective bargaining function in a college or university, since personnel administration encompasses diverse employee groups, such as faculty, administration, and staff. The personnel administration function frequently is divided between two administrators, one of whom is responsible for faculty and one for administration and staff. However, the institution should appoint one person to serve as spokesman for the purposes of collective bargaining, and that person should:

1. Establish, in collaboration with others, the philosophy and posture of the institution's relationships with labor or similar professional organizations representing, or seeking to represent, any group of employees for the purposes of collective bargaining.

2. Negotiate with local and international officers of unions or other organizations concerning such matters as wages, hours, work conditions, employee benefits, grievances, and draft contract language.

3. Provide advice to those responsible for resolution of grievances in the early steps of the grievance procedure, conduct grievance appeal hearings and render decisions, and plan and present the institution's case in arbitration proceedings or assist counsel in doing so.

4. Respond to union requests for exclusive recognition as bargaining representative and represent or assist in representing the institution at National Labor Relations Board or state agency hearings and pre-election conferences.

5. Respond or assist counsel in unfair labor practice charge proceedings.

6. Analyze and make recommendations concerning proposed labor relations legislation that may directly or indirectly affect the institution and keep abreast of significant trends in federal and state legislation, as well as court and arbitration decisions affecting employee relations. (The National Labor Relations Board issues a weekly bulletin on current decisions.)

7. Be sensitive to personnel policies and supervisory and managerial practices that may contribute to employee unrest and recommend appropriate changes in policies and practices.

8. Coordinate actions involving faculty and staff union matters, obtain necessary legal and other consultation, examine alternatives, and recommend proper courses of action.

In smaller institutions, the budget and workload may not justify the full-time services of a specialist in collective bargaining. Services required for representation elections, unfair labor practice charges, and arbitration proceedings may arise only infrequently, if at all. Accordingly, these specialized services can best be provided by labor relations consultants and lawyers specializing in labor law. Any comprehensive labor agreement contains a mechanism for resolving differences in understanding or failure to comply with terms of the agreement. This mechanism is described in the agreement.

Grievance and Arbitration Procedures

The conventional grievance procedure provides for internal review of alleged violations by various levels of administration and often includes progressively higher levels in the labor organization, beginning with the steward at the department level and ending with the international union representative. Grievances should be settled at the lowest possible level, and most are settled in the pre-arbitration steps.

Binding arbitration is often the final step in the grievance procedure, the result of a decision following a quasi-judicial hearing before a neutral person or panel having no attachment to either the institution or labor organization. The grievances processed in arbitration should involve only "rights" derived from the agreement, not "issues" to amend or modify the terms of the agreement. Issues are subject to negotiation and the various impasse procedures previously discussed.

The arbitrator usually is chosen from a panel of persons experienced in labor-management relations previously approved (by unions, managements, and other arbitrators) for referral by the American Arbitration Association, the Federal Mediation and Conciliation Service, or the arbitration panels of state dispute settlement agencies.

In arbitration hearings, the parties are given an opportunity to present testimony, evidence, and arguments, as well as to cross-examine opposition witnesses. Ordinarily the normal rules of evidence do not prevail at such a hearing, which tends toward informality rather than a rigid, judicial proceeding. The arbitrator rules on who should proceed first and who has the burden of proof. In complaints alleging discrimination because of race, sex, religion, age, or union membership before administrative agencies, the burden of proof theoretically is on the complainant.

A record may be made of the proceedings by a court reporter if either or both parties desire a transcript, which also is provided to the arbitrator. If both parties wish a copy of the record, they usually share the cost; otherwise, the requesting party pays the expense. The arbitrator's fee may be and usually is divided between the union and the institution. Some contracts specify that the fee be paid by the party that loses the award.

The most frequently arbitrated grievances are disciplinary actions (reprimands, warnings, suspensions, or discharges), which the employee and union believe were not for "just cause." Other common issues relate to seniority provisions for promotions and transfers, overtime work assignments, reductions in force, and recalls. Since every portion of the agreement is subject to controversial interpretation or application, grievances in arbitration even may extend to holiday, sick leave, or vacation benefits, assignments of work, wage rates and job classifications, safety, rules and regulations, and past practices.

Faculty collective bargaining agreements may involve additional disputes related to faculty functions, such as approved sick leave or granting of personal leaves, credits for graduate courses applied to horizontal increments of the index for salary schedule, extracurricular assignments and compensation (coaching, drama, concerts, newspaper, and yearbook), summer teaching assignments, pay for cancelled classes, involuntary transfers among campuses, elimination of positions, and charges of discrimination.

Not every complaint or grievance unresolved at a lower level is arbitrable, depending on the specific language of the negotiated agreement. The issue of arbitrability itself is decided by the arbitrator. The timeliness of filing, appealing, or responding to grievances at various levels also is frequently an arbitrated issue.

Discharge and Disciplinary Actions

Discharge and disciplinary actions are an important supervisory responsibility because of the effect on employee and supervisor morale, on productivity, and on the potential complications that may follow a poorly handled case. Managerial decisions concerning discharge and discipline are subject not only to the grievance and arbitration terms of the agreement, but to investigation by federal and state equal employment opportunity enforcement offices when racial, sex, religious, or age discrimination is alleged. In such cases an employee has recourse to both the grievance procedure and the federal and state agencies involved in discrimination. Managerial decisions also may be subject to charges of unfair labor practices before labor relations agencies if discrimination for union activity is contended.

There are many employee faults that motivate

management's decision to warn, reprimand, suspend, or discharge a person, including (for service and support staff) absenteeism, incompetence or negligence, insubordination, theft or dishonesty, falsification of employment records, intoxication, sleeping on the job, and violation of posted rules. The action taken against the employee usually is challenged by a union appearing before an arbitrator on such grounds as: the employee was not guilty as charged; the penalty was too severe for the infraction; the employee was not given adequate instruction or counseling; the foreman's attitude or conduct was a contributing or mitigating factor; the rule or order was not applied to all employees equally or the penalties were not meted out in a predictable and uniform manner; or the employee had long service with no previous infractions on his record. Most of these amount to rules of "procedural due process."

Faculty grievances processed through the various steps, including arbitration, have been different from those initiated by service and support staff, especially when the agreement excludes from third-party adjudication any action based on academic judgment, when tenure decisions by peers are excluded, and in those situations in which much of the academic governance is by an institutional entity such as a faculty senate rather than through the more adversary relationship established by many union agreements. However, issues of due process frequently arise from refusal to reappoint, termination of appointment, and denial of promotion; these grievances therefore can seriously affect promotions and tenure. Faculty issues in arbitration may include questions of timeliness and adequacy of academic and professional progress evaluations and counseling or alleged arbitrary or discriminatory use of the procedures. There is often frequent overlapping of academic judgment with contentions of procedural improprieties, which causes uncertainty about the protection of caveats limiting the arbitrator's authority or jurisdiction in dealing with refusals to reappoint or denials of promotion. These hazards are evident in various arbitrators' decisions handed down after the academic year has ended—the elapsed time from the original filing of the grievance to the date the award is rendered may be nine months or longer.

The Supervisor's Role in Labor Relations

The first-line supervisor (department head, supervisor, foreman, director, chairman) is the key to a successful labor-management relationship. His knowledge of the contractual obligations and responsibilities of all parties, his personal attitudes toward unions and shop stewards or other union officers, and the way he perceives his managerial position contribute substantially to the development of the labor-management "personality" of the institution. Supervisory errors may lead to excessive grievances, costly arbitration, and possible strikes. Supervisors require constructive training in both the letter and intent of the terms of union agreements. They also need an understanding of the extent and limitation of the legal rights of union stewards, union business managers, and international union representatives, as well as instruction in how to receive and respond to grievances.

Many persons in managerial positions find it difficult to adjust when they are overruled on a discipline or discharge action or in their application or interpretation of personnel policies. The first year or two after the introduction of collective bargaining can be especially traumatic. The institution's senior administration should devote special and immediate attention to helping supervisors recognize these changes and adjust to them.

Employee Relations Consultants and Labor Attorneys

Institutions, including those with knowledgeable and capable staff members, have turned to employee relations consultants and labor attorneys for several reasons:

1. To fill a gap in the technical competence of the staff.
2. To compensate for lack of experience in the face of new developments.
3. To obtain independent, objective judgment and recommendations.
4. To stimulate and broaden organizational viewpoints and thinking.
5. To draw on the consultant's resource information about trends and prospects.
6. To avoid enlarging the permanent staff.
7. To obtain the part-time services of expensive talent that the institution could not afford on a full-time basis.

Qualified consultants usually have an extensive library of labor relations reference materials to which reports of the latest developments in labor relations are added continually. They probably have a strong background in management and union philosophies, strategies, and tactics, and are familiar with most arguments and counterarguments associated with support of issues and grievances.

Of special value to many institutions is the ability of an employee relations consultant to serve as the devil's advocate before serious problems develop. This is most valuable to institutions seeking to minimize the probabilities of successful union recruitment by occasional "audits" of policies or practices the professional union organizer might be able to exploit. The consultant's services are most usable on a continuing retainer arrangement whereby he is available by telephone for idea testing, guidance, and review of proposed revisions of policy statements and employee handbooks. Employed on this basis, he is likely to be available when needed, to have a continuing interest in the institution, and to be equipped to anticipate and prevent problems.

During actual negotiations, the consultant or attorney may serve either as the chief negotiator or as a resource person, depending on the expertise available at the institution. Whenever possible, it is better to have as the spokesman a staff member who has intimate knowledge of the institution's operations and who will administer the agreement. The consultant in this case can serve as an adviser. In those instances when an attorney or consultant acts as spokesman for an institution first experiencing collective bargaining, the role gradually should be transferred to an administrator being developed for that purpose. One or more of the labor relations subscription services will be invaluable for the future administrator.

Before considering the services of an employee relations consultant or labor attorney, the institution must decide what it expects to gain from the expert and who should benefit from the services performed, beginning with the president and vice presidents. Only then is the selection of the consultant apt to be rewarding and satisfactory to everyone concerned.

In addition to the consultant's competence in the appropriate fields, inquiry should be made of other institutions concerning the quality of the relationship between consultant and client, his ability to assist with the problems, and his availability in helping to implement recommendations, if necessary. Moreover, one should know whether the consulting work will be assigned to a person in the firm other than the one with whom the subject was discussed.

SUMMARY

To anticipate future developments in the field of labor relations and collective bargaining, the president first must identify his institution's position in relation to current trends. Only then can he determine whether the institution is moving toward the best choice of the probable future options and whether the administration is preparing to cope with developments over which it may have little or no control.

Knowledge about the future of labor relations is essential for the president to cushion the impact of new developments and minimize the probability of occurrence of those that are unexpected. The competent employee relations officer or consultant should be working on solutions to potential problems before others have recognized they are developing.

There are advantages and disadvantages to unionization and collective bargaining, and some presidents ask the administration to maintain a completely neutral position on the subject, especially during organizing drives. Others recognize the probability that the extent of union organization among specific groups is likely to remain constant because of the corrections and improvements institutions make that diminish the severity of discontent. Still others expect an annual list: union demands with resulting changes in the agreements, most of which have an associated cost; mishandled grievances and occasional arbitration awards; more restrictions and less flexibility on management's right to manage; seniority in lieu of merit advancement; and rigidity in administration of contract terms. Positive considerations resulting from unionization are: more internal consistency in the interpretation and application of personnel policies; more equitable treatment of employees with less favoritism shown by certain supervisors; and earlier consideration of the employee relations impact on institutional planning.

Part 3

Business
Management

Purchasing

AN EFFECTIVE organization for purchasing promotes the basic objectives of an educational institution by providing faculty and staff members necessary supplies, equipment, and services. The purchasing function can be performed more effectively and economically by trained specialists than by those for whom purchasing is not a primary responsibility.

The basic objective of a purchasing department is to identify, select, and acquire needed materials and services as economically as possible within accepted standards of quality and service. This should be done in a timely and organized manner that provides for essential accountability of university expenditures. Although the purchasing process should be a joint effort among the using department, purchasing department, and vendor, the purchasing department must have the final authority to conduct and conclude negotiations concerning prices and conditions of sale. Institutional commitments should be made by the purchasing department in accordance with requisition/ordering procedure.

ORGANIZATION

The responsibility for purchasing should be centralized under the chief business officer. The complexity of an institution and the amount spent influence the sophistication of purchasing practices and techniques, but size should not prevent centralization of purchasing authority and responsibility in a senior administrator. Budget and staff support should be commensurate with the size of the annual expenditure and special purchasing needs at the time.

Some of the significant advantages of centralized purchasing are:

1. Definite economies resulting from the pooling and integrated, overall planning of the common requirements of various departments.
2. Development of standard specifications for the common commodities purchased, resulting in more uniform quality and less variety of materials, supplies, and equipment.
3. Better budgetary and financial control of departmental expenditures.
4. Development of qualified personnel through specialization in purchasing.
5. Reduction in administrative costs through elimination of multiple purchasing staffs, records, and procedures.
6. Reduction in inventories because of closer supervision regarding the quantity of materials on each purchase order and greater utilization of the available supply of materials through transfers and substitutions.
7. Provision for adequate testing and inspection of materials purchased.
8. Assurance of cash discounts by prompt handling of vendor's invoices and assurance of taking exemption for state sales tax and other taxes not applicable to colleges and universities.
9. Prompt delivery and better service by suppliers, resulting from more careful selection and better follow-up systems.
10. Benefits of competition, resulting in improved study of markets and other research.
11. Better public relations, resulting from consistent and equitable treatment obtained by dealing with one department.

Specialized purchasing operations may, under some circumstances, be delegated or assigned on an interim basis to persons outside the central purchasing organization. However, this delegated responsibility should be performed within the policy and procedure of the institution. For example, procurement of food commodities and supplies often is delegated to the director of food services; computer equipment rental or purchase, to the director of the computing center; library books, to members of the library staff; merchandise for resale in the student store, to the store manager; new construction, to an officer responsible for planning or supervision; hospital or health-related needs, to the hospital director or health sciences administrator. Specialized purchasing authority and responsibility should be delegated in writing by the chief business officer and should include any prescribed limits on types of purchases and dollar amounts.

ETHICAL CONSIDERATIONS

Effective purchasing in an educational institution is a cooperative undertaking between buyer and supplier and between the purchasing staff and other persons within the institution. The purchasing department must maintain satisfactory relationships with external suppliers and internal consumers. Satisfactory relations between the staff of the purchasing department and other staff members of the institution prevail if the purchasing functions are performed with understanding, dispatch, fairness, and competence. The purchasing staff must be sensitive to the problems and needs of departments and individuals, anticipate where controversies might arise and try to avoid them, and if not possible, resolve them promptly to maintain good public relations internally and externally.

An institution's reputation for fair and consistent treatment of suppliers can best be accomplished if purchasing is done solely on the merits of the transaction. Suppliers who have made gifts to an institution, whose officers or representatives are donors or alumni, or who are located in the same community occasionally request special consideration. Extreme care should be exercised in giving special consideration to these suppliers; if possible, the request should be denied. Institutions may prevent conflicts of interest through a policy of full disclosure. Departure from sound award procedures may eliminate competition or base it on political pressure or personal contacts, thus jeopardizing the image of the institution. If in doubt, legal advice should be obtained to avoid conflict.

The purchasing power of an institution should not be used for personal acquisitions for faculty and other staff members. Some institutions maintain lists of suppliers offering special considerations to institutional staff members, who then may deal directly with suppliers. Such an arrangement provides a service and relieves the institution of problems resulting from the special handling required for personal purchases. In these cases, the institution should not become a party to any dispute between buyer and seller.

A code of conduct for the staff members of the purchasing department, defining obligations and ethics, should be published; this code should be reviewed with the staff periodically. The following principles have been adopted by the National Association of Educational Buyers and can form the basis for such a code:

1. Give first consideration to institutional objectives and policies.
2. Obtain the maximum value for each dollar expended.
3. Cooperate with trade and industrial associations and government and private agencies engaged in promotion and development of sound business methods.
4. Demand honesty in sales representation whether offered through verbal or written statements, advertisements, or product samples.
5. Decline personal gifts or gratuities that might influence the purchase of materials.
6. Grant all competitive bidders equal consideration; regard each transaction on its own merit; foster and promote fair, ethical, and legal trade practice.
7. Use only by consent the original ideas and designs devised by one vendor for competitive purchasing purposes.
8. Be willing to submit any major controversy to arbitration.
9. Accord a prompt and courteous reception insofar as conditions permit to everyone calling on legitimate business.

STATEMENT OF POLICIES AND PROCEDURES

A statement of policies and procedures for the purchasing function is essential. The statement should define the responsibilities of the purchasing department and assignment of authority within the department; establish criteria for selection of vendors, for bidding procedures, and for determination of quality, standardization, and other operating policies; and formulate procedures for departments to use in requesting purchases.

The statement of policies and procedures should provide for regular audits of purchasing operations. These audits reveal such information as whether proper bidding procedures are followed, orders are awarded to the lowest and most responsible bidders, and competitive prices are obtained. Under special conditions, the audit may encompass a review of the ability of bidders to perform.

Some publicly controlled institutions must use purchasing procedures prescribed by statutes or government regulations. Certain states have established central purchasing departments to serve all state agencies, including educational institutions. Such totally centralized public purchasing agencies generally are not structured to meet the unique requirements of colleges and universities, and it is the obligation of administrators in these situations to properly identify the problems and offer remedial action. However, if economies would result from a state or other central department, it may be beneficial to utilize such purchasing agencies.

Many purchasing procedures may be relatively routine, requiring some technical skill. However, in two important areas, the purchasing agent must exhibit considerable judgment, based on knowledge and experience. These areas are development and use of specifications and selection of sources of supply. Judgments must be made that affect the entire purchasing organization and that determine to a large extent the degree of confidence the public has in the integrity of the institution.

FUNCTIONS OF THE PURCHASING DEPARTMENT

The following are to be considered in operating an effective purchasing department:

1. Prepare, with the cooperation of the using departments, delivery schedules and quality and quantity specifications for items and services to be purchased.
2. Provide using departments with current information on new products and services, alternative materials, and costs.
3. Encourage competition among vendors through negotiation, competitive bidding, and contract buying.
4. Insure that purchase orders and contracts contain all necessary conditions, such as guarantees, warranties, governmental regulations, shipping instructions, f.o.b. points, and credit terms and discounts allowed.
5. Develop records as needed to determine requirements of the institution for supplies, services, and equipment.
6. Maintain adequate records and files of requisitions, purchase orders, vendors, catalogues, product information, and prices.
7. Arrange for control and disposal of surplus equipment and supplies, salvage, and scrap.
8. Advise and assist other departments that have been delegated some purchasing functions.
9. Explore and use possible advantages of interuniversity, consortia, or cooperative purchasing programs.

In addition, the purchasing department should develop and encourage use of standard specifications for items performing the same functions in the various divisions of the institution. Standardization facilitates quantity purchasing, interchangeability in use of equipment, and reduction in service and inventory costs.

A continuous program of research and testing is generally a responsibility of the purchasing department. Testing may be performed by vendors, independent laboratories, or the institution, each under the direction of the purchasing department. Research activities include studies of sources of supply, adequacy of specifications, analyses of commodities in relation to specifications, analyses of substitute materials, and forecasts of market trends. The purchasing department should maintain a catalog file as extensive as practicable and files of specialized sources of information such as governmental publications, technical handbooks, and other books and magazines to aid in carrying out the purchasing function. Much helpful information is available from national laboratories, governmental agencies, and minority vendor directories.

Those responsible for purchasing should be knowledgeable of:

1. Government safety requirements such as the Occupational Safety and Health Act, as amended, and other safety requirements as they relate to purchased equipment or supplies.
2. Governmental requirements, where applicable, on developing minority suppliers and placing affirmative action clauses in construction contracts.
3. Imports, customs regulations, and duty considerations generally and specifically as they relate to Public Law 89-651, Education and Scientific and Cultural Materials Importation Act of 1966. Knowledge of the international monetary situation is also important.

ADDITIONAL FUNCTIONS OF THE PURCHASING DEPARTMENT

If the institution operates a central stores system and maintains an equipment inventory, these should be a function of the purchasing department. Other activities of some purchasing departments may include operation of typewriter repair shops, duplicating centers, and photographic departments, control of narcotics licenses and alcohol permits, handling of returnable containers and control and disposition of radiological materials, supervision of vending machines, and travel reservation and ticketing services. If these are part of the purchasing department, specific attention to internal control is mandatory and audits should be more frequent.

Contracts for construction and remodeling often are not a responsibility of the purchasing department, but it may cooperate in advertising, receiving, and analyzing bids, and in the review and award of contracts and their modification. To be effective, the purchasing department should participate at the appropriate time in construction planning in order to assist effectively in the review of preliminary plans. Reasonable access for deliveries to proposed buildings is a design feature that may be overlooked in the architectural planning. Since the purchasing department is responsible for the logistics of supply, it should interject opinions on this design feature. Interior design services for furniture, furnishings, and equipment for new buildings should be provided by contract through the purchasing department or from in-house sources under the direction of the purchasing department. This task requires close cooperation with the architects, future users of the facility, and physical plant officers. The purchasing department should assist in preparing both budget estimates and ordering and delivery schedules for furniture, furnishings, and equipment.

PURCHASING PROCEDURES

The usual purchasing cycle involves determining requirements by the using departments, communicating requirements to the purchasing department, conducting negotiations for purchases, selecting sources of supplies, issuing purchase orders or contracts, and receiving materials. The purchasing department should establish records and files of appropriate information and periodically review the entire cycle.

Communicating Requirements

There are basic forms to accurately communicate the using department's requirements to the purchasing department and to implement the purchasing procedure used in contracting with third parties. These forms are requisition, bid or quotation, and purchase order or contract.

Information about requirements of using departments is communicated to the purchasing department by issuance of a requisition on which the requirements are clearly stated. The format and content of requisition forms vary widely among institutions but, at a minimum, should provide for a description of the item to be purchased, quantity of materials requested, designation of the date required, designation of the account to be charged, and approval by appropriate academic officers and business or budget officers.

It is desirable for the requisition form to provide space for using departments to indicate preference for particular vendors, with reasons for such preference. Such suggestions, while not binding on the purchasing department, often are helpful in finding sources of supply and in evaluating special services offered by a particular vendor. The purchasing department should be aware of communications between the using department and any vendors.

The requisition should be designed by the purchasing department and should be printed and distributed to using departments. In some instances special requisitions are used for requests for food, printing, stores, or other needs. The requisition, by proper signature, authorizes the purchasing department to expend funds against a named account for equipment, goods, and services.

The bid or quotation form provides a uniform request to one or more suppliers to make an offer to the institution according to specified terms and conditions.

The purchase order is the formal contract to purchase goods or services offered. The purchase order should be designed carefully with the advice of legal counsel, keeping in mind accounting and computer needs where appropriate.

Determining Quality and Quantity

Determination of suitable quality for the intended purpose must be a cooperative decision of the using department and the purchasing department. The relative technical competence of each group concerning the product to be purchased should determine the degree of participation in this decision. Determination of the quality of commodities used throughout the institution, such as paper products, office supplies, and furniture and office equipment, is primarily the responsibility of the purchasing department, but determining the quality of specialized scientific equipment and supplies normally rests with the using departments.

Descriptions of quality should conform to recognized standards. Nonstandard specifications substantially increase costs, often without a corresponding increase in quality. Although nonstandard specifications and special restrictions may insure high quality, they should not be structured to eliminate qualified bidders.

Whenever possible, it is desirable to define quality in objective terms. Several methods may be used, such as competitively equivalent brand names, model or catalog numbers, standard market grades, performance or functional requirements, conformance to sample, and detailed written specifications and blueprints covering material and design. Specifications should contain reference to such governmental requirements as safety and affirmative action. Since purchasing officers of public institutions generally are not free to award

purchase orders on the basis of best value and lowest cost, the need for detailed specifications is particularly important.

If detailed specifications or performance requirements are used, provision must be made for inspection and testing to verify compliance with the specifications. If performance can be accurately and adequately defined and measured, performance specifications may be preferable to detailed engineering specifications. Under the latter, if the product meets detailed design specifications, the vendor has fulfilled his obligation, whether or not the performance is adequate. If performance specifications are used, the vendor is required to supply a product that will serve the specified purpose regardless of design.

The quantity of products to be ordered is a cooperative effort of the purchasing and using departments. Historical usage may be one criterion for quantities ordered. Rarely should the quantity ordered exceed the estimated usage required for an academic year, but at any rate, care should be taken not to encourage needless stockpiling of goods.

Source Selection

The materials selected must be satisfactory to the using departments, but selection of the source of supply is the responsibility of the purchasing department. Whenever possible, more than one supplier should be considered. Recruitment of new vendors should be a regular part of the buyer's job, and new suppliers, especially suppliers representing minority groups, should be developed to serve the requirements of the institution.

Purchasing department buyers must have acquired a knowledge of marketing and distribution channels for various types of materials and be capable of selecting the most economical and efficient level for each purchase, giving consideration to educational buying cooperatives. In addition to understanding production cycles and knowing the most propitious time to purchase certain items, buyers should be aware of the importance of anticipating price trends.

Determining Price

The circumstances of each purchase govern the procedures used in determining price and awarding orders. Where competitive bidding may be employed, the buyer has fair assurance that he is receiving the right price.

Price analysis can be used to determine the fair price in the case of items available from a single source or where competition is lacking. The price may be compared with a price formerly paid, with General Services Administration price levels, with published price lists from which an expected discount is available, or with that paid by other institutions using the same quantity and quality. Price analysis also should be used where preparation time is short or for items of small dollar value that are purchased infrequently.

Cost analysis is an analysis made on the vendor's cost to arrive at the proper price. This procedure usually is used when a large dollar contract is negotiated with a single source.

Negotiation may be used in the absence of criteria for competitive bidding to arrive at the correct price. Examples are occasions when the dollar expense involved does not justify the cost of specifications to the extent necessary for fairness to bidders, when the service or product is unique to one vendor, when real price competition is lacking, when equipment is being purchased for compatibility with existing equipment, or when an emergency exists and there is insufficient time to write specifications and take bids. All parts of a contract are negotiable, including price, delivery, elements of the specifications, and length of the contract. Negotiation implies arrival at a mutually acceptable arrangement through bargaining. An adequate documentation/audit trail is essential.

Informal quotations also may be used to obtain price estimates when early delivery is required, when specifications are not complete, or when the value of the purchase is nominal. Telephone inquiries and other informal contacts with sales representatives may provide prices quickly on required items; nevertheless, the request should include as many elements of a formal quotation as are feasible.

Formal quotations call for the preparation of a written bid document, generally known as "Request for Quotation" or "Invitation to Bid." Formal bidding may be either publicly advertised or invited, but in both cases the request for quotations or bids must be prepared with great care. Publicly advertised requests for bids involve more technical consideration of the legal aspects of bidding, including detailed clauses regarding time of opening bids and options for rejection. Requests for bids must stipulate that quotations or bids are to be firm prices unless, as circumstances sometimes dictate, cost bids or escalator clauses in the quotations are desirable.

When an institution is able to select bidders, the purchasing department should invite them to submit quotations only if it is willing to place an order with them. Unless public bidding regulations require disclosure, some institutions may elect not to tell unsuccessful bidders the details of quotations of other bidders.

A value analysis (or value techniques) program requires that the purchasing department be continually alert to economic advantages. Equipment should be selected that will increase productivity without increasing labor effort. Consumable supplies should be selected to provide the greatest utilization possible. Thought should be given not only to what a product is but how it is used, so that less costly substitutions can be recommended to achieve desired results at reduced costs. This constant probing and analysis of present usage can be extended beyond hard goods to business systems and procedures employed to accomplish the institution's objectives. Aggressive pursuit of value analysis should occasionally result in buying the best value even though a higher initial price is paid.

The Purchase Order

A purchase order is a legal document and, when accepted by the vendor, constitutes a contract between buyer and seller. It therefore should contain all pertinent details of the agreement, conditions of sale, and governmental legal requirements.

The format and content of purchase orders vary among institutions as do the number, distribution, and uses of the copies. Combination forms should be used whenever possible to reduce the number of forms used in the purchasing department. The purchase order forms should be prenumbered, identify clearly and completely both the institution and the vendor, describe the product adequately and specify the quantity of items ordered, provide delivery instructions, and show the required delivery date. The order should show prices. It also should include other information, such as terms of payment, discounts, account number to be charged, f.o.b. points, warranties, insurance requirements, and other items designed to protect the institution from defaults by vendors and negligence and accidents by carriers. It should include a statement that the vendor, upon acceptance of the purchase order, confirms that the product furnished meets safety standards of the state. Also included should be a statement that the vendor, by acceptance of the order, confirms that he is complying with the Civil Rights Act of 1964. A sufficient number of copies of purchase orders should be prepared to accommodate the needs of the institution and vendors.

After an order has been placed by the purchasing department and accepted by a vendor, subsequent changes must be mutually acceptable to buyer and seller. All changes must be specified in writing and copies distributed in the same manner as copies of the original purchase order. This principle applies also to cancellations. When the volume of changes warrants, development of a change order form is advantageous.

The responsibility of the purchasing department does not end with placing purchase orders. A follow-up and expediting system is needed to insure that materials are delivered in time to meet requirements of the using departments. Realistic delivery dates should be indicated on departmental requisitions by the using departments, and procedures must be established to insure observance of delivery dates indicated on subsequent purchase orders. Satisfactory supplier service should be documented; records also should be kept of unsatisfactory supplier service, so that those suppliers can be avoided in the future.

Emergencies arise that make orders for immediate delivery or commitment necessary, and procedures should be developed to provide emergency service. Although emergencies sometimes occur through failure of equipment or needs that cannot be anticipated, frequent emergency or confirmation orders may indicate poor planning, coordination, and organization. A formalized procedure should be established and documented for using departments to insure proper handling of commitments made under these circumstances. Also, corrective measures must be taken to reduce occurrences of emergencies.

Other Purchasing Procedures

A blanket (or standing) purchase order is awarded to a selected supplier for consumable goods or services to be released as needed. This technique should be used to facilitate receipt of items not available in the institution's stores system or to reduce inventory requirements. The order should be for a specific period and preferably on a predetermined price schedule. Monthly rather than individual invoices can be stipulated to reduce the volume of paperwork.

Limited dollar (or small) purchase orders reduce the volume of paperwork processed through normal business channels. Procedures, policies, and forms may be designed to enable departments to acquire items of small monetary value without formal purchasing action. In this way a large number of orders representing a small percentage of the expenditures can be processed without individual review by the purchasing staff. As a result, the purchasing department will have more time to spend on transactions for which opportunities for savings are greatest. It is important that the purchasing department select in advance those sources with which small orders are valid. Checks and balances can be built into the system to minimize direct, day-to-day involvement of the purchasing staff.

Requirements (or minimum) contracts usually provide for an institution to purchase all its requirements for specified materials, such as fuel oil, from a given source for a stated period of time. They may be used to obtain advantageous prices by combining the requirements over a period of time from many units within the institution into one large quotation and contract. The contracts provide flexibility in delivery terms, avoid bulk storage by the institution, and expedite filling individual requisitions. A simple release system may be used or a prearranged shipping schedule may be established for easy administration. Monthly billing may be more desirable than individual charges.

Systems contracting usually applies to an entire family of items used repetitively; such items are normally of low unit value. Examples are plumbing, electrical, and hardware supplies. The vendor has responsibility for providing designated materials to the institution at a prearranged price over a predetermined period within an agreed delivery response time. The objectives of systems contracting are to simplify ordering procedures and to reduce costs of carrying inventories.

The check-with-order technique, selectively employed, is one in which a blank check, valid in amounts up to $200 to $500, is sent with each order. Following the delivery of all specified materials, the supplier enters the amount due and deposits the check. Post-audit procedures are used to validate the expenditures.

Cash purchase might be appropriate for low-cost and infrequently used items that require personal selection or that are available only through retail cash sources. Policies and procedures for cash purchases should be established and made known to all staff members. Direct reimbursement for petty cash purchases may be made to staff members by the business office upon presentation of proper receipts. Limits on dollar amounts and other regulating criteria must be clearly stated to insure that this method is used only when it is economical and appropriate and when items are not in stock in stores.

Making In-House

In any "make in-house" or "buy open market" situation, a cost analysis of the "make" process should be conducted, with special attention to labor costs and fringe benefits. Since the decisions to make in-house often are made by the using departments, these departments should be encouraged to communicate with the purchasing department to assist in the decision. The purchasing department may be able to suggest commercial sources for the requirements.

Leasing

Outright purchase or borrowing to buy often will result in a lower total expenditure than leasing. In each lease proposal it is imperative that the charge for the use of funds be calculated and compared against all alternate methods of financing, including third-party leasing. Leasing may be advisable in fields with changing technology when obsolescence is a factor or the period of use is relatively short. Vendor responsibility for maintenance of complex equipment may be obtained more easily by leasing the equipment than by pur-

chase. When leasing is the only viable answer, care should be exercised to provide cancellation options that are least damaging to the institution's financial resources. The institution should identify the source of funds to cover payments of lease charges for its entire period of effectiveness.

Receiving Procedures

A central location may be provided for receiving supplies, or they may be delivered to various locations. Some factors that determine whether central receiving or random receiving is appropriate in a given situation are:

1. Loading dock facilities.
2. Control of traffic.
3. Capability to perform receiving functions at individual buildings.
4. Verification of delivery and control and payment of collect and freight charges.
5. Effectiveness of inspection and claim processing.
6. Identification of true costs in central receiving compared to the fragmentation of costs in random receiving.

Central Stores

Central stores are a desirable resource in effective purchasing. The needs of each institution must be determined by its location and the availability of vendors that can supply its needs, as well as institutional size and ability to combine needs into contracts or large purchases. The layout of the campus and the building facilities predetermine the feasibility and cost of distribution. The stocking of commonly used items can reduce repetitive purchasing, require smaller departmental inventories, effect quantity buying, accomplish standardization, and meet current needs more effectively. A department can use stores to obtain, on a single order and delivery, a variety of items that might normally require many individual orders and deliveries at higher prices. Whether the goods stocked are sold at cost or marked up to recover the cost of operation, periodic checks should be made to test the cost effectiveness of any centralized stores facility.

Against the advantages of central stores, the cost of space, personnel, inventory, delivery, and inventory loss must be considered.

Auxiliary Enterprises, Organized Activities, and Service Departments

SUPPORT or service activities often are classified in three separate but related categories: auxiliary enterprises, organized activities related to educational departments, and service departments. The classification of an activity depends on its relation to the educational process, its relation to the consumer, and the source of its revenue. The operations of the three activities should be shown separately in the operating statements, and each activity should be supported by detailed schedules of revenues and expenditures. Such statements are essential for internal use to ascertain the degree of self-support attained and to provide the basis for exercise of controls. Separate balance sheets may be prepared but need not be published.

AUXILIARY ENTERPRISES

An auxiliary enterprise furnishes a service to students, faculty, or staff, and charges a fee directly related to, but not necessarily equal to, the cost of the service. The public may be served incidentally in some auxiliary enterprises. They are essential elements in support of the educational program, and conceptually should be regarded as self-supporting. Little or none of the revenue generated comes from educational and general sources, but in the case of housing and food services, there may be a limited amount of sales to the institution. Other examples of auxiliary enterprises are college unions, college stores, rental facilities, institutionally operated vending services, recreational areas, faculty clubs, laundries, certain parking facilities, and, frequently, intercollegiate athletics. The need for specific auxiliary enterprises should be reviewed periodically.

The administration of auxiliary enterprises takes one of two basic forms. The customary form of administration is a division managed by an officer who is generally in the business office. He should have sufficient authority to develop procedures and practices to manage the enterprises effectively. Their special needs necessitate adjustment of practices of support departments such as purchasing, accounting, controller, and personnel. An exception to this form of administration, which has been adopted by public institutions in California and New York, consists of an administrative division managed by an officer who reports to a board representing the entire university community (students, faculty, administration, staff, and governing board).

Each auxiliary enterprise must have clearly written, detailed administrative policies. Otherwise, confused operating procedures and overlapping authority may result. If an outside agency conducts the activity, the written policy is replaced by a legal contract or agreement. Such contract services may include the operation of food services, housing, college stores, hospitals, and newspaper and other institutional printing. In such cases, the officer responsible generally serves as contract liaison between the institution and contract service agency. The contract services still are regarded individually as auxiliary enterprises, and collectively as an administrative division within the institution.

Auxiliary enterprises are related directly to the objectives of colleges and universities. They can contribute significantly to the realization of those objectives in direct relation to the quality of service rendered. For example, any totally self-supporting function satisfying the needs of its consumers (customers) contributes substantially to the effectiveness of the institution. Such a function provides needed services, allows the institution to benefit from the services without cost to the institution, and requires little involvement by the academic administration.

In developing policies for the program and management of auxiliary enterprises, advice and cooperation should be sought from representatives of the institutional community to be served. The objectives of the institution with regard to auxiliary enterprises should be articulated by all institutional interests. After the objectives are written, the officer responsible for auxiliary enterprises should be independent to operate within written policies such as civil service rules, purchasing policies, and required financial obligations. The activity should be evaluated for effectiveness by measuring performance against objectives.

Auxiliary enterprises should be expected to pay their share of general administrative expenses as well as direct operating expenses, including debt service and provisions for renewal and replacement. If a subsidy is received, the accounting records and reports should disclose the amount and source. Similarly, if revenues exceed expenditures after provision for reserves and any debt service, the amount of excess and its disposition also should be disclosed.

Housing and Food Services

Student dissatisfaction with traditional dormitories has resulted in significant changes in the residence halls of many institutions. Some residence halls have become living-learning units containing classrooms or other learning facilities. Dining areas or kitchen facilities often are included. There are coeducational residence halls, and some institutions have modern apartment complexes that accommodate faculty, staff, and single and married students in one facility. Still another form of housing is the student cooperative, which is owned or leased and managed by students.

Some institutions have housing boards, with student, faculty, and administration members. Such boards not only influence long-range housing plans and budget developments, but also provide a day-to-day liaison between students and housing administrators, thus dealing with problems as they arise.

Renovation of existing residence halls is more economical than new construction, and often is more pleasing to students, especially when done

according to student suggestions. Where new dwellings must be built, an alternative to the traditional sequence of separate design and construction is the package construction contract in which units are planned and built by one developer according to performance specifications. In some cases, a leaseback arrangement is used, in which a developer builds at his own expense and leases dwellings back to the institution.

The management of residence halls has both business and educational aspects. Close cooperation between business officers and student affairs officers is especially important in development of budgets and of provisions for counseling and other student services. Management of student housing usually comes under the direction of the chief business officer, but assignment of space, development of social programs, and establishment of regulations may be duties of the officer responsible for auxiliary enterprises, a student affairs officer, or another administrative officer.

The type, number, and frequency of operating reports vary with local factors. Some more significant periodic reports prepared for the administrative offices include the statement of revenues and expenditures, reports on occupancy, expenditures for repairs, custodial services, and utilities, and expenses for counseling, student government activities, and other programs.

Institutional food services have undergone changes similar to those in housing; one example of this is that voluntary board plans are available at many institutions. With the advent of apartment-type housing, smaller, family-style dining rooms and student kitchens have replaced some traditional dining halls. Some institutions have converted dining halls into cafeterias, and often the hours of serving meals have been relaxed or changed to allow for continuous service or service hours consistent with student styles. Student committees can perform a valuable service in developing menus and evaluating daily food quality.

A food services department serves the entire college or university community. Because this service is also a business operation, appropriate costs should be charged. Responsibility for a profitable business operation and the extent of services offered rests with the administration. For example, a snack bar-dining room might be the only place for commuting students to rest between classes or after lunch. This facility then functions as a lounge. Demanding a profit under these conditions—long serving hours with low dollar volume—is unrealistic.

While most institutions employ a director to manage food services, others rely on food service management companies for this function. Where such companies are employed, the institution gains from the company's professional competence. The institution negotiates, as part of its contract, fair prices and quality as well as space, equipment use, utilities, insurance, and all direct operating expenses.

The cost per meal served, according to the various components, is the most meaningful measure of comparison of food service costs as it eliminates the factors of absenteeism and sales volume. It also gives a reasonably accurate comparison among food services departments in various parts of the country.

Controls that are normally a part of business operations should be mandatory, such as monthly physical inventories, receiving and storage security, and control of cash. Audits by the internal auditor are useful to indicate to the food services director whether the department is adhering to institutional policies and whether there are any problems of which he is unaware.

A close working relationship should be created between the student housing and the food services departments. The application for housing should include information on food service plans. The appropriate time for indicating optional board arrangements is at the beginning of the student's first year. The boarding student is the basis for most successful food services departments because of the advantages of fixed income and a known number to be served at each meal. The student benefits because of the low cost per meal served.

College Unions

A college union is defined by the Association of College Unions—International as a "community center of the college for all members of the college family—students, faculty, administration, alumni, and guests" and is considered a building, an organization, and a program. Many unions use this definition or an adaptation of it in their statements of purpose. Union facilities should be designed to implement the purposes, which recognize several functions.

Unions are as diverse as the colleges and universities they serve. Their facilities can be divided into ten categories: recreation, social, cultural-hobby, meeting, service, food, commuter, organizational and administrative, stores, and adult education. Many unions are governed by a policy board, and the responsibilities delegated to union directors vary from complete responsibility for food service, bookstore, meeting rooms, budget control, purchasing, program, and maintenance to primary responsibility for housekeeping functions only, such as space assignment, cleaning, and games room operations. Many of the union buildings with debt service depend on a student fee for amortization; in others such a fee may not be necessary. Operating funds usually derive from a variety of sources, such as student fees, appropriations, and earned income.

College unions often include service operations in their programs. Good management is essential for these operations which, together with the bookstore and sometimes the athletics department, are the cash merchandisers of the institution. To be effective, union managers should have the same tools as those required by commercial managers, as well as immediate access to information on sales, cost of goods, inventory, cost of payroll, and indirect costs. The union system of accounts should be integrated with that of the institution.

Unions render an important service to the institutional community by remaining open during vacations and other periods when many facilities are closed, thus providing the only food and recreational services. This and other factors unique to the college union should be considered when comparing its revenue-generating operations with those of commercial enterprises. While the union enjoys the advantages of tax exemption and a captive market, these may be offset by unusual service demands, long operating hours, and the academic calendar.

College Stores

Every institution should evaluate carefully the services expected of its college store. Once the objectives are outlined, the institution must decide if its requirements are best met by service from privately owned, local stores; by a cooperative somewhat independent of the school; by store facilities leased to an operator; or by an institutionally operated store. If the store is operated by the institution, the store manager and chief business officer must decide which services to offer and how to finance them, in much the same manner as other budgets in the institution are prepared.

College stores have guidelines, commonly called retail accounting, with which to judge the effectiveness of their operations in comparison with the operation of regular retail stores. Normal retail accounting principles provide an excellent means for measuring the financial success of the store's operation. However, profitability is not the sole criterion of a successful operation.

Instructional materials frequently must be obtained without regard to the cost involved. When this occurs, the store is no longer merely a retailer, but an essential arm of the institution, serving educational needs. Cooperation between academic departments and the store manager is essential to insure accurate information regarding these needs. The college store needs the income from the sale of general merchandise to augment the small margin often incurred in the operation of essential merchandise departments, especially the textbook operation. Purchase of merchandise, control and evaluation of inventory, departmental evaluation, accounting, advertising, and display in college stores should follow established retail practices. The college store has the same physical requirements as a normal retail store, and it should be in the best traffic location possible. Standards for store size are available from the National Association of College Stores.

ORGANIZED ACTIVITIES RELATED TO EDUCATIONAL DEPARTMENTS

An organized activity related to an educational department is supportive of instruction and helps demonstrate to students the classroom or related educational techniques. Organized activities may generate some revenue, but their basic support usually is derived from the institution's general support—its appropriation and/or student fee income. Revenues generated by organized activities normally are considered incidental, since such

activities are operated primarily for demonstration purposes. Examples of organized activities are demonstration schools, college theaters, hotels or restaurants operated for the instruction of students enrolled in courses in hotel or restaurant administration, and stores that sell products of experimental farms and dairies. The goods or services created by these activities are incidental to the basic instructional or laboratory experience of the students. In the instruction or laboratory procedure, expenditures are incurred for raw materials, technical supplies, and service personnel.

Certain organized activities, such as laboratory schools and medical and dental clinics, complement the work of educational departments by providing program support for instruction and research. These activities may provide by-products or services available, for a charge, to students, faculty, and staff members, or to the general public.

Because these activities are closely related to education and research, their administration should conform to academic lines of control. The chief business officer's responsibility is, however, somewhat different from that in the usual educational and research activities, inasmuch as many organized activities involve more business management than do educational departments.

The direction of each organized activity generally is assigned to a member of the educational department, and normal business controls, accountability, and record systems should be maintained. Organized activities seldom are combined into a single administrative unit as in the case of auxiliary enterprises and service departments.

In some cases educational and research activities comparable to those classified as organized activities are of such small scope that they are performed as an integral part of the normal departmental activity. Should revenues result from such activities, they would be recorded as sales of the educational activity. An organized activity whose operations are of major magnitude may be shown in the financial reports separately from other organized activities. Even though its detailed accounting may be decentralized for purposes of institutional control, there should be central recording of revenues and expenditures. A large activity may justify special supervision within the educational or research department. In this case, the chief business officer should be consulted in the selection of the supervisor, and he should establish and supervise detailed accounting records and special operating reports as warranted by the size and character of the activity.

Hospitals and clinics administered in connection with medical or dental schools are a unique activity and offer special problems in the classification and reporting of operations. Frequently, hospitals or clinics are shown as a major item of both revenues and expenditures in a separate category.

The successful operation of organized activities requires cooperation and understanding between the chief business officer and academic officers. The primary objectives must remain the educational process and research activities. When an activity ceases to serve these objectives, it should be reclassified.

SERVICE DEPARTMENTS

A service department provides a specific type of service to various institutional departments rather than to individuals and is supported by internal transfers from the institution's operating budget. Such a service might be purchased from commercial sources, but for reasons of convenience, cost, or control, is provided more effectively through a unit of the institution. Examples are scientific apparatus repair shops, glassblowing shops, instrument-making shops, statistical and tabulating departments, addressograph and mailing services, secretarial pools, duplicating services, office-machine repair shops, laundries, photographic departments, printing shops, travel bureaus, audio-visual services, telephone systems, and motor pools.

Management and operation are usually the responsibility of the chief business officer, although some service departments, such as a computer center or a glass-blowing shop, may be under the direction of an academic officer or a department chairman.

The rates charged by a service department should reflect operating costs, including salaries, wages, staff benefits, costs of materials and supplies, operation and maintenance of the physical facilities occupied, provision for the renewal and replacement of equipment, provision for debt service, and a share of general administrative and

institutional expense.

The service may be provided on a direct (ownership) basis or on a contractual (rental) basis. In institutions large enough to support a staff to do so, assigning the administrative duties to one person as a director of services, or as a liaison for several contract services, is an efficient practice that promotes better management.

CLASSIFICATION OF ACTIVITIES

The classification of activities among the three categories may vary from institution to institution, reflecting differences in the purposes for which the activities exist. For example, at institutions where gate receipts are sizable, intercollegiate athletics should be classified as an auxiliary enterprise; where gate receipts are negligible and the athletic program is intended primarily for student participation, intercollegiate athletics may be classified as an organized activity or identified in the physical education department. Another example of variation in classification is the central duplicating service, which usually is a service department, but might be classified as an organized activity related to an educational department if it is operated as a practical laboratory for students specializing in printing technology.

BUDGETING AND COST ACCOUNTING

Each activity in the three categories should have its own budget and accounting system to identify salaries, wages, operating supplies, equipment, and other expenditures. Indirect costs, such as those for administration, plant operation, and maintenance, also should be apportioned to each activity. Only through cost accounting is it possible to establish appropriate rate schedules, identify subsidies, if any, and compare the resulting costs with commercial costs.

The three classifications lend themselves to budgeting and analysis techniques such as planning, programming, and budgeting systems (PPBS). Elements and subelements of costs, unit of product quality, or measure of service can be discerned readily. Cost accounting should relate the results of service evaluation to cost elements in a clear, timely manner, and should be employed to identify, analyze, and compare costs with commercial counterparts. Development of budgets, the establishment of prices pertinent to institutional policy related to the extent to which costs are to be recovered, and evaluation of service in terms of success in meeting pre-established goals (other than only financial ones) can be accomplished effectively regarding these services.

Budgets for auxiliary enterprises and service departments should be prepared by those responsible for these functions and should be approved by the chief business officer. Budgets for organized activities related to educational departments, while prepared by a cognizant academic officer, should be developed in consultation with the chief business officer or his representative. Institutional financial and business policies should be followed in the management of all three activities, and the disposition of any net revenues should be determined by institutional policy. Inasmuch as the primary objectives of these activities may change over time, they should be reviewed periodically to determine whether they are properly classified.

Facilities Operation and Maintenance

THE OPERATION AND MAINTENANCE of buildings, grounds, and other physical facilities of an educational institution are the responsibility of the physical plant organization. This function falls within the business administration of an institution and should be managed by a qualified person frequently designated "director of physical plant."

The physical plant organization is concerned fundamentally with timely service operations, maintenance, alterations, and related activity pertaining to the facilities portion of a total learning environment. The organization affects all segments of the institution and effectively must provide the level of service necessary in a manner compatible with institutional objectives. This activity requires efficient, courteous, and dedicated persons who also possess technical and professional capability. The manner in which they perform their services helps provide an effective, economical, and harmonious total operation. The public relations function of physical plant employees should not be underestimated. Personal contact with all departments, utilizing effective communication channels, is necessary to maintain good rapport within the organization and with all customers. There is frequently a correlation between level of maintenance and custodial service in buildings and respect shown the facilities by users. An effective educational program requires good, properly maintained facilities.

A small institution with only a few employees may consider a maintenance program using services of contractors as a means of obtaining varied skills needed for proper maintenance. Good specification preparation and maintenance program supervision by the physical plant office is necessary, but a quality maintenance program can be effected in this manner without maintaining skilled craftsmen in all trades on the physical plant staff.

Principles discussed in this chapter are universally beneficial, regardless of size or management philosophy of an institution.

ORGANIZATION AND ADMINISTRATION

For administrative purposes, the physical plant office should be organized according to functions. The head of the office should appoint a supervisor for each function that he does not personally direct. Normally there are at least six basic areas of responsibility in the physical plant office: administration, building and equipment maintenance, custodial services, utility systems, landscape and grounds maintenance, and major repairs and renovations.

Many institutions assign additional functions to the physical plant office, such as automotive service, construction planning and inspection, communications (telephone, telegraph, mail, and messenger service), risk management, purchasing and stores for the physical plant office, safety, security, traffic, fire-fighting, waste disposal, and trucking and moving.

The administrative group carries out the duties of management and administration for all areas under the jurisdiction of the physical plant office. This includes development of policy for use within the office, as well as operating guidelines within overall university policies. Daily decisions are necessary for effective use of staff, material, and money; effective scheduling is essential, with all work completed as required or promised. Effective management control requires persons with professional knowledge in labor relations, career training, data processing, buildings, and related systems, contracts, and record keeping. The physical plant administrative staff should be represented at the decision-making level on all matters affecting the office.

Effective budgeting for the complex functions of physical plant operations is critical. Competition for the limited funds available has caused state legislators, governing boards, and institutional councils to seek appropriation standards or formalization criteria to provide equitable distribution of funds to institutions within their charge. Although no widely accepted system has been developed, some states have determined formulas for allocation of their physical plant budget moneys. The system of unit cost allocation (cost per square foot) is the most widely used system for budget allocation, but has many inequities if used exclusively. Many other variables that bear heavily on physical plant costs are not taken into consideration by averaging them into a unit square footage cost.

The physical plant budget should provide for normal and recurring operation and maintenance of facilities. Funds for other purposes, such as building alterations for a particular department or college, should come from other sources, such as the department or college making the request. That is, no services other than routine operation and maintenance should be provided unless they are charged to the user department or college or to a special account provided for such projects.

Records related to payrolls, billing, material ordering, and dispatching of work orders are important to the conduct of physical plant operations and often can be maintained on data processing equipment. The director of physical plant must have effective production control and cost control and analysis, requiring rapid feedback with more detailed input and output information than is available on normal fund ledgers.

A record file of each building should be maintained in the office of the director of physical plant. The records should include name of the building; date of construction; original cost; date, nature, and cost of major renovations; utility systems; floor plans; record of painting and routine maintenance; and original architectural drawings and construction specifications. For accurate information and future use, the file also should include "as built plans" and the working drawings and plans of subcontractors and each mechanical trade.

Labor relations is increasingly important as more employee organizations, unions, and other bargaining units are formed. Good personnel records are necessary and in-house training programs for staff and supervisors are highly desirable to encourage the best motivating and managing techniques. Technical schools can be used in lieu of or in addition to in-house training. Apprenticeship programs are an alternative when instructors are not available from other sources. Although the labor relations function is often administered by a centralized personnel or labor relations office, that office should have the active cooperation of the director of physical plant. For a detailed treatment of this subject, refer to the chapter "Labor Relations and Collective Bargaining."

Effective management of buildings and systems requires professional and technical knowledge of such facilities and may necessitate having engineers, architects, draftsmen, and estimators on the staff or on a consulting basis. This group should analyze systems, modes of operation, and selection of replacement materials or systems; prepare documents for contractual maintenance and renovations; and recommend standards for construction.

BUILDING AND EQUIPMENT MAINTENANCE

Building and equipment maintenance includes all items related to routine repair of buildings, structures, and utility distribution systems, including normally recurring repairs and preventive maintenance. This service is provided by carpenters, electricians, plumbers, painters, roofers, steamfitters, tinsmiths, and other skilled workers. In large institutions, each of these skills may be represented by a separate staff with an appropriate number of supervisors. In small institutions the maintenance crew may be limited to one or two persons, including the director. The work should be planned, organized, and scheduled on the basis of regularly required servicing, emergency repairs, and annual requirements for painting, major repairs, and other preventive maintenance activities. When extensive repair or renovation projects must be completed during brief periods, such as between sessions and during vacation periods, additional help may be employed on a temporary basis or the projects may be performed under contract. If a particular project requires skills or costly equipment not available at the institution, the services and equipment should be obtained from outside sources on the basis of competitive bids.

Modern maintenance programs may include communication systems, two-way radio systems, and do-it-now capability, such as small crews with trucks fitted for their service specialty, with support crews to complete scheduled maintenance.

Formalized, planned maintenance programs for small and large operations are desirable and, in most instances, once organized and implemented, will provide the most economical operation. Such programs can be automated for greater efficiency. The need and the program should be comprehensively evaluated from a functional and economical point of view before work is initiated. In the long run, a well-planned maintenance program will save money. In the short run, it can be quite costly to organize and implement but if done well will reap benefits in addition to the financial considerations.

Consumption of utilities is a major item in physical plant budgets. Systems consuming these utilities must be in good operating condition to avoid an inflated financial burden. Diligent surveillance and maintenance are essential in keeping these systems in good operating condition. Maintenance mechanics must be well-trained, and a continuous retraining program is necessary to keep them abreast of changes in technology. Close attention to operating hours, peak loads, and waste of utilities also can have significant impact on the utility cost. Occasional review by consultants may indicate how to reduce costs. The control systems on modern heating and air conditioning systems are complex and require trained technicians to assist maintenance crews.

Many older buildings contain inefficient, uneconomical systems and obsolete structural components. There may be requirements for improved heating systems, addition of air conditioning, new office equipment, improved lighting, and increased electrical capacity. All proposed changes should be reviewed by professional engineers and practical solutions developed before decisions are made regarding replacements, modifications, and renovations.

CUSTODIAL SERVICES

Custodial care includes routine duties to keep interiors of buildings in a presentable condition. In addition to maintaining floors and restrooms, custodians also wash windows, walls, and venetian blinds, provide snow removal adjacent to building entrances, and may perform minor maintenance. The group may serve as a labor pool to provide assistance in moving and setup for special events. Custodial maintenance operations may include use of specialized crews for some operations, such as floor stripping and rewaxing. Regardless of their duties, custodians must know their job expectancy; that is, their duties should be defined.

Custodians usually report directly to their work assignment. This eliminates lost time in travel to and from the physical plant administration building. For maximum efficiency the cleaning portion of custodial services should be provided after normal class and office hours. Buildings with high weekend use should be on a seven-day schedule. Adequate training of new employees and a periodic retraining program directly influence quality and efficiency of service. Uniforms and identification badges may be provided for custodians.

The work assignment for each custodian and the cleanliness requirements of each building will vary, depending on the building's use. Each building should have its individual cleaning priorities by specific areas. This insures cleaning critical areas regardless of daily manpower fluctuation or traffic.

Supervisors must schedule the work effectively. If work schedules and acquisition of materials are planned in advance, efficient use of staff members can be achieved. Supervisors should prepare work assignments based on daily progress. Variations from the total time estimated for each assignment should be reviewed and explained as part of the supervisory responsibility. Proper scheduling requires careful evaluation of each building, awareness of the academic and administrative calendar, and seasonal considerations. Supervisors also must keep abreast of new products and equipment. This is especially important in view of high labor costs. They also should be consulted on design and on materials being considered for new construction or alteration projects. Their advice may save maintenance costs and years of complaining.

Local, state, and federal safety standards and institutional policies regarding facilities use will have an impact on the need for custodial services. A campus ordinance forbidding domestic animals in buildings, except seeing-eye dogs, is recommended.

OPERATION AND MAINTENANCE OF UTILITY SYSTEMS

Utilities include heating, cooling, power and light, water supply, sewage treatment, gas, and other utilities necessary for the operation of the institution. It is a major and costly item in the physical plant budget, and prudent management decisions are essential to obtain the most effective results. The director of physical plant must continuously analyze the systems to assure reliable, efficient, and economical operation. The utility system operation and maintenance procedures need to be closely correlated with the overall building maintenance program.

It is recognized that institutions may have various systems. These range from total purchase of utility services to the capability to produce and perform all services or a combination thereof. In some urban areas where buildings are in close proximity to a utility plant, it may be more economical to purchase both electricity and heat (steam or high-temperature hot water) from local utility companies rather than to generate them.

Because utility companies supply their products at various rates, a thorough study often is required to insure that the rate paid for a particular service is the most advantageous. Utility rates are controlled by state commissions. Utility companies are staffed with rate experts who usually will assist institutions in determining whether they are scheduled on the proper and most advantageous rate. An alternative is to have a professional rate engineer periodically review utility arrangements.

Construction involves long lead times and utility loads must be projected continuously for at least five to ten years in advance. Distribution systems should adhere to a master plan that projects into the future as far as possible. Voltages, steam pressures, and pipe and cable sizes selected for distribution systems must anticipate future load growth.

Utilities must be planned not only to meet expected maximum demands, but also to provide standby capacity as a back-up for equipment failure and to allow for equipment shutdown for mandatory annual overhaul. The decision to gen-

erate electricity in addition to heat must weigh the economics of the relatively simple heating system against the more complicated total energy system, that is, utilizing a turbogenerator to produce electricity at the same time it reduces the pressure of steam so that it may be distributed for campus heating and cooling loads. Electrical tie-ins with utility companies provide a back-up source for the total energy system. A record of the degree-days is a vital factor in the plant size required for heating and air conditioning.

In order to determine the most desirable air conditioning system, a thorough review of all costs— installation, operation, and maintenance—must be made of the available types of systems. These generally include central chilled-water plants, individual systems that cool one building, and individual room units such as window air conditioners. The central chilling plants or building units may be of the absorption, centrifugal, or reciprocating type.

Fuel systems include gas, oil, and coal. Gas is by far the most convenient fuel but is not always available. Its price can vary from the least to the most expensive, depending on the area and type of service. Oil has slightly better availability but less convenience. Coal is the most available fuel in most areas. Its evaluation must include freight, ash removal expense, purchase and maintenance of handling equipment, additional operators, and required storage space. Gaseous and particulate emissions must meet federal, state, and local laws. Minimal environmental problems arise from use of gas. The serious pollution problems resulting from the use of coal can be reduced by installation of effective precipitators.

Water may be purchased from a municipal source or the institution may operate its own water system, including supply. In either case, the water supply must be tested to assure that the chemical characteristics of the water will not adversely affect the plumbing system or laboratory apparatus through corrosion or deposition of solids. The water supply also must be checked frequently to assure purity and to guarantee a consistently acceptable product.

Sewage or waste water treatment normally is purchased from a municipal plant with the cost being proportional to water consumption. It therefore is desirable to review frequently the use of water and to implement water conservation programs to prevent waste.

Operation of the utility system requires technical competence and constant supervision. Plans for modification or expansion of utility systems should include the latest engineering developments and use of automatic control systems. Proposals for boilers and other high-pressure vessels should be reviewed by the insurance carrier's engineering and inspection divisions, because safety and risk features of systems have a direct bearing on premium rates.

Decisions in such matters must be made with the assistance of competent engineers. Larger institutions may have the competence on the staff, while smaller institutions may have to rely totally on a consulting engineer.

LANDSCAPE AND GROUNDS MAINTENANCE

Maintenance of attractively landscaped grounds will enhance the respect shown the institution by students, staff, and the general public. This responsibility requires a staff sufficient to maintain lawns, shrubbery, flower beds, walkways, and parking areas, and to remove snow and perform similar services. In addition, it may be advisable to obtain professional service for both landscape design and supervision of the groundskeepers. In large institutions, the responsibilities may require the attention of a full-time staff member; in institutions with limited requirements, the services may be obtained on a contract basis. Some institutions use local nurseries for all grounds maintenance work.

A master plan for campus landscape development and utilization should be prepared by a landscape architect engaged especially for the purpose or by the institution's supervising architect. The master plan should include projections of the location of future buildings, roads, parking lots, walkways, and playing fields and should give consideration to the location of subsurface utilities and the practical aspects of maintaining all items in the most efficient manner. Supervisors concerned with campus maintenance should be asked to study and approve any master plan and modifications of it before it is adopted. After a master plan has been adopted, all planting of lawns, trees, and shrubbery should proceed according to the plan in order to insure consistent development.

MAJOR REPAIRS, RENOVATIONS, AND ALTERATIONS

Major repairs and renovations to buildings are necessary from time to time to keep the condition of buildings and their systems at an acceptable level for use and to meet safety standards. This activity includes replacement of roofs, walls, floors, ceilings, and lighting; tuck pointing; and upgrading or replacement of electrical and mechanical systems. These activities are not considered normal maintenance, since they are usually large in scope and are performed infrequently. To the extent that funds are available, amounts are allocated to the physical plant office and identified under a separate category such as major plant projects.

These projects often require design and engineering plans accompanied by formal estimates. Estimating procedures that have proved to be most reliable are those that have utilized cost standards. These standards can be acquired or developed locally in accordance with the local market.

Academic departments and administrative offices may request room modifications and specify new environmental conditions due to change in program or function. This type of change is identified and funded under another category such as alterations and improvements. Information and costs for the development of these projects should be provided by the physical plant office.

Performance of major repairs, renovations, and alteration projects in addition to normal maintenance requires careful scheduling. It is important that the director of physical plant be apprised of the volume of this work simultaneously with release of operating budgets so that planned use of manpower is continually possible. At any rate, arrangements should be made in cooperation with —and normally under the direction of—the physical plant office.

One of the more successful ways of organizing the work process to accomplish major projects is by assigning a project supervisor. This fixes responsibility and provides a specific source for decision making and coordination.

If a project cannot be performed by the physical plant staff for any reason, the work may be assigned to an outside contractor selected on the basis of the lowest acceptable bid and such factors as timeliness, quality, and aesthetic considerations.

This procedure assigns responsibility for building modifications and repairs to the director of physical plant, with whom such responsibility should reside.

Building standards or codes should be developed to provide minimum requirements for all building and remodeling, and some institutions must comply with federal, state, and local codes, as applicable. This insures that the structural and architectural integrity of the campus buildings, grounds, and utilities will be maintained at a high level and provides for special needs concerning fire, safety, and accommodations for the handicapped. Without these standards, new buildings can be functionally and aesthetically depleted in a short time. Building and remodeling plans should take into consideration items previously standardized by the physical plant office, such as key systems, door closers, and items for which replacement parts are kept.

PHYSICAL PLANT SHOPS

The physical plant office must be provided with a shop equipped with the basic tools and machines required for the maintenance function. Its size and the variety and sophistication of equipment will be governed by the number of buildings and the extent of the grounds. Most institutions construct or assign a separate building exclusively for this purpose, usually on the periphery of the grounds.

It is beneficial to have a stores-supply operation and a salvage function associated with the shop to fully benefit handling of the large volume of supplies processed by this operation.

If practical, the service building should house the offices of the director of physical plant and his staff and also should serve as the headquarters for the maintenance staff. With the exception of custodians who go directly to and depart from their duty stations, all plant employees should report to a central point in the service building at both the beginning and end of their working hours. At large institutions there may be several reporting stations.

An essential adjunct of the physical plant shop is a storeroom or warehouse for supplies used in plant operation and maintenance. If possible, the storage area should be in the service building, and all shop supplies should be delivered there.

A person should be designated as receiving clerk

to verify shipments with purchase orders and place goods in storage or inventory according to a predetermined system for inventory control and for efficient service to those requiring goods. Withdrawals from stores should be by requisition identifying the buildings and work orders involved. This procedure provides data essential for cost accounting and for control of materials. The variety and volume of supplies stocked will be determined by the size and complexity of the institution and by local availability. The supervisor should review the inventory at least annually to determine that stock and proposed purchases are limited to essential and regularly used items.

OTHER PHYSICAL PLANT SERVICES

In addition to the responsibilities and functions described above, the physical plant office frequently is assigned responsibility for construction planning and inspection, risk management, purchasing and stores for the physical plant office, safety, security, traffic, fire-fighting, and trucking and moving. Other assigned activities are described below, such as automotive service, communications, and waste disposal.

Automotive Service

Responsibility for administrative control, maintenance, service, and repair of institutionally owned motor vehicles may be assigned to the physical plant office or may be assigned to a motor pool operated as a service department. Automobiles usually are available for use by faculty and staff on the basis of approved requisitions. The extent to which an institution maintains repair facilities for its motor vehicles and equipment depends on the number of units. If large numbers of vehicles are involved, institutional repair shops are economically feasible. Some institutions may use vehicle-rental agencies that supply cars, trucks, buses, and other types of motor units on an annual contract basis.

Communications

Responsibility for supervision of the communication systems may be assigned to the physical plant office, but the policy is determined by the administration. Included may be telephone systems, interoffice communication systems, and mail service. Requests for additional or expanded services should be evaluated according to the established need for them and with recognition of the cost involved. New and improved systems, such as Centrex switchboards and visual displays for information retrieval from central data banks, may be implemented where practical.

Handling of mail normally requires a central mail room in which mail is received and sorted for distribution to various departments. Large institutions will need persons to collect and distribute all mail.

Waste Disposal

The approaches used by colleges and universities for disposal of solid, liquid, and gaseous waste are no different from those used by most commercial organizations. The physical plant office may be responsible for storm and sanitary sewer lines on the institution's grounds and also for the runoff of rainwater beyond the institution's property lines. Although an institution may have its own sewage treatment system, this service usually is contracted with the local municipality.

Solid waste disposal is a complex and costly activity. Several methods can be used: incinerating, shredding, compacting, hauling to a landfill, or a combination of these methods. Institutions may elect to contract this service or handle it themselves, but a regional concept of solid waste disposal with other communities is recommended. An institution that handles its own solid waste disposal will find it necessary to make a sizable investment in containers, compacters, transporting vehicles, and other related equipment.

Recycling of waste paper and other recyclable materials for resale normally is not economically feasible, but when students have programs for this purpose, the physical plant office should cooperate as much as possible. The complexity of the problems of solid waste disposal and stringency in governing regulations make it apparent that individual solutions by small agencies are impractical and greater cooperation is necessary at the community level.

Facilities Planning, Design, and Construction

IN PLANNING NEW CONSTRUCTION, an institution first must establish general guidelines before more specific issues can be settled. New construction must be conceived in terms of a master plan— a compendium of the institution's educational philosophy and academic programs, administrative structures, kind and number of students served, rate of growth, facilities needed to accomplish these goals, and resources required. The physical plan, a component of the master plan, determines where a new structure will be built, and is an important part of the overall program of institutional growth. Questions concerning use of a proposed facility and its relationship to the academic master plan, relationship to other facilities, relationship of one department to another, and special requirements such as laboratories must be answered before architects can design an efficient building.

An institution may use its own staff in compiling a master plan, or it may hire a firm with total planning capability. Many architectural firms employ consultants in education, traffic, security, and other fields pertinent to colleges and universities. An institution possibly may obtain from such firms a more objective analysis than members of its own staff might provide. A disadvantage of this method is cost. However, institutions and large commercial concerns often have found that an in-house staff with total planning and design capability not only may result in false economies over the long term, but also may often function at greater cost, project by project, than the consultant-practitioner. Even if a college or university planning committee gathers most of the data, it may be advisable to obtain some advice from outside consultants. When hiring a consulting firm, an institution must clearly define the tasks delegated to it as well as those tasks to be handled by staff planners; the

engagement of a consultant does not lessen the responsibility of staff planners. Comprehensive planning is complex, and a detailed contract that benefits both parties is essential. For a detailed treatment of long-range planning, refer to the chapter "Institutional Planning."

LONG-RANGE FACILITIES PLANNING COMMITTEE

Responsibility for reviewing and revising the physical plan should fall to a long-range facilities planning committee. To be effective, this committee should have broad-based representation, with staff specialists and members of the administration and faculty.

Comprehensive physical planning is difficult for a new college or university, and even more so for an established institution, where the plan must contain a pattern for growth that is integrated with the past. Plans often must be revised because of changes in educational objectives, teaching techniques, and funding. Thus, planners regularly must schedule reviews and revisions of the physical plan.

In addition to maintaining the physical plan, the long-range facilities planning committee usually screens requests for new construction and major renovations. The committee periodically should examine the progress of new projects, and the president then should make recommendations to the governing board concerning relative priorities of construction and renovation projects and the best methods for implementation.

PROGRAMMING THE NEW PROJECT

Ad Hoc Planning Subcommittee

Once new construction or major renovations are approved, an ad hoc subcommittee should be appointed. The work of the subcommittee is to guide project planning and to assist in the development of a program for a specific building. Recommendations from future users should be submitted to the subcommittee with accompanying rationale. The physical plant office should provide technical data concerning the site and utilities and, later, evaluations of various structural, electrical, and mechanical systems recommended by designers. It is helpful for members of the subcommittee to visit recently built facilities similar to those they are planning. By this means, unsatisfactory features can be avoided and good features can influence the development of project design.

Project Program Requirements

The work of the subcommittee should culminate in a statement of user requirements, commonly known as the project program. Although some institutions work with documents such as notes from planning conferences, these records are seldom as effective as formal program documents, which help architects and engineers by providing three kinds of essential information. From the master plan, the project program uses guidelines in areas such as the institution's educational philosophy, academic and research programs, planning criteria, and projected growth. Specific features of the building are determined by the subcommittee, based on data collected. Finally, from technical information prepared by the physical plant office, the project program selects data pertinent to the project, including utilities locations, electrical characteristics, and test borings. Institutions sometimes have a construction standards handbook, which outlines administrative and planning information, specification documentation, design and construction requirements, and materials. The subcommittee continues to work after architects and engineers have been engaged, cooperating with them and the institution's facilities planning staff.

Selection of Architects and Engineers

An important responsibility in preparing for new construction is the selection of architects and engineers. The appearance, efficiency, and cost of a building—including operation and maintenance expenses—are largely a result of their design. With appropriate participation of the long-range facilities planning committee, the president will make recommendations to the governing board on the selection of architects and engineers. Normally, an architect will be hired, but some projects may require the services of an engineer alone.

Design competition is one method of selecting architects. However, this option often is too expensive and time-consuming to be useful. An alternative is a careful analysis of job requirements on the one hand and capabilities of available architects on the other. Among the important qualities to look for in selection of an architect are design integrity, technical competence, and interpretation of program requirements in the design. Evaluation of all these factors can be accomplished by personal inspection of completed projects. Architectural fees and services to be performed are additional factors to be considered in the selection of an architect.

Once the architect is chosen, the parties should sign a contract that states assistance the institution will render, services the architect will provide, and remuneration he will receive. Most architectural contracts are modifications of a standard model recommended by the American Institute of Architects. Architectural fees may conform to a scale established by a local political subdivision for work done at institutions under its control, or may be negotiated with the architect on an individual basis. In any event, the fee is based primarily on cost of construction, with some consideration given to the simplicity or complexity of the building. If an architect engages the services of engineers, the architect pays for their services from his fee.

The institution pays the architect according to a schedule agreed upon in advance. A typical arrangement might be:

Phase		Percent of Total Fee
1	Schematic Design	10-15
2	Design Development	15-20
3	Working Drawings and Specifications	40-50
4	Supervision of Construction	20-25

Another system in use is based on hourly rates for the architect, designers, draftsmen, specifications writers, and special consultants. The charge usually includes a markup for overhead costs and requires separate billing for out-of-pocket expenses such as travel, long-distance telephone calls, and blueprints. Under both arrangements, if the institution decides to terminate the project or discontinue the services of the architect, it pays only for services rendered, with a nominal amount added to cover the architect's final expenses.

DESIGN

It is primarily architects and engineers who carry a project through the design stage until the job is ready for bidding. They need considerable assistance from the ad hoc planning subcommittee and the facilities planning staff, and may require the aid of consultants. Architects conceive the design, while engineers are responsible for devising systems to fit the design. The process requires the exploration of all options, development of concepts and costs, and then refinement, correction, and coordination of all drawings and estimates. The major steps in the design process are schematic design, design development, and working drawings and specifications.

Consultants

Even in the earliest stages of design, architects and engineers may require help from consultants in solving complicated problems in special-purpose buildings and in specialties such as audiovisual equipment, acoustics, interior design, food services, and landscape architecture. The architect and institutional representative should interview the consultant, state his responsibilities, and require a memorandum from him that delineates services to be provided and their cost. The institution rather than the architect has final approval of consultants added to the design team. If a consultant is approved, his fee may be assumed by the architect or paid by the institution.

Coordination

With many persons working on the same project, close coordination of their work is important. As the architect moves the project from schematic drawings to final working drawings, he and his engineers and consultants should meet frequently with the institution's ad hoc planning subcommittee and facilities planning staff. Architects and engineers need firm decisions from the institution's planners as early as possible to perform expedi-

tiously. If a builder has been selected early through a negotiated contract, his representative also should be included in the planning process to advise on possible construction problems. The campus architect-planner and the physical plant representative may be especially helpful in communicating between academic or administrative planners and professional designers.

Review

At each important design stage, the ad hoc planning subcommittee (or campus architect) should require that the plans be examined by the director of physical plant and appropriate members of his staff. Physical plant representatives may be able to suggest design changes to simplify operation and maintenance and thus reduce the building's operating costs. A thorough plan review also covers code compliance and requirements of the federal Occupational Safety and Health Act or similar state program. Good architects are acquainted with most pertinent codes and with the Act's standards, but mistakes do occur.

Specifications

An important and complicated step is preparation of final specifications. Although the architect is responsible for this task, institutional officers must work closely with him and carefully review his work. The institution and architect must decide which specifications are appropriate for the building. Five methods of specifying construction products are:

1. Descriptive specifications, detailing the exact product characteristics desired.
2. Proprietary specifications, which allow the institution to control quality levels more easily by requiring brand name products.
3. Reference standards, which stipulate that products must meet quality levels established and published by authorities and testing institutes such as the American Society for Testing and Materials and the National Fire Protection Association.
4. Performance specifications, which require that products accomplish certain functions —for example, that the ventilating system change the air in the building five times an hour.

5. Cash allowances, which are a tactic to delay a specifications decision.

Proprietary specifications are a problem in competitive bidding because they eliminate competition by naming the brand to be used. As a result, they usually are prohibited on work done at public institutions or with public funds. Sometimes they are necessary; even federal and state projects may have to specify products by name in cases where new materials must match existing materials in quality and size or where new equipment must connect with systems previously installed.

In addition to instructing the architect about types of specifications to be used, the institution should provide technical and legal review of the work. Technical review is advisable because many architects rely heavily on manufacturers for help in writing specifications. Problems may arise with this method in competitive bidding. In such a case, the documents should be examined by institutional representatives to insure that specifications are not so restrictive that they eliminate all products except those supplied by the assisting company.

The institution's counsel should review nontechnical portions of the general and supplementary conditions before final approval is given. Sections of particular legal importance include insurance coverage and its relation to the institution's overall insurance program, conditions for release of liens, guarantees, and performance and payment bonds.

Although movable furniture and fixed furnishings for laboratories, libraries, physical education buildings, kitchens, and other facilities require specifications, they usually are excluded from the general contract. Their acquisition should be a responsibility of the institution's purchasing officer, who should work closely with the architect and the ad hoc planning subcommittee during the period of specifications, preparations, bid, and installation of equipment.

CONTRACT ADMINISTRATION

A list of reliable contractors is as important to an institution as a set of comprehensive specifications. Investigation of contractors under consideration and the subcontractors they will employ should include queries into their concern for quality, financial standing, reputation, integrity, the experience of the proposed construction superintendent, and ability to work well with architects and project supervisors representing the institution.

To aid the investigation, contractors should provide the following information:

1. Current financial statement.

2. Schedule of projects currently under contract, a list of those completed within the last five years, an estimate of their value, and names and addresses of clients and architects involved.

3. Statement of experience with projects similar to the one under consideration.

4. Number, names, and qualifications of the supervisors proposed for the job.

5. Name of bonding company.

6. Affirmative action policy.

A "Contractor's Application for Prequalification" may be developed by the institution. Such a form produces a complete record of the experience, capabilities, organization, and financial condition of every company that applies.

Bidding Versus Negotiation

With some exceptions, the most economical construction contracts are those awarded through competitive bidding procedures. To insure economy and avoid graft and favoritism, most federal and state agencies require competition on projects they fund. However, private and even public institutions may find it less expensive in certain circumstances to negotiate a construction contract with only one company. One reason for this savings is that competitive bidding requires preparation of many detailed documents and drawings that can be eliminated if a contractor is hired early in the design stage. Furthermore, good contractors, when participating at an early phase as members of the building team along with planners, architects, and engineers, can bring practical decisions into the design process for more economical construction.

Bidding Documents

Before calling for competitive bids on a project, the architect for the project must prepare certain documents, review them with the institution's personnel, and then provide an appropriate number to each invited contractor. Bidding documents prepared by architects usually include the following:

1. Working drawings.
2. Specifications, including general and supplementary conditions.
3. Bid proposal form, including spaces for total cost, breakdown by trades, any alternate and unit prices requested, and time needed for completion.

A refundable deposit usually is required for the loan of these bidding documents; if a contractor wishes additional copies, he purchases them. Single sets of the drawings and specifications should be on file with the ad hoc planning subcommittee, at the office of the director of physical plant, facilities planning and/or architect's office, and such other offices as may be required by state or local laws.

Upon submission of bid proposals, the following usually are also required from the bidder as part of the package of bidding documents:

1. Bid bond signed and returned by the contractor with a deposit as a guarantee to perform if selected.
2. Performance bond signed at contract settlement, insuring that if the contractor is unable to complete the job, his bonding company will.
3. Payment bond, often combined with the performance bond, insuring that subcontractors will be paid.
4. Contractor's affirmative action policy.
5. List of subcontractors.
6. Evidence of liability and workmen's compensation insurance.

Bidding Procedures

On those projects funded totally or in part by state and/or federal agencies, open bidding among any and all bondable bidders is normally required by such agencies. In situations where closed bidding is allowable, an institution should invite at least three contractors to submit bids, in order to make bidding competitive. A danger exists that some of the better companies may not risk preparation costs when a large number of bidders lowers their probability of award. Local conditions may help determine how many contractors to invite;

for example, some already may be committed to their full capacity.

An unresolved issue in bidding is the determination of which procedure produces the highest quality. The traditional system calls for a general contractor to submit a total price for the entire project (with alternates separately priced to allow some leeway for negotiation and change) and then to act as coordinator for both the work he performs and that of his subcontractors. This method simplifies administration: the contract establishes clear lines of authority running from the institution through the architect to the general contractor, subcontractors, suppliers, tradesmen, and laborers, while providing single responsibility through the guarantees following completion of the work.

However, the growing complexity of structural, mechanical, and electrical systems has popularized the multibid method in which as many as three to five subcontractors are awarded separate contracts for portions of the job. Proponents claim that the multibid method allows the institution to eliminate the general contractor's profit on certain complex work that is too technical for him to administer efficiently. General contractors counter that speed and coordination suffer as responsibility is dispersed. Institutions using multibids either must provide a staff member to supervise coordination or else award the architect an additional fee for this task.

Two weeks is the minimum time contractors should have for preparing bids; if other similar jobs are out for bid at the same time, a month might be appropriate. Due dates and delivery locations should be specified in the bid invitation and strictly adhered to. Bids should be opened and read in the presence of all bidders who wish to attend, and the architect should prepare a tabulation of all bids and distribute it to all the bidders.

Bidding Problems

Although competitive bidding determines the low bidder, award is never automatic or immediate. Before announcing the final decision, the architect and a representative of the institution should analyze all bids for the best combination of alternates and for certain danger signs, such as an extraordinarily low bid. Since most bids in a competitive market normally fall within a range of ten percent, a contractor whose bid falls below this range may have developed a particular efficiency or may have made a serious mistake. If a mistake has been made, the contractor should inform the institution promptly, and advise whether he intends to forfeit his bid bond or proceed with the contract as bid. When such circumstances arise, legal counsel should be sought by the institution.

Negotiations

Institutions not bound to competitive bidding may wish to negotiate with one general contractor or with several subcontractors. Advantages may include greater speed, economy, and quality, but these advantages can be maintained only if the contract is carefully administered. The key is selecting reliable firms. Major contract types are:

1. *Guaranteed maximum.* This arrangement requires the institution to pay for labor and materials and to reimburse the contractor for managing the project. The builder guarantees that the labor and materials expense will not exceed an agreed-upon maximum.

2. *Cost-plus.* This arrangement is similar to the first, but without a guaranteed maximum for the builder.

3. *Owner-builder.* Under this arrangement the institution authorizes one of its officers to act as general contractor, and designates an experienced staff member as construction supervisor. This system allows the institution to deal directly with subcontractors and to eliminate the general contractor's overhead and profit, but it places great demand on the staff and should be attempted only when an experienced supervisor is available.

Speed of construction is the primary advantage of a negotiated contract. By reaching an agreement with a builder, the institution can eliminate the two- to four-week bidding period and the one to two weeks for bid analysis. On some projects the process can be speeded further by beginning foundation work before detailed working plans for the later stages of construction have been drawn.

Change Orders

While change orders should be avoided if possible, they may be necessary for any of the follow-ing reasons: improvements, unanticipated site or building problems, and mistakes. Mistakes are most frequent, and usually it is the institution that suffers most, whether changes result in additional or reduced costs. If the architect or engineer makes a mistake, it usually is the institution's mistake under terms of the contract. Rarely does a designer return part of his fee because of inaccurate or incomplete work. For the institution, change orders mean delay and greater cost because of redesign, estimating extra construction, and perhaps even refinancing.

Common causes of changes are:

1. Errors of commission, which develop from design mistakes that make further construction or installation according to original plans impractical.

2. Errors of omission, which result in gaps in plans, such as omitting access panels for utility systems or safety hooks for upper-floor windows.

3. Substitutions, which may be warranted by newly developed materials or equipment or by the unavailability of specified products.

4. Changes in scope, which occur after construction has begun and planners decide that more space is required; availability of funds may necessitate increasing or reducing size or quality of the project.

5. Changes in personnel or administration.

6. Discovery of unknown site conditions or building problems.

The best way to control the number of changes is to engage good designers and to conduct rigorous plan reviews, using the original program as the constant control document. The institution must expect change orders and never sign a contract that leaves this expensive issue unresolved. All change orders must be in writing, approved by authorized personnel.

Construction Schedule

Construction contracts should require the contractor to submit a detailed financial breakdown and a proposed construction schedule soon after award. These may take the form of a bar chart or of a critical-path-method diagram, and should include estimates of the contractor's monthly billings to the nearer thousand dollars. This information allows the business officer to manage his cash flow more effectively.

CONSTRUCTION

Preconstruction Conference

The preconstruction conference is an on-site coordinating conference. The architect organizes this meeting to resolve any last-minute questions of contractors, suppliers, subcontractors, and institutional representatives. Detailed but important matters such as timing of subcontractors, use of power and water, parking, and the confines of the construction site often remain unsettled until major contract decisions are made, and this meeting should eliminate confusion and causes for delay.

Lines of Authority

The contract states the chain of authority controlling construction. The institution, which provides the site and bears the cost, is the ultimate authority, but the contract often empowers the architect to act as the institution's agent in matters related to construction. Depending on contract terms, he can inspect the contractor's work, reject unacceptable materials, and order the contractor to maintain the schedule. He can condemn portions of the work that are poorly executed, and order the contractor to rebuild. However, he cannot interfere with the way the contractor manages the job or deal directly with subcontractors or workmen under the contractor's control.

The institution should never bypass the architect if the contract gives the architect the authority to deal directly with the contractor. If the institution approves work, equipment, or materials that the architect disapproves, it may have no legal recourse against the architect or builder should problems develop during the guarantee period.

This does not mean that the institution should ignore its new building during the construction period; one experienced staff member should be appointed to work full-time as the institution's representative. If this is not possible, someone should be appointed to keep a daily construction log. The architect may employ his own representative to report to him, and the contractor undoubt-edly will have a project supervisor performing a similar function, but the institution still should have a staff member who keeps himself informed on the progress of the work. Some larger institutions find it economical and effective to employ their own inspectors and not require the architect to perform this function; this will result in a reduction of the architect's fee.

Construction in Progress

One of the architect's duties is to keep all parties informed on the status of the work. He can do this best by issuing bulletins on a regular schedule, perhaps once or twice a month. These bulletins should provide information on such items as work completed, financial situation to date, problems, cost revisions, and change orders. Periodic meetings of all parties also may be helpful in communicating progress or resolving problems.

During construction, the architect should make periodic inspections of the project. If any work is not being accomplished in accordance with the plans and specifications, the architect should undertake to have the contractor correct the problems. This may require tearing out existing work and having it redone. Physical plant representatives also may inspect the work for the owner and report any problem they see developing directly to the architect for him to resolve.

End of Construction

Near the end of construction, architects, engineers, and institutional representatives inspect the project and make a "punch list" of uncompleted items. The architect is not bound to include the institution's suggestions in the final punch list he compiles for the contractor unless those suggestions fall within the requirements of the construction contract. He then should send the punch list to all interested parties to inform them that the job will be complete as soon as the contractor finishes the remaining items satisfactorily.

When the contractor notifies the other parties that all items on the punch list have been completed, all principals convene for a tour of the facility. If, as a result of this tour, the architect and institution agree that the contractor has met all the stipulations of the contract, they then can collect any remaining releases of liens and accept the building. When disputes about the work occur between the client and contractor, the architect usually will act as mediator and judge. Most contracts also include an arbitration clause to cover especially complex situations.

ACCEPTANCE AND OCCUPANCY

Even in amicable cases, the "final inspection" often is not final. Demands for additional space sometimes force an institution to accept a building for "beneficial occupancy" before it is completed. In such a case it is important to clarify exactly when and how the builder will finish the work. It is standard procedure in such a situation for the institution to retain a portion of the funds as an incentive to the contractor to complete his work.

Certification by the architect that the contractor has completed his work and should receive final payment prepares the way for acceptance of a building by the governing board. Acceptance means that the institution legally owns and controls the building. Because most buildings open with a few incomplete items remaining on a punch list and many pieces of equipment under guarantees, it would be more accurate to speak of a "schedule of acceptances." The important point is that the transaction of acceptance should not be completed before certain administrative details in the original contract have been satisfactorily examined and executed. These include certificates, guarantees, operating manuals, test operations, and as-built drawings.

The contractor is responsible for preparing and collecting all certificates of inspection from public agencies and professional testing laboratories and delivering them to the architect for retention in contract files.

The contractor also should deliver—through the architect—all guarantees to the institution. The warranty period usually begins when equipment in satisfactory condition first is used by the institution in normal operations, but it is vital that the institution determine the start of each warranty period with written agreements from the contractor and architect concerning these dates.

For efficient use of equipment, the contract should require the contractor to compile for the institution a manual that includes manufacturer's literature, catalog cuts, and specifications sheets— all the technical data and instructions necessary for the operation and maintenance of the building. This manual should be approved by the architect.

If test operations are included in the contract, it is recommended that the architect designate the time for them. This usually occurs after the institution has accepted the building as substantially complete. One method of testing is to have the contractor supply the skilled personnel necessary to operate the building for five consecutive days of eight hours each. During this period the contractor will demonstrate the operation of all equipment to the architect and the director of physical plant and other interested persons.

One of the last contract details and one of the most important is the final set of as-built drawings. Because the process of construction inevitably requires changes from the original working drawings, it is essential that the institution acquire at least one set of revised, reproducible drawings that incorporates these alterations. It is usually the architect's responsibility to provide such drawings, and a stipulation to that effect should be included in his contract.

When a building is accepted, it should be included in the institution's schedule of insurance for buildings and contents.

Security

THE MISSION of a security, law enforcement, public safety, or police department is to provide a safe environment through excellence in protection of life and property. Regardless of whether an institution operates its own department, contracts for this purpose, or depends on local jurisdictions, the following services are essential:

1. Protection of constitutional rights.
2. Creation and maintenance of a feeling of security in the community.
3. Identification and elimination of hazards and of opportunities for crime.
4. Protective patrols to deter and detect crime, to detect fire and safety hazards, and to prevent traffic accidents and congestion.
5. First-aid and rescue capabilities.

In addition to these essential services, it is highly desirable to provide investigative capability to follow up on crimes, accident investigations (if not handled by another department), and emergency transportation of sick and injured. Other services sometimes provided are protective escort, parking enforcement, and lost and found operations. Whatever functions are assigned, members of the department also have a public relations role in rendering information and assistance to faculty, staff, students, and visitors.

The Open College or University

An important criterion in determining security requirements is the accessibility of the institution. The definition of an "open" college or university differs among institutions, but each college or university that falls into this category may experience increased security problems. Urban institutions often are open in the sense that public streets may cross the campus or an institution may have several locations. In this situation, access may be gained more easily than if the institution were "closed"—that is, enclosed by a single perimeter. If an institution operates its own security department, its officers often have authority only on institutional property, while protection on surrounding streets depends on local law enforcement or on the actions of security officers as private citizens.

Another concomitant of the open university concept is that the institution remains accessible at all hours, unrestricted by any barriers or system of permits, thus posing a challenge to security by outsiders even when the institution lies within a single perimeter.

AN INSTITUTIONAL SECURITY DEPARTMENT

The decision to create an institutional department rather than to rely on external agencies should be based on a firm commitment to the administrative, budgetary, and personnel requirements of such a department as well as on the following factors:

1. The extent of crime and security problems at the institution.
2. The ability and willingness of external agencies to deal with institutional problems effectively, consistently, and in a manner that is relevant and sensitive to the uniqueness of academic life.
3. The institution's desire to have control of and influence on security and law enforcement programs.
4. The institution's willingness to act as its own policeman and to accept the responsibilities, costs, and risks of engaging in law enforcement.
5. The extent to which the department will be

a viable, integral part of the institution, improving its quality of education, research, and public service.

Since the security department represents the institution and takes part in its functions, it too has a role in educating members of the community both by example and by service, thereby creating respect and goodwill for all such agencies.

College or university security requires many services that a local police force is not expected to provide. The department must be responsive to the needs of a young, intelligent, and often liberal and progressive community.

Organization of the Department

College and university security departments vary in organization. In some cases the security or public safety director is accountable directly to the president or to a chief administrative officer. The director also may advise other interested persons of his activities, such as the student services officer, who may be notified of an incident involving student conduct. In other cases, the security director may report to the director of physical plant, or there may be a dual reporting responsibility, such as to the student services officer on matters of investigation or patrolling and to the director of physical plant concerning such problems as thefts of institutional property.

Some states have designated a coordinator of security, who is responsible for reorganizing and improving security at all public institutions of higher education in the state. Among the coordinator's principal functions are the establishment of uniform training, general standards for staffing and equipment, and procedures for reporting and record keeping.

Policy and Procedure

A policy manual is essential to the security program. If an institution is developing its own department, the help of security consultants or other experts should be solicited in preparing the program and in drafting the manual. An excellent resource is institutions having such programs. When a security director is hired to set up a new department, he should prepare the first draft of the manual, subject to further review and approval of higher authority. Upon approval of the policy manual, the director should establish an operations manual, which provides specific guidance for the staff.

To be effective, policies and procedures of an institutional security department must be well-defined and should recognize the character of the institution and current crime problems. Enforcement policies must recognize the supremacy of the law and the principle of equal protection under the law. Department policy should not interfere with enforcement of unpopular laws or set quotas for arrests or traffic violations, but should include a minimum standard of performance for officers and stress prevention of crime, with arrest as a last resort.

If the department has police powers, at least upon the property of the institution, these should include:

1. Arrest by warrant, on view and upon probable cause.

2. Lawful searches.

3. Direction and control of traffic.

4. Investigation of crime.

5. Use of necessary force to perform its duties.

Such authority is most effective when granted by the appropriate state or local jurisdiction. If the department does not have police powers, there may be instances in which deputization of security officers is advisable.

Any changes in security regulations should be approved by the security director and his superior officers: however, any changes that affect the entire institutional community should be undertaken only by a principal administrator. The director should have the authority to establish procedures for the department, law enforcement objectives and priorities, and internal departmental controls. The program and staff should be evaluated on a regular schedule to make certain that desired levels of service are maintained. In cases where budgets have expanded and the record has improved, reductions may be in order.

The security department requires a uniform system of records, files, and reports. Monthly and annual statistical and financial reports should be submitted by the director to appropriate officers of the institution for use in crime analysis, budget justification, and administrative briefings.

Ideally, the reporting procedure also should provide:

1. Thorough initial and follow-up reports on every reported crime and incident.
2. Distribution of reports, on a need-to-know basis, to other agencies as intelligence items.
3. Inclusion of crime experience in the uniform crime reports.
4. Confidentiality of reports.
5. Permanent storage and ease of retrieval.

Qualifications and Training

The director of a college or university security department should be experienced in law enforcement or private security. There is no substitute for such experience, although proven leadership in another department of the institution is sometimes accepted in place of the experience requirement. A security director must be sensitive to the higher education environment, since it is essential that members of the institutional community, particularly students, have confidence in the security operation.

Officers working with the security director also should be sympathetic to the college or university environment. Some institutions require that all security officers be enrolled in a degree program and that their salaries be based on credits accrued as well as on their performance records. In certain institutions security officers may continue their education tuition-free, or they may be given other assistance in furthering their education.

Thorough training programs must exist to insure professional competence and development. Arrangements should be made for security officers to attend police training programs and workshops, and the resources of regional organizations are available in most states. In many jurisdictions a state training program is mandatory for all law enforcement officers, including security officers at colleges and universities. Requirements vary from state to state, and city or county regulations regarding law enforcement agencies often must be met as well.

The institution should sponsor a continuous, in-service training program that includes study of human relations and sensitivity training, thorough orientation concerning procedures to be used in event of emergencies, and familiarization with institutional philosophy, policies, and regulations. A new officer may work temporarily with a senior officer for specific, on-the-job training. In-service classes should be offered periodically, drawing on resources of the community. For example, an instructor from the institution may address security officers on human behavior; a local police officer may lecture on drug abuse; an attorney may discuss search and arrest laws with members of the department.

Since the basic role of the security officer is to observe, identify, and report, it is essential to provide instruction in report writing, proper procedures for interrogations, and the fundamentals of good investigative techniques.

Uniforms and Equipment

Security may be strengthened not only by stressing individual protective measures and by utilizing security devices such as locks and alarms, but also by the conspicuous presence of a uniformed force on foot and in mobile patrols.

Some institutions have accepted a uniform of blazer and trousers for its officers rather than the traditional police-type attire in the belief that community members find the former style of dress preferable. Concern must be given to this decision if the institution's experience shows that the major offenders are outsiders. The presence of a police uniform serves as a deterrent, particularly to an outsider who is unaware of a blazer-slacks police image. At some institutions there is a mix of the two types.

An institutional security department should purchase and issue all items of uniform and equipment for its officers to insure quality, uniformity, and its right to inspect and control usage. Where uniforms are used, they should be clearly distinguishable, even from a distance, from those of all other law enforcement agencies in the area.

Law enforcement falls into two general categories—visual and nonvisual. Visual law enforcement, such as the presence of uniformed officers walking posts or traveling in marked vehicles, is intended to prevent crime. Nonvisual enforcement is investigation of crime and apprehension of suspected offenders.

Many institutions do not permit weapons, but institutions that do issue weapons to security officers must provide training in their proper use. Rules must be established concerning the handling of weapons, and it must be emphasized that firearms are to be used only for protecting the officer's life or the life of another. Officers should requalify in the use of weapons at least every six months.

Many innovations have been formulated to meet specific security needs. One institution has installed a successful "blue light" program that involves a campus-wide emergency telephone system marked by blue lights and connected directly to the campus police dispatcher so that instant help may be summoned. Another innovation is the use of officers on horseback, who are especially useful in patrolling wooded and other less populated areas, and who also can be effective in controlling crowds. Some institutions have found the use of guard dogs beneficial.

An adequate communications system is essential to the security department, and should include a communications center operated on a 24-hour basis and a two-way radio provided to each security officer on duty. Radios having more than one frequency may be necessary if officers are to communicate with the local police jurisdiction as well as the institution's security department.

Electronics is recognized as a better means of controlling access and for protecting certain facilities than either watchmen or fixed guardposts. Central consoles in the security headquarters may monitor various types of alarms, closed-circuit television, remotely controlled electric strike-equipped doors, and also may perform other security, fire safety, and equipment control functions. Such devices are expensive initially, but may pay for themselves by eliminating labor costs while providing a uniform level of protection.

Use of Students in Security

Student Security Patrols. An effective aid to security in some institutions is the use of student security patrols. Both male and female students volunteer or are employed to patrol buildings and grounds, with special attention to problem areas such as parking lots. Although student patrols have no police authority and take no police action, they may be used to help with peaceful demonstrations and with crowd control at athletic and similar events.

Each prospective member of the patrol should be interviewed by the security director and should be able to pass a physical examination. Training in first aid, human relations, proper use of fire-fighting equipment, and other subjects should be provided. Members usually should not work more than four hours a day or between the hours of 10:00 p.m. and 6:00 a.m. except in unusual circumstances.

If uniforms are supplied to student security patrols, they should be distinctive, but not the same as those worn by the regular security staff; members should not wear badges. If uniforms are not supplied to patrol members, an armband or other type of identification may be used.

Each student should carry a flashlight, whistle, notebook or clipboard, and two-way radio to report observations and summon help from regular officers when necessary. Bicycles are useful, and students patrolling on foot or after dark should travel in pairs.

Student Police. Some institutions employ a security force comprised largely or entirely of students. Student police, while effectively checking crime, also may improve student-police relations and ease campus tensions.

Some student police have their tuition paid under a scholarship program administered by the Law Enforcement Assistance Administration, a crime-fighting agency of the federal government. Institutions having a student police force may use a cadet system, in which recruits direct traffic during athletic events, operate radio transmitters, and do other police work during apprenticeships that last a year.

Institutions with criminal justice degree programs may draw their student officers from these programs. Such students often intend pursuing law enforcement or criminal justice careers, and thus are highly motivated.

CONTRACT AND PART-TIME SECURITY SERVICES

Some institutions may prefer to contract for security services rather than to establish their own departments. While good results can be obtained with this method, there may be certain disadvantages: guards provided by contracting agencies may not always be as well-qualified as desired, and they may not be familiar with the special problems of the higher education environment.

Contract security officers and off-duty officers from other security agencies can be used as extra manpower on special occasions, such as athletic events.

LIAISON WITH OTHER AGENCIES

The security department must be largely self-sufficient, but able to work harmoniously with other institutional departments. It also should maintain effective liaison with other law enforcement agencies, the courts, the prosecuting agencies, and the press. It is advisable that the local chief of police be informed of public functions to be held at the institution, so that he may be prepared to assist if necessary.

All members of an institution must be assured at least the same degree of protection afforded anyone in the outside community. Students rightfully have demanded equal protection and prompt, intelligent response to their problems, and those colleges and universities with inadequate security programs must call upon outside agencies. Communication and cooperation with local police units foster mutual understanding and otherwise are helpful to both the institution and the community.

Safety

ALL INSTITUTIONS of higher education have the moral and legal obligation to provide safety —that is, freedom from health hazards and risk of injury. Apart from humanitarian and legal considerations, any accident represents an unwanted interruption in the normal course of business. Whether it is an injury, a property loss, or merely an interruption of normal procedure, it is costly, undesirable, and unnecessary.

Losses may be covered by insurance, but insurance premiums over the long term reflect actual losses, plus overhead and profit. In addition, many institutions operate with high deductibles or self-insure a large portion of losses. While the initial costs of a safety program may be high, the savings from good performance can be significant. An effective safety and accident prevention program can be self-supporting through savings in workmen's compensation losses and reduction of property damage.

The Williams-Steiger Occupational Safety and Health Act of 1970 affects almost every employer in the United States. It is administered by the U.S. Department of Labor through the Occupational Safety and Health Administration (OSHA). The Act was designed to operate through state governments, but until state standards are at least equal to those of the federal government, federal standards apply. OSHA does not directly affect public institutions; however, they will be subject to occupational safety and health standards as the programs of the various states are approved. All private institutions must comply—with federal standards if the state plan has not been approved, otherwise with state standards. OSHA safety standards cover most hazards. The law requires unannounced inspections by federal compliance officers, with potentially severe fines for noncompliance, prison sentences in certain circumstances, and specified periods of time for the abatement of hazards found.

An effective safety program enables institutions, large or small, to conserve resources and meet their legal obligations to provide a safe environment.

ADMINISTRATION POLICY

For a safety and accident prevention program to be effective, it must be the responsibility of the president. He should have a policy statement developed that reflects his acceptance of the moral and legal reponsibility for maintenance of a safe environment. This statement should be approved by the governing board. It should include provision for safety of employees, students, and the visiting public. The statement should provide guidelines for engineering, training, and motivation, and request the full cooperation of all involved. Finally, it should assign responsibility for safety to specific individuals. It should make clear that safety is important to management, and that there are persons accountable to the president for safe facilities and performance.

ORGANIZATION

Responsibility for coordinating the institutional safety program must be assigned to an individual who is part of line administration. He should have direct access to senior institutional officers and councils. Ideally, he should not have other operational assignments, such as physical plant or security, that might dilute his attention to safety. In small institutions, however, some combinations may be inevitable. Safety is an administrative function. The individual assigned responsibility for safety must be adequately supported by professionals in health and safety. In large institutions several may be needed. In small institutions faculty expertise may be used but decisions must be reserved to line administration.

Authority should be delegated to the safety officer to take immediate action when imminent danger exists. This authority necessarily must be used sparingly and with good judgment. In the academic environment, the safety officer accomplishes most goals by persuasion and persistence, as safety cannot be easily mandated, but must be "sold." A safety committee with faculty, staff, and student representation can be an effective adjunct to the program by providing guidance and approval for policies or by coordinating major projects.

ACCIDENT REPORTING, INVESTIGATION, AND RECORDKEEPING

A definite procedure must be established for reporting accidents, unsafe conditions and practices, and progress in the safety effort. OSHA requires that specific records on prescribed forms be maintained, and there are established fines for noncompliance. Injury and occupational illness reports are required for statistical and planning purposes. Such reports also may be the basis for legal protection of the institution or employee in court actions that may arise.

The basic reason for accident reports is accident prevention. Summary and analysis of accidents provide essential data for assigning resources to areas of greatest need and cost benefit. All members of the institutional community should be encouraged to report all injuries and accidents, no matter how minor. Reporting recommendations apply not only to faculty, administration, and staff, but also to students and visitors.

Accidents should be reported on a standard report form. Forms for reporting accidents usually are available from insurance carriers at no charge. If these are not suitable, such forms may be developed within the institution. A time limit for reporting and recording accidents must be specified to meet the requirements of OSHA and local laws. Reports should be sent directly to the safety officer for investigation, review, follow-up, and possible presentation to the safety committee. Included in the report should be a recommendation for prevention or other necessary corrective action. The review should be complete and accurate, include a statement concerning the most likely causes, and specify corrective action. A procedure for follow-up should be established. Department heads and supervisors can be trained in accident investigation and reporting techniques and should be shown the benefits of such reports.

Records may be useful in determining the trends or shortcomings of a program. For example, accident or incident records are important in specifying situations with a high probability for accident. Such situations can be defined as any "near miss," unsafe practice or condition, delayed treatment case, or accident that under similar circumstances could result in serious injury or damage.

Many elements are involved in the accident sequence, and seldom is an accident attributable to a single cause. Careful investigation may reveal an unsafe act, one or more unsafe conditions, personal factors, or a combination of the three.

Unsafe conditions are a primary focus of OSHA rules and regulations, and it is beneficial to establish a system for reporting unsafe conditions on a routine basis. Such a system may include a survey by the institution's safety officer and may incorporate a simple form for reporting or investigating unsafe conditions. A primary function of the department head or supervisor is maintenance of a safe environment. Therefore, he normally is involved if an unsafe condition is found, and corrective action should be initiated by him. More hazardous conditions may require immediate action.

Unsafe practices, although not stressed as strongly as unsafe conditions in safety laws, are the cause of the majority of accidents, and the reporting of unsafe practices should be included in the system developed for reporting hazards. As with safety of the environment, work techniques are a primary responsibility of the department head or supervisor, and corrective measures should be taken by him. The only exception to this procedure is an imminent danger requiring immediate action by the observer.

To prevent injuries and accidents, it is essential that rules governing the use and treatment of equipment and machines, as well as behavior in areas containing them, be understood and followed by all persons. Such rules should be posted in each department in a conspicuous place or beside the machinery or equipment to which they specifically refer. A check-out procedure should be conducted by the department head or supervisor before anyone is permitted to operate machines or equipment.

Progress reports on the effectiveness of the safety effort should be part of the program; they may include statistical and narrative information. In the past, primary focus on accident reporting was in use of the terms "frequency" and "severity." Although these may be of interest in comparing experience with other institutions, they are not meaningful to management. One of the most useful ways to report to management is in financial terms.

There are many systems of reporting; such systems may include the ratio of workmen's compensation costs to payroll dollars, insurance premiums paid, credits on premiums (or penalties) based on performance, or actual losses. A statistically valid system has been developed, supported by the National Safety Council, which includes the "hidden costs" of accidents.[1] This system results in a standard charge for each type of accident—lost time, medical treatment, first aid, and property damage. Once established, it is simple to maintain and update and provides an accurate appraisal of the true cost of accidents. To insure that they are read, progress reports should be relevant and interesting to all persons on the distribution list. This will broaden the base of support for the safety effort.

INSPECTIONS

The safety program should provide for periodic inspections of all departments. The inspections should be conducted by qualified persons, who record their findings in written reports for the safety officer. Also, self-inspection by individual departments is an important part of data collection, establishment of responsibility, and communication. Inspectors should examine the entire environment, not only for conditions that may result in injury, but also for conditions that may produce illness, such as improper use of laboratory chemicals. A check list is an important aid in conducting inspections, for even an experienced safety professional occasionally overlooks some items.

More frequent inspections and random observations should be scheduled for more hazardous areas.

Since the majority of accidents are caused by human failure, it is important that inspections include scrutiny of work practices and procedures as well as of the physical environment. The person responsible for an area or department should be informed of inspection results and be included in the formulation of recommended corrective action. Recommendations should be followed up to insure that hazards are corrected. The emphasis in all inspections must be on conditions or practices with a high potential for causing serious injury or property damage.

Review of all plans and specifications for new construction or renovation should be included in the safety program to avoid built-in hazards discovered only after the facility is in use. It is much less expensive to correct the hazard on paper than after the project is complete. In order to perform this function, the safety officer must be familiar with applicable codes and regulations, such as those of OSHA, local building or fire codes, and insurance company standards.

SAFETY STANDARDS

Standards established by governmental codes and laws must be considered minimum standards for safety, and it is often necessary and desirable to exceed the legal requirements. Many institutions provide such standards in booklet form to architects and engineers, representing those requirements that are unique to a particular organization.

Building standards should include not only the basic requirements to meet the needs of the particular building, but special requirements such as facilities for maintenance and housekeeping, fire protection, facilities for the handicapped, ventilation, illumination, and first aid or emergency needs. Grounds standards may be provided for walkways and roads, traffic control, and lighting. Plantings should be located such that they do not interfere with safe driving.

Special safety provisions apply to laboratories, depending on their use; for example, the requirements for a research laboratory are different from

---

[1]Rollin H. Simonds and John V. Grimaldi, *Safety Management: Accident Cost and Control* (Chapter 7), Homewood, Ill., Richard D. Irwin, Inc., 1963.

those for an undergraduate or teaching laboratory. The nature of the work also has an effect on safety requirements. General requirements for laboratories should specify adequate lighting and ventilation, alternate means of egress, safe and efficient storage and handling of materials, and appropriate protective devices for persons using the laboratory, such as safety showers and eye-wash facilities, emergency breathing apparatus, sprinkler systems, and explosion venting. These devices should be tested periodically and must be properly maintained. Limits should be set on the quantities of flammable and corrosive materials stored in the area at one time.

Motor vehicle standards should include the latest legal requirements for safety devices, a system of qualifications for drivers using institutional vehicles, a reporting system for vehicle defects, and follow-up procedures to insure that vehicles are maintained in safe condition.

Office areas should consider standards for electrical supply adequate for typewriters, desk lamps, and other electrical equipment. Floor loading and stability are a consideration for filing cabinets. Many modern files can be attached to a wall or to each other for stability. Since office workers vary in their requirements for comfort, minimum standards should be established to regulate office temperature and ventilation.

Shops and maintenance areas require attention to machine guarding, ventilation, dust collection, electrical grounding, use of flammable liquids, and adequate training of persons who operate the machinery and equipment. These requirements are detailed specifically in the OSHA regulations. There are other specialized requirements to be met in establishing or operating food services and similar occupancies that may be peculiar to educational institutions.

Large public assembly areas such as theaters and stadiums present the possibility of catastrophic accidents. Safety standards and inspections of these areas should be especially rigorous. Adequate emergency exits and lighting as well as emergency procedures should be provided.

Many institutions have standards for persons working alone in shops and laboratories. For the most part, these standards limit the functions that may be performed after normal working hours to office work, custodial duties, or nonhazardous laboratory procedures. Some require that no persons work alone or that persons working alone be monitored in some way, check in periodically, or sign in and out, with regular checks by security persons. The safety officer may wish to ask one or more members of the safety committee to assume specific responsibility for following up on compliance with established safety standards. In the event of an accident, those responsible for the follow-up procedure should make sure that corrective action is taken by the appropriate person, and that the safety officer receives a full report of the result.

EMERGENCY PROCEDURES

Numerous emergencies may be encountered, and it is necessary to establish special procedures for each type. Situations included in such planning are fires, bomb threats, gas leaks, tornadoes, floods, earthquakes, and hurricanes. Emergency procedures should include a chain of command establishing the authority and responsibility of various individuals. In emergencies, procedures sometimes must be changed at an instant's notice; therefore, responsible persons should be selected for this function.

Building evacuation is required for fires, explosions, bomb threats, hazardous atmospheres, and certain natural disasters. The evacuation plan should include responsibility for activating and executing the plan, with the necessary training and practice. It should include an assembly checkpoint to insure that all persons have been evacuated; this point should be free of the hazard causing the evacuation. For example, in the event of a bomb threat or fire, the sidewalk immediately adjacent to the building would not be satisfactory as an assembly checkpoint because of the danger from flying missiles or the interference with fire-fighting operations. Handicapped persons may require special assistance.

Disaster shelters should be designated, and all persons informed of their locations and the safe routes to reach them. It is important that shelter locations and routes be properly identified with easily understood signs. Depending on the estimated time persons may be required to spend in the shelters, provision must be made for food, ventilation, and sanitation. Designated persons, usually department heads and supervisors, require training in the management and operation of shelters.

Notification and alerting systems are required in any emergency plan. In addition, special communication systems such as telephones and radio beepers are necessary for alerting key persons. Depending on available resources and facilities, separate systems may be established for different types of emergencies. Periodic testing is required for operational readiness and training of personnel, and to insure that there are no "dead spots" where signals are inaudible.

First aid facilities, equipment, and training are essential for an emergency plan. Special stations, fire-fighting equipment, certain medical supplies, and personnel trained in some or all areas may be required. Shelf-life of supplies should be determined, with outdated supplies replaced as necessary. The institution's physicians probably will want to become involved in selection of supplies and training of personnel. The local fire department can be helpful in providing assistance and training in the use of extinguishers and other fire-fighting apparatus.

Rescue teams may be included in the plan to provide emergency rescue, radiation monitoring, and other services. Special equipment, as well as necessary protective clothing, should be made available to these teams. Such teams also must receive training and practice.

Part 4

Fiscal Management

Administration of Endowment Funds, Quasi-Endowment Funds, and Other Similar Funds

THE THREE principal categories of endowment and similar funds are endowment funds, term endowment funds, and quasi-endowment funds (sometimes referred to as funds functioning as endowment). The principal of an endowment fund is not expendable by an institution under the terms of the instrument creating the fund. Term endowment funds are like endowment funds, but all or part of the principal may be expended after a stated period of time or upon the occurrence of a certain event. A quasi-endowment fund may be totally expended at the discretion of the governing board. Many principles of fund administration apply to all funds in the endowment, quasi-endowment, and other similar funds group. All three types of funds—endowment, term endowment, and quasi-endowment—should be reported in the endowment and similar funds section of the balance sheet, and the identity of the groups should be clearly differentiated in the fund balance section.

The chief business officer or other designated officer is responsible for insuring that all funds are used in compliance with applicable restrictions until such restrictions are removed. Because of the relationship between good stewardship and long-range success in raising endowment funds, this is a most important function. The responsible officer therefore should have a thorough understanding of the legal framework within which he must act, and the funds must be used in compliance with legal restrictions.

THE LEGAL STATUS OF ENDOWMENT FUNDS

Endowment funds, sometimes called "true en-dowment funds," have been the subject of considerable legal discussion. The most serious question is whether fund appreciation, realized and unrealized, must be treated as principal and therefore be considered unexpendable. The answer depends on the extent to which the principles of private trust law are applicable to educational institutions, which are considered charitable corporations governed by a mixture of trust law, corporation law, and, to some extent, contract law.

There are two major concepts of the legal nature of endowment funds. The traditional concept is that an endowment fund is a trust fund and that all endowment funds are to be treated as held in trust. It is inconsequential to proponents of the trust concept that an institution may hold property in trust for itself (or in a broader sense, for the public), and that the three-way separation of trustee, life beneficiary, and remainderman—the cornerstone of private trust law—does not exist. The second concept, one adopted in 1972 by the National Conference of Commissioners on Uniform State Laws in the model Uniform Management of Institutional Funds Act, is that educational institutions hold endowment funds for their own benefit as their absolute property, that the laws applicable to charitable corporations apply, and that principles of private trust law are not applicable.[1]

The Endowment Fund as a Trust Fund

Under the trust fund theory, an endowment fund is viewed as being held in trust regardless of whether trust language is used in the instrument establishing the fund, and the principal of

---

[1] For a more complete discussion of the subject, see William L. Cary and Craig B. Bright, *The Law and the Lore of Endowment Funds*, New York, The Ford Foundation, 1969.

the endowment fund must be maintained inviolate in perpetuity. Principal, moreover, is construed to include not only the original value of the fund when established and the original value of any additions to the fund, but also appreciation in the value of investments of the fund. For example, if a donor established an endowment fund of $100,000, with the income to be used for faculty salaries, and over a period of ten years the value of the investments of the fund grew to $180,000, the full $180,000 would have to be kept inviolate and no portion of the $80,000 of appreciation could be expended.

To achieve as much flexibility as possible in a gift, educational institutions should discourage use of technical trust language in deeds of gift or wills. It is important that the officers responsible for fund raising and fund administration be aware of these implications. If it appears that an institution may be forced to serve as a trustee in the technical sense, the problem should be resolved in the courts as promptly as possible by applying for relief from the formal requirements of trusteeship.[2]

An anomaly in the trust fund approach to endowment funds is the practice of commingling assets for investment purposes. In private trust law, the rule forbidding a trustee to commingle investments of two or more separate trust funds is strictly applied. (Under special legislation, however, banks are permitted to commingle the assets of trusts of which they are the trustees.) If one accepts the concept that endowment funds are trust funds, pooling investments of endowment funds is not permissible. However, most educational institutions have pooled investments of endowment funds for many years, and this practice has never been challenged. This deviation from private trust law as applied to endowment funds of educational institutions seems to have gained universal acceptance.

Another consequence of viewing endowment funds as trust funds is that the governing board may not delegate responsibility for management of investments of endowment funds, even though it has freedom to delegate other important decision-making authority to officers of the institution. Therefore, in some jurisdictions the governing board, or at least an investment committee composed of governing board members, actually must decide to purchase or sell specific investments.

Absolute Ownership Theory of Endowment Funds

Several states have rejected the trust theory in favor of the doctrine that charitable corporations hold their endowment funds solely for their own benefit. It follows that the investment and administration of those funds are governed by the law of charitable corporations rather than by the law of private trusts. This does not result in clear-cut gains for educational institutions in those states, however, because the law of charitable corporations is loosely applied and often confusing, drawing on a mixture of corporate, trust, and contract principles. It is possible, for example, for a court in an "absolute ownership" state to reach the conclusion that appreciation must be considered part of principal as in private trust law, contrary to the general principle of corporation law that appreciation may be treated as earnings.

Moreover, subject to provisions to the contrary in the law of the state of incorporation or in the charter documents, the governing board of a charitable corporation does have some freedom to delegate authority in connection with investment functions to a committee of its members or to appropriate corporate officers, but the delegation of investment authority to professional investment managers who are not officers of the corporation should be made subject to the ultimate responsibility of the board.

Uniform Management of Institutional Funds Act

The model Uniform Act was proposed as a solution to the problems involved in administering endowment funds. This model Act permits prudent use of appreciation, specifies the nature of investment authority, allows the delegation of

---

[2]Colleges and universities should scrupulously avoid serving as executors or trustees of testamentary trusts and are legally foreclosed from serving in those capacities in most states. A donor may achieve the effect of naming the institution as an executor or testamentary trustee by naming an institutional officer (usually an investment or other financial officer) in his individual capacity. This procedure, however, should be adopted only when the donor is fully aware that conflicts may arise between the institution and other beneficiaries and when the institutional officer is fully aware of his fiduciary responsibilities.

power to make investment decisions, and prescribes a standard of business care and prudence to guide governing boards in exercising their duties.[3]

Important definitions included in the model Act are:

Institutional fund means a fund held by an institution for its exclusive use, benefit, or purposes, but does not include (1) a fund held for an institution by a trustee that is not an institution or (2) a fund in which a beneficiary that is not an institution has an interest, other than possible rights that could arise upon violation or failure of the purposes of the fund.

Endowment fund means an institutional fund, or any part thereof, not wholly expendable by the institution on a current basis under the terms of the applicable gift instrument. (Implicit in this definition is the continued maintenance of all or a specified part of the original gift.)

Historic dollar value means the aggregate fair value in dollars of (1) an endowment fund at the time it became an endowment fund, (2) each subsequent donation to the fund at the time it is made, and (3) each accumulation made pursuant to a direction in the applicable gift instrument at the time the accumulation is added to the fund.

Appreciation as used in the model Act means appreciation over historic dollar value. Therefore, if the market value is below the historic dollar value of the fund, the institution may spend only the yield.

LIFE INCOME AND ANNUITY FUNDS

Institutions also may receive gifts or bequests subject to payment of income or specified amounts to one or more beneficiaries for life. In this instance, the institution functions as a trustee for federal tax purposes. Such funds are not "institutional funds" within the scope of the model Uniform Act but will become such upon the death of the last beneficiary. They nevertheless possess many characteristics of institutional endowment funds for administration and investment purposes. Opinions vary regarding the proper method of classifying life income funds on the balance sheet,

but regardless of the reporting method used, the funds must be labeled clearly as subject to life income reservation by footnote or otherwise.

A life income agreement is an agreement whereby money or other property is made available to an institution on the condition that the institution bind itself to pay periodically to the donor or other designated individual(s) the income earned by the assets donated to the institution for the lifetime of the donor or of the designated individual(s). If the institution is obligated to pay stipulated amounts rather than only the income actually earned by the assets, the term "annuity agreement" should be used. An annuity agreement is an agreement whereby money or other property is made available to an institution on the condition that the institution bind itself to pay periodically to the donor or other designated individual(s) stipulated amounts, which payments are to terminate at a time specified in the agreement.

Prior to the passage of the Tax Reform Act of 1969, arrangements with donors were often informal. Many institutions sought to avoid the finding of a trust relationship under local law by use of "life income agreements" and scrupulous avoidance of use of the word "trust." The Tax Reform Act of 1969 clearly established the existence of a trust relationship (for Internal Revenue Service purposes) when educational institutions are trustees of life income funds. The Act stipulates that gifts or bequests subject to life income must be to qualified pooled life income funds or charitable remainder unitrusts or annuity trusts (as defined in the Act) in order to qualify for the income, estate, or gift tax charitable deductions. Definitions of these entities must include detailed provisions governing administration of various types of trusts. Donors may make additional gifts to their existing pooled life income or unitrusts. However, additions to annuity trusts are not permitted under the Act.

Institutions that now administer or plan to administer life income trusts should seek advice from counsel to insure compliance with relevant provisions of federal and state laws. The officer respon-

---

[3]As of 1 November 1973, the following states have used the model Uniform Act: California, Colorado, Connecticut, Illinois, Kansas, Maine, Maryland, Minnesota, New Hampshire, Tennessee, Vermont, Virginia, and Washington. In addition, New Jersey, Pennsylvania, and Rhode Island passed similar acts before the model Act was prepared.

sible for life income trust administration and investments should be thoroughly familiar with the practical considerations involved.

Although its relative importance has diminished because of a 1969 tax treatment change, the charitable gift annuity remains an additional deferred giving option.

Several basic policy decisions must be made by the governing board or investment committee of the institution with respect to each deferred-giving option offered. These policy decisions include:

1. The suitability of each particular type of agreement to the institution's needs and operating capabilities.
2. The minimum gift amount required to establish the type of trust in question.
3. The maximum number of life beneficiaries permitted.
4. The minimum age for life beneficiaries.
5. The cost of investment management and administration and whether to charge a fee to cover these costs.

Pooled Life Income Funds

A pooled income fund is a trust, defined in Section 642(c)(5) of the Internal Revenue Code, to which donors make irrevocable gifts of money or securities that are commingled with property of other donors who have made similar transfers. Each donor retains a life income interest for himself and/or one or more named beneficiaries living at the time the gift is made. Each beneficiary is entitled to his pro rata share of the pooled fund's earnings each year for his lifetime. At the death of the last beneficiary of any one donor, the charitable organization severs the donor's share of the pooled fund and uses it for its charitable purposes.

The assets of a pooled fund may be commingled with the assets of other institutional funds—such as assets of an associated endowment pool, unless the pool is invested and administered on a total return basis (total return is discussed in the chapter "Investment Management")—as long as detailed accounting records are maintained specifically identifying the life income portion of the pool and the income earned by and attributable to that portion. Tax law requires that the market value, unit method of accounting be used for all pooled life income funds, whether or not the

assets are commingled with assets of endowment funds.

The institution may delegate its trustee responsibility for the investment management of a pooled life income fund to a bank as long as it retains the power to change trustees. Moreover, a bank may use a common trust fund as an investment vehicle; by using this device, it may be possible for smaller institutions to effect considerable cost savings and achieve greater diversification of their pooled life income funds.

Investment management of a pooled life income fund presents no unique problems, but as with any investment pool, the institution should state clearly the investment objectives. Institutions operating only one pooled income fund usually opt for a balanced fund aimed at moderate income and some growth. Larger institutions may wish to operate more than one life income pool in order to give donors a wider choice of income and growth options; an individual donor's selection of a given option will depend on his charitable objectives for the institution and on the ages of the beneficiaries and their particular financial circumstances.

Charitable Remainder Unitrusts

Under Section 664(d)(2) of the Internal Revenue Code and attendant regulations, there are three variations of the unitrust.

In the "straight" unitrust a donor irrevocably transfers money, securities, or property to a separate trust having a charitable remainderman, with payments to be distributed to named beneficiaries at least annually in an amount equal to a fixed percentage (not less than five percent under the Act) of the net fair market value of the trust assets determined annually. On the death of the last beneficiary, the trust terminates and the assets are distributed to the charitable remainderman. The donor may designate himself and/or other beneficiaries to receive these payments as long as the designated beneficiaries are alive at the time the trust is created and payments are made for their lifetimes or for a term not to exceed twenty years.

The "net income" unitrust is like a straight unitrust except that payments to beneficiaries are limited to the actual income earned by the trust up to, but not exceeding, the fixed percentage stated in the trust agreement.

142

In the "net-plus-makeup" unitrust, payments are limited to ordinary earned income as in the case of the net income unitrust except that payments may exceed the stated percentage up to but not exceeding the amount required to make up any accumulated deficiencies from prior years (years in which the trust earned less than the stated percentage).

The net income and net-plus-makeup unitrusts differ from pre-1969 separately invested life income funds only in that the payout rate stated in the instrument imposes a ceiling on distributions, expressed as a percentage of the fair market value of the trust assets.

The net income unitrust will be used most frequently by older donors seeking maximum income when the institution has no income-oriented pooled fund, and this naturally will dictate the investment strategy. Once the initial investment is made, investment activity in such trusts must be executed with care in order that income payments are not reduced.

The net-plus-makeup option usually will be chosen by younger donors seeking capital appreciation until retirement and maximum income thereafter. The investment strategy therefore will be similar to that for a straight unitrust initially and shift to a net income strategy at a later date. The development office is responsible for informing the investment officer in detail of the donor's objectives in such cases.

The straight unitrust differs from the others in that a stated percentage of the market value of the trust assets must be distributed annually regardless of whether this amount is earned by the trust in the form of interest or dividends. To meet the payout obligation, tax law specifies that the trustee must first pay all ordinary income from the current year or prior years, then pay realized capital gains from the current year or prior years, and finally return principal to the beneficiary, if necessary. Moreover, the payments retain their character in the hands of the beneficiaries and are taxed to them accordingly. Hence the straight unitrust is primarily of interest to donors in high tax brackets who seek maximum appreciation and minimum ordinary income. This dictates an active, closely supervised, growth-oriented investments program.

Administratively, several options are available for the management of unitrusts. The institution can, in effect, run a small "trust department," making individual decisions with respect to the investment of each straight unitrust. This is difficult and costly for a large number of trusts. It may be possible, however, for the institution's investment adviser to prepare a list of a limited number of low-yield, growth-oriented securities in which all straight unitrusts will be invested. These ordinarily will be issues held in the institution's regular portfolio. Such a list should be monitored closely and reviewed regularly.

An institution may elect to have a bank serve as trustee of its unitrusts, in which case the investment vehicle for all but the largest trusts ordinarily will be the bank's growth-oriented common trust fund. Such an arrangement may permit an institution to accept smaller straight unitrusts than it could afford to accept if it retained direct investment responsibility.

An institution also may elect to invest its straight unitrusts in a minimum number of growth-oriented mutual funds.

Charitable Remainder Annuity Trusts

An annuity trust is defined in Section 664(d)(1) of the Internal Revenue Code as one created by a donor irrevocably transferring money or securities for the benefit of a charitable organization in exchange for a fixed dollar amount (at least five percent of the initial fair market value of the transferred property) to be paid at least annually to a designated beneficiary or beneficiaries for their lifetimes or for a fixed term not to exceed twenty years. At the death of the donor or the last surviving beneficiary, the trust terminates and the assets of the annuity trust are transferred to the charitable organization for which the trust was created.

Except that the amount of the annual payment is fixed at the outset, the annuity trust is essentially similar to a unitrust; the same "tiered" payout rules applies to it and straight unitrusts. Because of the fixed annual payment, the donor has interest in investment strategy only to the extent that (1) it affects the character of the payments and (2) the trustee pursues a strategy that, at a minimum, preserves sufficient assets to make the required payments for the life of the beneficiary.

It follows that the investment strategy for such a trust should be growth-oriented.

RESTRICTIONS ON USE OF ENDOWMENT EARNINGS

In accounting records and financial reports, funds in the endowment and similar funds group also should be classified according to any limitations placed on use of their earnings.[4] Earnings should be classified in the accounting records as unrestricted if no limitations are imposed by the donor and restricted if limitations are imposed by the donor. If the governing board, rather than a donor, establishes limitations on use of the earnings from any funds in this group, the term "designated" should be applied to such funds. "Designated" can refer only to unrestricted funds.

All endowment funds therefore should be classified according to limitations on (1) expenditure of principal and (2) use of earnings from the investment of the funds. For example, if a donor specifies that the principal must be retained but makes no stipulations concerning use of the earnings, the fund is an unrestricted endowment fund. If the donor specifies that the earnings from the fund be used for a certain instructional department or other identified purpose, the fund is a restricted endowment fund. If the governing board decides to use the earnings from an unrestricted endowment fund for a specific purpose, that fund becomes a designated endowment fund. The same situations may exist with respect to use of earnings from term endowment funds, which also may be classified as unrestricted, restricted, or designated term endowment funds.

If a donor makes a gift to an institution, specifying only that it be used for a specific institutional purpose and not stipulating that the assets of the fund be maintained in perpetuity or for a period of time, and if the governing board elects to invest the fund and expend only the earnings for the purpose stipulated by the donor, the fund becomes a restricted quasi-endowment fund. Other funds in this category may be classified as unrestricted or designated quasi-endowment funds,

depending on board action on use of earnings from the investments of such funds.

CY PRES PROCEDURE

In some instances a donor may, by the terms of his gift, have so limited either the purposes for which an endowment fund may be used or the manner in which it may be invested as to severely limit the value of the fund to the institution. In such cases it is often undesirable, impractical, and sometimes impossible for the institution to continue to comply with the donor's wishes. To gain relief from impractical restrictions, the institution may bring a *cy pres* action in an appropriate court, seeking to depart from the original terms to the extent necessary to make the fund useful while adhering, as nearly as possible, to the donor's original intent.

Cy pres has not been a satisfactory answer and is applied reluctantly in some states. Therefore, the model Uniform Act provides a statutory procedure for the release of restrictions with the consent of the donor. If the donor is deceased, unable to consent, or cannot be identified, the appropriate court may, upon application of the governing board, release a limitation shown to be obsolete, inappropriate, or impractical.

DONOR RELATIONSHIPS

Institutions should endeavor, when possible, to discuss terms of proposed gifts and bequests with potential donors. Conferences will help donors recognize the wisdom of making wholly unrestricted gifts—some of which may be treated as quasi-endowment funds—or of establishing term endowment funds, rather than funds for limited purposes that must be maintained in perpetuity. When a donor is reminded that restrictions may make achievement of his purpose difficult and administration of his fund impractical or impossible, he often is willing to grant broad latitude not only in the use of the fund and its earnings, but also in the manner in which it is invested. Most donors recognize that a fund causing administrative

---

[4]In this and subsequent sections, use of the term "income" to describe the amount allotted on a regular, periodic basis by the institution for current expenditure has been avoided, because many institutions have adopted "total return" spending formulas under which they may expend not only yield ("income" in the traditional trust law sense) but also a prudent portion of appreciation. Therefore, the neutral term "earnings" is more appropriate to this discussion.

problems ultimately is a poor memorial to their generosity.

A representative of the institution also should review gift instruments in draft form to suggest changes in terms or wording that will help the institution comply with the donor's wishes. While most gifts to institutions are motivated by charitable considerations, tax and legal considerations are also important. It is essential, however, that representatives of the institution avoid acts or statements that might be construed as tax or legal advice. The donor should refer such matters to his own counsel or financial adviser.

POLICIES FOR ADMINISTRATION OF ENDOWMENT AND SIMILAR FUNDS

Every institution should establish policies to insure compliance with all conditions, restrictions, and designations imposed by donors and the governing board on use of funds and their earnings. The chief accounting officer (usually the controller) and the independent auditors should periodically examine administrative policies and practices. Such examination should be supplemented from time to time with a review by legal counsel.

Assets of endowment funds must not be hypothecated or pledged for any purpose. Although quasi-endowment funds can be used for any purpose, true endowment funds should not be invested in property of the institution, whether income-producing or not.

Administration of endowment and similar funds requires maintenance of a register of all such funds. The register should include such information as (1) names of the donor and members of his family, with brief biographical comments, (2) amount and date of donation, (3) identification of the type of fund, (4) designations of, or restrictions on, use of the fund or its earnings, (5) identification of the source of such limitations (donor, grantor, or governing board), (6) limitations on investments, and (7) reference to formal acceptance and other actions by the governing board.

While such a register is a useful administrative tool, its limitations should be recognized. It may present terms and restrictions in summary form,

when in fact such terms and restrictions may have been developed through correspondence with a donor over a period of many years. It is therefore essential that an institution maintain complete files of all original gift instruments and related correspondence, as such documents provide an authoritative basis for resolving difficult interpretations.[5] The administrative officer and others responsible for fund raising must insure that information essential to the administration of an endowment fund is in writing at the time of donation of the original gift.

The institution's organizational units designated as recipients of revenue from restricted endowment, term endowment, and quasi-endowment funds should be informed of the amount of expendable revenue available for their use.

ADMINISTRATION OF ASSETS OF ENDOWMENT AND SIMILAR FUNDS

To the extent legally possible, colleges and universities may find it advantageous to pool investments of endowment and similar funds. An investment pool permits broad diversification with attendant protection of principal and relative stability of revenue. In addition, it permits economies in administration and accounting.

Even though assets are invested as a pool, the identity of separate funds must be maintained. Individual accounts must be kept, usually in subsidiary records, for the principal of each fund in the investment pool. This is particularly important if the pool is administered on a total return basis in conformity with the model Uniform Act or other applicable state law. While the market value of assets of the pool may exceed the aggregate historic dollar value of the funds invested, the value of the proportionate share of the pool's assets assigned to a particular fund may be greater or less than the historic dollar value of that fund. If the value of the fund's share of the assets is less than its historic dollar value, then only the yield may be utilized.

A consolidated pool is desirable for investment of endowment, term endowment, and quasi-endowment funds. It is preferable to have sep-

---

[5]As the term is used in the model Uniform Act, "gift instrument" means a will, deed, grant, conveyance, agreement, memorandum, writing, or other governing document (including the terms of any institutional solicitations from which an institutional fund resulted) under which property is transferred to or held by an institution as an institutional fund.

arate investment pools for funds such as life income and annuity funds, which have objectives and characteristics different from endowment and similar funds.

If an institution adopts a total return investment policy for its pooled endowment and similar funds, life income funds *must* be invested in a separate pool because of requirements of the Tax Reform Act of 1969. Institutions not using the total return method may continue to invest life income funds in a pool with other institutional funds as long as adequate accounting records are maintained. However, any institution with a significant number of life income funds should establish one or more separate life income pools to facilitate compliance with the stringent operating rules established by the Act.

The terms of some gift instruments may prohibit pooling or commingling of assets. Legal interpretation of complex language in gift instruments is often necessary, but generally the requirement that a fund be "held separate" is construed as meaning only that the fund balance be separately identified at all times and not that the assets of the fund be separately invested. Language to the effect that the fund be "invested separately" or that "its assets shall not be commingled" requires that the fund be separately invested. When it is possible to guide a donor in drafting a gift document, the benefits to the fund and to the institution of pooling investments should be explained and the donor's consent sought for participation in the pool.

Separate investment sometimes may be necessary because of special provisions in the gift instrument or because of the nature of the gift property. For example, a donor may require retention of a particular investment, limit investments of the fund to certain types of securities or other property, or contribute assets that are unmarketable (restricted stock), not income-producing, hard to value, or uncommonly risky. These characteristics might disqualify the gift property as a proper investment of an endowment pool. The only solution is to establish a separately invested fund in the donor's name. Then his fund alone will suffer the consequences of any change or loss in value occurring because of the nature of the gift property. If the character of the asset

changes, as when restrictions on the sale of securities are removed, the fund then may be invested in a pool.

Certain life income gift options available to donors since the passage of the Tax Reform Act of 1969 also require separate investment. These are discussed in the chapter "Investment Management."

OPERATING INVESTMENT POOLS

The operation of an investment pool necessitates procedures permitting equitable distribution of earnings and assignment of market values of the individual funds invested in the pool.

Investment earnings are distributed to the various participating funds on the basis of the assignment to each fund of a number of units calculated on the market value of the assets of the pool at the time of entry of each fund into the pool. This procedure is known as the "market value" or "unit" method of accounting for investment pools. Under this method, when an investment pool is inaugurated, or when a change is made from the historic dollar value to the market value method, an arbitrary value, perhaps $100, is assigned to a share or unit. Each institutional fund then is considered to have the number of units directly proportional to its historic dollar value at the time the market value method is inaugurated. For example, if $100 is assigned for each unit, a fund of $10,000 has 100 shares.

Thereafter, the pooled assets are valued at specific intervals, usually monthly or quarterly, and a new unit value is determined by dividing the new total market value by the total number of units. This new unit value is used to determine the number of units assigned to, or "purchased" by, a new fund as it enters the pool. The new unit value also is used in calculating the value of a fund that may be withdrawn from the pool. For example, the market value of assets of an investment pool having a total of 100,000 units may be $15 million at a given monthly or quarterly valuation date; the value of each unit, therefore, would be $150 ($15 million divided by 100,000 units). A new fund of $30,000 entering the pool on that date would be assigned 200 units ($30,000 divided by $150). Also, a fund holding 300 units being withdrawn from the pool would have a value of $45,000 (300 units multiplied by $150).

In making distributions from the pool, the total investment earnings are divided by the average number of units held by all funds participating in the pool during the year or period in order to determine the distribution per share. Earnings are distributed at this rate on the basis of the number of units held by each fund, with suitable adjustments made for units held for less than a full year or period.

Either of two procedures may be followed in admitting funds to or withdrawing funds from the pool. One is to admit funds to or remove them from the pool only on valuation dates. The other method is to admit or remove them at any time, the valuation of units being that of the latest valuation date. (Under provisions of the Tax Reform Act of 1969, this method cannot be used for pooled life income funds.) If the latter method is employed, unit values should be determined with sufficient frequency to avoid inequities resulting from undue variations in unit market value.

An account for realized gains and losses on investment transactions usually is established for each investment pool. This account is charged or credited for unit valuation adjustments upon withdrawal of participating funds from the pool. Upon withdrawal, a fund receives assets equal in value to the market value of the units it held in the pool at the withdrawal date or the last valuation date. The difference between the historic dollar value upon entry and the withdrawal value represents a portion of the aggregate of realized gains and losses and unrealized appreciation of the portfolio. Accordingly, upon withdrawal of a fund, the difference is charged to the realized gains and losses account as an appropriate disposition of the adjustment. If the aggregate of unit adjustments is material in relation to undistributed realized gains and losses, a separate account could be established and appropriate disclosure made in the balance sheet.

The realized gains and losses account is not assigned shares in the investment pool, and no revenue is distributed to it. Thus, the revenue otherwise allocated to the account is distributed to each of the funds participating in the pool in proportion to the number of units held by each fund.

An institution may distribute gains and losses annually to each fund in the pool. However, most institutions do not regard the additional work involved as justified.

Realized gains and losses on separately invested funds should be distributed directly to the funds; thus, the fund balance changes each time an investment is sold and a gain or loss is realized.

In the past, many colleges and universities followed the historic dollar value method of distributing revenue. When there was little or no change in the valuation of assets held, this method equitably distributed investment revenue. However, because equity securities and other assets that fluctuate in value are of increasing importance to investment pools, the market value method provides a more equitable distribution of revenue and realized and unrealized gains and losses to each fund. The historic dollar value method is no longer considered acceptable. As a collateral advantage, fluctuations in unit value of the pool provide a useful measure of performance of the investment pool, undistorted by additions or withdrawals of funds.

REVENUE STABILIZATION RESERVES

To minimize the impact of year-to-year fluctuations in the amount of current revenue available from an investment pool, many institutions have established revenue stabilization reserves by allocating current investment revenue. Historically, two methods have been followed in establishing such reserves.

Under one method, a portion of the total revenue from the investment pool is not allocated to the participating funds, but is set aside in a stabilization reserve; the balance of investment pool revenue is distributed to the participating funds as described in the preceding section. According to the American Institute of Certified Public Accountants, this method is not in accordance with generally accepted accounting principles.[6] Institutions having such reserves should dispose of any balances under the guidance of their independent auditors.

Under the other method, all earnings from the pool are distributed to the participating funds as described in the preceding section. The amount

---

[6]*Audits of Colleges and Universities*, New York, American Institute of Certified Public Accountants, 1973.

applicable to the unrestricted endowment funds is reported in full as unrestricted current funds revenue under a title such as Endowment Earnings, and the amount set aside for the stabilization reserve is shown in the same statement as a Transfer to Unrestricted Current Funds Balance—Allocated. Under this method, the reserve relates only to earnings from the unrestricted endowment funds and is reflected in the balance sheet as a separately listed equity of Unrestricted Current Funds Balance—Allocated. Amounts not spent in restricted fund accounts remain as balances to be carried forward to the next period.

This method is acceptable to the Institute and may be used by any institution in establishing such a reserve. The need for and size of the reserve is determined by each institution and should relate to institutional needs.

Investment Management

INVESTMENT management objectives and policies vary markedly. The principles that guide institutions of higher education differ from those of a bank, insurance company, foundation, pension fund, or mutual fund. The differences stem primarily from the basic characteristics of a college or university: that it is perpetual, is exempt from income and capital gains taxation, and needs both current income and indefinite future protection of its purchasing power.

Investment management for an educational institution involves endowment, term endowment, and quasi-endowment funds (the last also may be referred to as funds functioning as endowment). Normally, these funds are invested for relatively long periods to provide recurring income for institutional operating purposes. Life income and annuity funds also may be administered on a similar basis.

In addition, many institutions have current funds not needed immediately for operating purposes and other funds earmarked for use as needed for plant construction or other capital improvements. These funds are invested for relatively short periods for maximum current return and safety of principal, combined with sufficient liquidity to permit cash withdrawals for expenditures.

Some institutions manage the investment of employee pension funds, which require investment policies that may differ from those applicable to other institutional funds.

ORGANIZATION FOR INVESTMENT MANAGEMENT

Whatever the size of an institution's endowment, it is essential that the investment funds have continuous, professional supervision. Each institution should select the form of management organization best suited to its investment objectives and the size of its portfolio. The ultimate responsibility for managing an institution's investments rests with the governing board. This responsibility usually is delegated to an investment committee, which may be separate from a finance committee.

The investment committee should be small and composed of members of the governing board with knowledge of investments and related matters. Typically, this committee is a policy-making body and does not directly manage the institution's investments by attempting to select securities for the portfolio. The day-to-day management should be clearly and fully delegated to one or more professional portfolio managers, subject to investment guidelines and reporting requirements mentioned later in this chapter.

Some institutions may have a board member willing to manage the portfolio and serve as chairman of the investment committee. There are a number of risks in such an arrangement, however. Competent talent rarely is available on a volunteer and continuous basis; a possible conflict of interest may exist; and if investment performance proves to be unacceptable, it may be difficult to dissolve the arrangement.

It is important to consult legal counsel concerning delegation of investment responsibility to insure that such delegation is in conformity with state laws and institutional bylaws. In most cases it is possible for the governing board to delegate investment responsibility to an investment committee. In turn the investment committee may delegate to an officer of the corporation the discretionary authority to buy and to sell.

Institutions with sufficiently large endowments can achieve continuous supervision by hiring a full-time investment manager and supporting professional staff. Under this arrangement the investment committee should choose the manager and define investment objectives. Thereafter the com-

149

mittee should confine its work to reviewing policies and procedures and monitoring and evaluating performance, with the selection of individual investments left to the manager.

A common approach is to retain one or more outside investment management organizations to manage the portfolio. An arrangement using outside management has the advantages of minimizing interference, simplifying the problems of measuring results objectively, and changing managers. The role of the investment committee under this arrangement is similar to the one described above —choosing the adviser(s), defining policies and procedures, and judging results.

Individual managers and firms often have areas of special expertise. In making a sizable commitment to investments in common stocks and bonds, managers should be employed who are well-qualified in these investment media. Use of competent outside management also may extend to real estate and other specialized investments.

If an institution uses an outside investment manager, however, the extent of the power to delegate is not entirely clear. (This subject is discussed in the chapter "Administration of Endowment Funds, Quasi-Endowment Funds, and Other Similar Funds.") Regular reports to the investment committee concerning transactions and holdings as well as the power to terminate the agreement at any time are essential means of committee control. A common practice, even with an outside manager, is to delegate the discretionary power to buy and sell while retaining the investment committee's power to take compensating action for any transaction. In such a situation securities purchased would have to be sold or securities sold would have to be repurchased. This practice requires prompt reporting of transactions.

Institutions with small endowments ($10 million or less) will have a more limited choice of managers. They also may wish to choose less specialized firms. There are a number of mutual funds, some with no sales commission and others managed by well-established investment advisory companies, through which small portfolios can be managed with care and competence. The nonprofit investment organization created specifically to manage institutional endowment funds, the Common Fund for Nonprofit Organizations, offers small endowments the benefits of a pooled investment fund with multiple managers.

INVESTMENT POLICIES AND OBJECTIVES

Recommendations concerning investment policies are usually the responsibility of the investment committee, but the governing board should confirm these policies. The committee should recommend investment policies expected to provide maximum investment returns, within acceptable limits of risk and consistent with the purposes of the funds. The definition of maximum investment return for a given fund will depend on the investment objective of that fund, such as maximization of yield or growth. In establishing policy and in making specific investment decisions that have not been delegated, an investment committee should operate on the basis of a majority of its members.

Traditionally, the investment objective of most educational institutions has been the preservation of principal and the production of dividend and interest income. More recently, a broadened concept of return on investments has developed, which assumes that changes in market values of portfolio securities are also a part of the return on assets.

This concept, known as "total return"—the sum of net realized and unrealized appreciation or shrinkage in portfolio value plus yield (dividend and interest income)—is an accepted measure of investment results. The yield from dividend and interest payments on securities invested for total return is not the primary consideration.

Combined with an investment objective in terms of total return, there usually is a financial management and budgeting policy which recognizes that inflation is a consideration in preserving principal and that current expenditures must favor neither present nor future financial requirements. The choice between present and future must be made in the process of financial planning and budget making, and reflected in investment decisions.

Investment achievements in equities have resulted in increased emphasis on them—so much so that the average endowment portfolio is invested more heavily in equities than in fixed-income securities. This emphasis has created a dilemma for some governing boards and administrators. To what extent can an institution forgo current income for the benefit of greater income in the future? Many institutions have converted some growth equities into higher-yield equities to increase current income. This practice no longer can be considered the only or best investment strategy. The alternative to this strategy is the total return concept.

An institution should have as its long-term investment goal the striking of a reasonable balance between meeting present needs and providing for future needs. Achievement of this long-term goal calls for a policy of maximum investment productivity at an acceptable level of risk. Investing for total return ordinarily involves a portfolio containing both equities and fixed-income obligations, with the former, as noted above, usually predominating. Under certain conditions investing for total return might involve a portfolio 100 percent in equities, but under other conditions might involve a portfolio 100 percent in fixed-income obligations. Usually, however, there will be a mixture of the two.

Total return has a second, distinct aspect different from its investment aspect. This is determination of the "spending rate," the proportion of total return that may prudently be utilized by an institution for current operating purposes. Systematic logic is needed to determine the amount of appreciation to be used for current needs, and spending rules should be developed that reflect a consistent, prudent, and deliberate balance between meeting current needs and reinvesting to meet future needs. A change in investment strategy to obtain higher total return generally means lower current investment yield. If an institution adopts total return, it normally is faced with lower yield and therefore might need to use appreciation. A reasonable objective would be to insure, given the total return formula, that the real value of endowment funds is not depleted.

Any institution adopting total return as a policy requires the approval of legal counsel and formal approval by its governing board. The institution's funds should be classified with endowment funds separate from quasi-endowment funds. Usually an institution should undertake a careful re-examination of all endowment funds received in the past to identify those funds with no restraint on expenditure of appreciation.

When legal counsel is consulted, it should be with the knowledge that there are a growing number of legal opinions which take the position that appreciation, realized or unrealized, is available for expenditure unless the instrument of gift or bequest specifically prohibits the spending of appreciation. The model Uniform Management of Institutional Funds Act (discussed in the chapter "Administration of Endowment Funds, Quasi-Endowment Funds, and Other Similar Funds") provides that the governing board may use for expenditure for current needs, for purposes for which an endowment fund is established, so much of the net appreciation, realized and unrealized, of the assets of the fund over its historic dollar value (recorded value) as is prudent. Each institution through its governing board should satisfy itself that the spending of appreciation of endowment funds under its total return policy meets the vital test of prudence. A conceivable test of prudence might be the objective of maintaining the real purchasing power of the endowment. Quasi-endowment funds by definition may be withdrawn from an investment pool at any time at their market value and totally expended by the governing board of the institution at its discretion.

Institutions maintaining a balanced fund or holding substantial bonds and other fixed-income securities also may operate on a total return basis. In such cases, the institution still should spend only a prudent part of the total return. For example, if the yield alone is eight percent, the governing board must determine whether it would be prudent to spend the total amount or whether a portion of the interest is, in effect, compensation for inflation.

Whether a college or university adopts the long-term objective of seeking maximum total return as well as a policy of spending part of the appreciation, objectives must be clearly stated, approved by the governing board or its authorized committee, and communicated to its investment manager. In addition to the concept, the details of a total return plan must be approved, such as valuation basis and date for allocation of appreciation. Recognizing that the economy and stock market move in cycles, investment objectives should be oriented primarily to long-term investment opportunities with characteristics that enable the institution to attain at least the average total return of the market as measured by corporate earnings and appropriate market indexes.

THE INVESTMENT MANAGER

Selecting an investment manager may be the most significant action taken by the investment committee. An important criterion in selection should be the record of performance of the firm and particularly its individual staff members who will manage the account over several years. Each firm under consideration should provide information on the objectives of all accounts managed, and performance should be measured against these objectives. It is necessary to understand the philosophy, style, and method of operation of any firm under consideration. In addition to the proposed fee, specific aspects of an investment management organization that should be reviewed include:

1. Workload: the number and type of accounts and the degree to which the manager's time is spent in nonportfolio activities such as administration and marketing.

2. Organization: the depth, experience, and retention of key persons; for example, the number of persons, their backgrounds, and length of service.

3. Investment philosophy and style: the procedures used in making portfolio decisions, the criteria for selecting investments, the degree of concentration or diversification in a typical portfolio, the types of companies and industries favored, the degree of risk-taking, the expected performance during market rises and declines, and the changes in key strategies and methods of operation during recent periods.

4. Research: the quality and quantity of research and the ability to relate research to portfolio management.

5. Trading: the ability to execute purchase and sale orders and the use of commissions.

6. Control: the supervision of portfolio managers and their results, and adherence to stated objectives and company policy on strategy.

7. Communication: the frequency and manner of reporting and past success at retaining accounts.

It is impossible to select the one best manager, and any manager will have varying performance relative to the market. The investment committee should identify a group of managers whose investment objectives generally match those of the institution, select one or more, then develop with the manager the best overall policy to meet the institution's needs.

The investment committee should rely on the manager primarily for recommendations of portfolio strategy to fit the current investment environment and for selection of individual investments. The manager's responsibilities for supervising the portfolio include recommendations for changes or modifications in investment policy and surveillance of investments in the portfolio through review of information developed internally and from other sources such as investment bankers, brokers, and advisory services.

The investment manager, whether an employee of the institution or an outside firm, should meet regularly with the investment committee. Quarterly meetings usually should be considered the minimum. The investment manager should provide the committee with written reports, preferably monthly but at least quarterly, showing cost and market values as well as performance measurement. Where discretionary authority cannot be provided, or is not granted, procedures must be established to permit prompt action between meetings. These procedures may call for frequent contact between the manager and chairman of the committee and, in some circumstances, other committee members as well.

The investment authority granted by the governing board to the manager should be as broad as legally possible to provide the maximum amount of discretion in investment choices. The more restrictions placed on management, the less chance there is to take prompt action on timely investment opportunities. If it is believed necessary to have prior approval of all investment actions, the policy for interim action may include authority to change investments between meetings, provided the change is approved by the chairman or a specified number of committee members when no change in investment policy is involved.

Matters of policy should be discussed at meetings of the investment committee and the committee should explore and define with the manager and the chief financial officer the best policies and procedures to attain desired objectives. The committee should evaluate the degree to which policy is being followed and the effectiveness of that policy, as well as review results of investment decisions. Overall performance of the equities segment of the portfolio should be compared with several of the unmanaged indexes. The reasons for any pronounced deviation from the unmanaged indexes and investment objectives should be analyzed with the manager. The performance of managers should be evaluated on a three- to five-year moving average, unless it becomes obvious sooner that investment performance is unacceptable.

CUSTODIAL AND SAFEKEEPING SERVICES

A custodial or safekeeping arrangement with a bank or trust company can be advantageous and reduce risk and liability of trustees. Other services performed by a custodian may be preparation of up-to-date portfolio appraisals, timely exercise or sale of stock rights, presentation of called bonds for payment, and conversion or sale of convertible securities. Service also can be extended to include use of the custodian's nominee name. A nominee is an individual or a partnership established for the limited purpose of facilitating the transferability of record ownership of securities without regard to beneficial ownership or interest. This device facilitates compliance with the requirements of the organized securities markets. The delivery of securities endorsed by a corporation is not acceptable.

Arrangements for custodial services should be specified by written agreement. They may include safekeeping, receipt and delivery of securities, collection of interest coupons and dividends, voting of proxies (if desired), notification of calls and maturities of bonds, information about issuance of subscription rights and stock dividends, interest defaults, plans for recapitalization, reorganizations, formation of protection committees, and other information requiring institutional action. Also, the custodian statements should include classification of securities holdings, amounts of interest and dividends received, and amortization schedules, where applicable.

Under custodial arrangements, receipts and deliveries of securities may be from or to brokers against payments charged or credited to a designated bank account or received or remitted by check.

Costs of investment management include direct expenses such as costs of supervision of securities, investments in real estate, and other types of investments, plus the cost of custodial arrangements. Indirect costs also may be included. Each fund may bear its proportionate share or an institution may choose to accept such costs as part of general institutional expense.

The arrangement for buying and selling investments varies with the nature of the portfolio and form of management organization. When an institution has its own internal investment organization, the full-time manager employed by the institution should be responsible for executions. When an independent adviser is employed—whether a bank, trust company, or investment management firm—it should have its own trading department, with persons whose principal responsibilities are executing transactions, checking markets, and identifying prospective sellers or purchasers of particular securities. This arrangement provides for the most advantageous purchases and sales.

It is important to select investment banking and brokerage firms that execute orders promptly and efficiently; that have research divisions capable of providing investment information; that are active in underwriting new issues or in managing private placement; that make a market for, or deal in, certain securities; and that provide investment performance measurement service.

Even though the investment management firm executes transactions, the allocation of the institution's business should be determined by the manager in consultation with the institution. Care should be exercised to avoid conflicts of interest. It is not only appropriate but good practice to require allocation of commissions to those investment brokerage firms providing services. It is also good practice to review quarterly the allocation of brokerage commissions paid by the fund, including identification of individuals in the brokerage firms and reasons for using them.

INVESTMENT GUIDELINES

After an institution's investment objectives have been determined, the investment committee must translate the objectives into policy. Policy ordinarily will evolve over a period of time, often as the result of a series of decisions on specific investments. The initial policy action is a governing board resolution pertaining to purchases and sales of securities. As previously discussed, this action should authorize as full and complete delegation and discretion as is acceptable to legal counsel and the governing board.

Following this, it is appropriate to develop administrative guidelines for the manager, including the frequency of and recipients for reports of transactions (for example, monthly reports to the investment committee and custodian), other reporting requirements, investment performance measurement and evaluation techniques by which managers' results will be compared, and the expected frequency of meetings.

Common stock guidelines may include limits on the size and number of individual investments. Some institutions may wish to establish for any single investment a maximum percentage of the total portfolio and a maximum and minimum dollar amount to safeguard against overconcentration or a tendency to hold too many different issues. Percentage limits may be set for total equity positions in any one industry or group classification, over-the-counter securities, securities in foreign issues, and outstanding shares of any one company. A certain percentage may be invested in companies with growth potential.

For bonds, guidelines may include percentage limits on the total issues in any one industry or group, on securities of any one issuer, and on the amount of private placements. Limitations also should be set on the level of quality ratings of bonds. Consideration may be given to the distribution of maturities of investments, including commercial paper and other short-term securities. In establishing commitment limits for fixed-income investments, different issues of the same debtor properly may be classified together. These guidelines should be flexible and reviewed periodically.

The types of investments commonly held by educational institutions include bonds, debentures, notes, preferred stocks, convertible securities, common stocks, warrants, mutual fund shares, real estate, leasebacks, and mortgages. The list of investments should be reviewed continually. An unusually large appreciation in the value of a particular holding should not necessarily dictate a reduction in the investment. The size of a company, nature of its business, and quality of its management are relevant factors to be considered. Prompt sale of securities not accomplishing investment objectives should be encouraged.

There exists a basic tendency toward too many different holdings because of the volume of gifts and bequests received in the form of securities and the desire of some donors to have their gifts of securities retained. A common policy is to require that all securities received by gift or bequest be disposed of as promptly as possible unless prohibited by terms of the gift or bequest and unless a particular security is already held in the portfolio or is under consideration as an addition to the portfolio in the near future.

Diversification of investments is essential for protection against unforeseeable trends in the economy and the securities markets, ownership of securities not measuring up to expectations, and investment in enterprises involving greater than normal risk.

Investments in a portfolio should be diversified by number and variety of securities. Decisions on both aspects will depend on investment objectives. Proportions of the debt and equity holdings should not be defined too rigidly. Special factors affecting decisions on proportions include type and quality of fixed-income securities, trend of interest rates, future growth and present value of equities, income, availability of particular investments at a given time, and marketability.

The investment manager should be free to set an investment strategy within the limits established. During different periods of economic and market cycles, it may be preferable to make substantial shifts in securities holdings. While it may or may not be considered appropriate to hold certain types of securities, it is inappropriate to have rules that are too rigid.

The investment committee should monitor actions taken by the manager to implement investment strategy and insure that policy changes are not undertaken without prior approval.

SHORT-TERM INVESTING

Money is a commodity that should be used as carefully as any other asset of an institution. The peaks and valleys in the cash receipt and disbursement patterns create opportunities for short-term investing. The consolidation of bank accounts and similar use of excess balances, including some of the float (value of checks outstanding), can produce additional income. Cash flow patterns for individual institutions should be maintained and a daily cash report utilized in conjunction with a cash forecast of three to six months. All funds available for short-term investing may be pooled unless circumstances or legal requirements dictate otherwise. Generally there are three types of funds in a pool—funds to be spent in current operations, funds earmarked for specific project payments such as construction, and temporary investment of endowment funds. While specific project funds are often available for longer periods, flexibility and timing are important in investment considerations. Liquidity and limited exposure to price fluctuation are also of primary importance.

Because of the nature of short-term investing, the chief financial officer of the institution often is assigned the responsibility for making short-term investments. Authority for such investing should be defined and delegated by the investment committee of the governing board. In order to maximize return, the manager of endowment fund investments should be aware of and utilize, if appropriate, short-term investment activities whether or not under his purview.

The most common investment media for short-term investing are commercial paper notes, U.S. treasury bills, banker's acceptances, certificates of deposit, and short-term bonds of U.S. government agencies. Risk and reward are inseparable in any investment decision. Quality, liquidity, and safety must be considered in all short-term investments. Such investments should be made with maturities scheduled or repurchase agreements sufficient to meet cash needs. It is generally worthwhile to invest for any period in any amount when return exceeds the cost of staff effort.

LENDING SECURITIES

To enhance earnings, a substantial number of colleges and universities lend securities they own to broker-dealers. A security loan is a transaction in which the owner of securities gives up physical possession of certificates to the borrower and in return receives cash or other collateral equal to the full current market value of the securities. While continuing to receive the equivalent income from the securities, the lender also has the unrestricted use of collateral, representing the full value of the securities for the period they are on loan.

Several firms make a specialty of servicing large portfolio accounts by generating security loan arrangements. Although the practice of securities lending is well-established, any institution contemplating participation should first learn all of the procedures, including protective controls. In contracting for security loans, care should be exercised to evaluate the financial stability of the broker-dealers involved.

MEASURING INVESTMENT RESULTS

An important responsibility of the governing board is to insure that endowment and other funds of the institution are invested to produce stated objectives. Productivity depends on many factors, such as the degree of volatility and risk the trustees are prepared to accept in the market value of investments, restrictions imposed on investments by donors, and the relative emphasis on current income versus long-term growth. Whatever criteria are used to judge the return on investments, it is essential that the rate of return be properly measured and that timely reports be made to the trustees.

The historic dollar value accounting method does not provide the information required to compute investment returns in a manner that permits accurate analysis of investment results. The most practical method of providing the required information is use of a market value, unit method of accounting. For portfolios in an institution's pool, the same computations can be made on worksheets, purely for performance measurement purposes.

The rate of return on investments has two components, yield and market value change. Rate of yield is simply the income earned on investments from dividends, interest, and net rental income for the period, stated as a percentage of the fund's market value during the period. The market value change is the net increase or decrease in market value over a designated period, expressed as a percentage of the beginning market value. The combination of yield and market value change is the total return on the fund. It is important that both components of total return be computed and reported to the trustees at regular intervals.

Significant cash flows into or out of invested funds can seriously distort the rate of return earned on the total fund. Use of a unit method of accounting makes it possible to compute a rate of return that eliminates the effect of cash flows. The resulting "time-weighted" rate of return, as opposed to the "dollar-weighted" result, is the appropriate measure of results achieved by the fund's investment manager. In averaging rates of return over successive periods, arithmetic averages (adding the rates of return and dividing by the number of periods) should be avoided. The geometric average of rates of return is the best measure of how profitably the portfolio has been managed.

Many institutions are interested in comparing their investment results with the rate of return achieved on widely quoted indexes, such as the Standard & Poor's 500-Stock Index or the Dow Jones Industrial Average. In making such comparisons, it should be noted that these are common stock indexes, whereas most institutions have significant holdings of fixed-income securities. Furthermore, because of volume and price weighting, these indexes are not fully representative of the movement of the larger market of stocks. The unit values published each quarter by the Common Fund also provide a basis for comparison. There are several stock brokerage firms offering performance measurement services. Dartmouth College, through a project sponsored by the NACUBO Investments Committee, also will compute rates of return from unit value figures submitted by an institution and supply comparative performance results. These comparisons do not take into account variations in investment objectives or differences in portfolio composition.

In computing rates of return for the purpose of evaluating the quality of investment management, it is also important to exclude real estate not currently appraised and unmanaged investments, or those not under the control of the investment manager. Unmanaged investments include such items as unregistered or "letter" stock, gifts of securities that the donors require to be held in the portfolio as a condition of the gift, or funds invested in institutional buildings. It may be useful for other reasons to report earnings on all investments, including such items, but they should not be included for the purpose of evaluating investment management.

SOCIAL RESPONSIBILITY IN INVESTMENT MANAGEMENT

Although the basic objective of college or university trustees in managing endowment and other funds is to produce maximum long-term investment return without assuming inappropriate risks, trustees should be aware that many institutions also are concerned about the social responsibility of corporations in which they invest. The addition of social and political considerations to economic and market considerations makes the optimum choice of investments a more complex problem.

If a policy statement on investor responsibility is adopted by a governing board, it should include descriptions of the responsibilities of officers and committees and of the decision-making process related to social and political issues in investment decisions. Special committees have been created at some institutions to discuss proxy issues.

Colleges and universities may find it helpful to use the services of organizations whose purpose is to provide impartial, timely, in-depth analysis, without recommendations, of corporate social responsibility.

Budgets and Budgetary Accounting

EDUCATIONAL PROGRAMS, need for support services, and limits of resources all help to determine the institutional budget—an itemized, authorized, and systematic plan of operation, expressed in dollars, for a given period. Development of the budget of a college or university is the concern of the president and senior administrative officers as well as faculty and staff members responsible for carrying out the functions and programs of the institution. Some colleges and universities seek participation from students, usually through recognized and representative student associations.

LONG-RANGE PLANNING

Long-range planning is highly desirable for a college or university. Such planning should begin with a statement of the mission of the institution. A list of institutional objectives should follow the statement of mission, resulting in the programs to be pursued. Such objectives should encompass a period of five to ten years, with planning more detailed in the earlier years and later becoming more general. Once the academic objectives have been established, it is then possible to establish objectives for the support services.

The long-range plans based on established objectives include every significant aspect of the educational program and support services. Changes in curriculum and method of instruction must be considered, as well as changes in support for research and public service. Faculty salaries, workloads, student-faculty ratios, staffing patterns, class size, and use of space must be determined for the present and estimated for the future. The need for support services and the requirements for physical facilities depend on the academic plan, and all must receive adequate attention in the comprehensive long-range plan.

The budgetary process is used to insure the optimum allocation of resources to the academic program, while simultaneously insuring adequate support services. This process requires imagination, insight, and creative effort. The chief business officer is responsible for coordinating or managing the development of cost estimates and a long-range financial plan to support the academic program. This process should be carried out in cooperation with appropriate academic officers. The plan should include estimates of added costs arising from expansion, improvements, and new programs, as well as those for increases in salaries, employee benefits, utilities, and prices of supplies, equipment, and services.

In institutions where there exists an institutional research office, both academic and business officers should participate in the studies produced by this office. Data produced and/or collected by institutional research offices often may be utilized by academic and business officers in budget planning and preparation. Such an office not only accumulates data basic to long-range plans, but also engages in continuing analyses and research that are helpful both in the establishment of objectives and in periodic review and modification of plans when objectives are not being met. For a detailed treatment of long-range planning, refer to the chapter "Institutional Planning."

BUDGETING TECHNIQUES

Formula Budgeting

Formula budgeting is a technique by which the financial needs, or operating requirements, of an educational institution may be determined through the application of a formula. Most formulas are based on enrollment data and/or credit-hour production. The formulas are relatively simple to understand, objective in their application, and reasonably equitable to institutions that offer instruction only.

Some state coordinating boards or other state agencies have adopted a formula approach to budgeting that places all institutions under their control on the same basis and affords comparison to budget requests. These separate institutional budgets then can be consolidated into one overall budget request for an appropriation for higher education. Some of these formulas are more sophisticated than others and are quite accurate in projecting the funding needed for the institutions. However, legislatures often ignore institutions' requests because of other state needs or limited resources, or simply underfund them with the result that, in many cases, institutions receive less money than they need to carry out their plans.

Some state formulas are based on instruction only and therefore do not take into consideration activities of the more complex universities. These formulas make allowance for instruction, but make little or no allowance for organized activities related to instruction, sponsored research programs, and similar functions. In some states the indirect cost reimbursements deriving from sponsored research are included in revenues, but no appropriate offset is made for the related expenditures that the institution incurs. Thus, an institution engaging in sponsored research is penalized for engaging in programs other than instruction. In spite of the shortcomings of less sophisticated formulas, institutions may find them reasonably acceptable if programs are fully funded by state legislatures.

The formula approach may use the projected full-time-equivalent student enrollment and the established student-faculty ratio at each of the various levels of instruction to arrive at the number of full-time-equivalent teaching positions required. Total teaching salaries then are determined by multiplying number of positions by expected average salary. To this amount is added a percentage for other direct teaching expenses, resulting in an estimate of the total direct teaching costs, which is considered the budget base. The formula also must recognize all applicable indirect costs.

Varying percentages are applied to the budget base for administration, general expense, organized activities related to instruction, organized research, public service, library, and maintenance of physical plant. This total is the budget requirement to be funded from tuition and fees and other revenue sources. An example of the formula approach is provided at the end of the chapter.

Formula budgeting determines a dollar allocation for each activity to accomplish its institutional mission. These requirements then are met by estimating revenues to be received that can be applied to educational and general support, with the difference between that revenue and total support required being requested by way of appropriation. To include *all* revenues fails to recognize the differences in institutions and will penalize an institution that manages to increase its revenues from outside sources. Some state formulas do include in their revenues indirect cost reimbursements on grants and contracts. By including such reimbursements, the appropriation request would be reduced by a corresponding amount.

Program Budgeting[1]

Program budgeting is essentially a planning device that ultimately leads to a conventional, departmental budget for operation and control. A number of colleges and universities have been working with program budgeting for several years, and some state coordinating boards have adopted a program budgeting system for determining financial requirements of the institutions under their control. This system also is used for resource allocation by certain states, after funds are obtained. Since program budgeting is designed for long-range planning and budgeting, it usually is developed to cover five- or ten-year periods. Institutional *programs* are the central factor in program budgeting, rather than organizational *units* as in the traditional budget system. The program budget attempts to establish and clarify the resource requirements of these programs and determines the cost of achieving given objectives. It further contributes to the decision-making process by providing an analysis of alternative program decisions in terms of anticipated costs and expected benefits.

[1]Material from *Accounting for Colleges and Universities,* copyright © 1970 by Louisiana State University Press, is adapted with permission.

It should be pointed out that, because of the complexities involved, program budgeting often makes extensive use of computers and computer technology. However, the computer does not reduce the need for the human element in the final decision-making process.

In relating program budgeting to colleges and universities, it is essential to understand the basic concept of the system. Institutional goals should be stated in broadly defined terms. For example, the goals may be expressed in general terms such as instruction, research, and public service. Such statements are not specific enough to permit programs to be formulated and evaluated. Objectives therefore must be defined in terms of "program categories" that are identifiable end products. For example, one of the goals of an institution may be training or study in business-related techniques and principles. Here the end product becomes the degree program in the respective field, such as Bachelor of Business Administration in accounting.

A specific degree, such as the one just named, must be defined in terms of identifiable units generally referred to as "program elements." For a degree, the program elements usually consist of a specified set of courses; however, a degree program may consist of program elements from other than instructional functions — for example, student activities and student health services. A program classification structure (PCS) enables the institution to cut across program lines to obtain costs of a given degree.

The program classification structure is a mechanism that can be employed to do budgeting by the method commonly called PPBS (planning, programming, budgeting system). This type of structure may be illustrated as follows for the bachelor's degree as a product of an institution:

I. Instruction (program)
A. Instruction leading to a bachelor's degree (subprogram)
1. Instruction in department A (program subcategory)
a. Level of instruction by department (program sector)
(1). Courses (program elements)
(a). Personnel costs ⎰ measures of
(b). Supplies ⎱ program elements

2. Instruction in department B
a. Level of instruction by department
(1). Courses
(a). Personnel costs
(b). Supplies
Etc.
II. Academic Support (program)
Etc.
III. Student Services (program)
Etc.
IV. Institutional Support (program)
Etc.

Institutional programs, such as the ones listed above, will have inputs to the cost of a degree. This format will reflect the necessary input by each program area of an institution, thus defining the composition of a degree. It should be noted that end products other than degrees exist for an institution. For example, the composition of actions that lead to development of a new cure for a disease may be an end product for an institution.

Historically, budget making typically was concerned with decremental and incremental costs of continuing the same programs, operations, or functions, or with adding new ones. It generally is assumed that the expenditure base on which the budget-making process begins is correct. Program budgeting, on the other hand, makes no such assumption, but attempts to set out programs and apply analytical tools to measure the cost-benefit/cost-effectiveness before alternative decisions are made.

Program budgeting cuts across conventional department lines and measures the performance of a program in terms of its output. In this manner, program elements that are possible substitutes for others may be given full consideration. Thus, program budgeting introduces a degree of competition designed to achieve greater effectiveness. Effectiveness may be considered as a measure of the extent to which a general program accomplishes its objectives and is related to benefits, which may be considered as the utility to be derived from a given program. This is the cost-benefit/cost-effectiveness as employed in program budgeting.

Another objective of program budgeting is control. Historically, budget control was identified solely with expenditure control. Program budgeting implies monitoring of program achievement as well as control of expenditures.

The final objective of program budgeting involves data and information. The system, if properly designed, will produce certain data that were not previously in evidence. This will enable the institution to make its decisions in terms of total program rather than on a departmental basis, which is possible because the programs relate to end products rather than to the administrative organization or function of the institution. The incremental emphasis of program budgeting becomes more appropriate as a system in view of the increased orientation to interdisciplinary programs. As further study is given to program budgeting, it is likely that wide use will be made of this type of system as an approach to various institutional programs.

Zero-Base Budgeting

The zero-base budgeting technique assumes nothing about prior budgets, but starts from zero each year to build a new budget. This kind of budgeting establishes standard workloads for the respective departments or colleges. If credit-hour production in a given department or college decreases and is expected to continue to decline, fewer instructional personnel, travel allowances, and supplies would be required; thus less money should be budgeted than in the previous period. This is a partial adaptation of program budgeting and forces better management of the institution's resources. While the detail supporting an allocation in this type of budgeting is different, the final budget is prepared in the traditional manner. An alternate approach to zero-base budgeting would be to have each department list the lowest five or ten percent of its priorities.

Obviously, the reductions or additions called for in the zero-base budgeting approach cannot be achieved easily and sometimes not at all. This is so because the institution cannot readily adjust its costs in the organization quickly or easily. It may be extremely difficult to relocate or terminate personnel in a short period of time. Fixed costs that have been financed over a period of several years make budget changes difficult in the short run. Although zero-base budgeting has much to offer from a management point of view, the

inflexibility that college management faces makes its adoption and strict implementation difficult.

THE TRADITIONAL ANNUAL OPERATING BUDGET

While each of the three forms of budgeting mentioned above has its advantages, the traditional budget is the budget for fiscal operation and control. The traditional budget is constructed along organizational lines, with each departmental budget providing for personnel compensation, supplies and expenses, and capital expenditures. This kind of budget can be restructured along program lines with the aid of computers and appropriate software packages. This restructuring, often referred to as a crosswalk, permits management to consider the cost of different programs and possible trade-offs for more effective use of budget funds, while still maintaining the traditional budget system.

The annual budget is coordinated with the long-range institutional plan. In addition, it is specific and detailed and presents the plan to finance the approved academic program and support services for a fiscal year. The annual budget is determined largely by the academic program within the limits of resources available. Within institutional budget guidelines approved by the governing board, individual budgets are developed by department heads, with appropriate contributions by faculty and staff. The president, chief academic officer, and chief business officer all have responsibilities for its development. The governing board is responsible for major policies and for final approval of the comprehensive budget.

The traditional budget in use in the majority of colleges and universities is the incremental budget with a breakdown by functions, such as instruction, research, and library, with detailed expenditure breakdown by object. The current budget base is the starting point; the assumption is made that the budget base is correct and that annual changes are effected by increasing or decreasing appropriate objects as occasion and resources dictate. Some institutions have questioned the validity of the incremental approach and have adopted other approaches, such as zero-base budgeting.

The annual current funds budget should be

prepared and adopted well in advance of the fiscal period and should include all anticipated operating revenues, expenditures, transfers, and allocations. The anticipated revenues and expenditures should be applied to all operations and activities for the educational and general functions and auxiliary enterprises, including anticipated uses of current funds revenues for purposes other than current operations.

Budgets for restricted current funds should be included, even though their timing may not correspond to the fiscal year. The amount of estimated expenditures from restricted funds during the fiscal year should be shown so that total current operations will be disclosed in the annual budget.

Capital asset budgets for construction projects, plant expansion, plant improvement, and other plant fund activities should be prepared, but should not be reflected in the current funds annual budget.

Responsibility of Administrative Officers

The president usually will find it necessary to confer freely and frequently with other administrative officers, especially the chief academic officer and the chief business officer, in developing the operating budget. The president also may establish a budget committee to assist him in developing guidelines for the preparation of the budget. The governing board should be apprised of the president's plan for the new budget, particularly new programs, in broad outline so that general approval can be given prior to beginning the work on drafting the formal budget.

The chief business officer assumes a major role in development of the budget, and supplies financial and statistical data to assist the budget committee in the planning and policy recommendations on the proposed budget. Other administrative officials, such as the chief academic officer, also can be expected to have a major role in budget formulation and resource allocation.

Responsibility of the Governing Board

The governing board must assume ultimate responsibility for the budget. Because the board generally is composed of persons whose primary occupations are outside the field of education, they can devote only part of their time to the affairs of the institution. Consequently, the governing board can best serve by directing its attention to major policies and priorities. The board can effectively discharge its budgetary responsibilities by reviewing and approving general policies that determine the educational and financial programs of the institution.

Policy Decisions

In development of the budget, the president makes and recommends some major policy decisions. These decisions cover such items as salary and wage increases, improvements in certain programs, implementation of new programs, reduction or elimination of existing programs, and other items. Policy decisions are communicated by the president in a budget memorandum to deans, directors, and department heads, and serve to guide them in development of their budgets.

Estimating Current Funds
Revenues and Expenditures

The compilation of estimates of revenues is the responsibility of the business officer. For many of the revenue items, estimates should be based on information supplied by other administrative officials. As an example, anticipated revenues from tuition and fees generally are based on estimated enrollment data prepared by the registrar or director of admissions. These estimates should take into account general economic conditions, trends of enrollment both within the institution and in similar institutions, attrition rates, and demographic and other factors.

The estimate of earnings from investments requires thorough study. The earnings from each item in the portfolio should be projected, giving due consideration to economic trends, dividend records of stocks held, and the effect of any anticipated changes in the portfolio. The investment officer or investment counselor should assist in preparing such estimates.

Estimates of revenues from gifts and unrestricted grants should take into consideration past experience, plans for appeals for funds, and alumni activities.

Because of the significance of sponsored programs, separate estimates should be made of the revenues and expenditures related to such programs. The magnitude of these programs has an important impact on all other operating areas, such as plant space, personnel, and position control. Budgets for sponsored programs should be separately identified within the regular budget and adjusted during the year as new projects are undertaken and others are terminated.

Estimates of revenues from auxiliary enterprises should be based on enrollments and on past experience in the operation of such units. Revenues should be estimated on a gross basis, including value of allowances for such items as room and board furnished to counselors and for other emoluments to staff members employed in the various enterprises, which also must be shown as expense. The director or manager of each auxiliary enterprise should prepare a budget for review by the business officer.

Estimates of revenues from other sources should be based on past experience adjusted for probable future conditions. Estimates of the prior year's balances that may be available for rebudgeting and estimates of balances of quasi-endowment, term endowment, and other funds that might be transferred to current funds for operating purposes should be considered in the preparation of estimates of the availability of total unrestricted current funds.

Federal, state, and local appropriations must be estimated with the realization that such support ultimately depends on the actions of legislative bodies. If such appropriations are included in the federal, state, or local budget—and thus have the approval of the legislative body — the figures then can be accepted as final and the estimates can be used for institutional budget making. In those cases where the budget of the federal, state, or local government does not have the approval of the appropriate legislative body, the chief business officer or other administrator must communicate with someone in the respective legislative body who is knowledgeable with respect to the particular programs to be funded. In the state legislature, the chairman of the appropriations committee or its equivalent would have knowledge of the appropriation for higher education. Local government officials would know the amount of funds to be made available through the city or county government.

In estimating expenditures, the general policies established in the long-range plan and the specific policies and instructions of the president for the annual budget being developed will guide department chairmen and others in preparing their budget requests. Among such policies are plans for expansion, improvement of existing programs, and the development of new educational programs. Consideration must be given to the effect of fluctuations in prices, salary and promotion policies, vacations, leaves, and other employee benefits. Guidelines, such as student-faculty ratios, class size, teaching loads, and staffing patterns may be helpful, but the use of rigid formulas should be avoided.

Provision should be made in the annual operating budget for contingencies and emergencies. The amount provided in contingency accounts will depend on available resources, past experience, and the extent of economic and other uncertainties at the time the budget is prepared. If resources are insufficient to accomplish the objectives of the long-range plan, the base of support must be increased or the plan must be cut back. Authority for assigning contingency funds generally is vested in the chief academic officer and the chief business officer. In smaller institutions, such authority might rest with the president.

Once revenue has been estimated, budget hearings have been held, and expenditure guidelines have been determined, it is then possible to provide deans or other administrative officers with a predetermined total which their budget request should not exceed. This approach requires the lowest possible operating level to make choices within its scope of activities, and has the advantage of balancing the budget on the first tabulation rather than having to review and reduce to achieve a balance.

Budget Forms

The form, content, and arrangement of items in budget request forms vary according to institutional requirements. In general, the forms are most useful if they follow the pattern of the budget itself and if the account classifications correspond to those in the accounting records and in internal and annual financial reports.

Budget request forms and final budgets usually reflect the three major object classifications—personnel compensation, supplies and expenses, and capital expenditures. Supporting schedules prepared in the development of the budget may assign amounts within the major classifications for subordinate object categories. For example, personnel compensation might be subdivided in supporting schedules into separate amounts for faculty and professional salaries, supportive staff salaries, technician's wages, and student wages. Minor object classifications such as travel, telephone and communications, and printing, among others, might be detailed in supporting schedules under the major classification of supplies and expenses. Such subordinate categories are used for management information, with budget controls normally applying to the major object classifications and selected minor classifications.

The budget forms should include columns for comparative figures for at least the preceding fiscal period, the current-year budget projected to the end of the year, and the budget year. Before forms are distributed to department chairmen and others, historical figures, supplied by the business office, should be inserted. The forms also should provide space for amounts recommended at each level of review.

The budget request forms for personnel compensation should include more detailed information than do other expenditure items. Each individual position and its incumbent, if known, should be listed, along with the term of service, whether academic year, twelve months, or part-time. (If part-time, the degree of part-time should be indicated.) This information may be used, after the budget has received final approval, to establish payroll authorizations. In addition, personnel records should be available as budget requests are reviewed at various levels.

Departmental budget requests should be tabulated in summary form to show both the changes in amounts from the budget of the current year and the comparisons with actual expenditures of previous years. These summary reports permit the review of departmental budget requests with a minimum of effort.

Internal Budget Studies

Colleges and universities are increasingly turning to their institutional research staffs to provide data for the budget committee. In budget development, it is extremely helpful to know the student credit-hour production of colleges and departments over the last five years and to have a projection of at least the new budget year. Workload data for each faculty member also are useful. Studies of secretarial support for each full-time-equivalent faculty member are useful in identifying over- or under-staffed colleges or departments.

Many institutions find that space utilization studies are essential to assure taxpayers, donors, legislators, boards of control, and others that the institution is making effective use of its available space. Such data will serve to document the need for new space.

As program budgeting, management information systems, and other techniques are further developed, the staffs of institutional research offices will be called upon more to provide a part of the data required by the institution's managers.

Presentation and Adoption of the Budget

The form of various budget analyses prepared for consideration of the governing board, as well as the amount of detail included in them, will be determined by needs of the individual institution. Inasmuch as the governing board has the ultimate responsibility for the budget, members must have sufficient information to permit them to discharge this responsibility. However, the board should leave as many details as possible to the judgment of the president, and should concentrate its efforts on major policies.

The presentation to the board should include a comparison of the proposed budget with budgets of previous years, explanation of major changes, descriptions of programs added or eliminated, and salary and wage policies. In addition, the board should be informed of the extent to which the budget permits fulfillment of long-range plans.

The business office should send each head of a budgetary unit a copy of the unit's approved budget. Copies of the approved budget, or excerpts from it, should be sent to appropriate administrative offices and divisions of the business office. The approved budget constitutes authority to collect all revenues and incur all expenditures included therein.

BUDGETARY CONTROL AND ACCOUNTING

Budgetary Control

An essential element of budgeting is establishment of effective budget control. Without good control, the value of a budget is seriously decreased, regardless of how accurately or how carefully it is prepared. One of the main purposes of budgetary control is to insure that expenditures do not exceed allocations. The adoption of a budget does not guarantee realization of estimated revenues. The business officer must maintain records that will compare actual revenues with budget estimates, and he should report major variations in budget operations to the president. If it should become apparent that estimated revenues will not be realized, the budget should be formally amended.

Budget control starts with those responsible for each budgetary unit. The chief business officer has responsibility for overall budget control, including responsibility to call attention to major departures from budget estimates and to take appropriate follow-up action. The department chairman, however, has the primary responsibility for control of expenditures within his budgetary unit. Therefore, he must see that the appointment of staff members and the salaries involved in his department do not exceed budget allocations. He must restrict expenditures for supplies and equipment to amounts allocated for these purposes. He must plan expenditures for his unit so that allocations will last through the entire fiscal year. Otherwise, an institution may be in financial difficulty even though adequate controls are maintained in the business office. Once the budget has been approved, the educational and financial plan should not deviate without approval of appropriate authority.

Reports comparing actual results with budget projections should be prepared and sent to individual budget units at least monthly. These reports should be made available as early as possible after the end of the period covered. Summary reports should be prepared monthly and distributed to appropriate administrative officers for review and any needed action.

Budgetary Accounting

Since the budget is of vital importance in the operation and administration of an educational institution, many institutions make the recording of budgetary control accounts an integral part of the accounting system. This procedure brings under accounting control records relating to revenues not yet realized and unexpended balances of budget allocations.

After the budget has been approved by the governing board, total estimated revenues for the year are charged in the general ledger to an account for Estimated Revenues or Unrealized Revenues, and total estimated expenditures and allocations are credited to an account for Estimated Expenditures or Budget Allocations for Expenditures. The excess of estimated revenues over estimated expenditures is credited to an account that represents the free and unallocated balance of unrestricted current funds available for expenditure or allocation in the current budget year.

At the close of the fiscal period, the balances in the actual and estimated revenues accounts, and in the actual and estimated expenditures accounts, are closed into the Unallocated Balance of Unrestricted Current Funds account.

As a part of the budget system, provision must be made for outstanding obligations. There are a number of methods for handling these, any one of which is acceptable as long as it is part of a total budgetary system that provides for proper control points. These range from a highly detailed, central encumbrance system that is kept as a part of the formal accounting records to a decentralized, informal memorandum record of commitments kept by each budgetary unit. The method selected should provide effective control and useful information, but should not be inflexible or unreasonably expensive.

In the accounting and budgetary control system, there may be records that should be kept locally, that is, at the point of use. In these cases, local records should correlate with, but not duplicate, centrally kept summary records.

Budget Revisions

The budget consists of a series of estimates, many of which are prepared months in advance of the fiscal period to which they relate. Since conditions change with the passage of time, there should be continuous review of data on which the budget estimates were based. Periodic, formal revisions should be made in order that the budget always represents an up-to-date estimate of realizable revenues and a realistic plan for expenditures.

Responsibility, authority, and procedures for budget revisions should be a matter of written policy, adopted and approved by the governing board of the institution. The adopted policy should allow the greatest degree of flexibility at each level of authority consistent with the maintenance of proper administrative responsibility and adherence to approved policies and goals.

Revised estimates of revenues should be initiated by the same officers responsible for the original estimates, and should be subjected to the same general procedures of review before they are approved and recorded in the books of account.

Requests for increased expenditure allocations usually are initiated at the department level and reviewed by the respective deans before being submitted to the president. If the amounts are within the total of the contingent account, or accounts, in the approved budget, or are covered by increases in estimated revenues or decreases in expenditures, the president usually has authority to approve such requests. However, if the amounts involved are large enough to change the anticipated net results of the original budget, the governing board should give formal approval before increased expenditures are authorized.

Example of Application
of the Formula Approach to Budgeting

Enrollment Projection:

	Semester Credit-Hour Production			Total Semester Credit-Hours				Full-Time Equivalent Enrollment
	Summer	*Fall*	*Spring*					
Lower Division	6,200	119,550	108,800	234,550	÷	30	=	7,818
Upper Division	16,300	113,250	103,650	233,200	÷	30	=	7,773
Graduate	15,100	24,600	24,350	64,050	÷	24	=	2,669
Projected Full-Year, Full-Time-Equivalent Enrollment								18,260

Full Year Teaching Faculty Needs:

	Enrollment		*Student-Faculty Ratio*		*Full-Time Equivalent Teaching Positions*		*Recommended Annual Salary*	*Total Teaching Salaries*
Lower Division	7,818	÷	28	=	279.2			
Upper Division	7,773	÷	20	=	388.7			
Graduate	2,669	÷	8	=	333.6			
All Levels	18,260	÷	18.2	=	1,001.5	×	$14,800	$14,822,200

Financial Needs:

$14,822,200	+	$4,891,325	=	$19,713,526
Total Teaching Salaries		33% for Other Instruction Expenses		Budget Base

Resident Instruction	$19,713,526	Budget Base
Organized Activities Related to Instruction	394,271	2% of Base
General Administration	1,379,947	7% of Base
General Expense	1,379,947	7% of Base
Organized Research	1,971,353	10% of Base
Extension and Public Service	1,971,353	10% of Base
Library	1,379,947	7% of Base
Operation and Maintenance of Physical Plant	2,759,894	14% of Base
Total Educational and General Budget	$30,950,238	

Estimated Income:

Revolving Funds	$10,292,785	33.3%
State-Appropriated Funds	$20,657,453	66.7%
Total Income	$30,950,238	100.0%

Internal Control and Audits

INTERNAL CONTROL comprises the methods and procedures adopted by an institution to safeguard its assets, to insure the accuracy and reliability of its accounting data, to promote operational efficiency, to protect its personnel, and to help insure adherence to prescribed policies and institutional regulations. The obligation to administer financial affairs justifies the careful design, installation, and support of internal control procedures, regardless of the size of the institution. An effective and responsive system of internal control becomes increasingly important as a management tool as details of such a system become more remote from senior administrators because of institutional growth, more complex management problems and regulations, more sophisticated computerized processes, and more delegation of responsibility.

Characteristics of a satisfactory internal control system applicable to any size of institution are:

1. Organization plans that provide appropriate segregation of functional responsibilities.

2. Authorization and record-keeping procedures that give reasonable accounting control over assets, liabilities, and all changes in the balances of funds.

3. Clerical practices that insure a high degree of compliance with approved authorization and record-keeping procedures.

4. Employees with capabilities sufficient to execute their prescribed responsibilities.

Responsibility, authority, operating policies, and procedures should be clearly defined. Operating, custodial, accounting, and internal auditing functions should be independent of each other. Ancillary records existing outside a department may serve in many instances as controls over activities within the department. That is, opportunities for

reconciliation of records between offices should be pursued whenever possible.

There should be appropriate records and forms and a logical flow of record-keeping and approval procedures. Appropriate records include control accounts and subsidiary ledgers, a meaningful classification of transactions and, where it serves a useful purpose, document accountability.

Practices should be adopted that will enhance the integrity of authorizations, recordings, and custody. Office procedures should include a continuous review or internal check of routine transactions, whereby the work of one person is proved independent of or complementary to the work of another. There should be division of responsibilities so that no person has complete control over all aspects of a financial transaction. For example, a person who accepts cash should have no responsibility for, nor access to, control or subsidiary ledger accounts, bank reconciliations, disbursement media, or registration material. The same person should not authorize payroll documents, prepare payrolls, and issue paychecks. The same person should not initiate purchase requisitions, place orders with vendors, verify receipt of materials, approve invoices, and prepare and mail checks to vendors. In smaller institutions with limited staff, opportunities for separation of functions may be limited, but the principle still applies and should be respected if at all possible.

Mechanical equipment, such as cash registers with locked-in counters and listing tapes and accounting machines with automatic totaling capability, contribute to effective internal control. Devices are available that attach to cash registers or accounting machines to produce punched cards, punched paper tape, or magnetic tape, which can generate receipts, accounting distributions, and analyses. Remote stations capable of direct input to computers also are available. All machine systems must be regularly examined for proper controls and balances. Electronic data processing equipment offers many control devices, but an internal control system also must be concerned with evaluating the systems definition and related input and operating procedures to insure adequate checks on the processing and reporting functions of the equipment and the integrity of its operators. Effective programming, separation of responsibilities, internal and external security of equipment and programs, and periodic audits provide the means of achieving internal control in a computerized system.

Employees responsible for internal control should be formally trained in management and accounting, with experience in the field also desirable. Such employees should not lose sight of the objectives of internal control while performing their tasks. The ability to cooperate and communicate with others is also important.

The characteristics mentioned above, together with review by the internal auditor, should be present in offices performing a business or service function, where funds are billed, received, obligated, or disbursed, where fiscal accounts are maintained or reported, or where inventories or other institutional assets are carried.

Many transactions originate in academic, research, service, and other areas outside the business office and provide separation of responsibilities that should be utilized fully in designing internal control system safeguards to discourage or disclose fraudulent schemes and errors. Through checkpoints in the day-to-day operations and through regular reports produced and issued to operational and senior management, the system should point out areas of concern or weakness so that prompt, corrective action can be taken.

INTERNAL AUDITING

Internal auditing in colleges and universities is a staff function that serves management at all levels by reviewing and appraising the business activities of the institution, the integrity of its records, and the general effectiveness of operations. Because the internal auditing function traditionally has concerned financial and business matters, the person responsible for this function usually reports to the chief business officer. However, the traditional role of the internal auditor has broadened to include other types of audits as well, such as the operational audit (described in the section "Operational or Performance Audits"). Regardless of the extent of his responsibilities, the internal auditor is likely to continue reporting to the chief business officer as his primary task remains the auditing of financial affairs.

In some institutions and state systems the internal auditor may report to the president or to the governing board. Whatever the reporting practice, the position should be such that it is independent of the operations reviewed. For maximum effectiveness, especially in cases where the auditor's activities relate to the chief business officer's functions, he must have access to a senior administrator other than the chief business officer—ideally, the president. In his staff capacity, the auditor should not be assigned line or operating responsibilities. For example, day-to-day review of invoice-vouchers is not appropriate, nor is routine reconciliation of bank statements.

The auditor's work should include the following general objectives:

1. Determining that the overall system of internal control and the controls in each activity under audit are adequate, effective, and functioning.
2. Insuring that institutional policies and procedures, state and federal laws, contractual obligations, and good business practices are followed.
3. Verifying the existence of assets shown on the books of accounts and insuring maintenance of proper safeguards for their protection.
4. Determining the reliability and adequacy of the accounting and reporting systems and procedures.

As a liaison between institutional administration and operating departments, the internal auditor should prepare a formal report of the results of his examination, including recommended corrective action, and distribute it to concerned levels of administration. To aid in accomplishing these objectives, the chief business officer should establish policies regarding the objectives and scope of the audit program, develop awareness within the institution of the internal audit function, require action on the internal auditor's recommendations, and keep the auditor informed of operating plans and developments. Unresolved issues between audited units and the internal auditor should be resolved by the chief business officer.

Audit Reports and Follow-Up

The internal audit report presents to management and operating personnel the results of an independent appraisal of an operation. If the report is to be effective, it must clearly and concisely present timely, accurate data.

The format of the report may vary according to the audit situation. However, the report should:

1. Include an introductory paragraph describing the activity audited, the period covered by the examination, and, very briefly, the general scope of the audit and any limiting factors.
2. Present principal findings without bias and in sufficient detail for the reader to understand the situation.
3. Present recommendations to remedy the situations reported, if necessary.
4. Include commendatory remarks if they are warranted.
5. Include information relating to underlying causes of deficiencies reported in order to assist in implementing corrective action.
6. Place primary emphasis on improvement of operations rather than on criticisms of the past.

A preliminary draft of the audit report ordinarily should be discussed with the head and appropriate staff of the audited department prior to final distribution of the report. The exit interview provides an opportunity to discuss audit findings and recommendations, to agree on factual matters, and to obtain relevant comments from the department head for incorporation into the finished report.

The finished report should be transmitted to the chief business officer, who then should distribute it with his additional comments or recommendations, if any, to the appropriate department head. He should request that the department head respond to the report in writing, with a copy of the response sent to the auditor.

Follow-up on audit recommendations is essential. The follow-up should be done by the chief business officer, but in many institutions it is handled by the auditor through the chief business officer.

Operational or Performance Audits

A logical, important extension of the internal auditor's function is operational or performance audits. Operational auditing may be considered a manner of approach, analysis, and thought, not a separate type of auditing using special techniques.

The operational audit is a part of management's overall control system. The basis for evaluation of the operations of a department must be how well the department achieves objectives the institution's administration has set for it. Thus, departmental mission statements or some formal statement of objectives should be available to the auditor. The audit reviews personnel, departmental workload, productivity, and quality of output, and should help to prevent waste, loss of time, and errors. It should include an appraisal of the quality of management and the effectiveness of operating procedures. Costs and expenses are reviewed not only to insure that amounts are correct, but for justification as well. These concepts can be applied to other activities as well as to business related functions.

Operational auditing is gaining recognition and stature because efficiency demands that equal or better results be obtained with less cost. The goal of operational auditing is to recommend ways of accomplishing this objective without sacrificing the necessary financial controls. Unlike the internal financial audit, which often is initiated in a given department without prior notice, the operational audit normally should be undertaken only with the full knowledge and consent of the administrator in charge of the department subject to the audit.

Audit Program

A formal, written program for the internal auditing operation should be developed with the advice and approval of the chief business officer. This program should establish the general scope of audit coverage of the financial and business operations of the institution. A schedule of activities and departments to be audited during a fiscal period should be determined annually. The frequency of internal audits is determined by such factors as the nature of the activity, changes in personnel, significant changes in volume of work, introduction of new or revised procedures, and adequacy of controls.

The audit schedule should be flexible enough to accommodate special projects that the auditor might be called on to carry out. However, special and emergency projects should not interrupt the internal audit schedule for long periods, as institutional needs are best served by a comprehensive audit schedule continuously maintained. To keep pace with changing conditions, the audit program should be reappraised periodically and appropriate modifications made to the audit program when necessary.

Scope of Audit Coverage

The general scope of financial audit coverage should be institution-wide and should not exclude any function or activity of the institution. Management should recognize that any limitation placed on the general scope of coverage reduces the effectiveness of the internal audit function and its appraisal of the institution's system of internal control.

The scope of audit coverage for a specific department or function may be illustrated by reviewing the scope of coverage for the accounting function, which maintains all central financial records and prepares reports required by management and federal and state agencies. It also serves as a financial control point for most activities of the institution. Consequently, it becomes the focus of information concerning both financial and operational audits. This function must provide information concerning confirmation of accounts receivable, inventory verification, flow and recording of entries on expenditure and revenue accounts, reconciliation of bank accounts or official depositories, securities and investments, revenues, and expenditure classification and data needed to test compliance with policies and procedures. Therefore, the scope of audit coverage for this function should include an examination of each item listed above.

Relationship to Systems and Procedures Function

Generally, it is inappropriate for the auditor to design or to supervise the design of financial sys-

tems and procedures, since he should not audit his own work. Practically, however, auditing and systems design cannot be completely separated, as audits frequently disclose the necessity for systems revisions, either in internal control situations or for operating efficiency.

Changing conditions continually generate the need for new controls; however, controls are seldom removed even after they cease to be useful or practicable. Similarly, unnecessary work becomes less conspicuous the longer it exists. A continuing evaluation is therefore necessary to make certain that existing practices meet the institution's current needs. The internal auditor should help provide such an evaluation for the chief business officer.

An administrative manual is advisable for stability and uniformity. A fundamental core of instructions for the operation of any college or university can save time, correspondence, explanation, and misunderstanding. Such instructions become the vehicle for communicating to all members of the organization the guiding principles, administrative policies, standard practices, and operating directives of the administration. Ideally, a systems and procedures function is available to coordinate the efforts necessary to generate and maintain the administrative manual. A continuing source of information for the systematic revision of existing systems, procedures, and standard instructions is provided by routine communication between internal auditing and the systems group.

Design of complex financial systems should be undertaken by systems specialists. The role of the auditor in the design of these systems is to insure that adequate controls are being built into the systems as they develop; furthermore, in the case of computer systems, he should see that necessary data can be retrieved for audit purposes.

Use of the Computer in Internal Auditing

The expansion of computer systems will continue to affect the development and execution of audits. The internal auditor should have sufficient knowledge of electronic data processing to understand a computer-based system and offer a sound opinion regarding the adequacy of controls of the total system, both separate from and within the computer.

In the execution of the audit by computer, audit test data can be used to verify that the results of a computer program are as specified, or computer programs can be designed to select, retrieve, sort, and summarize actual "live" data from the computer files.

The audit test data method allows the auditor to simulate certain types of transactions with realistic, but hypothetical, data under specified conditions. This concept can be integrated into the design of a computer system to provide continuous monitoring capability, on request, in order to test transactions during normal production runs. This latter development offers the best benefits when used with complex management information systems that operate on an on-line, real-time basis.

Use of computer programs to retrieve data has been aided by the development of generalized computer audit programs by the larger public accounting firms; these programs usually are made available to their clients. Such general-purpose audit packages use actual "live" data and select, sort, calculate, and summarize the data for audit purposes. Use of these programs can save the auditor time in performing detail steps of the audit and improve the overall quality of the audit.

RELATIONSHIP TO EXTERNAL AUDIT AGENCIES

An educational institution is subject to audit or review by a number of external agencies at the request of the governing board or because of terms of agreements with extramural sponsors.

Independent Certified Public Accountants and State Auditors

The governing board of an institution should require an annual audit by independent certified public accountants experienced in auditing educational institutions. In the case of public institutions, this is sometimes performed by state auditors; or the state, rather than the governing board, may employ an accounting firm to audit the institution. Typically, independent auditors examine and express their professional opinion on the accuracy and integrity of the institution's financial reports. Independent auditors often are engaged for specialized audits or technical services. They can assist the business office with expert advice and an independent view of accounting, fiscal, systems,

and management problems.

The arrangements made with the public accounting firm should be in writing, and the institution should specify the objectives of such audits; the firm will determine the nature and extent of the review required to render a sound opinion. Institutions should avoid imposing limitations on the audit, as that would result in the accounting firm's qualifying its opinion.

The working relationship between the internal auditor and auditors of the independent accounting firm and the state should be close. In some institutions, all audits by external agencies are coordinated through the internal audit department. With advance planning, year-end work such as inventory and cash verification can be divided, information exchanged, and audit coverage expanded. Certain surprise cash counts may require a large staff; in such cases the count can be a mutual effort of the internal and external auditors. In student loan and accounts receivable confirmations, the independent or state auditors may review and approve the sampling technique, and their return envelopes may be used so that confirmation responses are sent directly to them. They will share the replies with the internal auditor. Coordination such as this can expand audit coverage, and considerable savings in fees may be realized by the institution.

Federal Auditors

In addition to the audits by public accountants and state auditors, the federal government continuously audits federal grants and contracts, sometimes to the extent of having resident auditors permanently located at an institution if volume warrants.

Federal auditors may audit any segment of the institution that initiates charges to or expends funds received, or to be received, from federal sources. This may involve purchasing, stores and services, payroll, and insurance as well as the federally funded programs themselves. Since the federal auditors normally operate in a more restricted field than independent and state auditors, the relationship of the internal auditor with the federal auditors is limited in range of activities, but is nevertheless close. Generally, it consists of allowing federal auditors to review pertinent internal audit working papers, and perhaps furnishing federal auditors with audit reports on certain activities within the scope of their audit.

Reports of External Auditors

After its examination is completed, the independent public accounting firm addresses a formal report of its findings and opinion to the governing board, agency, or administrator that contracted its services. This report often is accompanied by a management letter containing observations made in the course of the audit and recommendations for improving operations or controls.

State and federal auditors report to their superiors on areas of their particular interest and concern and also offer relevant comments and recommendations. It is the responsibility of the chief business officer to respond to the recommendations, stating the action taken or the reasons for not implementing the recommendations.

Individual comments and recommendations are forwarded to the administrative head of the function or activity concerned, with a request for a reply indicating the action taken or other comments. The reply forms the basis of the response to the external audit agency.

INTERNAL AUDIT STAFF

The director of the internal audit function should have mature judgment, formal training in the objectives, techniques, and procedures of internal auditing, and experience in the auditing field. He should be able to work harmoniously with people and to communicate effectively, orally and in writing, with all levels of management and operating staff. He should be capable of rendering clear and concise audit reports related to financial condition, internal control, and operational effectiveness. The internal auditor and his staff should be familiar with statistical sampling, flow charting techniques, and computer capability as an audit tool.

The size of the audit staff and the amount of time devoted to internal auditing depend on the size of the institution, complexity of the operations, and the form of administrative organization. In large institutions, the internal audit staff should include specialists in disciplines other than auditing, such as systems, computers, or industrial engineering. In small institutions, internal auditing may be performed by a person responsible for other business and financial duties.

Part 5

Financial Accounting and Reporting

Introduction to Part 5

THE CHAPTERS that follow comprise a revision of those chapters of Part 2, *College and University Business Administration* (American Council on Education, 1968), dealing with principles of accounting and reporting. They were prepared by NACUBO committees and consultants working with keen awareness of new burdens being placed on accounting and reporting functions in colleges and universities and with a strong sense of the need to be alert to contemporary forces tending to reshape thinking about institutional accountability and disclosure. They represent, in a new time and in response to new demands, the authority historically carried by the predecessor texts.

BACKGROUND OF THE REVISION

The new revision was under development for more than two years by the NACUBO Accounting Principles Committee. It was approved for publication by the NACUBO Board of Directors upon the joint recommendation of NACUBO's Accounting Principles and Publications committees. It reflects, accordingly, with respect to accounting standards and practices and to the forms and methods of financial disclosure, the consensus of experienced and knowledgeable professionals representing the association having a primary interest in the field of college and university financial management.

The authority of the revision rests, in addition, upon a broader base than that of the 1968 text. Not only has it had the benefit of management studies and improvements that have come along in recent years, but it is a statement developed in close communication and consultation between NACUBO, through its Accounting Principles Committee, and two other organizations with interests directly related to the accounting and reporting functions—the American Institute of Cer-

tified Public Accountants (AICPA) and the National Center for Higher Education Management Systems (NCHEMS) of the Western Interstate Commission for Higher Education. There was consistent liaison between NACUBO and AICPA in the more than three years in which AICPA's former Committee on College and University Accounting and Auditing was developing its industry guide, *Audits of Colleges and Universities,* published in 1973. Similarly, members of the Accounting Principles Committee maintained contact with the NCHEMS task force developing the *Higher Education Finance Manual,* an effort supported by the Department of Health, Education, and Welfare and of interest to the U.S. Office of Education's National Center for Educational Statistics because of its relevance to the Higher Education General Information Survey (HEGIS) questionnaire. All such contacts were brought together in regular fashion in 1973-1974 in the establishment of an interorganizational Joint Accounting Group composed of representatives of NACUBO, AICPA, and NCHEMS.

THE GENERAL OBJECTIVES

The revision of the "Principles" of 1968 was carried forward with attention to two broad objectives, the first to decide upon generally acceptable, rather than alternative, methods of recording and reporting financial data, and the second to settle upon revenue and expenditure categories that would be uniformly acceptable and applicable. These goals were substantially achieved in the course of the AICPA-NACUBO liaison during development of the audit guide. The AICPA sought uniformity and full disclosure, objectives that paralleled NACUBO's, while deferring to NACUBO and professional consensus the questions of account classifications and definitions. The definitions and classifications were further refined and confirmed by the Accounting Principles Committee as it continued its consultations with AICPA and NCHEMS.

The effort that produced the AICPA guide was a significant part of the total effort that went into this present revision. When the draft of the guide was ready for exposure in August, 1972, NACUBO was responsible for this exposure throughout higher education, distributing copies to some 3,000 institutions and other organizations and supporting the four Regional Associations in sponsorship of regional audit guide study sessions in October, 1972. All views or comments transmitted by institutions or flowing from the regional meetings were given to the AICPA for reference. In December, 1972, the Accounting Principles Committee prepared a formal response to AICPA, and this paper (NACUBO *Special Report* 72-13, December 18, 1972) was approved by the NACUBO Board at a special meeting in New Orleans and sent to AICPA as the definitive response of the college and university community. In its preparation of the final text of the audit guide, AICPA was responsive to NACUBO's recommendations in nearly every case.

The professional discussion stimulated by the exposure draft of the AICPA audit guide was without precedent in scope and intensity. No other such guide had been examined so broadly by the industry concerned. The degree of final consensus was such that the guide was distributed to member institutions by NACUBO, in August, 1973, for their reference until the present chapters could be made ready for publication.

Certain relationships must be understood, however.

First, the AICPA guide is controlling *only* upon the certified public accountant who, performing an audit at a college or university, wishes to give an unqualified opinion. The AICPA cannot *require* an institution to conform to practices prescribed by the guide.

Second, the chapters that comprise Part 5 of *College and University Business Administration* were prepared by persons professionally involved in financial management in higher education for use and reference by all colleges and universities. They stand as recommendations based on wide consensus. No institution is compelled to conform to patterns of financial accounting and reporting herein recommended, but institutions that do so will be following guidelines strongly supported by professional judgment. NACUBO hopes and expects that most institutions will so conform, and that state and other agencies will incorporate these recommendations, as many have in the past, into their regulations on financial management in higher education.

Fundamental Concepts of Financial Accounting and Reporting

AMONG THE OBJECTIVES of accounting, whether for a commercial enterprise or a college or university, is the providing of information to assist (1) management in the effective allocation and use of resources and (2) the general public, investors, creditors, and others in evaluating the effectiveness of management in achieving organizational objectives. The nature of the organization, its resources, and objectives all serve to influence the form and process by which the accounting is accomplished and information reported.

The predominant objective of a commercial enterprise is to increase the economic wealth of those who provide resources to finance its operations. These resources are intended to produce revenues that not only replace the resources consumed but provide, in addition, the profit margin for the investor. The objective of a college or university is to provide services that fulfill societal needs without regard for financial gain. Thus resources are consumed to attain service objectives rather than to make a profit. To provide its services a college or university must continually obtain new resources.

In spite of this basic difference, both types of organizations must concern themselves with the proper and effective use of scarce resources and employ common, generally accepted accounting principles and practices to assist in this mission. As a result of the difference, however, there are also some accounting principles and practices employed by colleges and universities that are unique. Departures from commercial practices are (1) fund accounting, (2) form and content of basic financial statements, (3) application of accrual accounting, (4) accounting for depreciation, (5) accounting for investments, and (6) accounting for institutions operated by religious groups.

In the commercial enterprise it can be stated as a generalization that the two principal sources of resources are the capital investment of the owners and the flow of revenues resulting from goods produced or services rendered. The profit objective serves as a regulator of management and permits a high degree of flexibility in the use of resources. The emphasis, then, in the accounting and reporting process is on the matching of expenses with revenues to determine net income (profit).

Since service, in which resources are consumed, is the objective of the college or university, the accounting and reporting process must address itself to accounting for resources received and used rather than to the determination of net income.

While charges for services are made, such as tuition or fees, there frequently is no direct relationship between such charges and actual expenditures for programs. Tuition and fees collected generally are intended to represent only a portion of the total resource needs of the institution, since society has chosen to share in the costs of higher education by contributions and other means. Therefore, a variety of sources of financial support have emerged to assist in satisfying the resource needs of colleges and universities. In the absence of the profit element as a control device, many of the funding sources exercise control by stipulating the purposes for which resources provided to management can be utilized. Thus for colleges and universities there is added to the above objectives of accounting the need for adequate disclosure of the stewardship of resources, in accordance with the wishes of the funding sources.

FUND ACCOUNTING

To satisfy the requirement to account properly for the diversity of resources and their use, the principles and practices of "fund accounting" are employed. Within this concept, there have evolved certain principles of classification and presentation of accounting data as well as standard terminology for institutions of higher education.

Fund accounting is the manner of organizing and managing the accounting by which resources for various purposes are classified for financial accounting and reporting purposes in accordance with activities or objectives as specified by donors, with regulations, restrictions, or limitations imposed by sources outside the institution, or with directions issued by the governing board. In this respect, a clear distinction between funds which are externally restricted and those which are internally designated by action of the governing board should be maintained in the accounts and disclosed in the financial reports.

A fund is an accounting entity with a self-balancing set of accounts consisting of assets, liabilities, and a fund balance. Separate accounts are maintained for each fund to insure observance of limitations and restrictions placed on use of resources. For reporting purposes, however, funds of similar characteristics are combined into fund groups. The fund groups generally found in an educational institution are as follows:

> Current funds
> Loan funds
> Endowment and similar funds
> Annuity and life income funds
> Plant funds
> Agency funds

In addition to the foregoing fund groups, there can be additional fund groups unique to particular institutions, such as employee retirement funds, which should be accounted for separately and reported in the annual financial statements.

Since each fund group is considered as a separate entity, there are numerous transactions among the fund groups, which must recognize this entity concept. When the movement of funds from one group to another is intended to be permanent, it should be recorded as an outright transfer between the fund entities. However, when the movement is intended to be temporary, with repayment contemplated within a reasonable period of time to the contributing fund group, the transaction should be recorded as an interfund borrowing. Such borrowings should be reported as assets of the fund groups making the advances and as liabilities of the fund groups receiving the advances.

In some instances, legal provisions and government regulations pertaining to certain funds may require accounting and reporting practices that differ from generally accepted accounting principles. It is recognized that in these instances such legal and regulatory provisions must take precedence. However, such restrictions do not obviate the need for adhering to generally accepted accounting principles for the purpose of reporting financial position, changes in fund balances, and current funds revenues, expenditures, and other changes.

BASIC FINANCIAL STATEMENTS

Colleges and universities generally utilize three basic statements: a balance sheet, a statement of changes in fund balances, and a statement of current funds revenues, expenditures, and other changes.

The balance sheet presents a series of fund groups, with each group having its own self-balancing assets, liabilities, and fund balances.

The statement of changes in fund balances portrays all the activity that changed the fund balances of the fund groups between the preceding and the current balance sheet dates. This statement includes all additions to, deductions from, and transfers among the fund groups.

The statement of current funds revenues, expenditures, and other changes supplements and presents in detail some of the information presented in summary form in the current funds section of the statement of changes in fund balances. It does not purport to match expenses with revenues to derive a net income—rather, it presents in detail the current funds revenues by source, the current funds expenditures by function, and other changes in current fund balances. Also, it does not report the total revenue and expenditure activity of the institution, but only that related to current funds. The reporting objectives achieved by this statement may be accomplished in other ways (see Chapter 5:5).

The emphasis in these basic financial statements is on the status of funds and on the flow of resources through the fund entities. In addition, an overview of the financial operations of the institution is provided. Consideration might be given to supplementary schedules that combine nonfinancial with financial information to assist in further evaluating the activity, achievements, and overall operations of the institution.

ACCRUAL ACCOUNTING

The accounts should be maintained and reports prepared on the accrual basis of accounting. Revenues should be reported when earned and expenditures when materials or services are received. Included in expenditures are (1) all expenses incurred, determined in accordance with generally accepted accounting principles except for the omission of depreciation, and (2) expenditures for the acquisition of capital assets, to the extent expended. Expenses incurred at the balance sheet date should be accrued and expenses applicable to future periods should be deferred. However, certain deferrals and accruals, such as investment income and interest on student loans, often are omitted. Nevertheless, the only basis for their omission should be that the omission does not have a material effect on the financial statements. Revenues and expenditures of an academic term that encompasses parts of two fiscal years, such as a summer session, should be reported totally within the fiscal year in which the program is predominantly conducted.

One of the practices which supplement accrual accounting is that of recording encumbrances. An encumbrance represents an obligation incurred in the form of an order, contract, or similar commitment on which liabilities will be recognized when goods are delivered or services rendered. It establishes a claim against a particular fund balance in anticipation of a future expenditure.

Encumbrances, representing outstanding purchase orders and other commitments for materials or services not received as of the reporting date, should neither be reported as expenditures nor be included as liabilities in the balance sheet. Designations or allocations of fund balances in the financial statements or disclosure in the notes to the financial statements should be made when such commitments are material in amount. Failure to disclose the distinction between liabilities and encumbrances could result in the presentation of misleading information.

ACCOUNTING FOR DEPRECIATION

Depreciation expense related to assets comprising the physical plant is reported neither in the statement of current funds revenues, expenditures, and other changes nor in the current funds section of the statement of changes in fund balances. The reason for this treatment is that one of the primary reporting objectives of college and university accounting is to disclose resources received and expended rather than net income realized. Thus capital asset acquisitions financed from current funds are reported as expenditures of that group in the year of acquisition.

That depreciation is not recorded in the current funds does not preclude the use of expired capital cost data in evaluating performance and making management decisions on a variety of operating activities. Also, for purposes of statement presentation, depreciation allowance may be reported in the balance sheet and the provision for depreciation reported in the statement of changes in the balance of the Investment in Plant subgroup of the Plant Funds group.

In the Endowment and Similar Funds group, depreciation should be provided on depreciable assets held as investments in order to maintain the distinction between principal and income in those funds.

ACCOUNTING FOR INVESTMENTS

Investments purchased usually are reported at cost and investments received as gifts usually are reported at the fair market or appraised value at the date of gift. As a permissible alternative, investments may be reported at current market or fair value, provided this basis is used for all investments in all funds. When using this alternative, unrealized gains and losses should be reported in the same manner as realized gains and losses under the cost basis.

Interfund sales of investments should be recorded by the purchasing fund at fair market or appraised value at date of sale. The differences between carrying value and fair market or appraised value should be accounted for in the selling fund as realized gains and losses.

Investments of the various funds may be pooled unless prohibited by statute or by terms of the gifts. Proper determination of equities and the basis of income distribution should be made by utilizing current market values on a share or unit plan. This determination can be made through the use of memorandum records and does not require the recording of each investment at current market value in the accounts.

ACCOUNTING FOR INSTITUTIONS OPERATED BY RELIGIOUS GROUPS

Accounting and reporting records of an institution should be adequately segregated from the records of the sponsoring religious group so that the educational entity is in fact accounted for as a separate entity. Facilities made available to the educational entity by the religious group should be disclosed in the financial reports together with any related indebtedness.

The monetary value of services contributed by members of the religious group should be recorded in the accounts and reported in the financial statements. The gross value of such services should be determined by relating them to equivalent salaries and wages for similarly ranked personnel at the same or similar institutions, including the normal staff benefits such as group insurance and retirement provisions.

The amounts so determined should be recorded as expenditures by department or division, following the same classification as other expenditures, and a like amount should be recorded as gift revenue. The gift revenue should be reduced by the amount of maintenance, living costs, and personal expenses incurred, which are related to the contributing personnel and have no counterpart in a lay employee relationship.

In some cases, checks are drawn to the religious group and charged to expenditure accounts in the same manner as payroll checks. The religious group then makes a contribution to the institution, which records it as a gift. The determination of the contribution would rest with the religious group, since the latter is a separate entity.

In some cases these institutions inform the reader of the financial report as to the relative value of such contributed services by comparison with the average return on endowment fund investment. Such information should be limited to the notes to the financial statements, and the imputed capitalized value of such contributions should not be reflected in the balance sheet.

Current Funds

THE CURRENT FUNDS group includes those economic resources of a college or university which are expendable for the purpose of performing the primary missions of the institution—instruction, research, and public service—and which are not restricted by external sources or designated by the governing board for other than operating purposes. The term "current" means that the resources will be expended in the near term and that they will be used for operating purposes.

The Current Funds group has two basic subgroups—unrestricted and restricted. Unrestricted current funds include all funds received for which no stipulation was made by the donor or other external agency as to the purposes for which they should be expended. Restricted current funds are those available for financing operations but which are limited by donors and other external agencies to specific purposes, programs, departments, or schools. Externally imposed restrictions are to be contrasted with internal designations imposed by the governing board on unrestricted funds. Internal designations do not create restricted funds, inasmuch as the removal of the designation remains at the discretion of the governing board.

The distinction between unrestricted and restricted funds is maintained through the use of separately balanced groups of accounts in order to provide acceptable reporting of stewardship to donors and other external agencies. This distinction also emphasizes to governing boards and other sources of financial support the various kinds of resources of the Current Funds group that are available to meet the institution's objectives.

Separate accounting entities may be provided for auxiliary enterprises, hospitals, and independent operations in either the Unrestricted Current Funds or Restricted Current Funds subgroup or both, as appropriate.

ASSETS, LIABILITIES, AND FUND BALANCES OF CURRENT FUNDS

Assets usually consist of cash, accounts receivable, including unbilled charges, notes receivable, undrawn appropriations, investments, amounts due from other fund groups, inventories, prepaid expenses, and deferred charges. "Unbilled charges" are those which have been earned but which, because of inadequate information, incomplete projects or programs, or the timing of the billing cycle, have not been formally billed at the balance sheet date. "Undrawn appropriations" are those to which the institution is entitled, but which have not been remitted or made available to the institution by the appropriating federal, state, or local agency. "Deferred charges" are expenditures that are related to projects, programs, activities, or revenues of future fiscal periods.

Liabilities usually consist of accounts and notes payable, accrued liabilities, deposits, amounts due to other fund groups, and deferred credits. Accrued liabilities include such items as interest, wages, salaries, and taxes. Deferred credits are those revenues of unrestricted current funds that are applicable to a future period, when they become earned.

The individual assets and liabilities, but not the fund balances, of unrestricted and restricted current funds are sometimes combined for reporting purposes, but if they are combined, the borrowings between unrestricted and restricted funds should be disclosed by footnote or other appropriate means.

The fund balances may be subdivided to show allocations applicable to auxiliary enterprises, hospitals, independent operations, outstanding encumbrances, other allocations by operating management or by the governing board, budget balances brought forward from prior fiscal periods, and the unallocated balance.

Changes in the balances of unrestricted current funds include the gross amount of all unrestricted revenues and expenditures applicable to the reporting period, as determined in accordance with the accrual basis of accounting, and transfers to and from other fund groups for the period. Significant allocations of unrestricted current fund balances should be disclosed.

The fund balances of restricted current funds should be classified in the accounting system to show the various classes and sources of funds and purposes of restriction. Such restrictions often relate to the use of endowment fund income; gifts, grants, and contracts from private and governmental sources; and legislative appropriations. Further breakdowns may be provided to show amounts restricted to auxiliary enterprises, hospitals, and independent operations, if such activities are the beneficiaries of restricted current funds.

Additions to fund balances of restricted current funds arise from the sources indicated in the preceding paragraph. Deductions from restricted fund balances result from:

1. Direct expenditures and mandatory transfers.
2. Refunds to donors and other external agencies.
3. Amounts transferred to unrestricted revenues representing indirect cost recoveries on appropriate programs.
4. Nonmandatory transfers.

CURRENT FUNDS REVENUES

Current funds revenues include (1) all unrestricted gifts, grants, and other resources earned during the reporting period and (2) restricted resources to the extent that such funds were expended. Current funds revenues do not include restricted current funds received but not expended or resources that are restricted by external persons or agencies to other than current funds.

Interdepartmental transactions between service departments and storerooms and other institutional departments or offices should not be reported as revenues of the service departments but rather as reductions of expenditures of such departments, since these transactions are essentially interdepartmental transfers of costs. The billed price of services and materials obtained from service depart-

ments and central stores by offices and departments of the institution should be accounted for as expenditures of those offices and departments, just as if they had been obtained from sources outside the institution. Any difference between costs and billed prices as recorded in the service department account, whether credit or debit, should be reported under the Institutional Support expenditures classification.

Certain intrainstitutional transactions, however, should be reflected in the operating statements of the institution as revenues and expenditures. Materials or services produced by an instructional department as a by-product of the instructional program and sold to other departments or to auxiliary enterprises or hospitals—for example, milk sold by the dairy department to the dining halls—should be treated as sales and services revenues of the selling department and as expenditures of the receiving department. Sales and services of auxiliary enterprises to other departments—for example, catering by the food services department in the entertainment of institutional guests and sales by the college store to instructional departments—should be treated as sales and services revenues of the respective auxiliary enterprises and as expenditures of the unit receiving the services or materials.

Unrestricted and restricted current funds revenues should be grouped into the following major classifications by source of funds:

Tuition and Fees
Federal Appropriations
State Appropriations
Local Appropriations
Federal Grants and Contracts
State Grants and Contracts
Local Grants and Contracts
Private Gifts, Grants, and Contracts
Endowment Income
Sales and Services of Educational Activities
Sales and Services of Auxiliary Enterprises
Sales and Services of Hospitals
Other Sources, *including expired term endowments and expired life income agreements, if not material; otherwise, separate category*
Independent Operations

Tuition and Fees

This category should include all tuition and fees assessed against students (net of refunds) for educational purposes. Tuition and fees should be recorded as revenue even though there is no intention of collection from the student. The amounts of such remissions or waivers should be recorded as expenditures and classified as Scholarships and Fellowships or as staff benefits associated with the appropriate expenditure category to which the personnel relate.

When specific fees are assessed under binding external restrictions for other than current operating purposes—for example, debt service on educational plant or on renewals, replacements, or additions to plant—they should be reported as additions to the appropriate fund group (in the above example, plant funds), since they are not legally available for current operating purposes. Fees normally are not considered as assessed under binding external restrictions unless there is an explicit representation to the individuals remitting the fees that the fee or a specific portion thereof can be used only for the specific nonoperating purpose.

If some portion of total tuition or fee receipts is pledged under bond indenture agreements, the total receipts should be reported as unrestricted current funds revenues and the pledged amount treated as a mandatory transfer to plant funds.

If some portion of tuition or fees is allocated by action of the governing board, or subject to change by the governing board alone, for other than operating purposes, such as financing construction, the whole of the tuition charges or fees should be recorded as unrestricted current funds revenues and the portion allocated should be treated as a nonmandatory transfer to the appropriate fund group (in the above example, plant funds).

Revenues pledged under bond indenture agreements should not be reported as additions to plant funds, but should be reported as unrestricted current funds revenues, and funding of debt service requirements treated as mandatory transfers.

If an all-inclusive charge is made for tuition, board, room, and other services, a reasonable distribution should be made between revenues for tuition and revenues for sales and services of auxiliary enterprises.

Revenues from tuition and student fees of an academic term that encompasses two fiscal years—for example, a summer session—should be reported totally within the fiscal year in which the program is predominantly conducted.

If tuition or fees are remitted to the state as an offset to the state appropriation, the total of such tuition or fees should be deducted from the total for state appropriations and added to the total for tuition and fees.

Governmental Appropriations

This category includes (1) all unrestricted amounts received for current operations from, or made available to an institution by, legislative acts or local taxing authority and (2) restricted amounts from those same sources to the extent expended for current operations. This category does not include governmental grants and contracts. Amounts paid directly into a state or local retirement system by the appropriating government on behalf of the college or university should be recorded as revenue of the institution. This category does not include institutional fees and other income reappropriated by the legislature to the institution.

The determination of whether a particular government appropriation should be classified as restricted or unrestricted funds is based on the ability of the governing board of the institution to effect a change in the intended use of the funds. If a change in a particular restriction can be made without having to go through the legislative process, the funds should be considered unrestricted. Funds are unrestricted even if they are distributed to the institution for purposes specified by an intermediate group, such as the governing board. In this case, if a change in the use of funds needs to be made, it can be made by the intermediate body without going through the legislative process; the funds therefore would be unrestricted. Such appropriations should be considered unrestricted funds unless the restrictions are so specific that they substantially reduce the institution's flexibility in financial operations. Appropriations in terms of major object classes or to colleges and branch institutions should be classified as unrestricted current funds.

Governmental appropriations should be classified to identify the governmental level—federal, state, or local—of the legislative body making the appropriation to the institution. The fundor level is the level of the agent that makes the decision that the moneys will be appropriated to the particular purpose for which they ultimately are expended. For example, if the federal government stipulates a specific use for some funds that merely flow through the state to the institution, the funds should be classified as federal funds. However, if the federal government distributes funds to the state for unspecified general purposes—for example, general revenue sharing—and the state then appropriates all or a portion of those funds, the funds received by the institution should be classified as state rather than federal funds.

Governmental Grants and Contracts

This category includes (1) all unrestricted amounts received or made available by grants and contracts from governmental agencies for current operations and (2) all amounts received or made available through restricted grants and contracts to the extent expended for current operations.

Amounts equal to direct costs incurred by restricted current funds should be recorded as revenues of those funds, while amounts equal to associated indirect cost recoveries should be reported as unrestricted current funds revenues.

The government fundor level should be disclosed using the same criterion described for governmental appropriations.

Private Gifts, Grants, and Contracts

This category includes amounts from nongovernmental organizations and individuals, including funds resulting from contracting for the furnishing of goods and services of an instructional, research, or public service nature. It includes all unrestricted gifts, grants, and bequests as well as all restricted gifts, grants, and contracts from nongovernmental sources to the extent expended in the current fiscal year for current operations. Gifts, grants, and contracts from foreign governments should be treated as private gifts, grants, and contracts. Income from funds held in revocable trusts or distributable at the direction of the trustees of the trusts should be reported as a separate revenue source under this classification. This category excludes revenues derived from contracts and other activities, such as utility services, that are not related directly to instruction, research, or public service.

Amounts equal to the direct costs incurred by restricted current funds should be reported as revenues of those funds, while amounts equal to the associated indirect cost recoveries should be recorded as unrestricted current funds revenues.

Endowment Income

This category includes:
1. Unrestricted income from endowment and similar funds.
2. Restricted income from endowment and similar funds to the extent expended for current operations.
3. Income from funds held by others under irrevocable trusts, which should be identified separately under this revenue heading.

The unrestricted income from investments of endowment and similar funds credited to unrestricted current funds revenues should be the total ordinary income earned (or yield), except for income that must be added back to the principal in accordance with the terms of the agreement of donation. If endowment fund investments include real estate, the income should be reported on a net basis after allowing for all costs of operating and managing the properties.

Income from investments of endowment and similar funds does not include capital gains and losses, since such gains and losses are accounted for in the Endowment and Similar Funds group as additions to and deductions from fund balances. If any portion of the gains of endowment or quasi-endowment funds is utilized for current operating purposes, the portion so utilized should be reported as a transfer rather than as revenue (see Chapter 5:3).

When investments of endowment and similar funds are pooled, the amounts reported as revenues of unrestricted current funds and as additions to restricted current funds should be substantially equal to the amounts earned during the fiscal period and attributable to the various funds.

Many institutions have established endowment income stabilization reserves to spread or allocate current investment income. Two methods have been followed in establishing such reserves.

Under one method, a portion of the total revenue from the investment pool is not allocated to the participating funds, but is set aside in a stabilization reserve; the balance of the investment pool revenue is distributed to the participating funds. This method is not in accordance with generally accepted accounting principles for the following reasons:

1. The balance in the stabilization reserve may represent undistributed income attributable to both restricted and unrestricted current funds. Thus the balance in the reserve cannot be reported accurately in the financial statements.

2. To the extent any of the undistributed income earned during the fiscal year is attributable to unrestricted current funds, an understatement of revenues of unrestricted current funds will occur.

3. Questions might arise as to the authority of the governing board to withhold amounts of income attributable to, but not distributed to, restricted current funds.

Institutions carrying balances in endowment income stabilization reserves created under this method should dispose of them as appropriate.

The second method, which conforms to generally accepted accounting principles, would distribute *all* income from the pools to the participating funds. The amount applicable to unrestricted current funds would be reported as endowment income. Any amounts set aside for a stabilization reserve should be shown as an allocation of the unrestricted current funds balance and appropriately reflected in the balance sheet as a subdivision of that balance. Amounts applicable to restricted current funds should be reported as an addition to those fund balances. The amounts expended from such balances should be shown as revenues of endowment income in the restricted current funds. Amounts unexpended would remain as balances to be carried forward to the next period.

Sales and Services of Educational Activities

This category includes (1) revenues that are related incidentally to the conduct of instruction, research, and public service and (2) revenues of activities that exist to provide an instructional and laboratory experience for students and that incidentally create goods and services that may be sold to students, faculty, staff, and the general public. The type of service rendered takes precedence over the form of agreement by which these services are rendered. Examples of revenues of educational activities are film rentals, sales of scientific and literary publications, testing services, and sales of products and services of dairy creameries, food technology divisions, poultry farms, and health clinics (apart from student health services) that are not part of a hospital. Revenues generated by hospitals (including health clinics that are a part thereof) should be classified as sales and services of hospitals.

If sales and services to students, faculty, or staff, rather than training or instruction, is the purpose of an activity, the revenue should be classified as sales and services of auxiliary enterprises or hospitals.

Sales and Services of Auxiliary Enterprises

This category includes all revenues generated through operations by auxiliary enterprises. An auxiliary enterprise is an entity that exists to furnish goods or services to students, faculty, or staff, and that charges a fee directly related to, although not necessarily equal to, the cost of the goods or services. The general public incidentally may be served by some auxiliary enterprises.

Auxiliary enterprises usually include residence halls, food services, intercollegiate athletics (if essentially self-supporting), college unions, college stores, and such services as barber shops, beauty parlors, and movie theaters. Even though they may serve students and faculty, hospitals are classified separately because of their size and relative financial importance.

This category is limited to revenues derived directly from the operation of the auxiliary enterprises themselves. Revenues from gifts, grants, or endowment income restricted for auxiliary enterprises should be reported under their respective source categories.

Sales and Services of Hospitals

This category includes revenues (net of discounts, allowances, and provision for doubtful accounts) generated by hospitals from daily patient, special, and other services. Revenues of health clinics that are part of a hospital should be included in this category. Not included are revenues for research and other specific-purpose gifts, grants, or endowment income restricted to the hospital. Such funds should be included in the appropriate revenue sources described above.

Other Sources

This category should include all sources of current funds revenue not included in other classifications. Examples are interest income and gains and losses on investments in current funds, miscellaneous rentals and sales, expired term endowments, and terminated annuity or life income agreements, if not material.

Note: It is appropriate to subtotal all revenues described above; the subtotal excludes revenues of independent operations.

Transfers from Other Funds

Unrestricted amounts transferred from other fund groups back to the Current Funds group are not revenues of the current funds. An example is the return of quasi-endowment funds from the endowment and similar funds to unrestricted current funds. Such amounts should be identified separately and included in Nonmandatory Transfers (see expenditure categories).

Independent Operations

This category includes all revenues of those operations which are independent of, or unrelated to, but which may enhance the primary missions of the institution—instruction, research, and public service. Included are revenues associated with major federally funded research laboratories and other operations not considered an integral part of the institution's educational, auxiliary enterprise, or hospital activities. This category does not include the net profit (or loss) from operations owned and managed as investments of the institution's endowment funds.

ADDITIONS TO FUND BALANCES

The term "additions" is in contrast to revenues and transfers. Additions are amounts received or made available to the restricted current funds during the reporting period as distinguished from the amounts of restricted funds expended during the fiscal period, which are reported as restricted fund revenues.

CURRENT FUNDS EXPENDITURES AND TRANSFERS

Current funds expenditures represent the costs incurred for goods and services used in the conduct of the institution's operations. They include the acquisition cost of capital assets, such as equipment and library books, to the extent current funds are budgeted for and used by operating departments for such purposes. If the amount of ending inventories or the cost of services benefiting subsequent fiscal periods is material (in terms of effect on financial statements), both inventories and deferred charges should be recorded as assets and previously recorded expenditures appropriately decreased. In a subsequent fiscal period these inventories and deferred charges as consumed should be included as expenditures of that period. Significant inventories of materials are usually present in central stores.

A capital asset is defined as any physical resource that benefits a program for more than one year. Capital expenditures therefore include funds expended for land, improvements to land, buildings, improvements and additions to buildings, equipment, and library books. Most institutional accounting systems provide for recording at least a portion of capital expenditures in the current fund expenditures accounts of the various operating units. Whether an expenditure is to be considered a capital expenditure is generally a matter for institutional determination, or in the case of some public institutions, it is prescribed by state regulation.

The general criteria for defining a capital asset are the relative significance of the amount expended and the useful life of the asset acquired, or in the case of repairs and alterations, the extent to which the useful life is extended. For expenditure reporting purposes, any item costing more than a specified amount, as determined by the institution or appropriate governmental unit, and having an expected useful life of more than one year generally should be classified as a capital expenditure.[1]

Interdepartmental transactions ordinarily should be accounted for as an increase in current fund expenditures of the department receiving the materials, services, or capital assets and as a decrease in current fund expenditures of the transferring department. Thus, total institutional expenditures are not inflated by the transactions. Examples are sales and services of service departments and central stores and transfers of material and equipment from one department to another. Any differences between the revenue from sales and services and the operating costs of service departments or central stores, whether debit or credit, are treated as Institutional Support expenditures. On the other hand, sales and services of an auxiliary enterprise to another department or auxiliary enterprise, or sales of materials produced by an instructional department to another department or auxiliary enterprise, would be reported as an expenditure of the department or auxiliary enterprise receiving the materials or services and as revenue of the department or auxiliary enterprise selling the materials or services.

Expenditures differ from transfers. Expenditures are the recognition of the expending of resources of the Current Funds group toward the objectives of each of the respective funds of that group. Transfers are amounts moved between fund groups to be used for the objectives of the recipient fund group. There are two types of transfers, mandatory and nonmandatory, which are fully described later in this chapter.

Expenditures and transfers may be classified in a variety of ways to serve a variety of purposes. Some of the factors bearing on the desired classification are:

1. The context in which appropriations, gifts, grants, and other sources of revenue are made to the institution.

2. The mode best suited for preparing and executing the budget.

3. The form that best serves the needs for financial reporting.

4. The presentation that will improve the quality of comparative studies among institutions.

Thus, expenditures and transfers may be classified in terms of programs, functions, organizational units, projects, and object classes.

Classifications by *program* often cut across organizational, functional, and even fund group lines and are useful in the planning processes. The *functional* classification pattern—educational and general, auxiliary enterprises, hospitals, independent operations, and their subcategories—provides the greatest comparability of data among institutions. The classification by *organizational units* provides data corresponding to channels of intra-institutional administrative responsibilities. Classification by *projects* serves to provide data corresponding to the pattern in which gifts, grants, and contracts are utilized by the institution. Classification by *object class*—that is, according to materials or capital assets purchased or services received, such as personal services, staff benefits, printing and stationery, travel, communications, food, fuel, utilities, repairs, equipment, and library books—serves internal management needs.

Published financial reports usually classify expenditures and transfers in terms of function, organizational unit, and object, in that order.

It is suggested that the following functional classification be followed:

Educational and General
    Expenditures
        Instruction
        Research
        Public Service
        Academic Support
        Student Services
        Institutional Support
        Operation and Maintenance of Plant
        Scholarships and Fellowships
    Mandatory Transfers
    Nonmandatory Transfers
Auxiliary Enterprises
    Expenditures
    Mandatory Transfers
    Nonmandatory Transfers

---

[1]The Cost Accounting Standards Board (CASB) has stipulated $500 and a useful life of more than two years as the threshold at which items must be considered capital assets, and Federal Management Circular 73-8 (formerly OMB Circular A-21) defines equipment as items having an acquisition cost of $200 or more and an expected service life of one year or more. Different limits which are reasonable and consistently applied are acceptable.

Hospitals
    Expenditures
    Mandatory Transfers
    Nonmandatory Transfers
Independent Operations
    Expenditures
    Mandatory Transfers
    Nonmandatory Transfers

Educational and General

Instruction. This category should include expenditures for all activities that are part of an institution's instruction program, with the exception of expenditures for remedial and tutorial instruction, which should be categorized as Student Services. Expenditures for credit and noncredit courses, for academic, occupational, and vocational instruction, and for regular, special, and extension sessions should be included.

Expenditures for departmental research and public service that are not separately budgeted should be included in this classification. This category excludes expenditures for academic administration when the primary assignment is administration—for example, academic deans. However, expenditures for department chairmen, in which instruction is still an important role of the administrator, are included in this category.

Research. This category should include all expenditures for activities specifically organized to produce research outcomes, whether commissioned by an agency external to the institution or separately budgeted by an organizational unit within the institution. Subject to these conditions, it includes expenditures for individual and/or project research as well as those of institutes and research centers. This category does not include all sponsored programs (training grants are an example) nor is it necessarily limited to sponsored research, since internally supported research programs, if separately budgeted, might be included in this category under the circumstances described above. Expenditures for departmental research that are separately budgeted specifically for research are included in this category.

Public Service. This category should include funds expended for activities that are established primarily to provide noninstructional services beneficial to individuals and groups external to the institution. These activities include community service programs (excluding instructional activities) and cooperative extension services. Included in this category are conferences, institutes, general advisory services, reference bureaus, radio and television, consulting, and similar noninstructional services to particular sectors of the community.

Academic Support. This category should include funds expended primarily to provide support services for the institution's primary missions—instruction, research, and public service. It includes (1) the retention, preservation, and display of educational materials—for example, libraries, museums, and galleries; (2) the provision of services that directly assist the academic functions of the institution, such as demonstration schools associated with a department, school, or college of education; (3) media, such as audiovisual services and technology such as computing support; (4) academic administration (including academic deans but not department chairmen) and personnel development providing administrative support and management direction to the three primary missions; and (5) separately budgeted support for course and curriculum development. For institutions that currently charge certain of the expenditures—for example, computing support—directly to the various operating units of the institution, such expenditures are not reflected in this category.

Student Services. This category should include funds expended for offices of admissions and registrar and those activities whose primary purpose is to contribute to the student's emotional and physical well-being and to his intellectual, cultural, and social development outside the context of the formal instruction program. It includes expenditures for student activities, cultural events, student newspaper, intramural athletics, student organizations, intercollegiate athletics (if the program is operated as an integral part of the department of physical education and not as an essentially self-supporting activity), supplemental educational services to provide matriculated students with supplemental instruction outside of the normal academic program (remedial instruction is an example), counseling and career guidance (excluding informal academic counseling by the faculty), student aid administration, and student health service (if not operated as an essentially self-supporting activity).

Institutional Support. This category should include expenditures for: (1) central executive-level activities concerned with management and long-range planning of the entire institution, such as the governing board, planning and programming, and legal services; (2) fiscal operations, including the investment office; (3) administrative data processing; (4) space management; (5) employee personnel and records; (6) logistical activities that provide procurement, storerooms, safety, security, printing, and transportation services to the institution; (7) support services to faculty and staff that are not operated as auxiliary enterprises; and (8) activities concerned with community and alumni relations, including development and fund raising.

Appropriate allocations of institutional support should be made to auxiliary enterprises, hospitals, and any other activities not reported under the Educational and General heading of expenditures.

Operation and Maintenance of Plant. This category should include all expenditures of current operating funds for the operation and maintenance of physical plant, in all cases net of amounts charged to auxiliary enterprises, hospitals, and independent operations. It does not include expenditures made from the institutional plant fund accounts. It includes all expenditures for operations established to provide services and maintenance related to grounds and facilities. Also included are utilities, fire protection, property insurance, and similar items.

Scholarships and Fellowships. This category should include expenditures for scholarships and fellowships in the form of outright grants to students selected by the institution and financed from current funds, restricted or unrestricted. It also should include trainee stipends, prizes, and awards, except trainee stipends awarded to individuals who are not enrolled in formal course work, which should be charged to instruction, research, or public service as appropriate. If the institution is given custody of the funds, but is not allowed to select the recipient of the grant—for example, federal Basic Educational Opportunity Grants program or ROTC scholarships—the funds should be reported in the Agency Funds group rather than in the Current Funds group. The recipient of an outright grant is not required to perform service to the institution as consideration for the grant, nor is he

expected to repay the amount of the grant to the funding source. When services are required in exchange for financial assistance, as in the federal College Work-Study Program, the charges should be classified as expenditures of the department or organizational unit to which the service is rendered. Aid to students in the form of tuition or fee remissions also should be included in this category. However, remissions of tuition or fees granted because of faculty or staff status, or family relationship of students to faculty or staff, should be recorded as staff benefit expenditures in the appropriate functional expenditure category.

Mandatory Transfers. This category should include transfers from the Current Funds group to other fund groups arising out of (1) binding legal agreements related to the financing of educational plant, such as amounts for debt retirement, interest, and required provisions for renewals and replacements of plant, not financed from other sources, and (2) grant agreements with agencies of the federal government, donors, and other organizations to match gifts and grants to loan and other funds. Mandatory transfers may be required to be made from either unrestricted or restricted current funds.

Nonmandatory Transfers. This category should include those transfers from the Current Funds group to other fund groups made at the discretion of the governing board to serve a variety of objectives, such as additions to loan funds, additions to quasi-endowment funds, general or specific plant additions, voluntary renewals and replacements of plant, and prepayments on debt principal. It also may include the retransfer of resources back to current funds.

Auxiliary Enterprises

An auxiliary enterprise is an entity that exists to furnish goods or services to students, faculty, or staff, and that charges a fee directly related to, although not necessarily equal to, the cost of the goods or services. The distinguishing characteristic of auxiliary enterprises is that they are managed as essentially self-supporting activities. Examples are residence halls, food services, intercollegiate athletics, (only if essentially self-supporting), college stores, faculty clubs, faculty and staff parking, and faculty housing. Student health services, when operated as an auxiliary enterprise, also should be included. The general public may be served incidentally by auxiliary enterprises. Hospitals, although they may serve students, faculty, or staff, are separately classified because of their relative financial significance.

This category includes all expenditures and transfers relating to the operation of auxiliary enterprises, including expenditures for operation and maintenance of plant and for institutional support; also included are other direct and indirect costs, whether charged directly as expenditures or allocated as a proportionate share of costs of other departments or units.

Expenditures. Expenditures of auxiliary enterprises are identified by using the same general criteria as for educational and general expenditures to distinguish them from transfers.

Mandatory Transfers. This type of transfer follows the same criteria of identification as for educational and general mandatory transfers to distinguish them from expenditures and nonmandatory transfers.

Nonmandatory Transfers. This type of transfer follows the same criteria of identification as for educational and general nonmandatory transfers to distinguish them from expenditures and mandatory transfers.

Hospitals

This category includes all expenditures and transfers associated with the patient care operations of the hospital, including nursing and other professional services, general services, administrative services, fiscal services, and charges for physical plant operations and institutional support. Also included are other direct and indirect costs, whether charged directly as expenditures or allocated as a proportionate share of costs of other departments or units. Expenditures for those activities which take place within the hospital, but which are categorized more appropriately as instruction or research, should be excluded from this category and accounted for in the appropriate categories.

Expenditures. The same criteria for identifying expenditures are used as in the case of educational

and general expenditures to distinguish them from transfers.

Mandatory Transfers. The same criteria for identifying mandatory transfers are used as in the case of educational and general mandatory transfers to distinguish them from expenditures and nonmandatory transfers.

Nonmandatory Transfers. The same criteria for identifying nonmandatory transfers are used as in the case of educational and general nonmandatory transfers to distinguish them from expenditures and mandatory transfers.

Independent Operations

This category includes expenditures and transfers of those operations which are independent of, or unrelated to, but which may enhance the primary missions of the institution. This category generally is limited to expenditures associated with major federally funded research laboratories. This category excludes expenditures associated with property owned and managed as investments of the institution's endowment funds.

Expenditures. The same criteria for identifying expenditures are used as in the case of educational and general expenditures to distinguish them from transfers.

Mandatory Transfers. The same criteria for identifying mandatory transfers are used as in the case of educational and general mandatory transfers to distinguish them from expenditures and nonmandatory transfers.

Nonmandatory Transfers. The same criteria for identifying nonmandatory transfers are used as in the case of educational and general nonmandatory transfers to distinguish them from expenditures and mandatory transfers.

DEDUCTIONS FROM FUND BALANCES

The term "deductions" is in contrast to expenditures and transfers. Deductions represent decreases in current fund balances, such as refunds to donors and grantors, and unencumbered or unexpended funds returned or returnable to the state treasury at fiscal year-end, depending on provisions of state statutes or appropriation acts.

Loan, Endowment, Annuity, Life Income, and Agency Funds

LOAN FUNDS

The purpose of this fund group is to account for the resources available for loans to students, faculty, and staff.

Loan funds are derived from many different sources such as:

1. Gifts of funds that are to be operated on a revolving basis, whereby repayments of principal and interest may be lent to other individuals.

2. Gifts and grants which provide that, upon repayment of principal and interest, the proceeds are to be refunded to the donors or grantors.

3. Endowment fund income restricted to loan fund purposes.

4. Refundable grants by the U.S. government to be matched with institutional funds for loans to students.

5. Institutional funds transferred from current funds to match refundable U.S. grants.

6. Unrestricted current funds designated by the governing board to function as loan funds.

7. Income and gains from investments of loan funds.

8. Interest earned on loans.

In view of this wide variety of fund sources and the diverse responsibilities for their use, separate accounts should be maintained to indicate these various accountabilities.

The assets may consist of cash, notes receivable, investments, accrued interest on notes receivable and investments, and amounts due from other fund groups.

The liabilities include amounts due to collection agencies for collection fees and to unrestricted funds for unremitted share of administrative costs, as well as refunds due to donors or on refundable loan funds.

Interest rates on loans are determined under a variety of conditions: the rate can be specified by the donor of the respective gift to the loan fund, by regulations of the institution, and by agreements with governmental grantors of loan funds.

Interest on loans should be credited to the specific fund balance account. The accrual basis should be employed for determining interest earned; however, if such an amount is immaterial, it may be accounted for on the cash basis.

Increases in fund balances of the loan funds arise from the sources mentioned above. Assets arising out of borrowings from the government, private sources, or other fund groups do not increase loan fund balances. Refundable grants, such as National Direct Student Loan grants, are not deemed to be borrowings, but rather to be additions to fund balances as long as the date of repayment to the grantor is uncertain.

Decreases in fund balances of loan funds result from losses on investments of the loan funds, provision for possible losses on loans or loans written off in whole or in part, administration and collection expenditures, transfers to other fund groups, and refunds to donors.

When loan losses are estimated, either of two procedures may be followed. Under one alternative the amount of the provision for loan losses is deducted from the total of the balances of the Loan Funds group at the close of the fiscal period and reversed at the beginning of the next fiscal period. Actual losses are charged against the specific loan fund balances to which the loans written off pertain. At the end of each succeeding fiscal year, a new provision is established. Under the second alternative, the amount of the provision for loan losses is deducted from each specific loan fund balance to which the doubtful loans relate. Loans written off are charged against the appropriate allowance for doubtful loans. Thereafter, the allowance is adjusted, based on the estimated collectibility of loans still outstanding.

While neither loan losses nor provisions for loan losses on government loans presently are recognized by the Department of Health, Education, and Welfare, such provisions are in accordance with generally accepted accounting principles and, if material, should be set forth in the institution's financial statements.

For appropriate disclosure, the sources of the funds available for loan purposes at the balance sheet date should be identified separately in the financial statements, such as donor- and government-restricted loan funds, including funds provided by mandatory transfers required for matching purposes, unrestricted funds designated as loan funds, and funds returnable to the donor under certain conditions.

The balance sheet may identify resources available for loans to students separately from those for faculty and staff and should identify unrestricted fund balances that may be reverted to other purposes. In view of the variety of conditions under which loan funds are established and managed, supplementary schedules may be required to fulfill particular needs.

ENDOWMENT AND SIMILAR FUNDS

The Endowment and Similar Funds group generally includes endowment funds, term endowment funds, and quasi-endowment funds.

The following concepts guiding the financial accounting and reporting of endowment and similar funds are intended to be consistent with the policies for administration of such funds as presented in Chapter 4:1, "Administration of Endowment Funds, Quasi-Endowment Funds, and Other Similar Funds." So far as financial accounting and reporting are concerned, provisions of Chapter 5:3 shall govern.

Endowment funds are those for which donors or other external agencies have stipulated under the terms of the gift instrument creating the fund that the principal of the fund is not expendable—that is, it is to remain inviolate in perpetuity and is to be invested for the purpose of producing present and future income, which may be expended or added to principal.

Term endowment funds are like endowment funds, except that all or part of the principal may be utilized after a stated period of time or upon the occurrence of a certain event.

Quasi-endowment funds (funds functioning as endowment) are funds that the governing board of the institution, rather than a donor or other external agency, has determined are to be retained and invested. Since these funds are not required by the donor to be retained and invested, the principal as well as the income may be totally utilized at the discretion of the governing board, subject to any donor-imposed restrictions on use.

Prevailing legal opinion in some states holds to the trust fund theory in which the term "principal" is construed to include not only the original value of the fund when initially established plus subsequent enhancements by additional donations, but also the appreciation in value of investments of the fund.

Traditionally, educational institutions account for yield (dividends, interest, rents, royalties, and the like) as revenue available for institutional purposes and exclude from that category capital appreciation on investment transactions. The majority of educational institutions follow this practice with reference to all endowment funds—true, term, and quasi. This follows the classical trust or fiduciary accounting principle.

Some legal opinions hold to the corporate law concept, under which all gains and losses in the value of investments are treated as income transactions.

A substantial number of states have adopted the model Uniform Management of Institutional Funds Act, which permits the *prudent* use of appreciation in the value of investments. Under the Act, appreciation means enhancement of the value of investments over the historic dollar value—that is, the fair value in dollars of an endowment fund at the time it became an endowment fund plus each subsequent donation at the time it was made plus each addition of income to principal made pursuant to the terms of the gift instrument at the time of the addition. If the market value of the net assets associated with the fund is below the historic dollar value of the fund, the institution may expend only the yield.

Many institutions have adopted "total return" spending formulas by which they expend not only the yield but also a prudent portion of the appreciation of the principal. Almost all of the total return approaches call for the protection of the endowment principal from its loss of purchasing power as a primary consideration before appropriating gains.

Some spending approaches employ spreading techniques to minimize the effect of extreme short-term fluctuations in realized gains and losses, which may occur under the timing of the completed transaction method. Others combine both realized and unrealized gains in the spreading technique. Many institutions have confined the appropriation of gains to quasi-endowment funds. Other institutions have appropriated gains of virtually all types of endowment and similar funds. Some institutions restrict gains for appropriation to only realized gains, while others consider unrealized gains as also available for appropriation.

In view of the variations in application of the total return concept, its use does not consistently produce results that are objectively determinable. The concept of "principal" is often indecisive; there is no clear redefinition of income; the exercise of prudence is subjective and not susceptible to measurement in an accounting sense, and the "spending rate" is often related to the market value of securities rather than to the total return actually experienced.

Until a general practice in the application of the total return concept evolves that produces results that are objectively determinable, institutions should report any appreciation utilized from investments of endowment and similar funds as a transfer. To the extent such a transfer is added to current funds, it should be reported separately from the traditional income from endowment and similar funds and should not be included in total current funds revenues.

Except for sales and purchase commissions, all expenses of holding and managing endowment investments, except real estate, should be treated as institutional support costs and not netted against income; expenses may be funded from both unrestricted and restricted current funds. However, this treatment does not preclude the allocation of all expenses against income in evaluating the effectiveness of investment management.

When endowment funds are invested in real estate, the income should be reported on a net basis after allocating all costs of operating and managing the properties.

Income from investments of endowment and similar funds should be reported as either for:

1. Restricted purposes, credited to the respective unexpended endowment income accounts in restricted current funds or to fund balances such as loan, endowment, or plant funds as specified by the terms of the gift instruments, or

2. Unrestricted purposes, credited to unrestricted current funds revenues.

Further discussion of restrictions on the use of income and gains from investments of endowment and similar funds may be found in Chapter 4:1.

Each endowment and similar fund should be accounted for separately. Each fund should have its own cash and investments accounts, unless the assets are pooled with the assets of other funds, in which case the fund would hold shares in the pool. Funds must be invested separately if required by the terms of the gift instrument.

Assets of endowment and similar funds usually consist of cash and investments, but also may include accounts receivable, prepaid items, deferred charges, and amounts due from other fund groups. Investments may include marketable and nonmarketable securities, real estate, patents, copyrights, royalties, and participations. Advances to finance institutional plant should be disclosed separately. Investments are valued and accounted for as indicated in Chapter 5:1, "Fundamental Concepts of Financial Accounting and Reporting."

Liabilities of endowment funds consist of any form of indebtedness against the assets representing investments, as well as amounts due to other fund groups.

Additions to the balances of endowment and similar funds are comprised of gifts and bequests restricted to endowment, income added to principal as provided in the gift instrument, gains on investments, and transfers to quasi-endowment from other fund groups. Deductions from the fund balances include losses on investment transactions and withdrawals or transfers to other fund groups. Fund-raising expenses should not be charged to the balance of endowment and similar funds unless they relate directly to the proceeds of a campaign for that purpose. If so charged, the expenses should be reported separately as deductions and not netted against gift proceeds.

Upon termination, the unrestricted principal of term endowments should be added to unrestricted current funds revenues and clearly identified or disclosed so that there is no inference that a new gift has been received. If the gift instrument specifies that the principal should be restricted to a fund other than unrestricted current funds, such addition should be made directly to that group.

All three types of funds—endowment, term endowment, and quasi-endowment—should be reported in the endowment and similar funds section of the balance sheet and the identity of the three types should be clearly differentiated in the fund balance section. All three types of funds in this group may be further subdivided according to the manner in which the income from their investments may or must be used.

Annuity and life income funds, if insignificant in amount, also may be included in this group. If significant, these funds should be reported in a separate fund group.

ANNUITY AND LIFE INCOME FUNDS

The Annuity and Life Income Funds group consists of two subgroups—Annuity Funds and Life Income Funds.

Annuity Funds

The Annuity Funds subgroup consists of funds acquired by an institution under agreements whereby money or other property is made available to an institution on condition that it bind itself to pay stipulated amounts periodically to the donors or other designated individuals, which payments are to terminate at the time specified in the agreement.

In many jurisdictions, the "selling" or accept-

ance of annuities by a nonprofit organization is subject to the regulation of the appropriate government agency or department. For example, the Tax Reform Act of 1969 states the conditions under which an annuity trust (for Internal Revenue Service purposes) may be established and administered. In some jurisdictions, annuity investments must be deposited or security deposits made with a government agency. The supervising government agency also may designate the types of investments that may be made from these funds.

Accounting for annuity funds requires the recording of assets at cost or at fair market value at the date of receipt. The liabilities should be stated at the present value of the aggregate liability for annuities payable, based on acceptable life expectancy tables. There may be a fund balance or deficit, depending on the relationship between assets and liabilities. Investment income and gains are credited and annuity payments and investment losses charged against the liabilities. Periodically, an adjustment is made between the liabilities and the fund balances due to recomputation of the liabilities, based on the revised life expectancies and anticipated return on investments.

The assets of annuity funds include cash, securities, and other types of investments. The assets may be pooled for investment purposes, depending on the frequency of the adjustment of shares owned by individual funds, the number of funds, and regulatory provisions (see Chapter 4:1).

The liabilities of annuity funds include indebtedness against any of the assets, annuity payments currently due, amounts due to other fund groups, and the actuarial amount of future annuities payable.

Increases in annuity fund balances include additions of new gifts in excess of actuarial liability for annuities payable. Decreases include transfers to other fund groups upon termination of annuity agreements. Additional changes in the fund balances occur when an adjustment is made between the liabilities and fund balances, representing changes to the revised life expectancies and anticipated return on investments.

Upon termination of an annuity agreement, the principal of the annuity fund is transferred to the fund group specified by the originator, or in the absence of such restriction, to unrestricted current funds revenues clearly identified and disclosed, so that no inference is drawn that a new gift has been received.

If immaterial in amount, annuity funds may be included in the Endowment and Similar Funds group.

Life Income Funds

The Life Income Funds subgroup consists of funds acquired by an institution under agreements whereby money or other property is made available to an institution on condition that it bind itself to pay periodically to the donors or other designated individuals the income earned by the assets donated, usually for the lifetimes of the income beneficiaries.

In order to qualify and maintain a tax-exempt status for pooled life income funds, compliance with relevant provisions of federal and state law is essential. The Tax Reform Act of 1969 clearly established the existence of a trust relationship for Internal Revenue Service purposes when educational institutions are trustees of life income funds. The Internal Revenue Code and attendant regulations provide for three variations of the life income unitrust—"straight," "net income," and "net plus makeup" (see Chapter 4:1).

Life income funds usually are accounted for as a separate subgroup but are combined with annuity funds for reporting purposes. The transactions of life income funds should be reported separately and not as current funds revenues or expenditures. A separate set of accounts must be maintained for each life income fund.

The assets of life income funds include cash, securities, and other types of investments. Assets of life income funds may be invested separately, pooled with assets of other life income funds, or pooled with assets of endowment and similar funds (unless the endowment pool is invested and administered on a total return basis), as long as detailed records are maintained that specifically identify the life income portion of the pool and the income earned for and attributable to that portion (see Chapter 4:1).

The liabilities of life income funds consist of indebtedness against the assets, the life income payments currently due, and amounts due to other fund groups for advances to income beneficiaries.

Changes in fund balances consist of additions of new gifts; income, gains, and losses on investments; and transfers to other fund groups upon termination of the agreements.

Upon termination of agreements, the balance of the fund is transferred to the fund group specified by the originator or, in the absence of a restriction, to unrestricted current funds revenues, clearly identified and disclosed, so that no inference is drawn that a new gift has been received.

AGENCY FUNDS

These funds account for the resources held by the institution as custodian or fiscal agent for individual students, faculty, staff members, and organizations. When agency assets are immaterial in amount, the assets and liabilities may be reported as assets and liabilities of the Current Funds group and need not be accounted for in a separate fund group.

The assets include cash, receivables, temporary investments, and amounts due from other fund groups.

The liabilities include accounts payable, amounts due to other fund groups, and the balances owing to individuals and organizations for which the institution is acting as fiscal agent, custodian, or depository. There are no fund balances in this fund group analogous to those of other fund groups. Separate accounts should be maintained for the transactions in the net deposit liability balance of each account with an organization or individual in this fund group.

The earnings on investments of these funds should be credited to the net liability balances of the respective agency funds.

The balance sheet showing assets and liabilities by major type, including the liability for deposits in custody for others, is the only basic financial statement prepared for the financial reporting of agency funds to the public and the governing board. Since the net balances in each agency fund are liabilities, not fund balances, a statement of changes in fund balances is not prepared for this fund group.

Accountability for agency funds usually requires the submission of periodic reports of transactions and balances to the individuals or organizations owning the assets.

OTHER FUND GROUPS

The accounting and reporting for other fund groups administered by the institution, such as pension funds, are comparable with procedures for endowment and/or agency funds, and in some instances with those of commercial pension funds.

FUNDS HELD IN TRUST BY OTHERS

Funds held in trust by others are resources neither in the possession of nor under the management of the institution, but held and administered by an external fiscal agent. They preferably should not be included in the balance sheet with other funds administered by the institution, but should be disclosed parenthetically in the Endowment and Similar Funds group in the balance sheet or in the notes to the financial statements. However, if the institution has legally enforceable rights or claims, including those as to income, such funds may be reported as assets, properly described in the financial statements. The value of such funds should be supported by annual trust reports available to the institution.

If the funds were established under irrevocable trusts with no discretionary powers resting with the trustees as to the distribution of income, the income should be included either as endowment income, with a notation of the amount, or should be separately stated. If the funds were established under revocable trusts, or if the trustees have discretion as to the amounts to be distributed to the beneficiaries, the discretionary amounts of income are tantamount to gifts and should be so reported with disclosure of the amounts.

Plant Funds

THE PLANT FUNDS group is used to account for (1) unexpended plant funds to be used for the acquisition of long-lived assets for institutional purposes, (2) funds set aside for the renewal and replacement of institutional properties, (3) funds set aside for debt service charges and retirement of indebtedness on institutional plant, and (4) the cost (or fair value at time of donation) of long-lived assets (other than those of endowment and similar funds) and the sources from which the cost is funded, including associated liabilities.

Four self-balancing subgroups are provided for the Plant Funds group: Unexpended Plant Funds, Funds for Renewals and Replacements, Funds for Retirement of Indebtedness, and Investment in Plant.

There are the following general sources of assets of the Unexpended Plant Funds, the Funds for Renewals and Replacements, and the Funds for Retirement of Indebtedness:

1. Funds from external agencies.

2. Student fees and assessments for debt service or other plant purposes, which create an obligation equivalent to an externally imposed restriction and which are not subject to the discretionary right of the governing board to use for other purposes.

3. Transfers, both mandatory and nonmandatory, from other fund groups.

4. Borrowings from external sources for plant purposes.

5. Borrowings by advances from other fund groups.

6. Income and net gains from investments in the unrestricted and restricted elements of each of the subgroups.

The distinction between unrestricted and re-

stricted sources and uses should be maintained in the accounting records in order to disclose the limitations on the use of funds and the appropriate disposition of any excess funds. For example, funds derived from transfers from unrestricted current funds at the discretion of the governing board may be retransferred in whole or in part from plant funds prior to commitment.

When funds are restricted by donors and other outside individuals and agencies for plant purposes, such funds should be credited directly to the respective fund subgroup and not passed through the Current Funds group.

Transfers from other fund groups to plant funds for the acquisition of properties, for renewals and replacements, and for debt service should be represented by appropriate amounts of cash and other liquid assets. Transfers from plant funds to other fund groups also should be represented by the appropriate transfer of liquid assets.

UNEXPENDED PLANT FUNDS

The purpose of this subgroup is to account for the unexpended resources derived from various sources to finance the acquisition of long-lived plant assets and the associated liabilities. This subgroup also may include construction in progress, if not accounted for in the Investment in Plant subgroup.

Assets of this subgroup may consist of cash, investments, accounts receivable, amounts due from other fund groups, and construction in progress. Liabilities may consist of accounts, bonds, notes, mortgages, and leaseholds payable and amounts due to other fund groups.

The fund balances represent amounts unexpended at the reporting date. The sources of additions to fund balances are the same as the sources of assets (see above) except borrowings. Deductions from fund balances include expenditures for plant purposes, losses on investments of unexpended plant funds, return of unrestricted balances to unrestricted current funds, and other appropriate charges such as fund-raising expenses related to a building fund campaign.

Encumbrances outstanding at the reporting date should be reported either as allocations of fund balances or by footnote to the balance sheet.

Separate project accounts should be maintained for each major item. Within each project account the sources of funds should be distinguished between restricted and unrestricted.

As funds are expended for construction, a control account for construction in progress should be maintained. All capital expenditures, together with related liabilities and fund balances, should be transferred to the Investment in Plant subgroup at each reporting date. Alternatively, the accounting for construction in progress may be maintained in the Unexpended Plant Funds until completion of the project.

Any noncapitalized project costs should be written off against the fund balance of Unexpended Plant Funds. The related liabilities, if any, should be transferred to the Investment in Plant subgroup. This will have the effect of reducing the fund balances of both the former and latter subgroups by the amount of the transferred liabilities.

FUNDS FOR RENEWALS AND REPLACEMENTS

The resources of this subgroup provide for the renewal and replacement of plant fund assets as distinguished from additions and improvements to plant. In some instances, there is a fine line of distinction between a renewal or replacement and an improvement. Some portion of renewals and replacements may be capitalized as additions to plant.

Assets of this subgroup may include cash, investments, deposits with others, amounts due from other fund groups, and construction in progress. Liabilities may consist of accrued liabilities; accounts, notes, and bonds payable; and amounts due to other fund groups.

Fund balances represent the unexpended resources of this subgroup, and should be maintained to distinguish between unexpended resources originating from board-designated unrestricted funds

transferred for the purposes of this subgroup and those restricted for these purposes by external parties. Separate accounts for each fund within each project often are maintained to assist in establishing this distinction.

Additions to fund balances are those generally included in the listing of sources of assets above, other than borrowings. Deductions from fund balances consist of expenditures for renewals and replacements, transfers of unrestricted resources back to unrestricted current funds, and losses on sales of investments held by the subgroup.

Encumbrances outstanding at the reporting date should be reported either as allocations of the fund balances or by footnote to the balance sheet.

If it is determined that certain expenditures in this subgroup should be capitalized, the costs and associated liabilities and fund balances, if any, are transferred to the Investment in Plant subgroup as in the case of transfers of capitalized assets from the Unexpended Plant Funds to the Investment in Plant subgroup.

FUNDS FOR RETIREMENT OF INDEBTEDNESS

The purpose of this subgroup is to account for the accumulation of resources for interest and principal payments and other debt service charges, including contributions for sinking funds, relating to plant fund indebtedness.

Fund sources that restrict their use to the objectives of this subgroup should be recorded as *direct* additions to the fund balances of this subgroup and not as revenues of the Current Funds group or additions to fund balances of other fund groups.

Assets of this subgroup may include cash, investments, deposits with others, accounts and notes receivable, and amounts due from other fund groups. Liabilities may consist of accruals and accounts payable for trustees' fees and other debt service charges, as well as amounts due to other fund groups.

Fund balances represent the net resources held to serve the objectives of this subgroup. Since there are varying degrees of restriction on the use of funds in this subgroup, separate accounts should be maintained for each debt to delineate those balances originating from board-designated transfers and those restricted by legal provisions and other agreements with donors and other outside agencies.

Additions to the fund balances are those generally included in the listing of the sources of assets above, other than borrowings. Deductions include expenditures for principal and interest, trustees' fees and expenses, and losses on investments of funds in this subgroup. Transfers of cash or other liquid assets to sinking fund trustees, as required by bond indentures, are transfers between asset accounts and do not reduce fund balances.

Expenditures that reduce debt principal represent the further investment of institutional resources in the net investment in plant. Accordingly, the appropriate indebtedness in the Investment in Plant subgroup is decreased and the net investment in plant (the fund balance) is increased.

INVESTMENT IN PLANT

Except for long-lived assets held as investments in endowment and similar funds and their associated liabilities, the Investment in Plant subgroup includes all long-lived assets in the service of the institution and all construction in progress (unless carried in the Unexpended Plant Funds and Funds for Renewals and Replacements subgroups until completion of the project), as well as all associated liabilities.

The sources of assets of this subgroup include:

1. The capitalized completion costs of projects transferred from the Unexpended Plant Funds and Funds for Renewals and Replacements subgroups.
2. Capitalized costs of construction in progress transferred from the Unexpended Plant Funds and the Funds for Renewals and Replacements subgroups at the reporting date, unless held in those subgroups until completion of the project.
3. Donations (at fair market value on date of gift) of plant assets.
4. The cost of long-lived assets financed by expenditures of current and other funds, except endowment and similar funds.

Depreciation allowances on long-lived assets may be reported in the balance sheet and provision for depreciation in the statement of changes in fund balances in the Investment in Plant subgroup.

The assets may consist of land, buildings, improvements other than buildings, equipment, and library books. In cases where the institution has elected to record depreciation as described in Chapter 5:1, the applicable reduction in value would be disclosed here. Liabilities may consist of accounts, bonds, notes, mortgages, and leaseholds payable and amounts due to other fund groups if associated with the acquisition, renewal, or replacement of plant assets.

The net investment in plant is the fund balance representing the excess of the carrying value of assets over liabilities. Net investment in plant is increased through the acquisition of plant assets less associated liabilities, as well as through liquidation of indebtedness incurred for plant purposes.

Net investment in plant is decreased through disposal of assets and through depreciation, if depreciation is recorded as discussed above. When plant assets are sold, exchanged, or otherwise disposed of, the carrying value is removed from the asset accounts and the net investment is reduced accordingly. Upon sale of plant assets, the proceeds may be used to reduce the outstanding associated liabilities and the remainder may be added to unexpended plant funds. The appropriate disposition of proceeds depends on the sources of funds for the original acquisition of the assets, the laws and administrative regulations of the respective states, and/or the terms of agreements with donors or grantors.

Consideration may be given to subdividing the fund balance to indicate fund sources such as appropriations, gifts, student fees, and federal, state, and local grants.

FINANCIAL REPORTS OF PLANT FUNDS

Some institutions prepare sectional balance sheets and statements of changes in fund balances for each of the four subgroups of the Plant Funds group; some combine the assets and liabilities of the four subgroups for reporting purposes; others combine the assets and liabilities of three of the subgroups (Unexpended Plant Funds, Funds for Renewals and Replacements, and Funds for Retirement of Indebtedness) and list the Investment in Plant subgroup separately. Any combination of the assets and liabilities of the four subgroups is acceptable as long as separate fund balances are reported for each subgroup.

Financial Reports

A MAJOR OBJECTIVE of financial reports of colleges and universities is to provide information useful for evaluating the management of resources in attaining the institution's goals. In fulfillment of this and other objectives, financial reporting for colleges and universities generally should include three basic financial statements. These are:

1. Balance sheet.
2. Statement of changes in fund balances.
3. Statement of current funds revenues, expenditures, and other changes.

The balance sheet is a statement of financial position or status of funds resources as of a given reporting date. A balance sheet should be presented that includes all of the appropriate fund groups. It may be prepared with fund groups arranged sequentially in vertical order (as illustrated in the chapter "Illustrative Exhibits") or it may be presented in columnar form with a column for each fund group.

If the columnar form is used, amounts in the various fund groups should not be cross-footed in a total column unless all necessary disclosures are made, including interfund borrowings. The balances of any fund subgroups necessary for fair presentation, particularly those subgroups segregating donor-restricted from board-designated resources, should be reported either in the balance sheet or in the statement of changes in fund balances.

The statement of changes in fund balances is essentially a statement of changes in financial position between reporting dates, and is presented for all fund groups except agency funds, which have no fund balances. This statement may be presented either in columnar form (as illustrated) or in individual statements for each of the fund groups.

If the statement of changes in fund balances is presented in columnar form, columns should not be cross-footed unless care is taken to avoid the mislabeling of cross-footed totals and duplication of gross changes.

When significant resources or expenditures such as financing activities and investments in plant are not included in the statement of changes in fund balances, such activities may be disclosed separately in a note or elsewhere in the financial statements.

The statement of current funds revenues, expenditures, and other changes is unique to the current funds. It shows the details of current funds revenues by source, expenditures by function, and all other changes in current funds. A columnar statement of current funds revenues, expenditures, and other changes should be used to distinguish between unrestricted and restricted current funds revenues and expenditures. In this statement an amount equal to the restricted fund expenditures is reported as restricted revenues.

The statement of current funds revenues, expenditures, and other changes presents required, detailed financial information that may not ordinarily be presented in the current funds section of the statement of changes in fund balances. The net increases or decreases in both restricted and unrestricted funds in the former statement should be the same as reported for the net changes in the balances of the unrestricted and restricted funds in the statement of changes in fund balances.

The reporting objectives of this statement may be met in other ways. One technique is to dispense with the statement of current funds revenues, expenditures, and other changes and report the detailed, classified information in the statement of changes in fund balances. Another technique is to dispense with the statement of current funds revenues, expenditures, and other changes, substitute a statement of current funds expenditures by function, and include the detailed sources of revenues as additions to current fund balances in the statement of changes in fund balances.

In following these reporting techniques, it should be pointed out that revenues arising from the use of restricted funds are not ordinarily the equivalent of restricted current fund additions, since only the amounts equal to restricted fund expenditures are reported as restricted fund revenues. Therefore, the amounts earned through the expenditures of such funds should be disclosed in the basic statements or in notes thereto. It is also necessary to report the total of unrestricted and restricted current funds expended for each of the functional categories so that the total level of financial activity for each such category is disclosed.

For more complete disclosure, institutions may wish to explore variations in format and presentation. For example, institutions wishing to report separately unrestricted gifts, auxiliary enterprises, hospitals, and special activities may use additional columns or provide separate fund subgroups to the three statements. In all cases the statements should clearly indicate the unrestricted nature of such funds and the related changes for the period. In addition, a total column for all unrestricted current funds resources, fund balances, and current funds revenues, expenditures, and other changes for the period should be included in the appropriate statements.

Reporting requirements singularly relevant to the balance sheet and the statement of changes in fund balances of the loan, endowment, annuity, life income, agency, and plant funds may be found in the appropriate preceding chapters.

REPORTING RESULTS OF CHANGES IN ACCOUNTING METHOD

Adjustments resulting from a change in accounting method to comply with the recommendations of this manual should be treated as adjustments of prior periods, and financial statements for affected prior periods should be appropriately restated.

A subsequent change in accounting method ordinarily is reported as follows:

1. Financial statements of prior periods should be presented as they were originally.

2. The effect of the change on the reporting of current and prior periods should be disclosed in the financial statements or in the notes thereto.

3. The cumulative effect of the change should be disclosed in the statement of changes in fund balances.

NOTES TO FINANCIAL STATEMENTS

To achieve the objectives of adequate disclosure, the basic financial statements should be accompanied by (1) explanatory notes on significant matters not adequately disclosed in the financial statements and (2) a commentary on the accounting policies adopted and followed by the institution, as well as the effect of any changes in accounting method to the extent not disclosed in the financial statements. (See "Summary of Significant Accounting Policies" in the chapter "Illustrative Exhibits.")

SUPPLEMENTARY SCHEDULES

Consideration should be given to the desirability of providing supplementary schedules to the basic financial statements, which might be useful to various groups interested in the management of an institution. Some of these might be:

1. Schedule of current funds expenditures and mandatory transfers and resources *utilized*. (This schedule would be especially useful to institutions employing the total return concept or managing unrestricted gifts as separate resources.)

2. Schedule of current funds revenues.

3. Schedule of current funds expenditures.

4. Summary of gifts received—by source and purpose.

5. Summary of investments.

6. Summary of property, plant, and equipment.

7. Schedule of long-term debt.

8. Details of balances of each fund and changes therein during the period.

9. Schedule of operations of auxiliary enterprises.

10. Schedule of operations of hospitals.

11. Schedule of operations of independent operations.

SUPPLEMENTARY MATERIAL

In addition, the basic financial statements may be accompanied by interpretive material such as:

1. A more complete statement of the principles and objectives of fund accounting and the relationships among fund groups.

2. An explanation of accrual accounting and its objectives; its application to the various fund groups.

3. Definitions of commonly used terms such as expenditures, expenses, mandatory transfers, nonmandatory transfers, other changes, encumbrances, and allocations.

4. An interpretation of the financial statements, schedules, and exhibits, referenced to charts, graphs, and other illustrative material. This interpretive material may include nonfinancial data associated with financial information to show trends in relationships such as:

   a. Educational and general expenditures per full-time-equivalent student.

   b. Expenditures for operation and maintenance of plant per square foot of floor space.

   c. Average full-time faculty compensation, including staff benefits, by ranks within colleges or other major academic divisions.

   d. Direct educational and general expenditures for instruction per semester or quarter hour by colleges and other academic divisions.

ANNUAL REPORT FOR PUBLIC DISTRIBUTION

Colleges and universities, whether publicly or privately controlled, depend on public understanding and support; consequently it is desirable for an institution to publish an annual financial report. The extent of distribution should be sufficient to insure that representatives of the public and members of groups responsible for the institution's support are adequately informed of its financial affairs.

The financial report should present fairly the essentials of the institution's financial activities for the period covered and its financial position at the close of the period. Although excessive detail should be avoided, the goal should be the disclosure of resources and their utilization to inform those users of the financial statements who rely on them as their principal source of financial information about the institution's activities. The financial information relating to separately incorporated units for which the reporting institution is fiscally responsible, such as university presses, intercollegiate athletics, and research foundations, should be (1) included in separate statements, accompanied by and cross-referenced to the basic institutional statements, (2) disclosed by footnotes, or (3) included in the financial statements of the institution.

The auditor's opinion should be included in the published annual financial report. If it becomes necessary to issue a report without an auditor's opinion, a complete explanation should be included in the report.

ANNUAL REPORTS FOR INTERNAL USE

A report more detailed than the annual report for public distribution should be prepared in permanent form for use by academic and financial administrative officers, for whom it can constitute a valuable reference. In this report the financial information should be arranged by major academic, administrative, and other operating divisions and should provide details to support the figures in the exhibits of the financial report for public distribution. A table of contents and an index are useful adjuncts.

In addition to the annual published report and the detailed internal report, other supporting schedules should be prepared for those responsible for carrying out specific functions, such as the director of auxiliary enterprises, director of a fund-raising program, superviser of construction projects, investment manager, and directors of research programs and activities.

INTERIM REPORTS FOR INTERNAL USE

The form, frequency, distribution, and content of reports for internal use vary among colleges and universities according to size and complexity. Every institution will find it useful to prepare a report each month comparing current funds revenues, expenditures, and encumbrances with budgeted amounts.

Other reports for management and the governing board should be prepared at regular intervals. Examples of these are reports concerning restricted current funds, research projects, gifts received, construction projects, inventories, and cash flow. Reports frequently are prepared to show trends in financial operations by means of historical data combined with projections. Such reports are especially valuable when important changes in operations are being considered.

Reports on special projects or areas of administration should be prepared as needed. Such reports may (1) evaluate the impact of fund sources on the institution's activities and vice versa, (2) compare revenues from tuition and fees paid by students residing within the state with those paid by out-of-state students, (3) analyze procurement and contracting procedures to ascertain whether sufficient safeguards are maintained, and (4) propose the indirect cost rates for sponsored programs.

Reports, usually monthly, on transactions in investments of all endowment funds should be prepared and transmitted to the manager of the investment portfolio, to the investment committee of the governing board, and to other committees and administrative officers of the institution. Discussion of the measurement of investment results may be found in Chapter 4:2, "Investment Management."

Operating reports should be prepared at least monthly for each auxiliary enterprise, hospital, and independent operation. Reports for some activities, such as food services and the college store, may be required at more frequent intervals.

Balance sheets should be prepared periodically —for current funds at least—showing current-date balances compared with the same date a year earlier. These statements are important to facilitate the required surveillance over receivables, unbilled charges, deferred charges, inventories, payables, and deferred credits. Daily reports of cash balances as well as cash receipts and disbursements are necessary to the proper exercise of treasury responsibilities.

The chief business officer should provide those internal reports that are needed and most effective, should be alert to the needs of the governing board, its committees, and the administrative officers, and furnish them with reports that will contribute to effective management. He should use every opportunity to educate the governing board and administrators concerning the content and meaning of all financial reports so that the reports will be most useful. Any internal reports that do not facilitate planning, operating, controlling, or evaluating should be discontinued.

INTEGRATION OF REPORTS
WITH THE ACCOUNTING CYCLE

There is continual need in the division of business affairs to examine different operations and activities. In order for financial reports to serve their purposes most effectively, they must be planned and scheduled as a regular part of accounting activities, rather than result from frequent emergency requests. The division must be staffed adequately to prepare the needed interim reports and the annual report.

Chart of Accounts

A SYSTEMATIC CLASSIFICATION of accounts is an essential part of an accounting system. The accounts should be developed to be compatible with the organizational structure of the institution, and their form and content should be arranged in agreement with the financial reports to be presented.

The arrangement should be formalized in a chart of accounts, and for ease of identification and reference, each account should be assigned an appropriate code number or symbol. Classification should be according to the funds and fund groups of the institution, as described in the preceding chapters of Part 5. Within each fund group, the accounts should be listed according to assets, liabilities, and fund balance accounts.

The illustrative chart of accounts for a college or university presented below shows those accounts usually found in the general ledger or carried in subsidiary ledgers with appropriate control accounts in the general ledger. This chart is presented as a guide for institutions in developing their own detailed charts of accounts and to help them set up their accounts in conformity with the principles of accounting and reporting presented in the preceding chapters of Part 5. The system of accounts may be expanded, contracted, or modified to meet the needs of the individual institution and to con-

form to its organizational structure, but in any case it should incorporate the basic elements common to all educational institutions.

In designing or revising a chart of accounts, the code numbers or symbols assigned to the accounts should progress in a logical order. Because each fund and fund group is carried in the accounting records as a separately balanced group, the accounts in any given group should be assigned a code number that, perhaps by a prefix, identifies that fund group—for example, all accounts related to current funds should be identifiable as such; all accounts for plant funds should be identifiable as such. Similarly, within the fund groups, consistent code numbers should identify subgroups, assets, liabilities, and fund balances. For revenue accounts, code numbers or symbols can be used to identify sources. For expenditure accounts, code numbers or symbols can be used to identify functions, organizational units, projects, programs, and objects of expenditures. The individual fund identity should be an integral part of the fund balance, revenue, and expenditure account codes.

In developing a chart of accounts, it is important to exercise economy in the use of digits and characters for code numbers, to plan a logical arrangement for the chart, and to make ample provision for future expansion of account numbers.

General Ledger Accounts

Current Funds—Unrestricted

Asset Accounts

Cash
Petty Cash
Investments
Accounts Receivable—*detailed as needed, for example:*
    Students
    Hospital Patients
    Governmental
    Unbilled Charges
Notes Receivable—*detailed as needed*
    Allowance for Doubtful Accounts and Notes—*credit balance account associated*
    with each type of receivable
Inventories—*detailed as needed, for example:*
    College Store
    Dining Halls
    Central Stores
    Plant Operation and Maintenance Supply Store
Prepaid Items and Deferred Charges—*detailed as needed*
Due from Other Fund Groups

Liability and Fund Balance Accounts

Notes Payable
Accounts Payable and Accrued Expenses—*detailed as needed*
Deferred Credits
Deposits
Due to Other Fund Groups
Fund Balances—Allocated—*detailed as needed, for example:*
    Auxiliary Enterprises
    Reserve for Encumbrances
    Reserve for Computer Use Survey
    Reserve for Faculty Self-Improvement Program
Fund Balance—Unallocated
Operating Accounts. The following control accounts in the general ledger for actual revenues, expenditures, and other changes are supported in detail by Current Funds Revenues and Current Funds Expenditures and Other Changes accounts in subsidiary ledgers. If desired, several control accounts may be provided in lieu of single control accounts:
    Revenues Control—*credit account*
    Expenditures and Other Changes Control—*debit account*
When budgetary accounts are carried in the general ledger, the following control accounts would appear in the chart of accounts. They are supported in detail by Current Funds Revenues and Current Funds Expenditures and Other Changes accounts in subsidiary ledgers:
    Estimated Revenues *or* Unrealized Revenues
    Expenditures and Other Changes Allocations *or* Budget Allocations for Expenditures and Other Changes
    Unallocated Budget Balance *or* Unassigned Budget Balance

Current Funds—Restricted

These accounts are to be used if the assets and liabilities of such funds are separated from those of Unrestricted Current Funds.

206

Asset Accounts

Cash
Investments
Accounts Receivable—*detailed as needed, for example:*
  Governmental
  Other
  Unbilled Charges
  Allowance for Doubtful Accounts—*credit balance account*
Due from Other Fund Groups

Liability and Fund Balance Accounts

Accounts Payable
Due to Other Fund Groups
Fund Balances—Allocated—*detailed as needed, for example:*
  Reserve for Encumbrances
  Auxiliary Enterprises
Fund Balances—Unallocated
  Both of the fund balance accounts may be control accounts supported by separate subsidiary ledger accounts for each restricted current fund and for each type of fund balance. Additional control accounts may be provided as required or desired.
Operating Accounts. *Expenditures of restricted current funds may be recorded in the operating accounts of unrestricted current funds, in which case transfers of restricted current funds to current funds revenues accounts would be made to finance such expenditures. When this is not done, operating accounts for each current restricted fund must provide for proper classification of expenditures by object, as well as providing for appropriate categorization of sources of additions, deductions other than expenditures, and transfers to and from other funds.*

Loan Funds

Asset Accounts

Cash
Investments
Notes Receivable from Students, Faculty, and Staff
  Allowance for Doubtful Loans—*credit balance account*

Liability and Fund Balance Accounts

Accounts Payable to Collection Agencies
Due to Other Fund Groups
Refunds Payable on Refundable Government Grants
Fund Balances—*This may be a control account supported by separate subsidiary ledger accounts for each fund. Separate accounts should be carried to identify the sources of funds available for loans, such as donor- and government-restricted loan funds, including funds provided by mandatory transfers required for matching purposes, unrestricted funds designated as loan funds, and funds returnable to the donor under certain conditions. Accounts to identify allocations of fund balances should be provided. Accounts may be maintained to identify resources available for loans to students separately from those for faculty and staff.*

Endowment and Similar Funds

Asset Accounts

Cash
Accounts Receivable
Notes Receivable
  Allowance for Doubtful Accounts and Notes—*credit balance account*
Prepaid Items

Investments—*detailed as needed, for example:*
  Bonds
    Allowance for Unamortized Bond Premiums
    Allowance for Unamortized Bond Discounts
  Preferred Stocks
  Common Stocks
  Mortgage Notes
  Real Estate
    Allowance for Depreciation—*credit balance account*
Due from Other Fund Groups

Liability and Fund Balance Accounts

The fund balance accounts should be classified as to Endowment, Term Endowment, and Quasi-Endowment Funds, even though the investments of the funds may be merged in one or more investment pools.
Payables—*detailed as needed, for example:*
  Mortgages Payable
  Notes Payable
  Accounts Payable
Collateral Due on Securities Loaned
Due to Other Fund Groups
Balances of Endowment Funds
Balances of Term Endowment Funds
Balances of Quasi-Endowment Funds—Unrestricted
Balances of Quasi-Endowment Funds—Restricted
In order to differentiate between the balances of funds for which the income is unrestricted and those for which the income is restricted, the following accounts may be employed:
Balances of Endowment Funds—Unrestricted
Balances of Endowment Funds—Restricted—*detailed as needed, for example:*
  Professorships
  Instructional Departments
  Scholarships
  Library
  Loan Funds
Note. The balances of term endowment funds also may be identified in this manner.
Undistributed Gains and Losses on Investment Transactions—*Separate accounts should be established for each investment pool.*
Undistributed Share Adjustments—*Separate accounts should be established for each investment pool.*

Annuity and Life Income Funds

If the funds in this section are pooled for investment purposes, accounts for the assets may be classified as shown below for each investment pool. If any funds are separately invested, accounts should be set up for the investment of such funds.

Asset Accounts

Cash
Accounts Receivable
Notes Receivable
  Allowance for Doubtful Accounts and Notes—*credit balance account*
Investments—*detailed as needed, for example:*
  Bonds
    Allowance for Unamortized Bond Premiums
    Allowance for Unamortized Bond Discounts
  Preferred Stocks
  Common Stocks

Mortgage Notes
Real Estate
    Allowance for Depreciation—*credit balance account*
Due from Other Fund Groups

Liability and Fund Balance Accounts

Accounts Payable
Annuity Payments Currently Due
Annuities Payable
Life Income Payments Currently Due
Due to Other Funds for Advances on Annuity Payments
Due to Other Funds for Advances to Income Beneficiaries
Undistributed Income—Annuity Funds
Undistributed Income—Life Income Funds
Balances of Annuity Funds
Balances of Life Income Funds
    These may be control accounts supported by subsidiary ledger accounts for each fund. Within the two categories the accounts may be listed alphabetically by name, or they may be classified in any other manner at the discretion of the institution.
Undistributed Gains and Losses on Investment Transactions—*Separate accounts should be established for each investment pool.*
Undistributed Share Adjustments—*Separate accounts should be established for each investment pool.*
Income, Expenditure, and Transfer Accounts
Income from Investments—*credit account, detailed by each agreement*
Expenditures and Transfers—*debit account, detailed by each agreement*

Plant Funds—Unexpended

Asset Accounts

Cash
Investments
Receivables—*detailed as needed*
    Allowance for Doubtful Accounts—*credit balance account*
Due from Other Fund Groups
Construction in Progress—*alternatively can be shown in Investment in Plant sub-group of Plant Funds*

Liability and Fund Balance Accounts

Accounts Payable
Notes Payable
Bonds Payable
Mortgages Payable
Due to Other Fund Groups
Fund Balances—*This may be a control account supported by subsidiary ledger accounts which should differentiate between unrestricted and restricted funds.*

Plant Funds—Funds for Renewals and Replacements

These accounts should be used if the assets of such funds are separated from the assets of other subgroups of Plant Funds.

Asset Accounts

Cash
Accounts Receivable
    Allowance for Doubtful Accounts—*credit balance account*
Investments
Deposits with Trustees
Due from Other Fund Groups

Liability and Fund Balance Accounts

Accounts Payable
Due to Other Fund Groups
Fund Balances—*This may be a control account supported by subsidiary ledger accounts which should differentiate between unrestricted and restricted funds.*

Plant Funds—Funds for Retirement of Indebtedness

These accounts should be used if the assets of such funds are separated from the assets of other subgroups of Plant Funds.

Asset Accounts

Cash
Accounts and Notes Receivable
   Allowance for Doubtful Accounts—*credit balance account*
Investments
Deposits with Trustees
Due from Other Fund Groups

Liability and Fund Balance Accounts

Accounts Payable
Due to Other Fund Groups
Fund Balances—*This may be a control account supported by subsidiary ledger accounts which should differentiate between unrestricted and restricted funds.*

Plant Funds—Investment in Plant

Asset Accounts

Land
Buildings
   Allowance for Depreciation—*credit balance account*
Improvements Other than Buildings
   Allowance for Depreciation—*credit balance account*
Equipment
   Allowance for Depreciation—*credit balance account*
Library Books
Art Museums and Collections
Construction in Progress—*alternatively can be shown in the Unexpended Plant Funds subgroup of Plant Funds*

Liability and Fund Balance Accounts

Accounts Payable
Notes Payable
Bonds Payable
Mortgages Payable
Leaseholds Payable
Due to Other Fund Groups
Net Investment in Plant—*detailed as needed*

Agency Funds

Asset Accounts

Cash
Accounts Receivable
Notes Receivable
   Allowance for Doubtful Accounts and Notes—*credit balance account*
Investments
Due from Other Fund Groups

Liability Accounts

Accounts Payable
Due to Other Fund Groups
Deposit Liabilities—*Accounts for each agency fund should be carried either in the general ledger or in subsidiary ledgers.*

Current Funds Revenues Accounts
(Separate Restricted and Unrestricted Accounts)

Tuition and Fees—*detailed as needed*

Federal Appropriations

State Appropriations

Local Appropriations

Federal Grants and Contracts

State Grants and Contracts

Local Grants and Contracts

Private Gifts, Grants, and Contracts—*detailed as needed*

Endowment Income—*detailed as needed, for example:*

Income from Funds Held by Others Under Irrevocable Trusts

Sales and Services of Educational Activities—*detailed as needed, for example:*

Film Rentals
Testing Services
Home Economics Cafeteria
Demonstration Schools
Dairy Creameries
Food Technology Divisions

Sales and Services of Auxiliary Enterprises—*detailed as needed, for example:*

Residence Halls
Faculty Housing
Food Services
College Union
Additional revenue accounts may be established for sources of sales, types of products and services, and cash and interdepartmental sales.

Sales and Services of Hospitals—*detailed as needed, for example:*

Daily Patient Services
Nursing Services
Other Professional Services
Health Clinics *if an integral part of the hospital*

Other Sources—*detailed as needed*

Independent Operations—*detailed as needed by organizational units*

Current Funds Expenditures and Transfers Accounts

Current funds expenditures accounts should bear identifying codes and symbols that will identify functions, such as Instruction, Institutional Support, and Scholarships and Fellowships; identify organizational units, such as Department of Physics, Controller's Office, and Registrar's Office; and identify the object of expenditures, such as Personnel Compensation, Supplies and Expenses, and Capital Expenditures. If desired, interdepartmental purchases, as contrasted with purchases from external sources, also may be identified by code or symbol. The object coding and symbols should be designed to provide for common usage of the objects throughout the entire chart of accounts, although, of course, there will be individual object codings that will be used only for particular functional categories.

Educational and General

Instruction

Accounts by divisions, schools, colleges, and departments of instruction following the administrative organization of the institution. The four functional subcategories are:
General academic instruction
Occupational and vocational instruction
Special session instruction
Community education

Research

Accounts by individual projects, classified by organizational units. The two functional subcategories are:
Institutes and research centers
Individual or project research

Public Service

Accounts by activities, classified by type of activity, such as:
Community Service
Conferences and Institutes
Cooperative Extension Service
Public Lectures
Radio
Television

Academic Support

Accounts by activities, classified by type of activity, such as:
Academic Administration and Personnel Development
Audiovisual Services
Computing Support *(excluding administrative data processing), unless distributed to using activities*
Course and Curriculum Development
Demonstration Schools
Libraries
Museums and Galleries

Student Services

Accounts by activities, classified by type of activity, such as:
Admissions Office
Counseling and Career Guidance
Cultural Events
Dean of Students

Financial Aid Administration
Health and Infirmary Services *if not an integral part of a hospital nor operated as an essentially self-supporting operation*
Intramural Athletics
Intercollegiate Athletics *if operated as an integral part of department of physical education and not essentially self-supporting*
Registrar
Student Organizations
Remedial Instruction

Institutional Support—*detailed as needed, for example:*

Governing Board
Chief Executive Office
Chief Academic Office
Chief Business Office
Investment Office
Legal Counsel
Administrative Data Processing
Alumni Office
Auditing, internal and external
Safety
Security
Catalogues and Bulletins
Commencements
Convocations
Development Office
Employee Personnel and Records
Fund Raising
General Insurance *other than Property Insurance*
Interest on Current Funds Loans
Legal Fees
Memberships
Printing
Provision for Doubtful Accounts and Notes
Publications
Public Relations
Purchasing
Service Departments
    There should be interim accounts for all organizational units classified in this category; these accounts should be closed out at the end of each fiscal year.
Space Management
Telephone and Telegraph *unless charged to departmental budgets*
Transportation *including motor pool, unless operated as a service department*

Operation and Maintenance of Plant

Accounts for all organizational units and functions, such as:
Administration
Custodial Services
Maintenance of Buildings
Maintenance of Grounds
Utilities
Trucking Services
Fire Protection
Property Insurance

Scholarships and Fellowships

Accounts as needed and desired for scholarships, fellowships, grants-in-aid, trainee stipends, prizes, and awards.
Tuition and Fee Remissions *unless properly classified as staff benefit expenditures*
Accounts may be set up for instructional divisions and departments, such as:
  School of Medicine
  Department of Physics

Mandatory Transfers, Educational and General—*detailed to show subcategories, such*

as:
  Provision for Debt Service on Educational Plant
  Loan Fund Matching Grants

Nonmandatory Transfers, Educational and General *(to and from)—detailed to show*

significant subcategories, such as:
  Loan Funds
  Quasi-Endowment Funds
  Appreciation on Securities of Endowment and Similar Funds
  Plant Funds
    Renewals and Replacements of Plant Assets
    Additions to Plant Assets
    Voluntary Payments on Debt Principal

Auxiliary Enterprises, Hospitals, and Independent Operations

Auxiliary Enterprises

Accounts as needed and desired for such enterprises as included in the Current Funds Revenues accounts.
Provision should be made for identification of mandatory and nonmandatory transfers—to and from—by significant subcategories.

Hospitals

Accounts as needed and desired. Provision should be made for identification of mandatory and nonmandatory transfers—to and from—by significant subcategories.

Independent Operations

Accounts as needed and desired for organizational units.
Provision should be made for identification of mandatory and nonmandatory transfers—to and from—by significant subcategories.

Classification of Expenditures by Object

The object classification of expenditures identifies that which is received in return for the expenditures. Object classification has importance as a tool for internal management, but should be considered complementary to the classification of expenditures by function and organizational unit and should not replace these classifications in the various schedules of current funds expenditures. The value of object classification will depend on the usefulness of the information it provides to management. The classifications may be omitted from published financial reports or they may be used to any degree considered desirable by the institution. The use of object classifications and the related identifying codes and symbols should not be carried to an extreme; the number of categories should be limited to those that will be of significant value to management.

Three major object classifications are found in most colleges and universities: Personnel Compensation, Supplies and Expenses, and Capital Expenditures. Breakdowns of objects within these major categories may be necessary or desirable in some situations.

Personnel Compensation

This classification includes salaries, wages, and staff benefits. In the various salary and wage expense accounts, it may be desirable to distinguish between groups of faculty and other staff members, such as full-time and part-time personnel; student and nonstudent workers; and professional, secretarial, clerical, skilled, and nonskilled employees. Appropriate code numbers and symbols within this category will aid in identifying, collecting, and summarizing information.

Supplies and Expenses

Because of their general significance to nearly all organizational units within an institution, it may be beneficial to identify significant categories of these expenditures, such as supplies, telephone, travel, and contractual services.

Capital Expenditures

The following object categories within this classification (which includes both additions to and renewals and replacements of capital assets) may prove helpful in the accounting and reporting systems of educational institutions: scientific equipment, laboratory apparatus, office machines and equipment, library books, furniture and furnishings, motor vehicles, machinery and tools, building remodeling, minor construction, and livestock.

Illustrative Exhibits

THE FIGURES used in the accompanying exhibits are illustrative only and are not intended to indicate any relationship among accounts. The summary of significant accounting policies and notes to financial statements relate to the illustrative statements. Modifications should be made thereto as appropriate to actual circumstances.

Material from the Industry Audit Guide, *Audits of Colleges and Universities,* copyright © 1973 by the American Institute of Certified Public Accountants, Inc., is adapted with permission.

Sample Educational Institution

Balance Sheet

June 30, 19_____

with comparative figures at June 30, 19_____

Assets

Current Funds

	Current Year	Prior Year
Unrestricted		
Cash	$ 210,000	$ 110,000
Investments	450,000	360,000
Accounts receivable, less allowance of $18,000 both years	228,000	175,000
Inventories, at lower of cost (first-in, first-out basis) or market	90,000	80,000
Prepaid expenses and deferred charges	28,000	20,000
Total unrestricted	1,006,000	745,000
Restricted		
Cash	145,000	101,000
Investments	175,000	165,000
Accounts receivable, less allowance of $8,000 both years	68,000	160,000
Unbilled charges	72,000	
Total restricted	460,000	426,000
Total current funds	1,466,000	1,171,000

Loan Funds

	Current Year	Prior Year
Cash	30,000	20,000
Investments	100,000	100,000
Loans to students, faculty, and staff, less allowance of $10,000 current year and $9,000 prior year	550,000	382,000
Due from unrestricted funds	3,000	
Total loan funds	683,000	502,000

Endowment and Similar Funds

	Current Year	Prior Year
Cash	100,000	101,000
Investments	13,900,000	11,800,000
Total endowment and similar funds	14,000,000	11,901,000

Liabilities and Fund Balances

Current Funds

	Current Year	Prior Year
Unrestricted		
Accounts payable	$ 125,000	$ 100,000
Accrued liabilities	20,000	15,000
Students' deposits	30,000	35,000
Due to other funds	158,000	120,000
Deferred credits	30,000	20,000
Fund balance	643,000	455,000
Total unrestricted	1,006,000	745,000
Restricted		
Accounts payable	14,000	5,000
Fund balances	446,000	421,000
Total restricted	460,000	426,000
Total current funds	1,466,000	1,171,000

Loan Funds

	Current Year	Prior Year
Fund balances		
U.S. government grants refundable	50,000	33,000
University funds		
Restricted	483,000	369,000
Unrestricted	150,000	100,000
Total loan funds	683,000	502,000

Endowment and Similar Funds

	Current Year	Prior Year
Fund balances		
Endowment	7,800,000	6,740,000
Term endowment	3,840,000	3,420,000
Quasi-endowment—unrestricted	1,000,000	800,000
Quasi-endowment—restricted	1,360,000	941,000
Total endowment and similar funds	14,000,000	11,901,000

Annuity and Life Income Funds

Annuity funds		
Cash	$ 55,000	$ 45,000
Investments	3,260,000	3,010,000
Total annuity funds	3,315,000	3,055,000
Life income funds		
Cash	15,000	15,000
Investments	2,045,000	1,740,000
Total life income funds	2,060,000	1,755,000
Total annuity and life income funds	5,375,000	4,810,000

Plant Funds

Unexpended		
Cash	275,000	410,000
Investments	1,285,000	1,590,000
Due from unrestricted current funds	150,000	120,000
Total unexpended	1,710,000	2,120,000
Renewals and replacements		
Cash	5,000	4,000
Investments	150,000	286,000
Deposits with trustees	100,000	90,000
Due from unrestricted current funds	5,000	
Total renewals and replacements	260,000	380,000
Retirement of indebtedness		
Cash	50,000	40,000
Deposits with trustees	250,000	253,000
Total retirement of indebtedness	300,000	293,000
Investment in plant		
Land	500,000	500,000
Land improvements	1,000,000	1,110,000
Buildings	25,000,000	24,060,000
Equipment	15,000,000	14,200,000
Library books	100,000	80,000
Total investment in plant	41,600,000	39,950,000
Total plant funds	43,870,000	42,743,000

Agency Funds

Cash	50,000	70,000
Investments	60,000	20,000
Total agency funds	110,000	90,000

Annuity and Life Income Funds

Annuity funds		
Annuities payable	$ 2,150,000	$ 2,300,000
Fund balances	1,165,000	755,000
Total annuity funds	3,315,000	3,055,000
Life income funds		
Income payable	5,000	5,000
Fund balances	2,055,000	1,750,000
Total life income funds	2,060,000	1,755,000
Total annuity and life income funds	5,375,000	4,810,000

Plant Funds

Unexpended		
Accounts payable	10,000	
Notes payable	100,000	
Bonds payable	400,000	
Fund balances		
Restricted	1,000,000	1,860,000
Unrestricted	200,000	260,000
Total unexpended	1,710,000	2,120,000
Renewals and replacements		
Fund balances		
Restricted	25,000	180,000
Unrestricted	235,000	200,000
Total renewals and replacements	260,000	380,000
Retirement of indebtedness		
Fund balances		
Restricted	185,000	125,000
Unrestricted	115,000	168,000
Total retirement of indebtedness	300,000	293,000
Investment in plant		
Notes payable	790,000	810,000
Bonds payable	2,200,000	2,400,000
Mortgages payable	400,000	200,000
Net investment in plant	38,210,000	36,540,000
Total investment in plant	41,600,000	39,950,000
Total plant funds	43,870,000	42,743,000

Agency Funds

Deposits held in custody for others	110,000	90,000
Total agency funds	110,000	90,000

See accompanying Summary of Significant Accounting Policies and Notes to Financial Statements

Sample Educational Institution

Statement of Changes in Fund Balances

Year Ended June 30, 19___

	Current Funds Unrestricted	Current Funds Restricted	Loan Funds	Endowment and Similar Funds	Annuity and Life Income Funds	Plant Funds Unexpended	Plant Funds Renewals and Replacements	Plant Funds Retirement of Indebtedness	Plant Funds Investment in Plant
Revenues and other additions									
Unrestricted current fund revenues	$7,540,000								
Expired term endowment—restricted						50,000			
State appropriations—restricted		500,000				50,000			
Federal grants and contracts—restricted		370,000							
Private gifts, grants, and contracts—restricted		224,000	100,000	1,500,000	800,000	115,000		65,000	15,000
Investment income—restricted			12,000	10,000		5,000	5,000	5,000	
Realized gains on investments—unrestricted				109,000		10,000	5,000	5,000	
Realized gains on investments—restricted			4,000	50,000					
Interest on loans receivable			7,000						
U.S. government advances			18,000						
Expended for plant facilities (including $100,000 charged to current funds expenditures)									1,550,000
Retirement of indebtedness									220,000
Accrued interest on sale of bonds								3,000	
Matured annuity and life income restricted to endowment				10,000					
Total revenues and other additions	7,540,000	1,094,000	141,000	1,679,000	800,000	230,000	10,000	78,000	1,785,000
Expenditures and other deductions									
Educational and general expenditures	4,400,000	1,014,000							
Auxiliary enterprises expenditures	1,830,000								
Indirect costs recovered		35,000							
Refunded to grantors		20,000	10,000						
Loan cancellations and write-offs			1,000						
Administrative and collection costs			1,000					1,000	
Adjustment of actuarial liability for annuities payable					75,000				
Expended for plant facilities (including noncapitalized expenditures of $50,000)						1,200,000	300,000		
Retirement of indebtedness								220,000	
Interest on indebtedness								190,000	
Disposal of plant facilities									115,000
Expired term endowments ($40,000 unrestricted, $50,000 restricted to plant)				90,000					
Matured annuity and life income funds restricted to endowment					10,000				
Total expenditures and other deductions	6,230,000	1,069,000	12,000	90,000	85,000	1,200,000	300,000	411,000	115,000

Transfers among funds—additions/(deductions)

Mandatory:									
Principal and interest	(340,000)							340,000	
Renewals and replacements	(170,000)						170,000		
Loan fund matching grant	(2,000)	2,000							
Unrestricted gifts allocated	(650,000)	50,000		550,000	50,000				
Portion of unrestricted quasi-endowment funds investment gains appropriated	40,000			(40,000)					
Total transfers	(1,122,000)	52,000		510,000	50,000		170,000	340,000	
Net increase/(decrease) for the year	188,000	25,000	181,000	2,099,000	715,000	(920,000)	(120,000)	7,000	1,670,000
Fund balance at beginning of year	455,000	421,000	502,000	11,901,000	2,505,000	2,120,000	380,000	293,000	36,540,000
Fund balance at end of year	643,000	446,000	683,000	14,003,000	3,220,000	1,200,000	260,000	300,000	38,210,000

See accompanying Summary of Significant Accounting Policies and Notes to Financial Statements

[221]

Sample Educational Institution

Exhibit C

Statement of Current Funds Revenues, Expenditures, and Other Changes

Year Ended June 30, 19____

	Current Year			Prior Year Total
	Unrestricted	Restricted	Total	
Revenues				
Tuition and fees	$2,600,000		$2,600,000	$2,300,000
Federal appropriations	500,000		500,000	500,000
State appropriations	700,000		700,000	700,000
Local appropriations	100,000		100,000	100,000
Federal grants and contracts	20,000	$ 375,000	395,000	350,000
State grants and contracts	10,000	25,000	35,000	200,000
Local grants and contracts	5,000	25,000	30,000	45,000
Private gifts, grants, and contracts	850,000	380,000	1,230,000	1,190,000
Endowment income	325,000	209,000	534,000	500,000
Sales and services of educational activities	190,000		190,000	195,000
Sales and services of auxiliary enterprises	2,200,000		2,200,000	2,100,000
Expired term endowment	40,000		40,000	
Other sources (if any)				
Total current revenues	7,540,000	1,014,000	8,554,000	8,180,000
Expenditures and mandatory transfers				
Educational and general				
Instruction	2,960,000	489,000	3,449,000	3,300,000
Research	100,000	400,000	500,000	650,000
Public service	130,000	25,000	155,000	175,000
Academic support	250,000		250,000	225,000
Student services	200,000		200,000	195,000
Institutional support	450,000		450,000	445,000
Operation and maintenance of plant	220,000		220,000	200,000
Scholarships and fellowships	90,000	100,000	190,000	180,000
Educational and general expenditures	4,400,000	1,014,000	5,414,000	5,370,000
Mandatory transfers for:				
Principal and interest	90,000		90,000	50,000
Renewals and replacements	100,000		100,000	80,000
Loan fund matching grant	2,000		2,000	
Total educational and general	4,592,000	1,014,000	5,606,000	5,500,000

Auxiliary enterprises

Expenditures		1,830,000	1,830,000	1,730,000
Mandatory transfers for:				
Principal and interest		250,000	250,000	250,000
Renewals and replacements		70,000	70,000	70,000
Total auxiliary enterprises		2,150,000	2,150,000	2,050,000
Total expenditures and mandatory transfers	1,014,000	6,742,000	7,756,000	7,550,000

Other transfers and additions/(deductions)

Excess of restricted receipts over transfers to revenues		45,000	45,000	40,000
Refunded to grantors		(20,000)	(20,000)	
Unrestricted gifts allocated to other funds		(650,000)	(650,000)	(510,000)
Portion of quasi-endowment gains appropriated		40,000	40,000	
Net increase in fund balances	25,000	188,000	213,000	160,000

See accompanying Summary of Significant Accounting Policies and Notes to Financial Statements

[223]

Sample Educational Institution
Summary of Significant Accounting Policies

June 30, 19_____

The significant accounting policies followed by Sample Educational Institution are described below to enhance the usefulness of the financial statements to the reader.

ACCRUAL BASIS

The financial statements of Sample Educational Institution have been prepared on the accrual basis except for depreciation accounting as explained in notes 1 and 2 to the financial statements. The statement of current funds revenues, expenditures, and other changes is a statement of financial activities of current funds related to the current reporting period. It does not purport to present the results of operations or the net income or loss for the period as would a statement of income or a statement of revenues and expenses.

To the extent that current funds are used to finance plant assets, the amounts so provided are accounted for as (1) expenditures, in the case of normal replacement of movable equipment and library books; (2) mandatory transfers, in the case of required provisions for debt amortization and interest and equipment renewal and replacement; and (3) transfers of a nonmandatory nature for all other cases.

FUND ACCOUNTING

In order to ensure observance of limitations and restrictions placed on the use of the resources available to the Institution, the accounts of the Institution are maintained in accordance with the principles of "fund accounting." This is the procedure by which resources for various purposes are classified for accounting and reporting purposes into funds that are in accordance with activities or objectives specified. Separate accounts are maintained for each fund; however, in the accompanying financial statements, funds that have similar characteristics have been combined into fund groups. Accordingly, all financial transactions have been recorded and reported by fund group.

Within each fund group, fund balances restricted by outside sources are so indicated and are distinguished from unrestricted funds allocated to specific purposes by action of the governing board. Externally restricted funds may only be utilized in accordance with the purposes established by the source of such funds and are in contrast with unrestricted funds over which the governing board retains full control to use in achieving any of its institutional purposes.

Endowment funds are subject to the restrictions of gift instruments requiring in perpetuity that the principal be invested and the income only be utilized. Term endowment funds are similar to endowment funds except that upon the passage of a stated period of time or the occurrence of a particular event, all or part of the principal may be expended. While quasi-endowment funds have been established by the governing board for the same purposes as endowment funds, any portion of quasi-endowment funds may be expended.

All gains and losses arising from the sale, collection, or other disposition of investments and other noncash assets are accounted for in the fund which owned such assets. Ordinary income derived from investments, receivables, and the like is accounted for in the fund owning such assets, except for income derived from investments of endowment and similar funds, which income is accounted for in the fund to which it is restricted or, if unrestricted, as revenues in unrestricted current funds.

All other unrestricted revenue is accounted for in the unrestricted current fund. Restricted gifts, grants, appropriations, endowment income, and other restricted resources are accounted for in the appropriate restricted funds. Restricted current funds are reported as revenues and expenditures when expended for current operating purposes.

OTHER SIGNIFICANT ACCOUNTING POLICIES

Other significant accounting policies are set forth in the financial statements and the notes thereto.

Sample Educational Institution

Notes to Financial Statements

June 30, 19_____

1. Investments exclusive of physical plant are recorded at cost; investments received by gift are carried at market value at the date of acquisition. Quoted market values of investments (all marketable securities) of the funds indicated were as follows:

	Current year	Prior year
Unrestricted current funds	$ 510,000	$ 390,000
Restricted current funds	180,000	165,000
Loan funds	105,000	105,000
Unexpended plant funds	1,287,000	1,600,000
Renewal and replacement funds	145,000	285,000
Agency funds	60,000	20,000

Investments of endowment and similar funds and annuity and life income funds are composed of the following:

	Carrying value	
	Current year	Prior year
Endowment and similar funds:		
Corporate stocks and bonds (approximate market, current year $15,000,000, prior year $10,900,000)	$13,000,000	$10,901,000
Rental properties—less accumulated depreciation, current year $500,000, prior year $400,000	900,000	899,000
	13,900,000	11,800,000
Annuity funds:		
U.S. bonds (approximate market, current year $200,000, prior year $100,000)	200,000	110,000
Corporate stocks and bonds (approximate market, current year $3,070,000, prior year $2,905,000)	3,060,000	2,900,000
	3,260,000	3,010,000
Life income funds:		
Municipal bonds (approximate market, current year $1,400,000, prior year $1,340,000)	1,500,000	1,300,000
Corporate stocks and bonds (approximate market, current year $650,000, prior year $400,000)	545,000	440,000
	2,045,000	1,740,000

Assets of endowment funds, except nonmarketable investments of term endowment having a book value of $200,000 and quasi-endowment having a book value of $800,000, are pooled on a market value basis, with each individual fund subscribing

225

to or disposing of units on the basis of the value per unit at market value at the beginning of the calendar quarter within which the transaction takes place. Of the total units each having a market value of $15.00, 600,000 units were owned by endowment, 280,000 units by term endowment, and 120,000 units by quasi-endowment at June 30, 19.........

The following tabulation summarizes changes in relationships between cost and market values of the pooled assets:

| | Pooled Assets | | Net Gains (Losses) | Market Value per Unit |
	Market	Cost		
End of year	$15,000,000	$13,000,000	$2,000,000	$15.00
Beginning of year	10,900,000	10,901,000	(1,000)	12.70
Unrealized net gains for year			2,001,000	
Realized net gains for year			159,000	
Total net gains for year			$2,160,000	2.30

The average annual earnings per unit, exclusive of net gains, were $.56 for the year.

2. Physical plant and equipment are stated at cost at date of acquisition or fair value at date of donation in the case of gifts, except land acquired prior to 1940, which is valued at appraisal value in 1940 at $300,000. Depreciation on physical plant and equipment is not recorded.

3. Long-term debt includes: bonds payable due in annual installments varying from $45,000 to $55,000 with interest at 5⅞%, the final installment being due in 19........., collateralized by trust indenture covering land, buildings, and equipment known as Smith dormitory carried in the accounts at $2,500,000, and pledged net revenue from the operations of said dormitory; and mortgages payable due in varying amounts to 19........ with interest at 6%, collateralized by property carried in the accounts at $800,000 and pledged revenue of the Student Union amounting to approximately $65,000 per year.

4. The Institution has certain contributory pension plans for academic and nonacademic personnel. Total pension expense for the year was $350,000, which includes amortization of prior service cost over a period of 20 years. The Institution's policy is to fund pension costs accrued, including periodic funding of prior years' accruals not previously funded. The actuarially computed value of vested benefits as of June 30, 19........ exceeded net assets of the pension fund by approximately $300,000.

5. Contracts have been let for the construction of additional classroom buildings in the amount of $3,000,000. Construction and equipment are estimated to aggregate $5,000,000, which will be financed by available resources and an issue of bonds payable over a period of 40 years amounting to $4,000,000.

6. All interfund borrowings have been made from unrestricted funds. The amounts due to plant funds from current unrestricted funds are payable within one year without interest. The amount due to loan funds from current unrestricted funds is payable currently.

7. Pledges totaling $260,000, restricted to plant fund uses, are due to be collected over the next three fiscal years in the amounts of $120,000, $80,000, and $60,000, respectively. It is not practicable to estimate the net realizable value of such pledges.

Part 6

Bibliography
and
Acknowledgments

Bibliography

THIS SELECTED BIBLIOGRAPHY is organized by chapter, and presents sources from which more detailed information may be obtained. The list shows some presumption on the part of the Editor, but should be useful to those who would like to have a starting point from which to review the literature.

In addition to the sources listed below, the reader is directed to the organizations with related interests and to the published proceedings of the regional associations of business officers. These organizations and associations are listed in the "Acknowledgments."

1:1 Business Administration in Higher Education

American Academy of Arts and Sciences. *The Assembly on University Goals and Governance.* Cambridge, Mass.: The Academy, 1971.

Berdahl, Robert O. *Statewide Coordination of Higher Education.* Washington, D. C.: American Council on Education, 1971.

Blackwell, Thomas E. *College and University Administration.* New York: Center for Applied Research in Education, Inc., 1966.

Bowen, Howard R. *The Financing of Higher Education.* New York: McGraw-Hill Book Co., 1970.

Brubacher, John S., and Rudy, Willis. *Higher Education in Transition.* Rev. ed. New York: Harper & Row, 1968.

Burns, Gerald P. *Administrators in Higher Education.* New York: Harper & Bros., 1962.

———. *Trustees in Higher Education.* New York: Independent College Funds of America, 1966.

Carnegie Commission on Higher Education. *Governance of Higher Education.* New York: McGraw-Hill Book Co., 1973.

———. *Institutional Aid: Federal Support to Colleges and Universities.* New York: McGraw-Hill Book Co., 1972.

———. *Priorities for Action: Final Report of the Carnegie Commission on Higher Education.* New York: McGraw-Hill Book Co., 1973.

Chambers, M. M. *Higher Education: Who Pays? Who Gains?* Danville, Ill.: The Interstate Printers & Publishers, Inc., 1968.

Cheit, Earl F. *The New Depression in Higher Education, A Study of Financial Conditions at 41 Colleges and Universities.* New York: McGraw-Hill Book Co., 1971.

———. *The New Depression in Higher Education: Two Years Later.* New York: McGraw-Hill Book Co., 1973.

Committee for Economic Development. *The Management and Financing of Colleges.* New York: The Committee, 1973.

Corson, John J. *The Governance of Colleges and Universities.* New York: McGraw-Hill Book Co., 1960. (Revision forthcoming.)

Council for the Advancement of Small Colleges. *The Trustee: A Key to Progress in the Small College.* Washington, D. C.: The Council, 1970.

Fecher, Roger James. *Career Patterns of Chief Administrative Services Officers.* Doctoral dissertation. Ann Arbor, Mich.: University Microfilms, 1972.

Glaze, Thomas E. *Business Administration for Colleges and Universities.* Baton Rouge, La.: Louisiana State University Press, 1962.

Huell, W. Frank, and Shapiro, Allen H. *The University Trustee in Law and Practice.* Toledo, Ohio: Center for the Study of Higher Education, 1973.

Hungate, Thad L. *Management in Higher Education.* New York: Bureau of Publications, Teachers College, Columbia University, 1964.

Jellema, William W. *From Red to Black?* San Francisco: Jossey-Bass, Inc., Publishers, 1973.

Jenny, Hans H., and Wynn, G. Richard. *The Golden Years: A Study of Income and Expenditure Growth and Distribution of 48 Private Four-Year Liberal Arts Colleges.* Wooster, Ohio: The College of Wooster, 1970.

———. *The Turning Point: A Study of Income and Expenditure Growth and Distribution of 48 Private Four-Year Liberal Arts Colleges.* Wooster, Ohio: The College of Wooster, 1972.

Kaplowitz, Richard A. *Selecting Academic Administrators: The Search Committee*. Washington, D. C.: American Council on Education, 1973.

Knowles, Asa S. (ed.) *Handbook of College and University Administration*. New York: McGraw-Hill Book Co., 1970. Two vols.

Lahti, Robert E. *Innovative College Management*. San Francisco: Jossey-Bass, Inc., Publishers, 1973.

Lawrence, Ben; Weathersby, George; and Patterson, Virginia W. *Outputs of Higher Education: Their Identification, Measurement, and Evaluation*. Boulder, Colo.: Western Interstate Commission for Higher Education, 1970.

Mason, Henry L. *College and University Government; A Handbook of Principle and Practice*. New Orleans: Tulane University, 1972.

Millett, John D. *An Outline of Concepts of Organization, Operation, and Administration for Colleges and Universities*. Washington, D. C.: Academy for Educational Development, Management Division, 1973.

Mood, Alexander M., et al. *Papers on Efficiency in the Management of Higher Education*. New York: McGraw-Hill Book Co., 1972.

Nance, Paul K. *Business Management Practices in Selected Colleges and Universities*. Office of Education Bulletin 1966, No. 12. Washington, D. C.: U.S. Government Printing Office, 1966.

Nance, Paul K.; Robbins, Leslie; and Cain, J. Harvey. *Guide to College and University Business Management*. Office of Education Bulletin 1965, No. 30. Washington, D. C.: U.S. Government Printing Office, 1965.

National Commission on the Financing of Postsecondary Education. *The Financing of Postsecondary Education*. Washington, D. C.: Government Printing Office, 1974.

O'Neill, June A. *Sources of Funds to Colleges and Universities*. New York: McGraw-Hill Book Co., 1973.

Perkins, James A. *The University as an Organization*. New York: McGraw-Hill Book Co., 1973.

Perry, Richard R., and Hull, W. Frank, IV. *The Organized Organization: The American University and Its Administration*. Toledo, Ohio: University of Toledo, 1971.

Rauh, Morton A. *The Trusteeship of Colleges and Universities*. New York: McGraw-Hill Book Co., 1969.

Robbins, Leslie F., and Nance, Paul K. *Business Management: Survey of Chief Business Officers of Colleges and Universities*. U.S. Department of Health, Education, and Welfare, 1965.

Rourke, Francis E., and Brooks, Glenn E. *The Managerial Revolution in Higher Education*. Baltimore, Md.: Johns Hopkins Press, 1966.

Scheps, Clarence, and Davidson, E. E. *Accounting for Colleges and Universities*. Baton Rouge, La.: Louisiana State University Press, 1971. (Revision forthcoming.)

Stanford, Edward V. *A Guide to Catholic College Administration*. Westminster, Md.: Newman Press, 1965.

Swanson, John E.; Arden, Wesley; and Still, Homer E., Jr. *Financial Analysis of Current Operations of Colleges and Universities*. Ann Arbor, Mich.: Institute of Public Administration, 1966.

Wilson, Logan (ed.) *Emerging Patterns in American Higher Education*. Washington, D. C.: American Council on Education, 1965.

Wilson, Logan. *Shaping American Higher Education*. Washington, D. C.: American Council on Education, 1973.

Wilson, Logan, and Mills, Olive. *Universal Higher Education: Costs, Benefits, Options*. Washington, D. C.: American Council on Education, 1972.

Woodburne, Lloyd S. *Principles of College and University Administration*. Palo Alto, Calif.: Stanford University Press, 1958.

Yee, Albert H. *Perspective on Management Systems Approaches in Education: A Symposium*. Englewood Cliffs, N. J.: Educational Technology Publications, 1973.

A Chronological, Historical Bibliography

Harper, William Rainey. *The Trend in Higher Education*. Chicago: University of Chicago Press, 1905. (Chapter X, "The Business Side of a University.")

Christensen, J. C. "University Business Administration." Manhattan, Kansas: Kansas State Agricultural College, 1913.

Bumpus, H. C. "Standard Form for Receipts." *Proceedings of the Midwest Association of Business Officers*, 1913.

LeFevre, Arthur. *The Organization and Administration of a State's Institutions of Higher Education*. Austin, Texas: Von Boeckmann-Jones Co., 1914.

Goodspeed, Thomas Wakefield. *A History of the University of Chicago—1891-1916*. Chicago: University of Chicago Press, 1916.

Drury, Horace B. *Scientific Management*. 2nd ed. New York: Columbia University, 1918.

Burrus, Julian Ashby. "Business Administration of Colleges." Unpublished Ph.D. dissertation, University of Chicago, 1921.

Arnett, Trevor. *College and University Finance*. New York: General Education Board, 1922.

Franke, W. B. "College and University Accounting." *Journal of Accountancy*, March 1925.

Reeves, Floyd. "Standards for Accrediting Colleges." *North Central Association Quarterly*, Vol. III, No. 2 (September 1928).

Hungate, T. L. "A Study of Financial Reports of Colleges and Universities in the United States." Urbana, Illinois: National Committee on Standard Reports for Institutions of Higher Education, 1930.

Klein, Arthur J. *Survey of Land Grant Colleges and Universities*. Vol. 1, Pt. III, pp. 123-132, 195-197. U.S. Office of Education Bulletin No. 9, 1930.

Morey, Lloyd. *University and College Accounting.* New York: John Wiley & Sons, Inc., 1930.

Hungate, T. L. "Principles of Accounting in American Colleges and Universities in Relation to Present Practices." Unpublished master's thesis, Columbia University, 1931.

Morey, Lloyd. "Suggested Forms for Financial Reports of Colleges and Universities." Urbana, Illinois: National Committee on Standard Reports for Institutions of Higher Education, 1931.

————. *Financial Reports for Colleges and Universities.* Chicago: University of Chicago Press, 1935.

Scroggs, Schiller. "Systematic Fact-Finding and Research in the Administration of Higher Education." Ph.D. dissertation, Yale University, 1935.

Duffus, R. L. *Democracy Enters College.* New York: Charles Scribner's Sons, 1936.

Eells, Walter C. *Surveys of American Higher Education.* New York: Carnegie Foundation for the Advancement of Teaching, 1937.

Morey, Lloyd. *A Decade of Progress in Accounting and Financial Reporting for Colleges and Universities.* Washington, D. C.: American Council on Education, 1940.

Russell, John Dale. *The Finance of Higher Education.* Chicago: University of Chicago Press, 1944. (Chapter VII, "Analysis of Expenditures.")

Hungate, T. L. *Financing the Future of Higher Education.* New York: Bureau of Publications, Teachers College, Columbia University, 1946.

Scheps, Clarence. *Accounting for Colleges and Universities.* Baton Rouge: Louisiana State University Press, 1949.

Sherer, Harvey. *Progress in Financial Reporting in Selected Universities Since 1930.* Urbana, Illinois: University of Illinois, 1950.

National Committee on the Preparation of a Manual on College and University Business Administration. *College and University Business Administration.* Washington, D. C.: American Council on Education, 1952 (Vol. 1) and 1955 (Vol. 2).

Tickton, Sidney. *Needed: A Ten-Year College Budget.* New York: The Ford Foundation, 1961.

Millett, John D. *The Academic Community: An Essay on Organization.* New York: McGraw-Hill Book Co., 1962.

Van Dyke, George E. (ed.) *College and University Business Administration.* Washington, D. C.: American Council on Education, 1968.

Periodicals

American Education
Change
The Chronicle of Higher Education
College and University
College Management
Community and Junior College Journal
Community College Review
Education Abstracts
Educational Administration Abstracts
Educational Record
The Education Digest
A Fact Book on Higher Education
Higher Education
Higher Education and National Affairs
The Journal of Higher Education
Nation's Schools and Colleges
New Directions for Community Colleges
New Directions for Higher Education
Research in Higher Education

NACUBO *Professional File*

"Dynamics of Higher Education in Times of Change, Challenge—Reflections from the 1973 Annual Meeting" (July 1973)

"The Management Dilemma: Shared Authority" by Robert P. Lisensky (December 1971)

"The Management of Change in Higher Education" by Donald S. Holm (June 1972)

"Old Assumptions and New Uncertainties in the Planning Process" by James I. Doi (July 1973)

"An Opportunity for Positive and Creative Leadership in the Business Management of Higher Education" by Allan W. Barber (February 1972)

"The Role of the Business Officer in Managing Educational Resources" by William G. Bowen (December 1971)

NACUBO *Studies in Management*

"The Management of Change in Higher Education" by Glen R. Driscoll (February 1974)

"Social Pressures on Management: Disadvantaged Students" by William M. Birenbaum (February 1972)

"Universities as Management Arenas" by Donald E. Walker (August 1973)

2:1 Institutional Planning

Arthur, William J. *A Financial Planning Model for Private Colleges: A Research Report.* Charlottesville, Va.: University Press of Virginia, 1973.

Casasco, Juan A. *Planning Techniques for University Management.* Washington, D. C.: American Council on Education, 1970.

Commission on Independent Colleges and Universities, State of New York. *1972 Statewide Master Plan for Private Colleges and Universities of the State of New York.* New York: The Commission, 1972.

Dressel, Paul L., et al. *Institutional Research in the University: A Handbook.* Washington, D. C.: Jossey-Bass, Inc., Publishers, 1971.

Hartley, Harry J. *Educational Planning, Programming, Budgeting: A Systems Approach.* Englewood Cliffs, N. J.: Prentice-Hall, Inc., 1968.

Johnson, Charles B., and Katzenmeyer, William G. *Management Information Systems in Higher Education: The State of the Art.* Proceedings of the Seminar on Management Information Systems, EXXON Educational Foundation. Durham, N. C.: Duke University Press, 1969.

Knorr, Owen A. (ed.) *Long-Range Planning in Higher Education.* Boulder, Colo.: Western Interstate Commission for Higher Education, 1965.

Knowles, Asa S. (ed.) *Handbook of College and University Administration.* New York: McGraw-Hill Book Co., 1970. (Section 4, Planning, Space Requirements, and Institutional Research.)

Koenig, H. E.; Keeney, M. G.; and Zemach, R. *A Systems Model for Management, Planning, and Resource Allocation in Institutions of Higher Education.* East Lansing, Mich.: Michigan State University, 1968.

McGrath, Earl J. (ed.) *Cooperative Long-Range Planning in Liberal Arts Colleges.* New York: Columbia University Teachers College, 1964.

Mason, Thomas R. "Synthetic Output by Simulation." In *Institutional Research and Academic Outcomes,* edited by Cameron Fincher. Athens, Ga.: Association for Institutional Research, 1968.

Millard, Richard; Sweeney, Karen; and Eklund, Nancy. (eds.) *Planning and Management Practices in Higher Education: Promise or Dilemma?* Denver, Colo.: Education Commission of the States, 1972.

National Association of College and University Business Officers. *Planning, Budgeting, and Accounting, Section II of A College Operating Manual.* Washington, D. C.: The Association, 1970. (Revision forthcoming.)

Newton, R. D., et al. *Models for University Systems Planning.* University Park, Pa.: Office of the Vice President for Planning, Pennsylvania State University, 1970.

Odiorne, George S. *Management by Objectives: A System of Managerial Leadership.* New York: Pitman Publishing Corp., 1965.

O'Neill, June A. *Resource Use in Higher Education.* Carnegie Commission on Higher Education. New York: McGraw-Hill Book Co., 1971.

————. *Sources of Funds to Colleges and Universities.* Carnegie Commission on Higher Education. New York: McGraw-Hill Book Co., 1973.

Parsons, Kermit C., and Lang, Jon T. *An Annotated Bibliography on University Planning and Development.* New York: Society for College and University Planning, 1968.

Pinnell, Charles. *Guidelines for Planning in Colleges and Universities.* Austin, Texas: Coordinating Board, Texas College and University System, 1968.

Shoemaker, William A. *Systems Models and Programs for Higher Education.* Washington, D. C.: Academy for Educational Development, 1973.

Wagner, W. C., and Weathersby, G. B. *Optimality in College Planning: A Control Theoretic Approach.* Ford Foundation Program for Research in University Administration, Paper P-22. Berkeley, Calif.: University of California, 1971.

Periodicals

Planning for Higher Education

NACUBO *Professional File*

"Assumptions and Expectations in Higher Education" by E. Laurence Chalmers, Jr., (August 1972)

"Budget Planning and Administrative Coordination: A Case Study—the University of Minnesota" by Malcolm C. Moos (July 1972)

"Cost Analysis in Higher Education" by Fred E. Balderston (October 1972)

"Making the Most of Institutional Resources" by Thomas E. Tellefsen (April 1973)

"Management Planning: Innovation on Campus" by Stephen S. J. Hall (October 1973)

"Old Assumptions and New Uncertainties in the Planning Process" by James I. Doi (July 1973)

NACUBO *Studies in Management*

"The Business Officer's Role in Solving the Admissions Problem" by Robert H. Barnett (September 1973)

2:2 Management Information Systems and Data Processing

Andrew, Gary M., and Moir, Ronald E. *Information-Decision Systems in Education.* (Management Series in Education, No. 1). Itasca, Ill.: Peacock, F. E., Publishers, Inc., 1970.

Arnold, Robert R., et al. *Modern Data Processing.* 2nd ed. New York: John Wiley & Sons, Inc., 1972.

Automated Education Center. *Computers in Education: Their Use and Cost.* Clair Shores, Mich.: Management Information Services.

————. *Establishing an Educational Data Processing Center.* Clair Shores, Mich.: Management Information Services.

Awad, Elias M. *Automatic Data Processing: Principles and Procedures.* 2nd ed. Englewood Cliffs, N. J.: Prentice-Hall, Inc., 1970.

Barron, D. W. *Computer Operating Systems.* New York: Halsted Press, 1971.

Bassler, Richard A., and Joslin, Edward O. *An Introduction to Computer Systems.* 2nd rev. ed. Arlington, Va.: College Readings, Inc., 1972.

Bower, James B., et al. *Financial Information Systems: Theory and Practice.* Rockleigh, N. J.: Allyn & Bacon, Inc., 1969.

232

Brandon, Dick. *Data Processing: Organization and Manpower Planning.* New ed. Philadelphia, Pa.: Auerbach Publishers, Inc., 1974.

Brandon, Dick, et al. *Data Processing Management: Methods and Standards.* New ed. New York: MacMillan Publishing Co., Inc., 1973.

Caffrey, John, and Mosmann, Charles J. *Computers on Campus: A Report to the President on Their Use and Management.* Washington, D. C.: American Council on Education, 1967.

Cogan, Carl. *Data Management Systems.* New York: John Wiley & Sons, Inc., 1973.

Contracting for Computers: A Checklist of Terms and Clauses for Use in Contracting with Vendors for Computing Resources. Princeton, N. J.: EDUCOM, 1973.

Gupta, R. *Electronic Information Processing.* New York: John Wiley & Sons, Inc., 1973.

Harris, M. L. *Introduction to Data Processing.* New York: John Wiley & Sons, Inc., 1973.

Hussain, Khateeb M. *Development of Information Systems for Education.* Englewood Cliffs, N. J.: Prentice-Hall, Inc., 1973.

Jancura, Elise, and Berger, Arnold. *Computing and Auditing.* Philadelphia, Pa.: Auerbach Publishers, Inc., 1973.

Johnson, Charles B., and Katzenmeyer, William G. (eds.) *Management Information Systems in Higher Education: the State of the Art.* Durham, N. C.: Duke University Press, 1969.

Knowles, Asa S. (ed.) *Handbook of College and University Administration.* New York: McGraw-Hill Book Co., 1970. (Section 3, Chapter 8, Information Systems for Administrative Control.)

Minter, John, and Lawrence, Ben (eds.) *Management Information Systems: Their Development and Use in the Administration of Higher Education.* Boulder, Colo.: Western Interstate Commission for Higher Education, 1969.

O'Brien, James L. *Management with Computers.* New York: Van Nostrand Reinhold Co., 1972.

President's Science Advisory Committee. *Computers in Higher Education.* Washington, D. C.: The White House, 1967.

Saxon, James A., and Steyer, Wesley W. *Basic Principles of Data Processing.* 2nd ed. Englewood Cliffs, N. J.: Prentice-Hall, Inc., 1970.

Schnake, Marilyn. *Data Processing Concepts.* New ed. New York: McGraw-Hill Book Co., 1973.

Shoemaker, William A. *Systems Models and Programs for Higher Education.* Washington, D. C.: Academy for Educational Development, 1973.

Sweeney, Robert B. *Use of Computers in Accounting.* Englewood Cliffs, N. J.: Prentice-Hall, Inc., 1971.

Tyran, Michael. *Computerized Accounting Methods and Controls.* Englewood Cliffs, N. J.: Prentice-Hall, Inc., 1971.

Wilkinson, Joseph W. *Accounting with the Computer.* Homewood, Ill.: Richard D. Irwin, Inc., 1972.

Periodicals

EDUCOM Bulletin

NACUBO *Professional File*

"Making the Most of Institutional Resources" by Thomas E. Tellefsen (April 1973)
"Management Reporting: Who Really Needs What?" by Jerry Dermer (March 1974)

NACUBO *Studies in Management*

"The Management of Change in Higher Education" by Glen R. Driscoll (February 1974)
"Management Systems and Budgeting Methodology: Do They Meet the Needs and Will They Work?" by Peggy Heim (September 1972)
"A Philosophy of Computer Utilization in Higher Education" by Eugene E. Cohen (October 1972)
"Techniques in the Use of Systems and Budgeting Methodology: A Conceptual Overview" by Ben Lawrence (August 1972)

2:3 Risk Management and Insurance

Adams, John F. *Risk Management and Insurance: Guidelines for Higher Education.* Washington, D. C.: National Association of College and University Business Officers, 1972.

Allen, C. H. *School Insurance Administration.* Riverside, N. J.: MacMillan Publishing Co., Inc., 1965.

Allen, Tom C., and Dotterweich, W. William. *Risk Management in Theory and Practice.* New York: Appleton-Century-Crofts, 1974.

American Association of School Administrators. *School Administrator's Guide to Insurance Buying.* Washington, D. C.: The Association, 1969.

Greene, Mark R. *Risk and Insurance.* 3rd ed. Cincinnati, Ohio: South-Western Publishing Co., 1973.

Huebner, Solomon S., et al. *Property and Liability Insurance.* New York: Appleton-Century-Crofts, 1968.

Knowles, Asa S. (ed.) *Handbook of College and University Administration.* New York: McGraw-Hill Book Co., 1970. (Section 8, Chapter 14, Insurance.)

Kulp, C. A., and Hall, John W. *Casualty Insurance.* 4th ed. New York: Ronald Press Co., 1968.

Lenz, Matthew, Jr. *Risk Management Manual.* Santa Monica, Calif.: Insurors Press, Inc., 1971.

MacDonald, Donald L. *Corporate Risk Control.* New York: Ronald Press Co., 1966.

Marquart, Eugene D., and Scarcliff, Charles W. *University and College Insurance Administration.* San Diego, Calif.: Auxiliary Organizations Association and the California State University and Colleges, 1973.

Mehr, Robert I., and Cammack, Emerson. *Principles of Insurance.* 5th ed. Homewood, Ill.: Richard D. Irwin, Inc., 1972.

Mehr, Robert I., and Hedges, Bob A. *Risk Management in the Business Enterprise.* Homewood, Ill.: Richard D. Irwin, Inc., 1963.

Osler, Robert W., and Bickley, John S. *Glossary of Insurance Terms.* Santa Monica, Calif.: Insurors Press, Inc., 1972.

Riegel, Robert, and Miller, J. S. *Insurance Principles and Practices.* 5th ed. Englewood Cliffs, N. J.: Prentice-Hall, Inc., 1966.

Webb, Bernard L., and Addicks, R. C., Jr. *Municipal Risk Management.* Cincinnati: The National Underwriter, 1971.

Webb, Bernard L.; Addicks, R. C., Jr.; and Lilly, Claude C. *Risk Manager's Guide.* Cincinnati: The National Underwriter, 1973.

Williams, C. Arthur, Jr., and Heins, R. M. *Risk Management and Insurance.* 2nd ed. New York: McGraw-Hill Book Co., 1971.

Periodicals

Best's Review
Business Insurance
The National Underwriter

NACUBO *Professional File*

"The Governing Board's Role in Risk Management and Insurance for Higher Education" by the Insurance and Risk Management Committee, NACUBO (March 1973)

2:4 Administration of Sponsored Programs: Instruction, Research, and Public Service

Allen, Jonathan (ed.) *March 4: Scientists, Students, and Society.* Cambridge, Mass.: Massachusetts Institute of Technology Press, 1970.

American Association of State Colleges and Universities, Office of Urban Programs. *A Guide to Federal Funds for Urban Programs at Colleges and Universities 1972-1973 edition.* Washington, D. C.: The Association, 1973.

American Council on Education. *Direct and Indirect Costs of Research at Colleges and Universities.* Washington, D. C.: The Council, 1969.

————. *Sponsored Research in American Universities and Colleges.* Washington, D. C.: The Council, 1967.

Association of American Universities. *The Federal Financing of Higher Education.* Washington, D. C.: The Association, 1968.

Caldwell, Lynton K. *Science, Technology, and Public Policy: A Selected and Annotated Bibliography in*

Three Volumes. Bloomington, Ind.: Department of Government, Indiana University. Vol. 1, 1968; vol. 2, 1969; vol. 3, 1972.

Commission on Resource Allocations. *Indirect Costs of Research.* Ann Arbor, Mich.: University of Michigan, 1972.

Committee on Governmental Relations. *Copyrights at Colleges and Universities.* Washington, D. C.: National Association of College and University Business Officers, 1972.

————. *Patents at Colleges and Universities: Guidelines for the Development of Policies and Programs.* Washington, D. C.: National Association of College and University Business Officers, 1974.

Danhof, Clarence H. *Government Contracting and Technological Change.* Washington, D. C.: Brookings Institution, 1968.

Dressel, Paul L., and Come, Donald R. *Impact of Federal Support of Science on the Publicly Supported Universities and Four-Year Colleges in Michigan.* Washington, D. C.: National Science Foundation, 1969.

Fried, Edward R., et al. *Setting National Priorities: The 1974 Budget.* Washington, D. C.: Brookings Institution, 1973.

Hall, Mary Jo. *Sources of Information on Funds: An Annotated Bibliography.* Eugene, Ore.: Office of Federal Relations, Oregon State System of Higher Education, 1971.

Knowles, Asa S. (ed.) *Handbook of College and University Administration.* New York: McGraw-Hill Book Co., 1970. (Section 3, Chapter 9, Federal Relationships.)

National Association of College and University Business Officers. *Federal Regulations and Employment Practices of Colleges and Universities: A Guide to the Interpretation of Federal Regulations Affecting Personnel Administration on Campus.* Washington, D. C.: The Association, 1974.

National Institutes of Health. *Grants for Research Projects: Policy Statement.* DHEW No(NIH) 72-8. Washington, D. C.: U.S. Government Printing Office, 1972.

————. *A Guide to the NIH Research Contracting Process.* U.S. Government Printing Office, 1973.

————. *The Institutional Guide to DHEW Policy on Protection of Human Subjects.* Washington, D. C.: U.S. Government Printing Office, 1972.

National Science Foundation. *Federal Support to Universities, Colleges and Selected Nonprofit Institutions, Fiscal Year 1972.* Washington, D. C.: U.S. Government Printing Office, 1973.

————. *NSF Grant Administration Manual.* NSF 73-26. Washington, D. C.: U.S. Government Printing Office, 1973.

————. *Resources for Scientific Activities at Universities and Colleges, 1971.* Washington, D. C.: U.S. Government Printing Office, 1973.

234

Orlans, Harold. *Ethical Problems in the Relations of Research Sponsors and Investigators*. Washington, D. C.: Brookings Institution, 1967.

————. *The Nonprofit Research Institute: Its Origin, Operation, Problems and Prospects*. New York: McGraw-Hill Book Co., 1972.

————. (ed.) *Science Policy and the University*. Washington, D. C.: Brookings Institution, 1968.

Research Foundation of State University of New York. *Sponsored Fund Administration: A Bibliography*. New York: The Foundation, 1973.

Strickland, Stephen. *Sponsored Research in American Universities and Colleges*. Washington, D. C.: American Council on Education, 1970.

U.S. Department of Health, Education, and Welfare. *A Guide for the Care and Use of Laboratory Animals*. Washington, D. C.: U.S. Government Printing Office, 1972.

U.S. Department of Health, Education, and Welfare, Health Services and Mental Health Administration. *A Guide to Institutional Cost Sharing Agreements for Research Grants and Contracts Supported by the Department of Health, Education, and Welfare*. Washington, D. C.: U.S. Government Printing Office, 1973.

U.S. Department of Health, Education, and Welfare, Office of the Assistant Secretary, Comptroller, Division of Grants Administration Policy. *A Guide for Colleges and Universities—Cost Principles and Procedures for Establishing Indirect Cost Rates for Research Grants and Contracts with the Department of Health, Education, and Welfare*. Washington, D. C.: U.S. Government Printing Office, 1971.

Westrate, Lee. *The Administration of Government Supported Research at Universities*. Washington, D. C.: Bureau of the Budget, 1966.

Willner, William, and Hendricks, Perry B., Jr. *Grants Administration*. Washington, D. C.: National Graduate University, 1972.

Other Publications

Federal Management Circulars
  FMC 73-3 Cost Sharing (formerly OMB A-100).
  FMC 73-6 Coordinating Indirect Cost Rates and Audit at Educational Institutions (formerly OMB A-88).
  FMC 73-7 Administration of College and University Research Grants (formerly OMB A-101).
  FMC 73-8 Cost Principles for Educational Institutions (formerly OMB A-21).
Armed Services Procurement Regulations.
National Aeronautics and Space Administration Grant Handbook.
Booklets on grant administration from National Science Foundation, United States Public Health Service, and Air Force Office of Scientific Research.

Services

Commerce Clearing House, Inc. *College and University Reporter*.
————. *Government Contracts Reporter*.

NACUBO *Studies in Management*

"Indirect Costs: A Problem in Communication" by the Subcommittee on Government Costing Policies, Committee on Governmental Relations, NACUBO (July 1974)

"Preparing the Indirect Costs Case for Federal Grants and Contracts" by James C. Gilfert (December 1972)

"What's So Special About Higher Education?" by Howard P. Wile (March 1974)

2:5 Legal Services

Alexander, Kern, and Solomon, Erwin S. *College and University Law*. Charlottesville, Va.: The Michie Company, 1972.

American Civil Liberties Union. *Academic Freedom and Civil Liberties of Students in Colleges and Universities*. New York: The Union, 1970.

Blackwell, Thomas E. *College Law: A Guide for Administrators*. Washington, D. C.: American Council on Education, 1961.

Brubacher, John S. *The Courts and Higher Education*. San Francisco: Jossey-Bass, Inc., Publishers, 1971.

Carbone, Robert F., et al. *Students and State Borders: Fiscal/Legal Issues Affecting Nonresident Students*. Iowa City: American College Testing, 1973.

Carr, Robert K., and VanEyck, Daniel K. *Collective Bargaining Comes to the Campus*. Washington, D. C.: American Council on Education, 1973.

Cary, William L., and Bright, Craig B. *The Developing Law of Endowment Funds: "The Law and the Lore" Revisited*. New York: The Ford Foundation, 1974.

————. *The Law and the Lore of Endowment Funds*. New York: The Ford Foundation, 1969.

Chambers, M. M. *The Colleges and the Courts, 1973*. Danville, Ill.: The Interstate Printers & Publishers, Inc., 1967.

————. *The Colleges and the Courts, 1962-1966*. Danville, Ill.: The Interstate Printers & Publishers, Inc., 1967.

————. *The Colleges and the Courts Since 1950*. Danville, Ill.: The Interstate Printers & Publishers, Inc., 1964.

Committee on Governmental Relations. *Copyrights at Colleges and Universities*. Washington, D. C.: National Association of College and University Business Officers, 1972.

_____. *Patents at Colleges and Universities: Guidelines for the Development of Policies and Programs.* Washington, D. C.: National Association of College and University Business Officers, 1974.

Denver Law Journal, Vol. 45, No. 4 (Special 1968): *Legal Aspects of Student-Institutional Relationships.* Denver: University of Denver College of Law, 1968.

Elliott, Edward C., and Chambers, M. M. *Charters and Basic Laws of Selected American Universities and Colleges.* New York: The Carnegie Foundation for the Advancement of Teaching, 1934.

Holmes, Grace W. (ed.) *Law and Discipline on Campus.* Ann Arbor, Mich.: The Institute of Continuing Legal Education, 1971.

_____. *Student Protest and the Law.* Ann Arbor, Mich.: The Institute of Continuing Legal Education, 1970.

Johnson, George M. *Education Law.* East Lansing, Mich.: Michigan State University Press, 1969.

Knowles, Asa S. (ed.) *Handbook of College and University Administration.* New York: McGraw-Hill Book Co., 1970. (Section 1, Legal Aspects of General Administration, and Section 1, Legal Aspects of Academic Administration, of Companion Volume on Academic Administration.)

Mills, Joseph L. *The Legal Rights of College Students and Administrators—A Handbook.* Washington, D. C.: Lerner Law Book Publishing Co., Inc., 1971.

O'Hara, William T., and Hill, John G., Jr. *The Student/The College/The Law.* New York: Teachers College Press, 1972.

Rose, Arnold M. *Libel and Academic Freedom, A Lawsuit Against Political Extremists.* Minneapolis: University of Minnesota Press, 1968.

Tice, Terrence N., and Holmes, Grace W., (eds.) *Faculty Bargaining in the Seventies.* Ann Arbor, Mich.: The Institute of Continuing Legal Education, 1973.

Williamson, E. G., and Cowan, John L. *The American Student's Freedom of Expression, A Research Appraisal.* Minneapolis: University of Minnesota Press, 1966.

Periodicals

College Law Digest
Journal of College and University Law
Journal of Law & Education

Services

The College Student and the Courts. Young & Gehring; College Administration Publishers, Inc.
Higher Education Administration Law Service. Educational Testing Service.

NACUBO *Professional File*

"Court and Campus—Striking a New Balance" by Robert M. O'Neil (August 1973)

2:6 Student Aid

Adams, Frank C., and Stevens, Clarence W. *A Student Job Classification Plan for Colleges and Universities.* Carbondale, Ill.: Southern Illinois University Press, 1972.

American College Testing Program. *Handbook for Financial Aid Administrators.* Iowa City: American College Testing, 1973.

Bowen, Howard, and Serville, Paul. *Who Benefits from Higher Education—and Who Should Pay?* Washington, D. C.: American Association for Higher Education, 1972.

Carnegie Commission on Higher Education. *Higher Education: Who Pays? Who Benefits? Who Should Pay?* New York: McGraw-Hill Book Co., 1973.

Cartter, Allan M. *New Approaches to Student Financial Aid.* New York: College Entrance Examination Board, 1971.

Cheit, Earl. *The New Depression in Higher Education.* New York: McGraw-Hill Book Co., 1971.

College Entrance Examination Board. *CSS Need Analysis: Theory and Computation Procedures.* New York: The Board, 1973.

_____. *Financing Equal Opportunity in Higher Education.* New York: The Board, 1972.

_____. *Report of the Committee on Student Economics.* New York: The Board, 1972.

Ford Foundation. *Pay-As-You-Earn, Summary Report and Recommendation.* New York: The Foundation, 1972.

Hansen, W. Lee, and Weisbrod, Burton A. *Benefits, Costs, and Finance of Public Higher Education.* Chicago: Marbham Publishing Company, 1969.

Hartman, Robert W. *Credit for College: Public Policy for Student Loans.* New York: McGraw-Hill Book Co., 1971.

Haven, Elizabeth, and Horch, Dwight. *How College Students Finance Their Education: A National Survey of the Educational Interests, Aspirations, and Finances of College Sophomores in 1969-70.* New York: College Entrance Examination Board, 1972.

Johnstone, D. Bruce. *New Patterns for College Lending: Income Contingent Loans.* New York: Columbia University Press, 1972.

Lamson, George, et al. *Income Contingent Loans: Conceptual and Applied Framework for the Small College,* MASFAA Monograph No. 2. Bloomington, Indiana: Midwest Association of Student Financial Aid Administrators, 1971.

North, Walter M. *The Relationship of Aid to Fee Increases and Enrollment Growth,* MASFAA Monograph No. 1. Bloomington, Indiana: Midwest Association of Student Financial Aid Administrators, 1970.

Orwig, M. D. (ed.) *Financing Higher Education: Alternatives for the Federal Government.* Iowa City: American College Testing, 1971.

236

Willingham, Warren W. *Free-Access Higher Education*. New York: College Entrance Examination Board, 1970.

Periodical

The Journal of Student Financial Aid

2:7 Personnel Administration

Beach, Dale S. *Personnel: Management of People at Work*. 2nd ed. Riverside, N. J.: MacMillan Publishing Co., Inc., 1970.

Benton, Lewis. *Supervision and Management*. New York: McGraw-Hill Book Co., 1972.

Chruden, Herbert J., and Sherman, Arthur W. *Personnel Management*. 4th ed. Cincinnati, Ohio: South-Western Publishing Co., 1972.

College and University Personnel Association. *A Classification Plan for Staff Positions at Colleges and Universities*. Urbana, Ill.: The Association, 1968.

————. *Personnel Practices in Colleges and Universities*. University Park, Pa.: Pennsylvania State University, 1966.

Dunn, J. D., and Rachel, Frank. *Wage and Salary Administration*. New York: McGraw-Hill Book Co., 1971.

Dunn, J. D., and Stephen, Elvis. *Management of Personnel*. New York: McGraw-Hill Book Co., 1972.

Eggert, C. Lee, and Williams, James O. *Personnel Management: A Systems Approach*. Midland, Mich.: Pendell Publishing Co., 1973.

Famularo, Joseph J. *Handbook of Modern Personnel Administration*. New York: McGraw-Hill Book Co., 1972.

Harkness, Charles A. *College Staff Personnel Administration*. Urbana, Ill.: College and University Personnel Association, 1965.

Ingraham, Mark H. (with the collaboration of Francis P. King). *The Mirror of Brass: The Compensation and Working Conditions of College and University Administrators*. Madison, Wis.: Association of American Colleges, University of Wisconsin Press, 1968.

Johnson, H. W. *Selecting, Training, and Supervising Office Personnel*. Reading, Mass.: Addison-Wesley Publishing Co., Inc., 1969.

Jongeward, Dorothy, and Scott, Dru. *Affirmative Action for Women: A Practical Guide*. Reading, Mass.: Addison-Wesley Publishing Co., Inc., 1973.

Jucius, Michael J. *Personnel Management*. 7th ed. Homewood, Ill.: Richard D. Irwin, Inc., 1971.

Knowles, Asa S. (ed.) *Handbook of College and University Administration*. New York: McGraw-Hill Book Co., 1970. (Section 6, Nonacademic Personnel Administration, and Section 6, Academic Personnel Administration, of Companion Volume on Academic Administration.)

McFarland, D. E. (ed.) *Personnel Management Theory and Practice*. Riverside, N. J.: MacMillan Publishing Co., Inc., 1968.

Margulies, Newton, and Wallace, John. *Organizational Change: Techniques and Applications*. Glenview, Ill.: Scott, Foresman & Co., 1973.

Megginson, Leon C. *Personnel: A Behavioral Approach to Administration*. Rev. ed. Homewood, Ill.: Richard D. Irwin, Inc., 1972.

Miner, Mary G., and Miner, John B. *A Guide to Personnel Management*. Washington, D. C.: Bureau of National Affairs, Inc., 1973.

National Association of College and University Business Officers. *Federal Regulations and the Employment Practices of Colleges and Universities: A Guide to the Interpretation of Federal Regulations Affecting Personnel Administration on Campus*. Washington, D. C.: The Association, 1974.

————. *Wage and Salary Administration for Smaller Institutions of Higher Education*. Washington, D. C.: The Association, 1974.

Pigors, Paul, and Myers, Charles. *Personnel Administration*. 7th ed. New York: McGraw-Hill Book Co., 1973.

Ritterbush, Philip C. (ed.) *Talent Waste: How Institutions of Learning Misdirect Human Resources*. Washington, D. C.: Acropolis Books, Ltd., 1972.

Rock, Milton L. (ed.) *Handbook of Wage and Salary Administration*. New York: McGraw-Hill Book Co., 1972.

U.S. Department of Health, Education, and Welfare. *Higher Education Guidelines: Executive Order 11246 "Nondiscrimination Under Federal Contracts."* Washington, D. C.; U.S. Government Printing Office, 1965.

Yoder, Dale. *Personnel Management and Industrial Relations*. 6th ed. Englewood Cliffs, N. J.: Prentice-Hall, Inc., 1970.

Periodical

The Journal of the College and University Personnel Association

NACUBO *Studies in Management*

"A Comprehensive Personnel System for Colleges and Universities" by Owen R. Houghton (January 1974)

"Equal Employment Opportunity on Campus: A Case Study of the University of Pittsburgh" by Edward J. Blakely (December 1973)

"Humanizing Business and Financial Affairs" by Stanford R. Bohne (January 1973)

2:8 Faculty and Staff Benefits

Adams, John F. *Risk Management and Insurance: Guidelines for Higher Education.* Washington, D. C.: National Association of College and University Business Officers, 1972.

Allen, Donna. *Fringe Benefits: Wages or Social Obligation.* New York: State School of Industrial and Labor Relations, 1969.

Benefit Cost Analysis, 1972: An Aldine Annual on Forecasting, Decision-Making, and Evaluation. Chicago, Ill.: Aldine Publishing Co., 1973.

Boulton, A. Harding. *Law and Practice of Social Security.* South Hackensack, N. J.: Rothman, Fred B. and Co., 1972.

Brown, J. Douglas. *An American Philosophy of Social Security.* Princeton, N. J.: Princeton University Press, 1972.

Day, James F. *Teacher Retirement in the United States.* North Quincy, Mass.: Christopher Publishing House, 1971.

Deric, Arthur J. (ed.) *Total Approach to Employee Benefits.* New York: American Management Association, 1967.

George, Victor. *Social Security and Society.* Boston, Mass.: Routledge and Kegan Paul, 1973.

Greenough, William C., and King, Francis P. *Benefit Plans in American Colleges.* New York: Columbia University Press, 1969.

Gregg, Davis W., and Lucas, Vane B. *Life and Health Insurance Handbook.* 3rd ed. Homewood, Ill.: Richard D. Irwin, Inc., 1973.

Harkness, Charles A. *College Staff Personnel Administration.* Urbana, Ill.: College and University Personnel Association, 1965.

Hold, William T., and Todd, Jerry D. *Foundations of Life and Health Insurance.* Austin, Texas: University of Texas Bureau of Business Research, 1971.

Ingraham, Mark H., and King, Francis P. *The Outer Fringe: Faculty Benefits Other Than Annuities and Insurance.* Madison, Wis.: University of Wisconsin Press, 1965.

King, Francis P. *Benefit Plans in Junior Colleges.* Washington, D. C.: American Association of Junior Colleges, 1971.

Knowles, Asa S. (ed.) *Handbook of College and University Administration.* New York: McGraw-Hill Book Co., 1970. (Section 8, Chapters 7 and 8, Fringe Benefits—Faculty, Administration, and Administrative Staff *and* Compensation and Fringe Benefits—Nonacademic Personnel.)

Mackin, John P. *Protecting Purchasing Power in Retirement: A Study of Public Employee Retirement Systems.* New York: The Academic Editions, Inc., 1971.

Melone, Joseph J., and Allen, Everett T. *Pension Planning.* Rev. ed. Homewood, Ill.: Dow Jones-Irwin, Inc., 1972.

National Association of College and University Business Officers. *Federal Regulations and the Employment Practices of Colleges and Universities: A Guide to the Interpretation of Federal Regulations Affecting Personnel Administration on Campus.* Washington, D. C.: The Association, 1974.

National Education Association. *Salary Schedules and Fringe Benefits for Teachers.* Washington, D. C.: The Association, 1972-1973.

————. *Teacher Retirement Systems.* Washington, D. C.: The Association, 1972.

U.S. Department of Health, Education, and Welfare. *History of the Provisions of Old-Age Survivors Disability and Health Insurance, 1935-1972.* No. 7311510. Washington, D. C.: U.S. Government Printing Office, 1972.

2:9 Labor Relations and Collective Bargaining

Andree, Robert G. *The Art of Negotiation.* Lexington, Mass.: Heath Lexington Books, 1971.

Barbash, Jack. *Academicians as Bargainers with the University.* Madison, Wis.: Industrial Relations Research Institute, 1970.

Beal, Edwin F., et al. *Practice of Collective Bargaining.* 4th ed. Homewood, Ill.: Richard D. Irwin, Inc., 1972.

Belcher, A. Lee; Avery, Hugh P.; and Smith, Oscar S. *Labor Relations in Higher Education.* Washington, D. C.: College and University Personnel Association, 1971.

Benson, Charles S. *Productivity and Collective Bargaining in Higher Education.* Madison, Wis.: Industrial Labor Relations Association, 1973.

Carlton, Patrick W., and Goodwin, Harold I. *The Collective Dilemma: Negotiations in Education.* Worthington, Ohio: Charles A. Jones Publishing Company, 1969.

Carr, Robert K., and VanEyck, Daniel K. *Collective Bargaining Comes to the Campus.* Washington, D. C.: American Council on Education, 1973.

Chamberlain, Neil W., and Kuhn, J. W. *Collective Bargaining.* 2nd ed. New York: McGraw-Hill Book Co., 1965.

Cole, Stephen. *The Unionization of Teachers: A Case Study of the UFT.* New York: Praeger Publishers, Inc., 1969.

"Collective Bargaining in Higher Education." Madison, Wisconsin: *Wisconsin Law Review,* February 1971

College and University Personnel Association and National Association of College and University Business Officers. *Faculty Collective Bargaining Seminar.* Washington, D. C.: The Associations, 1973.

Commons, John R. *Economics of Collective Action.* Edited by Kenneth H. Parsons. Madison, Wis.: University of Wisconsin Press, 1970.

Davey, Harold W. *Contemporary Collective Bargaining*. 3rd ed. Englewood Cliffs, N. J.: Prentice-Hall, Inc., 1972.

Duryea, E. D., and Fisk, Robert S. *Faculty Unions and Collective Bargaining*. San Francisco: Jossey-Bass, Inc., Publishers, 1973.

Elam, Stanley, and Moskow, Michael H. (eds.) *Employment Relations in Higher Education*. Bloomington, Ind.: Phi Delta Kappa, Inc., 1969.

Elkouri, Frank, and Elkouri, Edna A. *How Arbitration Works*. 3rd ed. Washington, D. C.: Bureau of National Affairs, Inc., 1973.

Gilroy, Thomas, and Russo, A. *Bargaining Unit Issues: Problems, Criteria, Tactics*. Chicago: International Personnel Management Association, 1973.

Hughes, Clarence R., et al. *Collective Negotiations in Higher Education: A Reader*. Carlinville, Ill.: Blackburn College Press, 1973.

Institute of Continuing Legal Education. *Faculty Bargaining in the Seventies*. Ann Arbor, Mich.: The Institute, 1973.

Knowles, Asa S. (ed.) *Handbook of College and University Administration*. New York: McGraw-Hill Book Co., 1970. (Section 6, Chapter 3, Nonacademic Personnel Labor Relations, and Section 6, Chapter 8, Collective Negotiations, of Companion Volume on Academic Administration.)

Kochan, Thomas. *Resolving Internal Management Conflicts for Labor Relations*. Chicago: International Personnel Management Association, 1973.

Ladd, Everett Carll, Jr., and Lipset, Seymour Martin. *Professors, Unions, and American Higher Education*. New York: McGraw-Hill Book Co., 1973.

Marceau, Leroy (ed.) *Dealing with a Union*. New York: American Management Association, 1969.

Marshall, Howard D., and Marshall, Natalie J. *Collective Bargaining*. Westminster, Md.: Random House, College Division, 1971.

Morris, Charles (ed.) *Developing Labor Law*. Washington, D. C.: Bureau of National Affairs, Inc., 1970. (Annual Supplements.)

Moses, Stephan. *Collective Bargaining Agreements in Higher Education*. Columbia, Mo.: University of Missouri, 1973.

National Association of College and University Business Officers. *Federal Regulations and Employment Practices of Colleges and Universities: A Guide to the Interpretation of Federal Regulations Affecting Personnel Administration on Campus*. Washington, D. C.: The Association, 1974.

National Center for the Study of Collective Bargaining in Higher Education. *Proceedings of the First Annual Conference on Collective Bargaining in Higher Education: April 1973*. New York: CUNY, Baruch College, 1973.

National Education Association. *Comprehensive Negotiation Agreement Provisions*. Washington, D. C.: The Association, 1972.

Saso, Carmen D. *Coping with Public Employee Strikes: A Guide to Public Officials*. Chicago: International Public Personnel Association, 1970.

Shulman, Carol H. *Collective Bargaining on Campus*. Washington, D. C.: American Association for Higher Education, 1972.

Simkin, William E. *Mediation and the Dynamics of Collective Bargaining*. Washington, D. C.: Bureau of National Affairs, Inc., 1971.

Skjei, Stephen S. *Information for Collective Action*. Lexington, Mass.: Heath Lexington Books, 1973.

Sloane, Arthur, and Whitney, F. *Labor Relations*. 2nd ed. Englewood Cliffs, N. J.: Prentice-Hall, Inc., 1971.

Taylor, Benjamin J., and Whitney, Fred. *Labor Relations Law*. Englewood Cliffs, N. J.: Prentice-Hall, Inc., 1971.

Tice, Terrence N., and Holmes, Grace W., (eds.) *Faculty Power: Collective Bargaining on Campus*. Ann Arbor, Mich.: The Institute of Continuing Legal Education, 1972.

U.S. Department of Labor. *Dispute Settlement in the Public Sector: The State of the Art*. Washington, D. C.: U.S. Government Printing Office, 1972.

————. *Scope of Bargaining in the Public Sector: Concepts and Problems*. Washington, D. C.: U.S. Government Printing Office, 1972.

Wollett, Donald H., and Chanin, Robert H. *The Law and Practice of Teacher Negotiations*. Washington, D. C.: The Bureau of National Affairs, Inc., 1970.

Woodworth, Robert T., and Peterson, Richard B. *Collective Negotiation for Public and Professional Employees*. Glenview, Ill.: Scott, Foresman & Co., 1969.

NACUBO *Professional File*

"The National Labor Relations Act and Higher Education: Prospects and Problems" by Robert E. Doherty (June 1973)

NACUBO *Studies in Management*

"Emerging Trends in Faculty Collective Bargaining Agreements" by John O. Andes and Harold I. Goodwin (June 1972)

3:1 Purchasing

Alijian, George W. *Purchasing Handbook*. 2nd ed. New York: McGraw-Hill Book Co., 1966.

Ammer, D. S. *Materials Management*. 2nd ed. Homewood, Ill.: Richard D. Irwin, Inc., 1968.

Anyon, G. J. *Managing an Integrated Purchasing Process.* New York: Holt, Rinehart & Winston, 1963.

Bacon, Paul A. "The Role of the Educational Purchasing Agent in Colleges and Universities of the United States." Doctoral dissertation. Ann Arbor, Mich.: University Microfilms, 1969.

Bolton, Ralph A. *Systems Contracting, a New Purchasing Technique.* New York: American Management Association, 1966.

Briggs, Andrew J. *Warehouse Operation Planning and Management.* New York: John Wiley & Sons, Inc., 1960.

Burns, H. S. *Purchasing and Supply Management Manual for School Business Officials.* Evanston, Ill.: Association of School Business Officials, 1962.

Dowst, Sommerby R. *Basics for Buyers.* Boston, Mass.: Cahners Publishing Co., Inc., 1971.

England, Wilbur B. *Procurement: Principles and Cases.* Homewood, Ill.: Richard D. Irwin, Inc., 1962.

Gravereau, Victor P., and Konopa, Leonard J. *Purchasing Management: Selected Readings.* Columbus, Ohio: Grid, Inc., 1973.

Haas, George H.; Mack, Benjamin; and Krech, E. M. *Purchasing Department Organization and Authority.* AMA Research Study 45. New York: American Management Association, 1960.

Heinritz, Stuart F., and Farrell, Paul V. *Purchasing: Principles and Applications.* 5th ed. Englewood Cliffs, N. J.: Prentice-Hall, Inc., 1971.

Knowles, Asa S. (ed.) *Handbook of College and University Administration.* New York: McGraw-Hill Book Co., 1970. (Section 8, Chapter 10, Purchasing in an Educational Institution.)

Kollios, A. E., and Stempel, Joseph. *Purchasing and EDP.* New York: American Management Association, 1966.

Kotschevar, Lendal H. *Quantity Food Purchasing.* New York: John Wiley & Sons, Inc., 1961.

Lee, J. Lamar, and Dobler, Donald. *Purchasing and Material Management.* New York: McGraw-Hill Book Co., 1965.

Pooler, Victor H. *The Purchasing Man and His Job.* New York: American Management Association, 1964.

Ritterskamp, James J.; Abbott, Forrest L.; and Ahrens, Bert C. *Purchasing for Educational Institutions.* New York: Bureau of Publications, Teachers College, Columbia University, 1961.

Report of the Commission on Government Procurement. Washington, D. C.: U.S. Government Printing Office, 1972.

Zemansky, Stanley D. *The Purchasing Job: Dimensions and Trends.* AMA Bulletin No. 11. New York: American Management Association, 1961.

3:2 Auxiliary Enterprises, Organized Activities, and Service Departments

Association of College Unions-International. *Standards for Professional Staff Preparation and Compensation in College Union Work.* Stanford, Calif.: The Association, 1974.

Brothers, Joan, and Hatch, Stephen. *Residence and Student Life: A Sociological Inquiry into Residence in Higher Education.* Scranton, Pa.: Barnes and Noble, Inc., 1971.

Butts, Porter. *The College Union Idea.* Stanford, Calif.: Association of College Unions-International, 1971.

————. *Planning College Union Facilities for Multiple Use.* Stanford, Calif.: Association of College Unions-International, 1966.

————. *Planning and Operating College Union Buildings.* Stanford, Calif.: Association of College Unions-International, 1967.

Durrett, Paul K., and Robinson, Ronald R. *Governance of the College Union.* Stanford, Calif.: Association of College Unions-International, 1972.

Ebbers, Larry H.; Marks, Kenneth E.; and Stoner, Kenneth L. *Residence Halls in U.S. Higher Education: A Bibliography.* Ames, Iowa: Iowa State University, 1973.

Educational Facilities Laboratories. *Student Housing.* New York: The Laboratories, 1972.

Higgins, Eleanor. *Food Training Routines 1 and 2.* New ed. Boston, Mass.: Cahners Publishing Co., Inc., 1973.

Jenkins, Jack, and McQueen, Sidney. *College Unions at Work: Administration and Operation of the College Union.* Stanford, Calif.: Association of College Unions-International, 1973.

Knowles, Asa S. (ed.) *Handbook of College and University Administration.* New York: McGraw-Hill Book Co., 1970. (Section 8, Business and Financial Administration.)

Kotschever, Lendal H. *Quantity Food Production.* 2nd ed. Berkeley, Calif.: McCutchan Publishing Co., 1966.

Mullins, William, and Allen, Phyllis. *Student Housing: Architectural and Social Aspects.* New York: Praeger Publishers, Inc., 1971.

National Association of College and University Food Services. *Guide to Food Service Management.* Edited by Frances Cloyd. Boston, Mass.: Cahners Publishing Co., Inc., 1972.

Riker, Harold C. *College Housing as Learning Centers.* Washington, D. C.: American Personnel and Guidance Association, 1965.

Smith, E. Evelyn, and Crusius, Vera C. *Handbook on Quantity Food Management.* 2nd ed. Minneapolis, Minn.: Burgess Publishing Co., 1970.

Stokes, John W. *Food Service in Industry and Institutions.* 2nd ed. Dubuque, Iowa: William C. Brown, 1973.

Terrell, Margaret E. *Professional Food Preparation: Techniques and Equipment for Large Quantity.* New York: John Wiley & Sons, Inc., 1970.

Periodicals

The College Store Journal
The Journal of College and University Student Housing
School Foodservice Journal

NACUBO *Studies in Management*

"Negotiation, Administration, and Measurement of Food Service Contracts in Higher Education" by H. Donald Scott (May 1973)

3:3 Facilities Operation and Maintenance

Allphin, Willard. *Primor of Lamps and Lighting.* Salem, Mass.: Sylvania Electric Products, Inc., 1959.
Association of Physical Plant Administrators. *Comparative Staffing and Operations Study for Physical Plant Functions of Universities and Colleges.* Washington, D. C.: The Association, 1973.
————. *Comparative Unit Cost and Wage Rate Report on Maintenance and Operation of Physical Plants of Universities and Colleges for 1973.* Washington, D. C.: The Association, 1974.
————. *Energy Conservation Checklist.* Washington, D. C.: The Association, 1974.
Berkeley, Bernard. *Floors: Selection and Maintenance.* Chicago: Library Technology Program, American Library Association, 1968.
Betz Handbook of Industrial Water Conditioning. 6th ed. Trevose, Pa.: Betz Publishing Co., 1972.
Buyers Laboratory, Inc. *Test Reports on Plant Products.* Hackensack, N. J.: The Laboratory, 1973-1974.
Conover, H. S. *Grounds Maintenance Handbook.* 2nd ed. New York: F. W. Dodge Corporation, 1958.
Educational Facilities Laboratories. *The Economy of Energy Conservation in Educational Facilities.* New York: The Laboratories, 1973.
Feldman, Edwin B. *Housekeeping Handbook for Institutions, Business, and Industry.* New York: Frederick Fell, Inc., 1969.
Fink, Donald G., and Carroll, John M. *Standard Handbook for Electrical Engineers.* 10th ed. New York: McGraw-Hill Book Co., 1968.
Green, John L., and Barker, Allan W. *A System of Cost Accounting for Physical Plant in Institutions of Higher Education.* Athens, Georgia: University of Georgia Press, 1968.
Haines, John E. *Automatic Control of Heating and Air Conditioning.* 2nd ed. New York: McGraw-Hill Book Co., 1961.

Illuminating Engineering Society. *IES Lighting Handbook.* 5th ed. New York: The Society, 1972.
Knowles, Asa S. (ed.) *Handbook of College and University Administration.* New York: McGraw-Hill Book Co., 1970. (Section 7, Physical Plant Administration.)
Maintenance Guide for Commercial Buildings. Cedar Rapids, Iowa: Stamats Publishing Company, 1970.
Morrow, L. C. (ed.) *Maintenance Engineering Handbook.* New York: McGraw-Hill Book Co., 1957.
National Fire Protection Association. *NFPA Handbook of the National Electrical Code.* 3rd ed. New York: McGraw-Hill Book Co., 1971.
Price, Seymour G. *A Guide to Monitoring and Controlling Utility Costs.* Washington, D. C.: BNA Books, 1973.
————. *Air Conditioning for Building Engineers and Managers; Operation and Maintenance.* New York: Industrial Press, Inc., 1963.
Sack, Thomas F. *A Complete Guide to Building and Plant Maintenance.* Englewood Cliffs, N. J.: Prentice-Hall, Inc., 1963.
Terry, Harry. *Mechanical-Electrical Equipment Handbook for School Buildings; Installation, Maintenance, and Use.* New York: John Wiley & Sons, Inc., 1960.
Weber, George O., and Fincham, Michael W. (eds.) *A Basic Manual for Physical Plant Administration.* Washington, D. C.: Association of Physical Plant Administrators, 1974.

NACUBO *Studies in Management*

"The Business Officer as Campus Environmentalist" by C. Ray Varley (October 1973)

3:4 Facilities Planning, Design, and Construction

Clough, Richard H. *Construction Contracting.* New York: John Wiley & Sons, Inc., 1960.
Flynn, John E., and Segil, Arthur W. *Architectural Interior Systems: Lighting, Air Conditioning, Acoustics.* New York: Van Nostrand Reinhold Co., 1970.
General Services Administration. *Construction Contracting Systems: A Report on the Systems Used by PBS [Public Building Service] and Other Organizations.* Washington, D. C.: U.S. Government Printing Office, 1970.
Heller, Edward D. *Value Management: Value Engineering and Cost Reduction.* Reading, Mass.: Addison-Wesley Publishing Co., Inc., 1971.
Knowles, Asa S. (ed.) *Handbook of College and University Administration.* New York: McGraw-Hill Book Co., 1970. (Section 7, Physical Plant Administration.)

241

McKaig, Thomas H. *Field Inspection of Building Construction*. New York: F. W. Dodge Corporation, 1958.

Metcalf, Keyes D. *Library Lighting*. Washington, D. C.: The Association of Research Libraries, 1970.

Planning and Management Systems Division, Western Interstate Commission for Higher Education, and The American Association of Collegiate Registrars and Admissions Officers. *Higher Education Facilities Planning and Management Manuals*. Boulder, Colorado: The Commission and Association, 1971.

Priluck, Herbert M., and Hourhan, Peter M. *Practical CPM for Construction*. Duxbury, Mass.: R.S. Means Co., Inc., 1968.

Russell, John Dale, and Doi, James. *Manual for Studies in Space Utilization in Colleges and Universities*. Athens, Ohio: Ohio University, 1957.

U.S. Department of Health, Education, and Welfare. *Academic Building System (ABS)—Higher Education*. Washington, D. C.: U.S. Government Printing Office, 1971.

————. *Technical Handbook for Facilities Engineering and Construction Manual*. Washington, D. C.: U.S. Government Printing Office, 1972.

Weber, George O., and Fincham, Michael W. (eds.) *A Basic Manual for Physical Plant Administration*. Washington, D. C.: Association of Physical Plant Administrators, 1974.

Periodical

American School and University

NACUBO *Studies in Management*

"Academic Building Systems" by Donald H. Clark (April 1972)
"The Business Officer as Campus Environmentalist" by C. Ray Varley (October 1973)

3:5 Security

Gelber, Seymour. *The Role of Campus Security in the College Setting*. Washington, D. C.: U.S. Government Printing Office, 1972.

Knowles, Asa S. (ed.) *Handbook of College and University Administration*. New York: McGraw-Hill Book Co., 1970. (Section 7, Chapter 7, Security, Safety, Fire Protection, and Civil Defense.)

The President's Commission on Campus Unrest. Washington, D. C.: U.S. Government Printing Office, 1970. (Chapter 4.)

Sims, O. Suthern. *New Directions in Campus Law Enforcement: A Handbook for Administrators*. Athens, Ga.: The University of Georgia Center for Continuing Education, 1971.

Weber, George O., and Fincham, Michael W. (eds.) *A Basic Manual for Physical Plant Administration*. Washington, D. C.: Association of Physical Plant Administrators, 1974.

Periodical

Campus Law Enforcement Journal

3:6 Safety

American Conference of Governmental Industrial Hygienists. *Industrial Ventilation*. 10th ed. Lansing, Mich.: The Conference, 1968.

American Industrial Hygiene Association. *Industrial Noise Manual*. Akron, Ohio: The Association, 1966.

————. *Respiratory Protection Devices Manual*. Lansing, Mich.: The Association and the American Conference of Governmental Industrial Hygienists.

Best's Safety Directory. 14th ed. Morristown, N. J.: A.M. Best Company, 1973.

DeReamer, Russell. *Modern Safety Practices*. New York: John Wiley & Sons, Inc., 1958.

Factory Mutual System. *Handbook of Industrial Loss Prevention*. 2nd ed. New York: McGraw-Hill Book Co., 1967.

International Conference of Building Officials. *Uniform Building Code*. Whittier, Calif.: The Conference, 1973.

————. *Uniform Fire Code*. Whittier, Calif.: The Conference, 1973.

Knowles, Asa S. (ed.) *Handbook of College and University Administration*. New York: McGraw-Hill Book Co., 1970. (Section 7, Chapter 7, Security, Safety, Fire Protection, and Civil Defense.)

Manufacturing Chemists Association. *Guide to Safety in the Chemical Laboratory*. 2nd ed. New York: Van Nostrand Reinhold Co., 1972.

————. *Laboratory Waste Disposal Manual*. Rev. ed. Washington, D. C.: The Association, 1973.

Matheson Gas Data Book. 4th ed. East Rutherford, N. J.: The Matheson Company, Inc., 1966.

National Fire Protection Association. *Fire Protection Guide on Hazardous Materials*. 5th ed. Boston, Mass.: The Association, 1973.

————. *Fire Protection Handbook*. 13th ed. Boston, Mass.: The Association, 1969.

————. *Manual of Hazardous Chemical Reactions, No. 491M*. 4th ed. Boston, Mass.: The Association, 1971.

————. *National Fire Codes*. Vols. 1-10. Boston, Mass.: The Association, 1971-72.

National Safety Council. *Accident Prevention Manual for Industrial Operations*. 6th ed. Chicago: The Council, 1969.

————. *Fundamentals of Industrial Hygiene.* Chicago: The Council, 1971.

————. *Supervisors Safety Manual.* 3rd ed. Chicago: The Council, 1967.

Patty, F. A. *Industrial Hygiene and Toxicology.* Vol. II. 2nd rev. ed. New York: John Wiley & Sons, Inc., 1963.

Plunkett, E. R. *Handbook of Industrial Toxicology.* New York: Chemical Publishing Company, Inc., 1966.

Sax, N. Irving. *Dangerous Properties of Industrial Materials.* 3rd ed. New York: Van Nostrand Reinhold Co., 1968.

Simonds, Rollin H., and Grimaldi, John V. *Safety Management: Accident Cost and Control.* Rev. ed. Homewood, Ill.: Richard D. Irwin, Inc., 1963.

Steere, Norman V. (ed.) *Handbook of Laboratory Safety.* 2nd ed. Cleveland, Ohio: The Chemical Rubber Company, 1972.

Tarrants, William E. *A Selected Bibliography of Reference Materials in Safety Engineering and Related Fields.* Park Ridge, Ill.: American Society of Safety Engineers, 1967.

U.S. Department of Labor. *Occupational Safety and Health Standards, Code of Federal Regulations, Title 29, Part 1910.* Washington, D. C.: U.S. Government Printing Office, 1972.

4:1 Administration of Endowment Funds, Quasi-Endowment Funds, and Other Similar Funds
and

4:2 Investment Management

Advisory Committee on Endowment Management. *Managing Educational Endowments.* 2nd ed. New York: The Ford Foundation, 1972.

American Alumni Council. *Guide to the Administration of Charitable Remainder Trusts.* Washington, D. C.: The Council, 1974.

Amling, Frederick. *Investments: An Introduction to Analysis and Management.* 2nd ed. Englewood Cliffs, N. J.: Prentice-Hall, Inc., 1970.

Bellemore, Douglas H., and Ritchie, John C., Jr. *Investments: Principles and Analysis.* 3rd ed. Cincinnati, Ohio: South-Western Publishing Co., 1969.

Brealey, Richard A. *Introduction to Risk and Return from Common Stocks.* Cambridge, Mass.: Massachusetts Institute of Technology Press, 1969.

————. *Security Prices in a Competitive Market: More About Risk and Return from Common Stocks.* Cambridge, Mass.: Massachusetts Institute of Technology Press, 1971.

Cary, William L., and Bright, Craig B. *The Developing Law of Endowment Funds: "The Law and the Lore" Revisited.* New York: The Ford Foundation, 1974.

————. *The Law and the Lore of Endowment Funds.* New York: The Ford Foundation, 1969.

Dougall, Herbert E. *Investments.* 8th ed. Englewood Cliffs, N. J.: Prentice-Hall, Inc., 1968.

The Endowment Conference. *Managing Endowment Capital.* New York: Donaldson, Lufkin & Jenrette, Inc., 1972.

Ford Foundation. *Managing Educational Endowments.* Report to the Ford Foundation by the Advisory Committee on Endowment Management. New York: The Foundation, 1969.

Graham, Benjamin; Dodd, David L.; and Cottle, Sidney. *Security Analysis Principles and Techniques.* 4th ed. New York: McGraw-Hill Book Co., 1962.

Knowles, Asa S. (ed.) *Handbook of College and University Administration.* New York: McGraw-Hill Book Co., 1970. (Section 8, Chapters 24 and 25, Investment Policies and Procedures *and* Portfolio Management by Professional Counsel.)

Longstreth, Bevis, and Rosenbloom, H. David. *Corporate Social Responsibility and the Institutional Investor.* A Report to the Ford Foundation. New York: Praeger Publishers, 1973.

Lorie, James T., and Hamilton, Mary. *The Stock Market: Theories and Evidence.* Homewood, Ill.: Dow Jones-Irwin, Inc., 1973.

Nelson, Ralph L. *The Investment Policies of Foundations.* New York: Russell Sage Foundation, 1967.

Sauvain, Harry C. *Investment Management.* 4th ed. Englewood Cliffs, N. J.: Prentice-Hall, Inc., 1973.

Simon, John G.; Powers, Charles W.; and Gunneman, Jon P. *The Ethical Investor: Universities and Corporate Responsibility.* New Haven, Conn.: Yale University Press, 1972.

Stephenson, Gilbert T., and Wiggins, Norman A. *Estates and Trusts.* 5th ed. New York: Appleton-Century-Crofts, 1973.

Torgerson, Harold W. et al. *Investment Principles and Practices.* 6th ed. Englewood Cliffs, N. J.: Prentice-Hall, Inc., 1969.

Williamson, J. Peter. *Performance Management and Investment Objectives for Educational Endowment Funds.* New York: The Common Fund, 1972.

NACUBO *Studies in Management*

"Current Trends in College and University Investment Policies and Practices" by Rodney H. Adams (March 1972)

"Investment Policies and Concepts for Pools" by Robert L. Ellis (February 1973)

"Techniques for Improving Cash Management" by Ronald G. Lykins (April 1973)

"Unit Method of Accounting for Investments" by Leigh A. Jones (December 1971)

4:3 Budgets and Budgetary Accounting

Budig, Gene A. *Dollars and Sense: Budgeting for Today's Campus.* Chicago: College and University Business Publications, McGraw-Hill Book Co., 1972.

The Coordinating Board, Texas College and University System. *Designation of Formulas.* Austin, Texas: The Board, 1970.

Green, John L., Jr. *Budgeting in Higher Education.* Athens, Georgia: University of Georgia Business and Finance Office, 1971.

Green, John L., Jr., and Ohanian, Garbis. *A New Approach to Budgeting in Higher Education.* Detroit: Wayne State University Business and Finance Office, 1972.

Halpern, Jonathan. *Bounds for New Faculty Positions in a Budget Plan.* Berkeley: University of California, 1970.

Hartley, Harry J. *Educational Planning, Programming, Budgeting; A Systems Approach.* Englewood Cliffs, N. J.: Prentice-Hall, Inc., 1968.

Jones, Reginald L., and Trentin, H. George. *Budgeting: Key to Planning and Control.* Rev. ed. New York: American Management Association, 1971.

Knowles, Asa S. (ed.) *Handbook of College and University Administration.* New York: McGraw-Hill Book Co., 1970. (Section 8, Chapter 3, Budgets and Reports for Financial Control.)

Miller, James L. *State Budgeting for Higher Education.* Ann Arbor, Mich.: Institute of Public Administration, University of Michigan, 1964.

National Association of College and University Business Officers. *Planning, Budgeting, and Accounting, Section II of A College Operating Manual.* Washington, D. C.: The Association, 1970. (Revision forthcoming.)

Pyhrr, Peter A. *Zero-Base Budgeting.* New York: John Wiley & Sons, Inc., 1973.

Said, Kamal el-Dien. *A Budgeting Model for an Institution of Higher Education.* New ed. Austin, Texas: University of Texas Bureau of Business Research, 1973.

Vaughn, Donald E., et al. *Financial Planning and Management: A Budgetary Approach.* Pacific Palisades, Calif.: Goodyear Publishing Co., Inc., 1971.

NACUBO *Professional File*

"Assumptions and Expectations in Higher Education" by E. Laurence Chalmers, Jr. (August 1972)

"Making the Most of Institutional Resources" by Thomas E. Tellefsen (April 1973)

NACUBO *Studies in Management*

"Management Systems and Budgeting Methodology: Do They Meet the Needs and Will They Work?" by Peggy Heim (September 1972)

"Techniques in the Use of Systems and Budgeting Methodology: A Conceptual Overview" by Ben Lawrence (August 1972)

4:4 Internal Control and Audits

American Institute of Certified Public Accountants. *Accounting and the Computer.* New York: The Institute, 1966. (Chapter 4, Auditing the Computer; Chapter 5, The Impact of EDP on Internal Control.)

————. *Auditing and EDP.* New York: The Institute, 1963.

————. *Auditing Standards and Procedures.* New York: The Institute, 1963.

————. *Audits of Colleges and Universities.* New York: The Institute, 1973.

Association of College and University Auditors. *Internal Auditing for Colleges and Universities.* Evanston, Ill.: The Association, 1968.

————. *A Budget and Progress Report for a College or University Auditing Department.* Evanston, Ill.: The Association, 1971.

Brink, Victor Z., and Cashin, James A. *Internal Auditing.* New York: Ronald Press Co., 1958.

Brown, Harry L. *EDP for Auditors.* New York: John Wiley & Sons, Inc., 1968.

Cadmus, Bradford. *Operational Auditing Handbook.* New York: Institute of Internal Auditors, 1964.

Cadmus, Bradford, and Child, Arthur J. E. *Internal Control Against Fraud and Waste.* New York: Prentice-Hall, Inc., 1953.

Institute of Internal Auditors. *A Guide to Organization and Administration of an Internal Auditing Department.* New York: The Institute, 1967.

————. *Internal Auditing of Electronic Data Processing Systems.* New York: The Institute, 1967.

————. *Sampling Manual for Auditors.* New York: The Institute, 1967.

Knowles, Asa S. (ed.) *Handbook of College and University Administration.* New York: McGraw-Hill Book Co., 1970. (Section 8, Chapter 5, Auditing—Internal.)

Lazzaro, Victor. *Systems and Procedures: A Handbook for Business and Industry.* 2nd ed. Englewood Cliffs, N. J.: Prentice-Hall, Inc., 1968.

Sawyer, Lawrence B. *The Practice of Modern Internal Auditing.* Orlando, Fla.: The Institute of Internal Auditors, 1973.

Scheps, Clarence, and Davidson, E. E. *Accounting for Colleges and Universities.* Baton Rouge, La.: Louisiana State University Press, 1970. (Revision forthcoming.)

Vance, Lawrence L., and Neter, John. *Statistical Sampling for Auditors and Accountants.* New York: John Wiley & Sons, Inc., 1956.

Wixon, Rufus; Keil, Walter G.; and Bedford, Norton M. (eds.) *Accountants' Handbook*. 5th ed. New York: Ronald Press Co., 1970.

NACUBO *Studies in Management*

"Program Review and Evaluation in the Business and Financial Area" by Wilbur K. Pierpont (July 1973)

Part 5: Financial Accounting and Reporting

American Institute of Certified Public Accountants. *Audits of Colleges and Universities*. New York: The Institute, 1973.
————. *Hospital Audit Guide*. New York: The Institute, 1973.
Gross, Malvern J. *Financial Accounting Guide for Nonprofit Organizations*. New York: Ronald Press Co., 1972.
Knowles, Asa S. (ed.) *Handbook of College and University Administration*. New York: McGraw-Hill Book Co., 1970. (Section 8, Business and Financial Administration.)
National Association of College and University Business Officers. *Planning, Budgeting, and Accounting, Section II of A College Operating Manual*. Washington, D. C.: The Association, 1970. (Revision forthcoming.)
Scheps, Clarence, and Davidson, E. E. *Accounting for Colleges and Universities*. Baton Rouge, La.: Louisiana State University Press, 1970. (Revision forthcoming.)
Wixon, Rufus; Keil, Walter G.; and Bedford, Norton M. (eds.) *Accountants' Handbook*. 5th ed. New York: Ronald Press Co., 1970.

NACUBO *Professional File*

"Accounting Principles and Financial Statements" by Daniel D. Robinson (May 1973)

NACUBO *Studies in Management*

"Financial Reporting by Colleges and Universities in 1971" by Harvey Sherer (May 1974)
"Recent Developments Impacting Financial Reports of Colleges and Universities" by Robert B. Gilmore (May 1972)
"The University Treasurer's Report Can Make Sense Without Abandoning Fund Accounting or Stewardship" by William M. Wilkinson (June 1973)

Acknowledgments

THE PROCESS of revising *College and University Business Administration* was initiated by the National Association in 1969, when a new Committee on the Revision of the Manual began to develop recommendations as to the procedures and schedules under which the work would be accomplished. Chairman of the Manual Revision Committee was Robert B. Gilmore, of the California Institute of Technology, who served in that capacity from 1969 until the committee was merged, in 1973, with the Publications Committee which, thus enlarged, carried the program into the publication phase. Planning was coordinated at all times with Publications Committees serving during the period, the first the committee under the chairmanship of W. A. Zimmerman, of the University of Oregon Medical School, 1969-1970; the second the committee under the leadership of Vincent Shea, of the University of Virginia, 1970-1973; and the third the combined Publications-Manual Revision group headed by Kurt M. Hertzfeld, of Amherst College, 1973-1974. The development of the program thus went forward during the administrations of six national presidents: James J. Ritterskamp, Jr., Vassar College, 1967-1969; Kenneth D. Creighton, Stanford University, 1969-1971; Harold M. Myers, Drexel University, 1971-1972; Thomas A. McGoey, Columbia University, 1972; William T. Haywood, Mercer University, 1972-1973; and Robert W. Meyer, Ohio Wesleyan University, 1973-1974.

The revision project benefited during the course of its development by awards from The Ford Foundation, the U.S. Steel Foundation, Inc., and the General Motors Corporation.

THE CENTERS OF RESPONSIBILITY

The production of materials for this revision depended heavily on the interest and dedication of certain groups and organizations. Other associations were deeply involved, not only the regional associations of business officers, but associations in fields related to college and university business. However, associations that sponsored manuscripts for chapters do not necessarily endorse the chapters as published.

Within the Association, final authority for approval of materials rested with the Board of Directors. For the 1973-1974 revision this responsibility fell altogether, and heavily, upon Directors serving with President Meyer. In addition to other duties, both in the Association and at their institutions, the Directors reviewed manuscripts for final approval, making their individual comments upon them and their recommendations concerning them.

Finally, there are the committees that carried central responsibility during the final preparations for publication. Many of the Association's committees contributed heavily to the development of materials with regard to their fields of interest. It fell to two committees, however—the Manual Revision Committee of 1972-1973 and the Publications Committee of 1973-1974—to see that manuscripts were made ready for recommendation to the Directors.

Listed on the following pages are organizations and individuals whose contributions reflect the scope and nature of the professional relationship that resulted in this revision.

Regional Associations

Central Association of College and University Business Officers

Eastern Association of College and University Business Officers

Southern Association of College and University Business Officers

Western Association of College and University Business Officers

Organizations with Related Interests

American Council on Education

American Institute of Certified Public Accountants

Association of College and University Auditors

Association of College and University Housing Officers

Association of College Unions—International

Association of Physical Plant Administrators

Campus Safety Association

College and University Personnel Association

College and University Systems Exchange

International Association of College and University Security Directors

National Association of College and University Attorneys

National Association of College and University Food Services

National Association of College Auxiliary Services

National Association of College Stores, Inc.

National Association of Educational Buyers

National Center for Higher Education Management Systems

Society for College and University Planning

University Insurance Managers Association

NACUBO Board of Directors, 1973-1974

ROBERT W. MEYER, *President*
Vice President of Business Affairs
Ohio Wesleyan University

ROBERT B. GILMORE, *Vice President*
Vice President for Business Affairs
California Institute of Technology

MERRILL A. EWING, *Secretary*
Treasurer and Business Manager
Mount Holyoke College

JESSE B. MORGAN, *Treasurer*
Business Manager and Comptroller
Tulane University

LLOYD GOGGIN
Vice President for Business and Finance
Miami University

GLEN E. GUTTORMSEN
Director of Business Affairs
California State University, San Jose
(Appointed October 1973)

WILLIAM T. HAYWOOD
Vice President for Business and Finance
Mercer University

PAUL W. HODSON
Vice President
University of Utah
(Resigned September 1973)

PAUL R. LINFIELD
Vice President for Finance and Treasurer
Franklin and Marshall College

LESTER G. LOOMIS
Vice President and University Treasurer
Brandeis University

ROGER D. LOWE
Vice President for Business Affairs
Wichita State University

ANTHONY D. LAZZARO
Vice President for Business Affairs
University of Southern California

DONALD MARBURG
Vice President for Business Operations
Beloit College

W. HAROLD READ
Vice President for Business and Finance
University of Tennessee

CHARLES C. TEAMER
Vice President for Fiscal Affairs
Dillard University

H. S. THOMSON
Director, Facilities Planning and Construction
University of Washington

Manual Revision Committee, 1972-1973

ROBERT B. GILMORE, *Chairman*
California Institute of Technology

E. E. DAVIDSON
Oklahoma State University

WILLIAM C. ERSKINE
University of Colorado

KURT M. HERTZFELD
Amherst College

W. HAROLD READ
University of Tennessee

248

Publications Committee, 1973-1974

KURT M. HERTZFELD, *Chairman*
Amherst College

E. E. DAVIDSON
Oklahoma State University

WILLIAM C. ERSKINE
University of Colorado

RICHARD W. GREENE
Wesleyan University

W. H. NIKKEL
Oakland Community College

W. GEORGE PINNELL
Indiana University

W. HAROLD READ
University of Tennessee

JAMES W. WOOD
Millsaps College

THE CONTRIBUTIONS OF THE MANY

The development of a single manuscript involved, between the initial planning and drafting and the ultimate approval, the contributions of scores of professionals—committee members, consultants, representatives of professional associations, and individual business officers—whose judgments are highly valued. The production of the complete revision involved hundreds of such persons. The service of these hundreds was voluntary and, however the services may have differed in degree, the total is an impressive contribution of professional knowledge and experience. Further, the service is essentially anonymous; even the authors of basic drafts scarcely can be adequately recognized, since the development of a final text was by consensus and "authorship" was by many hands and many minds.

Nevertheless, the National Association wishes to recognize, as fully and as accurately as possible, all those whose contributions are identifiable. These names appear below, as a record and reflection of the breadth of professional participation that has given *College and University Business Administration* its authority. The Association acknowledges specifically:

1. Persons who participated in the revision in appointive capacities, as authors, members of evaluation groups, representatives of other associations, members of Association committees, or consultants.

2. Persons who, as readers of manuscripts during exposure processes, contributed written comments on or critiques of the draft texts submitted to them.

But even as it attempts this broad acknowledgment, the Association is aware that there doubtless are still others, unidentified, whose assistance was less formal but nevertheless important. To them goes a general expression of thanks.

PART 1: BUSINESS ADMINISTRATION IN HIGHER EDUCATION

Contributors and Participants (Authors of Original Drafts, Members of Evaluation Subcommittees, and Members of Exposure Panels Submitting Comments in Writing): Howard R. Bowen, The Claremont Colleges; J. R. Brick, Los Angeles Community Colleges; A. Dean Buchanan, California Lutheran College; Eugene E. Cohen, University of Miami; Edward K. Cratsley, Swarthmore College; F. R. Ford, Purdue University; John L. Green, Jr., Rensselaer Polytechnic Institute; Norman H. Gross, University of California; J. Leslie Hicks, Jr., Denison University; Donald S. Holm, Jr., University of Missouri; Merl M. Huntsinger, Washington University; George Kaludis, Vanderbilt University; D. H. Kelsey, Albright College; Reuben H. Lorenz, University of Wisconsin System; Thomas A. McGoey, Columbia University; W. N. McLaughlin, University of Oregon; John F. Morack, Broward Community College; Harold M. Myers, Drexel University; F. E. Oliver, University of Michigan; Clarence Scheps, Tulane University; Fred S. Vorsanger, University of Arkansas.

PART 2: ADMINISTRATIVE MANAGEMENT

2:1 Institutional Planning

The manuscript for this chapter was submitted by R. Orin Cornett, of Gallaudet College, on behalf of the Society for College and University Planning.

Contributors and Participants (Authors of Original Drafts, Members of Evaluation Subcommittees, and Members of Exposure Panels Submitting Comments in Writing): Edwin G. Beggs, Brevard Community College; Frank R. Borchert, Jr., Case Western Reserve University; J. R. Brick, Los Angeles Community Colleges; Robert L. Carr, Evergreen State

College; W. Carter Childress, Virginia Commonwealth University; R. Orin Cornett, Gallaudet College; R. Clark Diebel, Texas A&M University; John M. Dozier, Macalester College; J. Leslie Hicks, Jr., Denison University; Roy O. Kallenberger, Marquette University; D. H. Kelsey, Albright College; Carl M. Lehman, Bluffton College; Joseph W. McGuire, University of California; Allen McKenzie, Oregon Department of Higher Education; Paul Magali, Long Island University; John F. Mitchell, Tufts University; Louis W. Moelchert, Jr., University of North Carolina at Charlotte; John F. Morack, Broward Community College; David W. Morrisroe, California Institute of Technology; Leotis Peterman, Alabama State University; C. T. Pettus, Peabody Institute; David W. Phipps, University of Denver; John B. Price, Brown University; R. R. Reid, Whitman College; D. L. Russell, University of Mississippi; Sam P. Satterfield, Oklahoma State University; Joe L. Saupe, University of Missouri; Clarence Scheps, Tulane University; David M. Smith, University of Pittsburgh; B. R. Venters, Del Mar College; Marwin O. Wrolstad, Lawrence University.

2:2 Management Information Systems and Data Processing

Contributors and Participants (Authors of Original Drafts, Members of Evaluation Subcommittees, and Members of Exposure Panels Submitting Comments in Writing): Glenn Andersen, University of Nebraska; George W. Baughman, Ohio State University; Joseph E. Callihan, Northrop Institute of Technology; Robert L. Carr, Evergreen State College; John A. Cole, Seton Hall University; Donna M. Denton, Baylor University; J. A. Diana, State University of New York at Stony Brook; Roger D. Green, Boise State University; J. Leslie Hicks, Jr., Denison University; Thomas E. Hoover, Management Horizons, Inc., Columbus, Ohio; W. J. Hustedt, University of Wisconsin System; A. J. Jaeger, University of Southern Mississippi; George Kaludis, Vanderbilt University; D. H. Kelsey, Albright College; W. S. Kerr, Northwestern University; Carl M. Lehman, Bluffton College; Louis R. Leurig, University of New Mexico; Paul Magali, Long Island University; Allen McKenzie, Oregon Department of Higher Education; John F. Morack, Broward Community College; David W. Morrisroe, California Institute of Technology; Edward L. Pine, University of Nevada-Reno; Howard L. Rhodes, University of South Carolina; O. J. Rinnert, University of Arkansas; Claude J. Rizzo, University of San Francisco; John C. Robertson, Junior College District of St. Louis; Joe L. Saupe, University of Missouri; Harvey Sherer, Medical University of South Carolina; David M. Smith, University of Pittsburgh; Charles R. Thomas, College and University Systems Exchange; Clarence E. Wolfinger, Hofstra University.

2:3 Risk Management and Insurance

The manuscript for this chapter was submitted by Stanley R. Tarr, of Rutgers University, on behalf of the University Insurance Managers Association.

NACUBO Insurance and Risk Management Committee (1972-1973): David R. Baldwin, Temple University, *Chairman*; John F. Adams, Georgia State University; Robert H. Barnett, Goucher College; Anthony D. Lazzaro, University of Southern California; Warren R. Madden, Iowa State University of Science and Technology.

Contributors and Participants (Authors of Original Drafts, Members of Evaluation Subcommittees, and Members of Exposure Panels Submitting Comments in Writing): O. D. Barksdale, Jacksonville University; Edwin G. Beggs, Brevard Community College; Robert Beth, Stanford University; D. N. Biello, Cuyahoga Community College; Kenneth Brown, Knox College; Joseph E. Callihan, Northrop Institute of Technology; Sherwood E. Carr, University of Arizona; Ernest M. Conrad, University of Washington; William B. Cutler, Foothill Community College District; C. Russell de Burlo, Jr., Tufts University; W. L. Dunsworth, University of Oklahoma; James R. Gallivan, University of Illinois; John Philip Goree, Florida Technological University; John E. Hesen, Bay Path Junior College; J. Leslie Hicks, Jr., Denison University; W. J. Hustedt, University of Wisconsin System; Richard L. Johnson, University of Washington; D. H. Kelsey, Albright College; W. S. Kerr, Northwestern University; H. Felix Kloman, Risk Planning Group, Inc., Darien, Conn.; Lawrence W. Larson, Mills College; Carl M. Lehman, Bluffton College; R. E. Marriott, Sr., University of Missouri; Edward W. Murrow, University of Colorado; Elmer Nix, Pima College; Joe L. Saupe, University of Missouri; Hart Slater, Virginia Military Institute; Marion Snider, John Brown University; John H. Stanford, University of California; J. Robert Sulmar, Webster College; Stanley R. Tarr, Rutgers University; John L. Watson, Oregon State Board of Higher Education; Marwin O. Wrolstad, Lawrence University.

2:4 Administration of Sponsored Programs: Instruction, Research, and Public Service

NACUBO Committee on Governmental Relations (1972-1973): Norman H. Gross, University of California System, *Chairman*; John F. Adams, Georgia State University; R. L. Anderson, The University of Texas System; Harry L. Baker, Jr., Georgia Institute of Technology; Robert T. Baker, California Institute of Technology; R. H. Bezoni, University of Missouri; Max A. Binkley, Colorado State University; Harry E. Brakebill, California State University and Colleges; Earl G. L. Cilley, Stanford University; Paul V. Cusick, Massachusetts Institute of Technology; W.

Clyde Freeman, Texas A&M University System; A. B. Hicks, University of Michigan; William S. Kerr, Northwestern University; Richard G. Leahy, Harvard University; Jesse B. Morgan, Tulane University; Reagan A. Scurlock, University of Pennsylvania; Robert C. Stephenson, Ohio State University; Linda S. Wilson, Washington University.

Contributors and Participants (Authors of Original Drafts, Members of Evaluation Subcommittees, and Members of Exposure Panels Submitting Comments in Writing): Allan W. Barber, University of Georgia; James A. Blissit, Medical College of Georgia; J. R. Brick, Los Angeles Community Colleges; Raymond S. Bugno, Ohio State University Research Foundation; Ernest M. Conrad, University of Washington; George H. Dummer, Massachusetts Institute of Technology; Paul Ebaugh, Pennsylvania State University; Robert N. Faiman, University of New Hampshire; G. Willard Fornell, University of Minnesota; L. J. Freehafer, Purdue University; Thomas E. Glaze, Louisiana State University; Margaret P. Greene, George Washington University; J. Leslie Hicks, Jr., Denison University; C. T. Johnson, University of Minnesota; E. T. Jolliffe, University of Iowa; E. J. Junior, Jr., Meharry Medical College; D. H. Kelsey, Albright College; Ernest W. Leggett, Ohio State University; Clark A. McCartney, University of Southern California; John C. Robertson, Junior College District of St. Louis; John E. Spires, Ohio State University Research Foundation; C. J. Stathas, University of Wisconsin System; Gerald W. Vonder-Brink, University of Dayton; Joseph C. Wagner, Ball State University; Alton E. Windsor, University of Mississippi Medical Center; John E. Wise, Medical University of South Carolina; Raymond J. Woodrow, Princeton University.

2:5 Legal Services

The manuscript for this chapter was submitted by Norman L. Epstein, of the California State University and Colleges, on behalf of the National Association of College and University Attorneys.

Contributors and Participants (Authors of Original Drafts, Members of Evaluation Subcommittees, and Members of Exposure Panels Submitting Comments in Writing): Marlene L. Barfield, Mount Mercy College; K. C. Batchelor, West Georgia College; J. Rufus Bealle, University of Alabama System; Robert L. Carr, Evergreen State College; John L. Carter, Jr., North Texas State University; Roderick K. Daane, University of Michigan; James R. Decker, Wichita State University; George H. Dummer, Massachusetts Institute of Technology; Norman L. Epstein, California State University and Colleges; Robert N. Faiman, University of New Hampshire; Carl M. Franklin, University of Southern California; W. C. Freeman, Texas A&M University System; Caspa L.

Harris, Jr., Howard University; J. Leslie Hicks, Jr., Denison University; John P. Holloway, University of Colorado; C. T. Johnson, University of Minnesota; E. T. Jolliffe, University of Iowa; Nathaniel H. Karol, Hebrew Union College-Jewish Institute of Religion; Lloyd A. Keisler, Indiana University; Ernest W. Leggett, Ohio State University; James E. Maberly, University of Corpus Christi; William S. Mason, Jr., Pembroke State University; Clay Maupin, University of Kentucky; John F. Morack, Broward Community College; Robert M. O'Neil, University of Cincinnati; John D. Phillips, Eckerd College; James J. Ritterskamp, Jr., Vassar College; Neal R. Stamp, Cornell University; Jule R. Stanfield, Armstrong State College; C. J. Stathas, University of Wisconsin System; Linda S. Wilson, Washington University; Raymond J. Woodrow, Princeton University; Marwin O. Wrolstad, Lawrence University; John F. Zeller, Bucknell University.

2:6 Student Aid

NACUBO Student Aid Committee (1972-1973): Lloyd A. Keisler, Indiana University, *Chairman*; Grant Curtis, Tufts University; William Jones, North Carolina Central University; William H. McMillion, West Virginia University; R. R. Reid, Whitman College.

Contributors and Participants (Authors of Original Drafts, Members of Evaluation Subcommittees, and Members of Exposure Panels Submitting Comments in Writing): J. R. Brick, Los Angeles Community Colleges; Paul Ebaugh, Pennsylvania State University; H. Graves Edmondson, Stetson University; Robert N. Faiman, University of New Hampshire; Suzanne C. Feeney, University of Washington; Lola J. Finch, Washington State University; W. C. Freeman, Texas A&M University System; Mark Heffron, University of Colorado; Kenneth W. Heikes, Eastern Montana College; J. Leslie Hicks, Jr., Denison University; C. T. Johnson, University of Minnesota; E. T. Jolliffe, University of Iowa; D. H. Kelsey, Albright College; Edwin O. McFarlane, Reed College; Dallas Martin, University of Northern Colorado; Alan P. Maynard, Brown University; Curtis Redden, Coker College; Charles C. Rowe, Jacksonville State University; Donald R. Ryan, California State University-San Jose; Reagan A. Scurlock, University of Pennsylvania; Charles J. Sheehan, University of New Mexico; C. J. Stathas, University of Wisconsin System; Richard L. Tombaugh, National Association of Student Financial Aid Administrators; Jack Wagner, University of Wisconsin System; Joseph C. Wagner, Ball State University; William Walters, Indiana University; Albert R. Whittle, Troy State University; L. A. Williams, Tuskegee Institute; Raymond J. Woodrow, Princeton University; Frank I. Wright, Carleton College.

2:7 Personnel Administration *and*

2:8 Faculty and Staff Benefits

The manuscript for "Personnel Administration" was submitted by Arlyn C. Marks, of Fordham University. The manuscript for "Faculty and Staff Benefits" was submitted by Russell W. Reister, of the University of Michigan. Both submissions are on behalf of the College and University Personnel Association.

NACUBO Personnel Committee (1972-1973): Carl Kasten, Drake University, *Chairman*; Jerry Anderson, College and University Personnel Association; Wilbur G. Holladay, Miami-Dade Community College; Robert F. Kerley, University of California-Berkeley; Mary M. Lai, Long Island University; Bernard Mintz, Bernard Baruch College; Orie E. Myers, Jr., Emory University.

Contributors and Participants (Authors of Original Drafts, Members of Evaluation Subcommittees, and Members of Exposure Panels Submitting Comments in Writing): John F. Adams, Georgia State University; Hugh P. Avery, University of Houston; Joe Baker, Meredith College; Edwin G. Beggs, Brevard Community College; A. Lee Belcher, University of Missouri; Harold Bland, Roosevelt University; E. E. Bretzman, University of Wisconsin-Madison; L. R. Brice, American Society for Personnel Administration; H. LeRoss Browne, University of Virginia; A. Dean Buchanan, California Lutheran College; Robert L. Carr, Evergreen State College; E. C. Clark, Rutgers University; Ernest M. Conrad, University of Washington; William B. Cutler, Foothill Community College District; B. A. Daetwyler, University of South Carolina; Philip L. Davis, University of Denver; Ray T. Fortunato, Pennsylvania State University; Roger D. Green, Boise State College; John H. Hargrove, North Texas State University; Albert J. Hoban, University of Rhode Island; Thomas B. Hogancamp, Murray State University; Harold Jacobsen, Seattle Community College District; E. J. Junior, Jr., Meharry Medical College; D. H. Kelsey, Albright College; Allen McKenzie, Oregon Department of Higher Education; Arlyn C. Marks, Fordham University; Keith L. Nitcher, University of Kansas; John A. Perkins, University of California; Lewis E. Profit, Eastern Michigan University; Russell W. Reister, University of Michigan; John C. Robertson, Junior College District of St. Louis; Stuart H. Simpson, Kalamazoo College; Clifford M. Van Buskirk, Wayne State University; Marwin O. Wrolstad, Lawrence University.

2:9 Labor Relations and Collective Bargaining

The manuscript for this chapter was submitted by A. Lee Belcher, of the University of Missouri, on behalf of the College and University Personnel Association.

NACUBO Personnel Committee (1973-1974): Carl Kasten, Drake University, *Chairman*; John F. Adams, Georgia State University; Robert A. Alesch, University of Wisconsin System; Max A. Binkley, Colorado State University; James H. Colvin, University of Texas at Austin; John F. Embersits, Yale University; Wilbur G. Holladay, Miami-Dade Community College; Robert F. Kerley, University of California-Berkeley; R. Frank Mensel, College and University Personnel Association; Bernard Mintz, Bernard Baruch College; D. K. Willers, Cornell University; Linda S. Wilson, Washington University.

Contributors and Participants (Authors of Original Drafts, Members of Evaluation Subcommittees, and Members of Exposure Panels Submitting Comments in Writing): A. Lee Belcher, University of Missouri; Emroy E. Bretzman, University of Wisconsin-Madison; J. T. Brogdon, University of Houston; Neil S. Bucklew, Central Michigan University; Robert L. Carr, Evergreen State College; E. C. Clark, Rutgers University; James M. Corley, University of California-Berkeley; Robert A. Currie, Davidson College; Timothy H. Czerniec, Barry College; M. Wayne Davis, University of Alabama in Birmingham; Philip L. Davis, University of Denver; George A. Evanoff, University of Arizona; C. Nelson Grote, Schoolcraft College; J. Leslie Hicks, Jr., Denison University; Albert J. Hoban, University of Rhode Island; M. C. Keith Jones, Mercer County Community College; William T. Joseph, Virginia Wesleyan College; Robert E. Keane, University of Maine; D. H. Kelsey, Albright College; Mary M. Lai, Long Island University; Allen McKenzie, Oregon Department of Higher Education; John F. Morack, Broward Community College; Keith L. Nitcher, University of Kansas; Joseph P. Nye, Columbia University; Homer A. Ooten, Florida State University; John M. Outler III, Emory University; Hubert B. Parker, University of Georgia; Lewis E. Profit, Eastern Michigan University; Sanford Schneider, Burlington County College; Morley Walker, University of California System; William M. Weinberg, Rutgers University.

PART 3: BUSINESS MANAGEMENT

3:1 Purchasing

The manuscript for this chapter was submitted by Eugene O. Ingram, of the University of Michigan, on behalf of the National Association of Educational Buyers.

Contributors and Participants (Authors of Original Drafts, Members of Evaluation Subcommittees, and Members of Exposure Panels Submitting Comments in Writing): Forrest L. Abbott, Barnard College; Reed Andrae, Northern Illinois University; Homer Ball, University of Colorado; D. N. Biello,

Cuyahoga Community College; J. R. Brick, Los Angeles Community Colleges; H. John Cantini, Jr., George Washington University; John A. Cole, Seton Hall University; Robert T. Crauder, Wilberforce University; J. A. Diana, State University of New York at Stony Brook; W. E. Donaldson, Texas A&M University System; Charles H. Elder, South Georgia College; H. H. Gilbert, Jr., North Georgia College; J. Leslie Hicks, Jr., Denison University; Eugene O. Ingram, University of Michigan; Kermit A. Jacobson, California Institute of Technology; Richard P. Jeffrey, Mount Wachusett Community College; Harold D. Keefover, University of Nebraska at Omaha; D. H. Kelsey, Albright College; Herbert E. Kimball, Rochester, New Hampshire; Jack Kompare, DePaul University; Richard Lichtenfelt, Central Michigan University; William H. McMillion, West Virginia University; Joseph Megliola, National Association of Purchasing Management; John F. Morack, Broward Community College; Gene Mosiman, Washburn University of Topeka; Paul Nestor, University of Kentucky; Jacqueline H. Payne, Dalton Junior College; Raymond P. Pipkin, Memphis State University; James J. Ritterskamp, Jr., Vassar College; John C. Robertson, Junior College District of St. Louis; Edward F. Smith, City University of New York; M. T. Tracht, Illinois Institute of Technology; C. E. Wolfinger, Hofstra University.

3:2 Auxiliary Enterprises, Organized Activities, and Service Departments

The manuscript for this chapter was submitted by Reed Andrae, of Northern Illinois University, on behalf of the National Association of College Auxiliary Services; with sections by Chester A. Berry, on behalf of the Association of College Unions—International; by John C. Birchfield, of the University of Tennessee, on behalf of the National Association of College and University Food Services; by Welker Bishop, of Ball State University, on behalf of the Association of College and University Housing Officers; and by Russell Reynolds, on behalf of the National Association of College Stores, Inc.

Contributors and Participants (Authors of Original Drafts, Members of Evaluation Subcommittees, and Members of Exposure Panels Submitting Comments in Writing): Reed Andrae, Northern Illinois University; Homer Ball, University of Colorado; Chester A. Berry, Association of College Unions—International; Jules W. Beuret, Berwyn, Pa.; D. N. Biello, Cuyahoga Community College; John C. Birchfield, University of Tennessee; Welker Bishop, Ball State University; Donald W. Brooks, Simpson College; J. Dillon Cherry, Technical Institute of Alamance; John A. Cole, Seton Hall University; Ernest M. Conrad, University of Washington; Robert T. Crauder, Wilberforce University; Arthur W. Danner, Tennessee State University; W. M. Dewberry,

Georgia Southern College; J. A. Diana, Jr., State University of New York at Stony Brook; Harold J. Forner, Muhlenberg College; C. W. Hancock, University of North Florida; J. Leslie Hicks, Jr., Denison University; Richard P. Jeffrey, Mount Wachusett Community College; D. H. Kelsey, Albright College; Herbert E. Kimball, Rochester, N.H.; Richard J. Lichtenfelt, Central Michigan University; Sidney McQueen, Carroll College; J. F. Mele, Bradley University; Gene Mosiman, Washburn University of Topeka; R. L. Mulligan, California Institute of Technology; Homer A. Ooten, Florida State University; Russell Reynolds, National Association of College Stores, Inc.; Edward F. Smith, City University of New York; John M. Wilson, Prince George's Community College; C. E. Wolfinger, Hofstra University.

3:3 Facilities Operation and Maintenance

The manuscript for this chapter was submitted by T. B. Simon, of Michigan State University, on behalf of the Association of Physical Plant Administrators.

NACUBO Facilities Committee (1972-1973): Charles E. Diehl, George Washington University, *Chairman;* Harry E. Brakebill, California State University and Colleges; Clyde B. Hill (deceased), University of South Florida; James L. Hunt, Southern University; Roy O. Kallenberger, Marquette University.

Contributors and Participants (Authors of Original Drafts, Members of Evaluation Subcommittees, and Members of Exposure Panels Submitting Comments in Writing): W. G. Anderson, Hamline University; Daniel D. Beatty, Kansas State University; Edwin G. Beggs, Brevard Community College; D. N. Biello, Cuyahoga Community College; Warren A. Bishop, Washington State University; Daniel E. Black, Fort Lewis College; Kenneth Brown, Knox College; Mary Jane Calais, U. S. Department of Health, Education, and Welfare, Region IV; Gordon B. Carson, Albion College; Eugene E. Cohen, University of Miami; James H. Colvin, University of Texas at Austin; Ernest M. Conrad, University of Washington; Gene B. Cross, University of Utah; William B. Cutler, Foothill Community College District; Dan DeYoung, Stanford University; Lloyd Durrow, Washburn University of Topeka; F. R. Ford, Purdue University; John W. Harding, University of Washington; S. C. Harward, Duke University; J. Leslie Hicks, Jr., Denison University; Harold Jacobsen, Seattle Community College District; E. J. Junior, Jr., Meharry Medical College; D. H. Kelsey, Albright College; D. T. Kosek, Florida Atlantic University; Lawrence W. Larson, Mills College; R. E. Latchaw, Carroll College; F. W. Miller, University of California-Berkeley; Edward L. Pine, University of Nevada-Reno; Harry J. Prior, Harry J. Prior & Associates, Inc., Seattle; Frank Rice, Jr., University of Wisconsin-Madison; John C. Robertson, Junior College District of St. Louis; Vincent Shea, University of Virginia; V. A. Shurm, University of Colorado; T. B. Simon, Michigan State University; Edmund P. Sliz, University of Tampa; Clarendon Smith, MacMurray College; Thomas B. Smith, Ohio State University; L. Terry Suber, Colorado State University; Alan K. Tarr, University of Washington; C. D. Thomas, University of Toledo; Ray Varley, University of Utah; Fred S. Vorsanger, University of Arkansas; R. L. Whitacre, Adrian College; Alfred Wilson, Clemson University; Marwin O. Wrolstad, Lawrence University; H. Evan Zeiger, Samford University.

3:4 Facilities Planning, Design, and Construction

The manuscript for this chapter was submitted by George O. Weber, of the University of Maryland, on behalf of the Association of Physical Plant Administrators.

NACUBO Facilities Committee (1973-1974): Charles E. Diehl, George Washington University, *Chairman*; James L. Hunt, Southern University; Roy O. Kallenberger, Marquette University; Elmo Morgan, University of California-Berkeley; T. B. Simon, Michigan State University.

Contributors and Participants (Authors of Original Drafts, Members of Evaluation Subcommittees, and Members of Exposure Panels Submitting Comments in Writing): M. L. Adams, Atlantic Christian College; Wallace G. Anderson, Hamline University; J. R. Brick, Los Angeles Community Colleges; William R. Campbell, Jr., Binnicker-Graves, Oklahoma City; John M. Compton, University of South Alabama; A. L. Cotton, Oberlin College; Dan DeYoung, Stanford University; F. R. Ford, Purdue University; Solon Gentry, East Tennessee State University; Kenneth W. Heikes, Eastern Montana College; J. Leslie Hicks, Jr., Denison University; D. H. Kelsey, Albright College; Lawrence W. Larson, Mills College; R. E. Latchaw, Carroll College; Edwin O. McFarlane, Reed College; John F. Mitchell, Tufts University; John F. Morack, Broward Community College; Earl L. Muir, Washington State University; T. E. Peeks, Troy State University; W. L. Prather, Amarillo College; John B. Price, Brown University; John C. Robertson, Junior College District of St. Louis; H. W. Scott, University of Houston; Joseph S. Soto, Marshall University; W. Cecil Steward, University of Nebraska-Lincoln; M. T. Tracht, Illinois Institute of Technology; D. L. Vaughan, Jr., University of the South; John L. Watson, Oregon Department of Higher Education; George O. Weber, University of Maryland; J. E. Westphal, California Institute of Technology; R. L. Whitacre, Adrian College; Paul M. Young, Kansas State University.

3:5 Security

The manuscript for this chapter was submitted by John W. Powell, on behalf of the International Association of College and University Security Directors.

Contributors and Participants (Authors of Original Drafts, Members of Evaluation Subcommittees, and Members of Exposure Panels Submitting Comments in Writing): Jack F. Albrecht, The Claremont Colleges; Wallace G. Anderson, Hamline University; Daniel E. Black, Fort Lewis College; D. L. Brooks, Jarvis Christian College; H. John Cantini, Jr., George Washington University; Darrell D. Christiansen, Tulsa Junior College; Philip L. Davis, University of Denver; Paul J. Dumas, Jr., Duke University; Harry Geiglein, George Washington University; Harold Gibbons, Miami University; Walter L. Hall, Montreat-Anderson College; R. M. Harper, Virginia Military Institute; Don S. Hasty, McCormick Theological Seminary; Kenneth W. Heikes, Eastern Montana College; J. Leslie Hicks, Jr., Denison University; D. H. Kelsey, Albright College; Raymond M. Krehel, Colgate University; R. E. Latchaw, Carroll College; LaVerne A. Lopes, University of California-San Francisco; John F. Mitchell, Tufts University; John F. Morack, Broward Community College; Elmer Nix, Pima College; Joseph P. Nye, Columbia University; Robert F. Ochs, Rutgers University; John A. Perkins, University of California System; Edward L. Pine, University of Nevada-Reno; John W. Powell, International Association of College and University Security Directors; Frank J. Rice, University of Wisconsin-Madison; Sidney S. Rubenstein, Chevy Chase, Md.; R. Eugene Smith, Memphis State University; M. T. Tracht, Illinois Institute of Technology; Charles H. Wheeler III, University of Richmond; R. L. Whitacre, Adrian College; Paul M. Young, Kansas State University.

3:6 Safety

The manuscript for this chapter was submitted by Eric W. Spencer, of Brown University, on behalf of the Campus Safety Association and the National Safety Council.

Contributors and Participants (Authors of Original Drafts, Members of Evaluation Subcommittees, and Members of Exposure Panels Submitting Comments in Writing): John F. Adams, Georgia State University; Eugene Barry, University of Pittsburgh; Daniel D. Beatty, Kansas State University; J. R. Brick, Los Angeles Community Colleges; C. W. DeMent, Purdue University; Badgett Dillard, Southern Baptist Theological Seminary; J. P. Eaker, University of Wisconsin-Milwaukee; John O. Fish, University of Washington; F. R. Ford, Purdue University; Ray Hall, University of Colorado; Derwood L. Hawthorne, Trinity University; J. Leslie Hicks, Jr., Deni-

254

son University; Roy O. Kallenberger, Marquette University; D. H. Kelsey, Albright College; John P. Lambert, Kansas State University; Kenneth F. Licht, National Safety Council; John F. Morack, Broward Community College; William H. Pott, University of North Carolina at Asheville; R. R. Reid, Whitman College; Frank Rice, Jr., University of Wisconsin-Madison; John C. Robertson, Junior College District of St. Louis; Lawrence L. Schmelzer, University of California-Berkeley; Clarendon Smith, MacMurray College; Eric W. Spencer, Brown University; R. H. Sudmann, University of Oregon; Walter W. Wegst, California Institute of Technology; R. L. Whitacre, Adrian College; Charles B. Wingstrom, University of Illinois.

PART 4: FISCAL MANAGEMENT

> 4:1 Administration of Endowment Funds, Quasi-Endowment Funds, and Other Similar Funds *and*

4:2 Investment Management

NACUBO Investments Committee (1972-1973): John M. Dozier, Macalester College, *Chairman*; Owsley B. Hammond, University of California System; Stephen C. Harward, Duke University; John F. Meck, Dartmouth College; George D. Stewart, Johns Hopkins University.

Contributors and Participants (Authors of Original Drafts, Members of Evaluation Subcommittees, and Members of Exposure Panels Submitting Comments in Writing): Rodney H. Adams, Stanford University; Harold E. Bell, University of Chicago; J. R. Brick, Los Angeles Community Colleges; Glen E. Brolander, Augustana College; Richard M. Burridge, University of Chicago; A. L. Cotton, Oberlin College; John E. Ecklund, Yale University; Gordon P. Freese, Stephens College; G. C. Henricksen, Duke University; J. Leslie Hicks, Jr., Denison University; Merl M. Huntsinger, Washington University; Leigh A. Jones, Berea College; D. H. Kelsey, Albright College; Raymond M. Krehel, Colgate University; H. K. Logan, Tuskegee Institute; R. M. Lynch, University of Notre Dame; Ricardo A. Mestres, Princeton, New Jersey; Roger H. Miller, Florida Atlantic University; Andrew J. Osborne, Southern Methodist University; John A. Osborne, University of Tulsa; W. Leslie Peat, Dartmouth College; Kenneth J. Plant, Rensselaer Polytechnic Institute; Richard G. Vogel, Washburn University of Topeka.

4:3 Budgets and Budgetary Accounting

Contributors and Participants (Authors of Original Drafts, Members of Evaluation Subcommittees,

and Members of Exposure Panels Submitting Comments in Writing): Carl C. Baratta, Essex County College; Joe H. Barber, Jr., Mississippi College; John W. Bartram, University of Colorado; R. H. Bezoni, University of Missouri; Robert W. Broughten, Colorado College; W. E. Butler, Elon College; Donald B. Clapp, University of Kentucky; L. J. Freehafer, Purdue University; Robert E. Gentry, University of Wisconsin System; Dud Giezentanner, University of Oklahoma; John L. Green, Jr., Rensselaer Polytechnic Institute; Ronald D. Hamilton, University of Kansas; J. Leslie Hicks, Jr., Denison University; W. D. Holland, Valencia Community College; Fred S. Johns, Eastern Washington State College; D. H. Kelsey, Albright College; Paul Magali, Long Island University; John F. Mitchell, Tufts University; John F. Morack, Broward Community College; David W. Morrisroe, California Institute of Technology; John P. O'Connor, Aquinas College; John B. Price, Brown University; Paul V. Rumpsa, Michigan State University; David M. Smith, University of Pittsburgh; Robert A. Wright, University of Alabama.

4:4 Internal Control and Audits

The manuscript for this chapter was submitted by J. D. Griggs, of the University of Washington, on behalf of the Association of College and University Auditors.

Contributors and Participants (Authors of Original Drafts, Members of Evaluation Subcommittees, and Members of Exposure Panels Submitting Comments in Writing): R. L. Anderson, University of Texas System; Paul J. Apt, University of Miami; Philip E. Arnold, State of Kansas Board of Regents; Larry G. Aungst, Franklin and Marshall College; Edwin G. Beggs, Brevard Community College; J. Marvin Bennett, University of Missouri; Lawrence D. Bibbee, Baldwin-Wallace College; Larry R. Bruner, University of Iowa; A. Dean Buchanan, California Lutheran College; John J. Carpini, Oregon Department of Higher Education; Robert L. Carr, Evergreen State College; Ernest M. Conrad, University of Washington; Fred L. Drake, University of Alabama; Myles Geer, Rutgers University; Robert E. Gentry, University of Wisconsin System; Roger D. Green, Boise State College; J. D. Griggs, University of Washington; Ronald D. Hamilton, University of Kansas; Claude M. Hamrick, Jr., Alexander Grant & Company, Atlanta; J. Leslie Hicks, Jr., Denison University; Robert Huebschman, Miami University; Harold Jacobsen, Seattle Community College District; Walter R. Jahn, Creighton University; William L. Jones, Tennessee Technological University; E. J. Junior, Jr., Meharry

255

Medical College; D. H. Kelsey, Albright College; C. W. Lambert, Foothill Community College District; Allen McKenzie, Oregon Department of Higher Education; Paul Magali, Long Island University; Lee J. Maisel, University of Maryland; George B. May, Amherst College; John F. Mitchell, Tufts University; John P. O'Connor, Aquinas College; J. R. Persons, Rice University; Louis Petito, Denison University; John B. Price, Brown University; Carroll Rikert, Jr., Middlebury College; John C. Robertson, Junior College District of St. Louis; Paul V. Rumpsa, Michigan State University; Paul F. Ryan, University of Michigan; Robert S. Shaw, University of Mississippi; Vincent Shea, University of Virginia; David M. Smith, University of Pittsburgh; Thomas Taylor, Junior College District of St. Louis; Wilbur J. Thom, University of Illinois; Richard G. Vogel, Washburn University of Topeka; John W. Woltjen, Dickinson College; J. A. Woodcock, Central Michigan University; Marwin O. Wrolstad, Lawrence University; W. M. Young, Princeton University.

PART 5: FINANCIAL ACCOUNTING AND REPORTING

NACUBO Accounting Principles Committee (1973-1974): W. Harold Read, University of Tennessee, *Chairman;* Harold Bell, University of Chicago; Norman H. Gross, University of California System; Jerry Leonard, St. Petersburg Junior College; Reuben H. Lorenz, University of Wisconsin System; David W. Phipps, University of Denver; Carroll Rikert, Jr., Middlebury College; Daniel D. Robinson, Peat, Marwick, Mitchell & Co.; Clarence Scheps, Tulane University; Robert Skelton, Mercer University; William M. Wilkinson, University of Rochester; Lucius A. Williams, Tuskegee Institute.

Consultant: Daniel Borth, Phoenix, Arizona.

AICPA Representatives to the Joint Accounting Group: Jay Anderson, Price, Waterhouse & Co.; Delford W. Edens, Haskins & Sells; Daniel D. Robinson, Peat, Marwick, Mitchell & Co.

256

Index